Unit Issues in Archaeology

Foundations of Archaeological Inquiry

Unit Issues in Archaeology
Measuring Time, Space, and Material

Edited by

Ann F. Ramenofsky and Anastasia Steffen

THE UNIVERSITY OF UTAH PRESS
SALT LAKE CITY

FOUNDATIONS OF ARCHAEOLOGICAL INQUIRY
James M. Skibo, editor

LIBRARY OF CONGRESS CATALOGING-IN-PUBLICATION DATA

Unit issues in archaeology : measuring time, space, and material / edited by Ann F. Ramenofsky
  and Anastasia Steffen.
        p.   cm. — (Foundations of archaeological inquiry)
    Includes bibliographical references and index.
    ISBN 0-87480-547-3 (alk. paper). — ISBN 0-87480-548-1 (pbk. : alk. paper)
    1. Archeometry.   2. Antiquities—Measurement.   3. Archaeology—Methodology.
  4. Landscape archaeology—Methodology.   I. Ramenofsky, Ann F. (Ann Felice), 1942–   .
  II. Steffen, Anastasia, 1963–   .   III. Series.
  CC75.U53   1997
  930.1'028—dc21   97-36485

For my mother Elizabeth Lantin Ramenofsky (1908–1996), whose love of knowledge will always be a beacon for me —A.F.R.

For Roger Steffen—my father, teacher, and friend (FFO)—A.S.

Contents

CONTENTS

Figures

Tables

Preface

The idea for this volume grew out of a graduate laboratory methods course the senior editor teaches at the University of New Mexico. The junior editor was the teaching assistant in the course for several years, and it was clear from the outset that our interaction would be both stimulating and productive; this volume is the outcome. There were numerous conversations on the kinds of readings and exercises to use in the course, and how little there was in archaeological literature that combined the methodological concerns of unit construction with clear examples of applications. The idea of creating a volume that could work in this course and might also be of use to the general community germinated over a period of several years. Finally, the volume seemed not only feasible but also important. It was just one of those projects that must be done.

Although there was much to accomplish between conceiving the idea and producing a volume, at each stage the project became more polished. Because preliminary drafts by selected authors were quite good, we asked the authors to participate in a Society for American Archaeology symposium held at the Minneapolis meetings in 1995. We thank all those who participated in that phase of the project. We especially thank Fraser Neiman and Mike Schiffer for their thoughtful comments. In spring 1996, students in Ramenofsky's laboratory course read the papers. Comments and discussions from those readings were incorporated into the final set of revisions. We thank all the students who read and helped in the clarification process.

We also thank Jeff Grathwohl, our editor at the University of Utah Press, for his help and support. His belief in what we were trying to accomplish helped immeasurably. The comments from the outside reviewers, especially Alan Sullivan, who read the entire manuscript, were very useful. Our contributors worked hard throughout seemingly endless revisions to create a coherent package, and we are grateful to them.

Finally, none of this could have happened without the support of our loved ones. Tom, Ben, and Kate put up with more grumpiness and "my mind is somewhere else" than they deserve. The folks in St. Louis have continued their unflagging support; and John Christopher's patience will be rewarded.

Part 1
Introduction

Units as Tools of Measurement

Ann F. Ramenofsky and Anastasia Steffen

In grade school we learned that scientists were people who measured things. The process of measurement not only unlocked truths about the world, but the measurements themselves, whether centimeters, pounds, decibels, or ohms, were absolute. Only later, when we actually tried to measure the edge angle of a projectile point or the thickness of a ceramic sherd did we discover the "awful truth" about science and measurement: "Nothing is more absolute than the fact that nothing is absolute" (Strauss 1994:4).

The implications of this statement are enormous when we try to make sense out of the archaeological record, a thing of shreds and tatters. Because interpretation of 99.9 percent of that record does not come prepackaged, we must make and organize measurements in order to say something intelligible. Yet, as suggested by the debates regarding the meaning of archaeological types, our measurement tools are not absolute. They are simply one way of slicing up the archaeological record.

The relativity of measurement is one of the paradoxes of science. We want to know something about the world. However, the nature of that knowledge depends on the tools we use. The paradox between what we know and how and what we measure explains the importance of scientific method within the structure of science. Method is the bridge between ideas and entities, translating and defining concepts so that the research process can move forward.

This volume emphasizes one part of scientific method: units and unit construction. If scientific method bridges ideas and entities, then units are the tools that construct the bridge. We use "unit" in its most inclusive and generic sense, to describe any and all divisions of variation, at all scales of observation or complexity. Although other terms (e.g., class, taxa, group) have some of the properties of units, they designate particular kinds of units and have more of a history within archaeology. *Units* are the packages that we create to measure the world. They are the means by which we partition and specify a range of variability that is relevant for particular research interests (see Read [1982] for a similar but more restricted definition of unit).

Unit construction is the process of specifying and creating these measurement tools. As with units, other more familiar terms—classification, taxonomy, clustering, or paradigm—refer to particular methods of partitioning. Unit construction, though unwieldy, emphasizes the conceptual aspects of the process and incorporates all partitioning methods. Single attributes, attribute aggregates, artifact classes, locational designations, temporal periods, sampling universes, culture stages, socioeconomic groupings, and geographic regions are all examples of constructed units.

Despite the fundamental importance of units in science and the continuing plea for science among (at least) some archaeologists, unit discussions are not well represented in the archaeological literature (Aldenderfer 1987b; Cowgill 1990a; Dunnell 1986b; Hodson 1982). Concerns about our tools of measurement are dispersed across a number of topics, including classification (Adams 1988; Adams and Adams 1991; Doran and Hodson 1975; Dunnell 1971; Klejn 1982; Whallon and Brown 1982), spatial sampling (Ammerman 1981; Mueller 1975), and quantitative methods (Aldenderfer 1987b; Shennan 1988; Thomas 1976; Voorrips 1990). The new wrinkle here is making units the focus of discussion. The following chapters exemplify how units are defined, described, and evaluated within specified archaeological research contexts, making this volume the first general treatment of archaeological units as they relate to the research process.

The relative indifference to units in archaeology is explained by a series of factors, including archaeological history, the lack of theoretical coherence in the discipline, and the nature of graduate training (see Dunnell [1986b] for a discussion of some of these points as regards classification). More fundamental than these factors, however, is the intellectual inconsistency regarding the nature of units. This inconsistency is evident in the recent book on archaeological classification by Adams and Adams (1991). On the one hand, they view units as arbitrary structures informed by purpose. On the other hand, they describe this construction as a practical pursuit and unit structures as "sets of pigeon-holes, or sorting categories" (1991: 77). If unit structures are pigeonholes, then unit construction is procedural. Compared to the "flash" of ideas, procedural discussions are drab and colorless.

Although units are categories that facilitate sorting, viewing units as only a set of pigeonholes reduces the process of unit formation and evaluation to a routine set of tasks. As part of scientific method, however, units are ideational, a concept we emphasize

throughout this volume. Before variation can be partitioned, units must be constructed and a range of variation specified. That process of definition and specification is conceptual; sorting categories are the result of the construction effort.

In our framework then, units are not the routinized phase of archaeology. Units are the heart of scientific measurement. Without measurement there is no science and without units there is no measurement. This volume is a treatise on the relationship between science and archaeological unit construction as a methodological endeavor. Before discussing our conceptual framework of unit construction and the elements critical to the evaluation of unit structures, we need to describe "unit" in greater detail.

THE STRUCTURE OF UNITS

Units are most frequently discussed within the literature pertaining to classification and typology (Adams 1988; Adams and Adams 1991; Doran and Hodson 1975; Dunnell 1971; Klejn 1982; Whallon and Brown 1982). Dunnell's 1971 volume on archaeological systematics marks the first in-depth treatment of archaeological classification, and his other works on the subject are seminal (Dunnell 1971, 1978, 1986b). Although acknowledging our debt to Dunnell's ideas regarding classification, we conceive of units as more inclusive than classes, types, or groups; unit schemes incorporate a greater range of structures than do paradigms, taxonomies, and object or attribute clusters.

Because units encompass such a broad range of classificatory tools, several concepts are useful for describing and distinguishing between different kinds of unit structures. There are three of these concepts: scale, unit content, and unit definition.

We recognize two notions of *scale*. In the first meaning, scale refers to both inclusiveness and resolution. Inclusiveness (Dunnell 1971) indicates the scope of material measured and described by units—be it chemical elements, traits, artifacts, features, sites, or regions. The second property of scale, resolution, refers to the degree of detail or fineness of grain of a unit. Resolution and inclusiveness are inversely correlated. As scale increases, for example, inclusiveness increases, while resolution decreases. Likewise, less inclusive units have greater resolution.

Accordingly, as the scale of investigation changes, units change. The same material analyzed at different scales will be measured using different units. Archaeological soils, for instance, can be studied mineralogically, by means of which the attributes of soil content are measured. The same soils can also be measured using textural classes, and this description occurs at the scale of particle. Then, if soils are examined as pedogenic units, layers of soil development are delineated.

The second meaning of scale refers to scales of measurement: nominal, ordinal, interval, and ratio. Classifications and typologies are nominal scale measurement tools. The Richter scale is an ordinal tool for measuring the relative intensity of earthquakes. Latitude is an interval scale measurement of space. Measurements of length or weight are ratio scales. Different scales of measurement permit different kinds of analyses. An important example is the different kinds of statistical manipulation possible with data collected using continuous variables (usually interval or ratio scale measurements) versus nominal scale frequency data. Different scales of measurement are usually found together in any analysis. Analyzing archaeological soils at the scale of region, for instance, might involve plotting textural classes (nominal or ordinal scale units) by latitude (interval scale) and altitude (ratio scale). This example involves superimposing one unit scheme onto another.

The *content* of units can be either empirical entities or concepts. Empirical units derive from direct observation, whether macroscopic or microscopic, and the resulting units are correlated with something physical. For instance, there are objects that match the empirical units "Clovis point" and "metate," whereas conceptual units are abstractions with no direct empirical referent. "Civilization," "community," or "chiefdom" are excellent examples of abstract units. The lack of empirical referents for abstract units places great weight on the selection criteria and means of measurement.

Whether the content is empirical or abstract, creating units involves *definition*. Two sorts of definitions are recognized (Dunnell 1971:15–17). Extensional definitions are defined in relation to specific groups of things, and frequently derive from sorting (see Neff [1993] for a clear discussion of sorting). Intensional definitions are developed from concepts and are imposed on phenomena. Because empirical units are directly observable, they are frequently defined extensionally. Conceptual units are not observable, and tend to be defined intensionally. However, these common combinations of empirical with extensional and conceptual with intensional should be seen as generalizations rather than necessary linkages.

There is also a tendency to associate types of definitions with kinds of units. Dunnell (1971, 1986b) equates intensionally defined units with classes. However, classes refer exclusively to nominal scale units. In our framework, intensional definitions are not restricted to nominal scale measurements. Defining a unit of length as 1.0 mm and a ceramic class as the co-occurrence of white slip, black lines, and everted rim are intensional definitions that result in different sorts of units.

Distinguishing between empirical or conceptual content and intensional or extensional definition has implications for understanding the historical tendency to equate archaeological units with discrete objects, such as ceramics, stone, or bone. Discrete objects are entities that can be physically sorted into groups; these groups can be examined for similarities and differences. Definitions arise from these comparisons. Because we can refer back to sorted groups, it is relatively easy to think of these units as real. Thus, empirical units are frequently perceived as natural units, and are the archaeological examples that come to mind most readily.

"Culture" is also a unit but, unlike ceramic or projectile point types, it is wholly abstract. There is no bounded empirical entity, comparable to a pottery sherd, that corresponds to "culture," which has resulted in hundreds of definitions of the concept (Kroeber and Kluckhohn 1952). Because culture is inferred from many traits and is not directly observable, definitions tend to be intensional, driven either implicitly or explicitly by a research goal.

In sum, a unit is a tool that can be defined at differing scales of inclusion and with different scales of measurement. Units may refer to observable entities or to concepts. All units require definition. That definition can arise from the sorting process and be limited to the set of things. Alternatively, an intensionally defined unit begins with definition.

THE CONSTRUCTION PROCESS

Unit construction is the process of creating a set of units or of selecting preexisting unit schemes. In addition, unit construction includes the implicit or explicit evaluation of those units for the relevant research. Three issues are germane to unit construction: the ontology of materialism, the role of ideas, and the means of evaluation.

MATERIALISM

At the heart of the typological debates in archaeology is the question of whether types are natural kinds (e.g., Adams and Adams 1991:67–68; Binford 1973; Binford and Binford 1966; Bordes 1961, 1969; Bordes and de Sonneville-Bordes 1970; Brew 1946; Doran and Hodson 1975; Dunnell 1986b, 1995; Ford 1954a, 1954b, 1954c, 1962; Hill and Evans 1972; Read 1982, 1989; Read and Russell 1996; Spaulding 1953a, 1953b, 1954; Taylor 1948; Whallon 1982). If types are natural, then they are discoverable, and unit construction refers to the means of uncovering natural boundaries. In that context, it becomes appropriate to use techniques that discriminate ever more accurate boundaries. If, however, types are artificial, then units are imposed on variation, and a different logic governs the construction process.

In evolutionary biology, the distinction between packaged nature and limitless varia-

tion is defined as *essentialism* and *materialism* (Hull 1967, 1970, 1989; Mayr 1994; Sober 1980). The ontology of essentialism contends that nature is packaged and discoverable, whereas a materialist ontology (also called population thinking) contends that only variation is real. Since Darwin, evolutionary biologists have debated whether species are natural kinds or constructed abstractions (Clark 1956; Ghiselin 1966, 1969; Hull 1969, 1989; Mayr 1942, 1949, 1969). This question, in fact, is at the heart of the materialist-essentialist controversy.

Evolutionary explanations demand a materialist ontology, so it makes sense that the conceptual distinction between materialism and essentialism arose in biology. Variation is the stuff of life; without it, there is no evolution, and nothing to explain (Ereschefshy 1991). Nonetheless, it is important for archaeologists to recognize that, although evolutionary theory requires materialism, the ontology of materialism is methodologically independent of that theoretical framework. It is possible to be a materialist methodologically without having the slightest interest in evolution. Ontological materialism, not evolution, is fundamental to our framework regarding unit construction.

Bringing materialism to bear on unit construction has several implications for how we conceive of measurement and how we organize our ideas about units. First, because only variation is real, measurement is not simply the act of wielding an instrument. Rather, measurement tools are constructed and imposed on some assortment of material. As a result, measurement is "deciding which value to record" (Bernard 1994:24). Second, the patterns generated are a result of this specification and definition of units. A different set of definitions would result in different patterns. The patterns "discovered" are not inherent to the material. Third, a materialist ontology highlights the role that ideas play in the construction process. The reality of limitless variation requires that we stipulate why only a certain suite of variables has been selected and only certain kinds of units constructed. In short, a materialist ontology regarding unit construction necessitates that we specify the fit between our ideas and the units created to measure those ideas.

The Role of Ideas

Unit construction begins with ideas because ideas are the rationale behind measurement (Adams 1988; Adams and Adams 1991; Cowgill 1990a; Dunnell 1971, 1986b). Ideas, themselves, take many forms, including theory, assumptions, hypotheses, or questions. Of these forms, theory is arguably the most effective and most elegant way to structure measurement. Theory provides the ground rules behind measurement, stipulating the problems to be investigated and the relevant kinds of variation (Binford 1972, 1981; Dunnell 1986b; Lewontin 1974; Teltser 1995b). Importantly, however, unit construction does not depend on theory. Coherent ideas, not theory, are required to build units.

Archaeological history provides the clearest illustration that unit construction does not demand theory. As a discipline, archaeology is more than 100 years old (Daniel 1976), and we have never had a coherent theoretical structure to guide investigation. If, despite the theoretical ambiguity, the discipline has functioned and been productive, then it is obvious that we have operable tools—many types of units at all scales. As Dunnell has pointed out for classification (1986b:150), these tools are largely divorced from discussions of theory and could benefit enormously from such discussions. The very presence of archaeological measurement instruments, however, means that unit construction is not dependent on theory.

The argument that units can be constructed without theory does not imply that we advocate blind description. Describing the world haphazardly is a dead-end activity (Binford 1972:109; Dunnell 1982; Hull 1970; Lewontin 1974). In the absence of theory, assumptions and research goals must be employed. The hard intellectual work begins with building a logical structure, specifying research questions, and identifying assumptions.

The importance of research design objectives for structuring archaeological inquiry

has been widely recognized for at least 30 years (Binford 1964; Hill 1972; Redman 1973), and we do not want to belabor the obvious. Identifying research goals, however, is not enough. In order to facilitate adequate measurement and description, the specification of research must be linked with the conceptual framework of units.

Imposing units onto material will always create a pattern. Whether that pattern is what we want to study is a fundamentally different question. Measuring the abundance and size of tempering materials in ceramic pastes, for instance, may be useful for addressing ceramic use; it is of doubtful utility for investigating social hierarchies.

G. A. Clark (1994) recently provided a lucid analysis of the relationship between common-sense ideas and incompletely specified units. He first critiques archaeological use of migration and diffusion as explanatory concepts for studying the Upper Paleolithic. He dissects the conceptual framework by showing that both migration and diffusion are empirical generalizations about the course of human history rather than explicitly formulated ideas. He then describes how these generalizations resulted in an assumed linkage between lithic artifacts and "identity-conscious social units" (1994:329).[1] Bordes's Upper Paleolithic typology is a methodological expression of that relationship. Given that the conceptual framework was not well formulated, it is no wonder that Clark declares that the units "have not fared very well" (1994:331). Incomplete delineation of the ideas resulted in units not measuring what it was hoped they would measure.

Especially when coupled with the theoretical ambiguity of archaeology, ontological materialism means that the number of measurements we can create is limitless. This recognition could be beneficial in the construction process. Unlike such disciplines as biology, unit construction in archaeology is not constrained by theory; this lack of structure allows for creativity. At the same time, our descriptions of the world must proceed systematically within a specified logical structure that incorporates measurement tools.

The adequacy of a given set of units depends on explicitly defined goals to inform on the business of building units that will work for a specified research endeavor.

EVALUATING UNITS

Because units are our measurement tools, the utility of the tools we select must be evaluated. The evaluation process begins with a clear identification, or description, of the unit structure, and then proceeds with an assessment of the performance and the relevance of those units within a particular research structure.

Analytic and Synthetic Units

Of particular importance is that the role of units within the research framework is either analytic or synthetic. Units are frequently referred to as "analytic tools," emphasizing that they partition and measure some larger whole. Units, however, have additional functions, and Dunnell's distinction between analysis and synthesis (Dunnell 1971: 154–55; see also Binford 1972:111–12) is helpful in specifying differing roles.

Analytic units segment actual observations and are used to describe the properties being measured. Synthetic units organize these analytic observations into categories used in interpretation or explanation. Whether a unit is analytic or synthetic is not a property of the unit, but rather identifies its role in the unit structure.

The distinction between analytic and synthetic reveals that unit construction consists of a number of layers, or levels, and rarely do we evaluate all the layers. The units employed as criteria in defining larger units are not typically evaluated. For instance, if we want to create units to categorize kinds of burials, perhaps to formulate interpretations about prehistoric status, then we create units to describe the burials using specified traits of those burials. Those traits (e.g., positioning of bodies within interments, characteristics of the individuals interred, and burial furniture or grave goods) become the criteria for creating burial units. When evaluating the utility of the burial units for inferring prehistoric status, the overall burial units typically are evaluated with more rigor than is the distinction between flexed and extended positions of the body. The layered nature of units is important because it emphasizes both the construction process and the impossibility of evaluating all layers. How much research would be accomplished if we had to evaluate the definition of the unit "millimeter" every time we used it? Instead, we evaluate whether it is the most useful measure for our purpose given its accepted definition.

Reliability and Validity

The second and most important part of evaluation concerns the adequacy of units. Reliability and validity are two concepts used in assessing their adequacy. Although well established within social science (Blalock 1979; Carmines and Zeller 1979; Cunningham 1986), anthropology (Bernard 1994), and archaeology (e.g., Amick et al. 1989; Beck and Jones 1994; Nance 1987; Nance and Ball 1986; Wandsnider and Camilli 1992), we argue that reliability and validity should be routinely employed to evaluate units from conceptualization through performance.

Reliability addresses the consistency and replicability of a measurement instrument. If units, designed for whatever purpose, are sufficiently specified, then they will obtain comparable results each time they are employed (Beck and Jones 1994; Fish 1978). Reliability describes the performance of units in producing precise and accurate measurements. Therefore, reliability assessment necessarily focuses on the empirical aspects of units. Given this definition, an evaluation of reliability is possible regardless of whether the unit is quantitative or qualitative. A watch, for instance, is reliable when temporal measurement is unaffected by the observer or the conditions under which the measurement is made. A ceramic type is reliable if it is sufficiently defined so as to facilitate consistent discrimination of one specimen from another. An unreliable unit, by contrast, is one that produces error.

Reliability and random error are inversely

correlated: as the amount of random error increases, reliability necessarily decreases (e.g., Nance 1987:246–47). Because reliability pertains to actual measurements, it may be possible to describe the reliability of a measurement instrument without considering the research context in which it is applied.

Validity, on the other hand, addresses the relevance of units to the goals of research. Unlike reliability, which is wholly phenomenological, the validity of units is considered within the ideational realm. Validity assessment concerns the fit between units and research, and is particularly important within social science where many of the interesting research questions concern such abstract concepts as "group identity" or "power." If, for instance, an empirical unit like temperature can be measured two ways, then consider all the ways that an abstract unit like "state" can be measured.

Archaeology may be the more empirical of the social sciences, yet we have sustained research interests in such abstract topics as settlement, subsistence, technology, specialization, behavior, and social identity. Thus, assessing the fit between concepts and units is both a logical and important aspect of our methodological process. Because research questions vary, the validity of a unit must be assessed on a case by case basis. Because the units we construct are ultimately what we study, there is a continuous need for assessing validity (Bernard 1994).

Validity is frequently described and linked with *bias*, or nonrandom measurement error (Bernard 1994:38–39; Carmines and Zeller 1979:13–15). This kind of systematic error greatly diminishes the validity of the measurement. The effect of bias is that the measurements obtained represent something other than the intended concept. Clearly, systematic error of an intolerable level invalidates the outcomes of the applied units.

Two points are pertinent here. First, reliability and validity can be described or estimated in terms of either random or systematic error, or both. Although useful for demonstrating the concepts, we consider an exclusive correspondence between kind of

error and either reliability or validity to be overly simplistic. Second, both reliability and validity are expressed along a continuum. The determination of how much error can be tolerated is a research decision, and, in the case of validity, is ultimately an ideational concern.

Rather than equating validity exclusively with systematic error, we find it helpful to define types of validity assessment. Although social scientists agree that validity assessment is crucial, there is no consensus on the breadth or nature of that assessment.[2] As Bernard put it: "Ultimately, we are left to decide, on the basis of our best judgment, whether an instrument is valid or not" (1994:40). Given that this volume is a first effort toward explicitly and systematically integrating validity assessment into the methodology of units, we define only two types of validity: "empirical validity" and "abstract validity."[3]

Empirical validity assesses whether the unit performs within a research context. In this sense, empirical validity is a kind of "outcomes assessment." The focus is actual unit performance relative to the larger research structure. When prehistoric land use became a research focus, archaeologists discovered that "site" was an invalid spatial unit (e.g., Dunnell and Dancey 1983; Thomas 1975). Knowledge of the distribution of artifacts across large tracts of land, rather than the distribution of sites, was required. Accordingly, the analytic unit shifted scale to the artifact rather than concentrations of artifacts (e.g., Camilli and Ebert 1992; Ebert 1992; Foley 1981b, 1981c; Jones and Beck 1992), and new units were created.

Abstract validity, by contrast, addresses the conceptual coherence between research goals and unit concepts. How strong is the relationship between the conceptual goals, or theory, and the unit concepts? Rather than describing the performance of units, abstract validity addresses whether the units actually measure the concept of interest. The nature of stone tool manufacture, for example, is frequently used to examine whether a population was mobile (e.g., Binford 1979b; Kelly 1988). Assessing the abstract validity of this linkage means asking whether lithic reduction units are appropriate units for measuring mobility. If the conceptual frameworks are not coherent, then selecting another sort of unit scheme is necessary.

Abstract validity has been part of our evaluative arsenal for a long time. When, as in all typological debates, the meaning of units is questioned, deep concerns about the coherence between goals and units are being aired. Such concerns (i.e., are we measuring what we intend to measure?) are at the heart of abstract validity assessment.

In conclusion, the conceptual aspect of units begins with identifying and refining ideas. Units are then constructed and become the surrogate measure for ideas. Regardless of what we want to study, measurement determines what we end up studying.

The last component of unit construction attends to how well our unit structures work. Reliability and validity assessment focus on different aspects of measurement and are, therefore, important approaches to undertaking evaluation.

Reliability concerns the performance aspects of units, their precision and accuracy. Using a precise and accurate tool is important, but an evaluation of only reliability is incomplete. Accurate measurement of distance between Albuquerque and Taos is irrelevant if the research goal is estimating the population size of New Mexico. Validity, in contrast, addresses the fit between units and research goals. While empirical validity considers the application of measurement relative to goal, abstract validity focuses on the conceptual fit between method and research goals.

HISTORICAL TREATMENT OF ARCHAEOLOGICAL UNITS

In this review we use reliability and validity to assess unit construction in Culture History, New Archaeology, Behavioral Archaeology, and Selectionism. Because the concepts of reliability and validity are neutral with respect to such loaded archaeological

contrasts as real and artificial, emic and etic, or style and function, they can be used to illustrate the long-term struggle in archaeology to build units that work in the context of research. Moreover, these concepts make it clear that through time we have moved toward increasing sophistication and awareness of the importance of our tools of measurement.

Although underrepresented in the literature generally, unit issues punctuate archaeological discussions during periods of paradigmatic growth or change. In the case of Culture History, units were the focus of many discussions because the culture historians were ordering the prehistoric record. Unit concerns heralded the change from Culture History to the New Archaeology, and the new archaeologists experimented with constructing new sorts of units that were both replicable and valid. In the current period there is emphasis on integrating theory and method.

CULTURE HISTORY

Culture History was the first successful paradigm of North American archaeology (Dunnell 1986a, 1986b; Trigger 1989; Willey and Sabloff 1993). The reasons for this success lie not only in recognized and agreed-upon goals for the discipline—constructing chronologies to order regional prehistoric records—but also in having developed a set of units that worked in the context of their agenda (e.g., Bordes 1969; Brew 1946; Colton and Hargrave 1937; Ford 1936, 1952, 1962; Gifford 1960; Gladwin and Gladwin 1930b; Gorodzov 1933; Griffin 1952b; Kidder 1962; Kreiger 1944; McKern 1939; Phillips 1958, 1970; Phillips, Ford, and Griffin 1951; Rouse 1939, 1960; Wheat et al. 1958; Willey and Phillips 1958). Culture historians built artifact units at two scales. Analytic units—usually types—were constructed at the scale of object and described empirical entities. Culture historians also created larger units at the scale of culture. These units were synthetic and based on generalizations derived from analytic units that tended to co-occur temporally and spatially. Both sorts of units were named. Binomial nomenclature was used for empirical types (Ford 1962), and type site names (e.g., Fort Ancient, Poverty Point, or Mogollon) were used for the larger synthetic units. The names of the latter appeared in the time-space charts for which culture historians were so famous.

Although both Culture History analytic and synthetic units have survived and routinely appear in the literature, the analytic units had greater reliability and empirical validity than did the synthetic units. The analytic units were based on empirical sorting, making the verification of criteria for separation relatively easy to evaluate. Type descriptions were codified following the initial development of the units (Colton and Hargrave 1937; Ford 1936; Griffin 1952b; Phillips et al. 1951), and this standardization was an effort toward increased reliability. These descriptions identified and regularized the criteria employed to construct empirical units in the first place.

Seriation was the means by which culture historians established empirical validity of units (Dunnell 1970, 1971, 1981; Ford 1962; Phillips et al. 1951). The criterion of "historicity" (Krieger 1944) dictated that analytic units had to sort temporally. Those units that sorted performed well in the context of chronological construction; those that did not sort were invalid.

That large-scale units were more difficult to construct is demonstrated by the iterations required to construct them (Deuel 1937; Kidder 1962; McKern 1939; Wendorf 1954). The McKern system was the first effort to construct large-scale units, but the system did not succeed. The tautology between component and focus meant that the units were not reliable. Despite McKern's goal of creating a structure based on "the culture factor alone" (1939:303), the taxonomy sorted cultural units by time and space (Deuel 1937). Consequently, the taxonomy lacked empirical validity. The system promoted by Willey and Phillips (1958) capitalized on these shortcomings. Terms were clarified, and the structure was redesigned to incorporate time and space. As a result, the Willey and Phillips system had greater reliability and empirical validity than did the McKern system.

Measured in terms of reliability and empirical validity, the units constructed for Culture History goals were largely successful. In particular, the analytic units have persisted. On the one hand, there was a clear rationale behind the development of these units. On the other, despite ever-changing goals and paradigms, the empirical entities being described remain constant. Moreover, certain Culture History synthetic units—the time-space charts, for example—survived and are still employed as organizational tools of the discipline.

Ultimately, the shift away from Culture History occurred because there was little abstract validity between the chronological goal and the analytic units. Analytic units performed, but, without a theory of style, culture historians could not explain why they performed (Teltser 1995a). Because culture historians could not justify why their units worked, the meaning of units came under fire. The Ford-Spaulding debate expressed this abstract-validity issue most succinctly (Ford 1954a, 1954b, 1954c, 1962; Spaulding 1953a, 1953b, 1954, 1977). Ford could not counter Spaulding's statistical elegance, and the result was the development of new analytic units, such as nonrandom attribute clusters as well as types and varieties (Gifford 1960; Hill and Evans 1972; Phillips 1958; Wheat et al. 1958), that explicitly incorporated cultural meaning into their definitions.

NEW ARCHAEOLOGY

In contrast to Culture History, the unit structures of the New Archaeology were neither uniform nor simple. The range and complexity of these units can best be understood by focusing on Binford's seminal contributions to the revolution. Although Binford (1982b) envisioned the New Archaeology as a change in paradigm, the change was methodological rather than theoretical (Meltzer 1979). Given the importance of units in scientific method, many of the innovations concerned the development and manipulation of units. Moreover, the breadth of Binford's vision for archaeology—science, logical positivism, and cultural behavior—resulted in the creation of units at all scales, from attribute to region.

The relationship between science and culture was particularly important in unit construction. Binford believed that cultural behavior was real and knowable archaeologically. If explaining cultural behavior was an explicit goal, then the inherent contradiction between this goal and the nature of the archaeological record had to be addressed. Because the archaeological record was "a static and contemporary phenomena" (Binford 1981:25), the key issue was how to assign meaning to the static, noninteractive matter? The resolution to this dilemma came through a science that employed models, hypotheses, midrange theory, quantification, and evaluation. Although the units were both qualitative and quantitative, the initial methodological breakthroughs occurred in the development of quantitative tools.

At the scale of object and attribute, for instance, new archaeologists employed statistics (e.g., chi-square and numerical taxonomy) for constructing and evaluating artifact units (Aldenderfer 1987a; Doran and Hodson 1975; Read and Russell 1996; Spaulding 1953a, 1977; Whallon 1982). Distance measures, including multidimensional scaling (Cowgill 1972; Marquardt 1978) and time series analysis (Braun 1985), became useful tools in seriation. Suites of quantitative units were introduced to analyze artifact structure at both site and regional scales (Carr 1985, 1987; Hodder and Orton 1976, Whallon 1984; see Wandsnider [1996] for review). Finally, probability sample designs were introduced as large-scale spatial units (e.g., Binford 1964; Mueller 1975). The New Archaeology provided a bounty of new units and powerful new procedures for unit construction.

Reliability assessment played a crucial evaluative role in the New Archaeology. Testing the replicability of units was a kind of reliability assessment, but reliability within the New Archaeology incorporated more than replicability. The assessment included precision, accuracy, and empirical validity. For instance, in "blind test" experimental studies of use-wear on stone tools (Keeley and Newcomer 1977; Newcomer and Keeley 1979; Odell and Odell-Vereecken 1980), reliability was the criterion for assessing the researcher's ability to identify such behavioral units as wear type, material worked, and action. Statistical replicability worked much the same way as the qualitative assessment. Statistical procedures assessed the reliability of traditional types (e.g., Binford 1973; Binford and Binford 1966; Whallon 1972) and the statistical units themselves (Christenson and Read 1977; Thomas 1978).

Reliability was also important for assessing the behavioral agenda of the New Archaeology. Pattern recognition at all scales of inclusion emerged as a viable strategy for discovering cultural patterns. Because the goal was explaining behavior, the units constructed were often interpreted as demonstrating cultural values. If chi-square tests demonstrated statistical significance, then real cultural combinations had been isolated (Read 1989; Spaulding 1953b, 1977). The discovery of meaningful spatial patterns was more challenging because "noise" (or extraneous observations) increased with the scale and number of measurements. The heuristic approach to spatial analysis (Kintigh and Ammerman 1982), for instance, was meant to reduce this noise and to create a closer fit between spatial sampling techniques and archaeological interests.

Within the New Archaeology, then, assessing reliability was an explicit part of the research process. Reliability assessment addressed precision, accuracy, and empirical validity. There was no independent assessment of abstract validity nor did the programmatic goals require such an assessment. If cultural behavior was real, then the purpose of the units was to discover cultural patterning. Assessment involved verifying that the patterns were inherent to the data.

Yet, the gap in assessing abstract validity had implications for the long-term success of the New Archaeology. As with Culture History, questions of unit meaning were voiced. Were the patterns generated truly cultural? How should variables be selected to guarantee that outcomes addressed past organizational properties?

Early on, Binford recognized both the importance and the arbitrary nature of variable selection, stating:

> A classification system depends upon a selection by the investigator of criteria considered "significant" for use in classifying data. Selection of different criteria may result in a "conflicting definition of artefact types." *If an investigator specifies the criteria to be used and applies them consistently, then differences or similarities noted are "real" and demand explanation. Simply because another investigator selects another set of criteria and generates a different taxonomy by whatever consistent method is no basis for an argument against the "validity" of the first evaluation of differences and similarities.* (1972:114; emphasis added)

Binford's rationale behind midrange theory and research was to overcome the inherent contradictions between variable selection and pattern recognition. He hoped through this methodological effort to build a data language bridge that would connect the static archaeological record to past dynamics. Simultaneously, quantitative archaeologists worked toward fitting their sophisticated tools into a behavioral structure (e.g., Aldenderfer 1987a; Carr, ed. 1985, 1987; Christenson and Read 1977; Clark 1987, 1994; Cowgill 1982; Nance 1987; Thomas 1978).

In the end, the initial, narrow definition of science and the simple equation of cultural behavior, measurement, and explanation challenged the programmatic goals of the New Archaeology. The weaknesses were confronted and the discipline was propelled forward. Although the New Archaeology is no longer the only ideational structure in archaeology, many of its methodological innovations have survived. Explaining behavior (see below) continues to be an important archaeo-

logical goal, and unit structures, such as spatial analysis, midrange theory, quantitative methods, and research design, are included as routine aspects of graduate training.

Theoretical Archaeology

As suggested by Schiffer's phrase the "thousand archaeologies" (1988:479), the issue of meaning continues to plague our discipline. Each of these archaeologies has a set of goals that guide research, but few originate from an explicit ideational structure. Fewer still have clearly defined methods. Behavioral and Selectionist archaeology are two of Schiffer's minor archaeologies with clearly defined ideas and method. In both programs, units play a significant role. Examining contrasts in unit issues between these two is useful on two fronts: it illustrates (1) how unit structures vary in the presence of different ideational structures and (2) the difficulties and challenges that obtain between theory and method.

Although, according to Schiffer (1995: 14), "behavioral theory has moved at a glacial pace," there have always been nomothetic goals: building laws that link behavior and artifacts (Reid et al. 1975; Schiffer 1996). Because the archaeological record is not behavioral, many of the most important contributions of Behavioral Archaeology are methodological: building units that work in the context of their interests (Schiffer 1988b, 1995). Schiffer's contrast between *systemic* and *archaeological* contexts designates the conceptual units that describe this distinction (1972).

Behavioral archaeologists construct units within three research domains: formation processes (Schiffer 1987), ethnoarchaeology (Longacre and Skibo 1994; Rathje and Murphy 1992; Skibo 1992), and experimental archaeology (Schiffer 1990a; Schiffer and Skibo 1987; Schiffer et al. 1994). The scale and nature of units varies according to the research domain. In formation processes, c- and n-transforms are conceptual units; in historical or ethnoarchaeology, artifacts in action are units; technological and functional units loom large in experimental archaeology. Eventually, behavioral archaeologists hope to integrate knowledge across these domains into explanatory nomothetic statements that pertain to past cultural behavior.

Like the New Archaeology, reliability and empirical validity are important foci of unit assessment in Behavioral Archaeology. The breadth of research endeavors using c- and n-transforms suggest that these conceptual units have great replicability (Kroll and Price 1991; Schiffer 1987; Wandsnider 1996). Assessing the performance characteristics of alternative technological variables is evaluating the empirical validity of technological units. Summary matrices that compare performance outcomes of technological alternatives are synthetic units, and these become the basis for explaining trajectories of technological change.

There are two ways to evaluate whether there is conceptual coherence (i.e., abstract validity) within Behavioral Archaeology. First, there is clear integration between behavioral goals and units. Behaviorists know where they are headed, and they know how they want to get there. Indeed, the coherence between behavioral theory and units is a strong point of the program. Despite the coherence, however, the jury is still out on whether general nomothetic goals are obtainable (see O'Brien and Holland 1995). Schiffer is upbeat on this point, arguing that the recent efforts at building sound inferences are moving the program in the direction of a true behavioral science (Schiffer 1995). Yet, as demonstrated in Binford's program, there are formidable obstacles to explaining behavior archaeologically. Because human behavior is more variable than the artifact record, there can never be perfect concordance between the two. Also, there are scalar differences in the temporal span of a human generation (systematic context) and that of the archaeological record. Such differences immediately raise questions about what we want and are able to measure. If the nomothetic goals are not obtainable, then conceptual coherence between goals and measurement is insufficient for what behaviorists want to know. Inferences will remain useful descriptions in search of larger ideational frameworks.

Selectionism is founded on the grand explanatory theory of biology. The goal of Selectionism is to explain differential persistence of variation (Dunnell 1980:38; 1982). Selectionists want to know why some variants survive and increase while other sorts of variation become extinct. Drift and selection are two widely recognized causal mechanisms of persistence and extinction.

Although the theoretical premises of Selectionism have been actively discussed since 1980, methodological discussions and evolutionary applications have only recently appeared (Jones et al. 1995; Neiman 1995; Teltser 1995a, 1995b; but see Rindos 1984). Dunnell's conceptual units of style and function (1978) early stipulated the relevant sorts of variation to be investigated. The definition of these terms as evolutionary units made it possible to study the archaeological record in fundamentally different ways. Subsequent unit construction efforts have been slow.

Making variation the centerpiece of explanation requires units that measure variation. Yet, most available archaeological units describe central tendencies rather than variances (Dunnell 1992a, 1995; Thomas 1988). Consequently, as a number of authors have noted, existing units are largely inadequate for creating evolutionary descriptions (Dunnell 1980, 1995; Leonard and Jones 1987; O'Brien and Holland 1995). Thus far, evolutionists have constructed units at the scale of attribute (Neiman 1995; Neff 1992, 1993, 1995a; Ramenofsky 1997), object (Abbott et al. 1996; Dunnell and Feathers 1991), and population (Graves and Ladefoged 1995; Leonard and Reed 1993; Maxwell 1995).

Given that evolutionary descriptions require different kinds of units, it is unfortunate, and a little surprising, that unit assessment has not been uniformly employed in evolutionary studies. Indeed, among Selectionists unit assessment can be scaled from underrepresented (reliability) to common (abstract validity). Although this emphasis on abstract validity makes sense given the relationship between theory and method, the long-term success of the program will require more attention to unit construction and reliability assessment.

To date archaeologists have identified certain sticking points in the Selectionism program (Bettinger et al. 1996; Boone and Smith 1998; Schiffer 1995). In terms of units, none are larger than the two assumptions that artifacts are part of the phenotype (Leonard and Jones 1987; O'Brien and Holland 1992) and that selection operates on the phenotype (O'Brien and Holland 1992, 1995). Because of these assumptions, artifact change can be tracked and analyzed as a product of selection or drift. As Teltser (1995b:6) and others (O'Brien and Holland 1995:158–59) have stated, these assumptions are clearly first approximations. While there is precedence in biology for the assumption that evolutionary processes operate on the phenotype, this is not a settled issue. Competing definitions of replicator, interactor, and vehicle (Dawkins 1982, 1994; Hull 1980, 1988; Williams 1992) or the matter of reintroduction of group selection (Williams 1965; Wilson and Sober 1994) would suggest that biologists themselves are not united on the crucially important topic of the unit of selection.[4] To move the Selectionism program forward, considerable attention should be paid to the linkage between artifact, phenotype, and evolutionary change.

Continued growth of the Selectionism program will require meeting a major methodological challenge: to create units that appropriately incorporate the dimension of time into the descriptions of variation and the modeling of change. For archaeology, evolutionary theory offers distinct kinds of explanations of variational change that span vast reaches of time. However, archaeologists cannot import the theoretical package from biology without reassembling it and adding key empirical components. Even if the assumptions identified above can be accepted, *archaeologists* must take on the task of creating units to describe the empirical variation of the human phenotype in terms

that can be measured at the temporal scales relevant to trait innovation, equilibrium, replacement, etc. For example, while biologists can rely on lengths of reproductive generations as a metronome of genetic transmission, what similar rates of transmission are relevant for those human phenotypic traits we measure archaeologically? In what ways do the nature of the traits under study influence the ways we should calibrate the description of functional persistence versus stochastic fluctuations? To date, Neiman's work (e.g., 1995) is the most sophisticated and creative effort to tackle the difficult methodological mandate of a theoretical perspective focused on explaining the distinctly temporal phenomenon of human change.

Thus, as suggested by Behavioral Archaeology and Selectionism, there currently is deep archaeological concern for ideational structures—a concern that extends to the construction and specification of units. On the one hand, behavioralists work methodologically in an effort to link human cultural behavior with artifacts. Selectionists, on the other, are only beginning to build units that measure their ideas. In both cases, however, it is clear that conceptual coherence between goals and units is a good beginning, but it is not sufficient. Whether the explicit coherence between ideas and units will facilitate the kinds of explanation each program seeks or whether the coherence will affect a larger and more thoughtful integration within the discipline remain open issues.

More generally, using reliability and validity to examine the history of archaeological unit construction has resulted in the demonstration of an interesting and logical progression. Cultural historians were most successful with empirical units at the scale of object. New Archaeologists were methodologically skilled, and they exploited that skill in the construction and manipulation of units. In both of these programs, the problems of conceptual coherence between goals and units created serious obstacles to further growth. Currently, theoretical coherence is being brought to bear on these problems of meaning, and there is significant investment directed toward integration between research programs and measurement.

OVERVIEW OF CONTRIBUTIONS

Thus far, our introduction has established a general methodological framework for units and unit construction, which serves as a backdrop for the individual contributions, where many of the issues we have raised are further elaborated. These chapters are case studies in that their authors consider particular kinds of archaeological phenomena. The chapters are, however, more than descriptions of units. In each one, specific unit structures are examined, and the performance of those units is evaluated. The general message presented in this introduction is reinforced by the particulars explored in the individual chapters.

That unit construction and manipulation is fundamental to all we do archaeologically is illustrated in a number of ways. These chapters span the range of phenomena size. At the small end, Hughes and Neff focus on chemical composition; Wandsnider, by contrast, considers landscape units. Furthermore, different sorts of units are described, constructed, and analyzed. Three of the chapters (Ramenofsky, Reed and Stein, and Wandsnider) focus wholly on conceptual units, while the other seven contributions assess empirical units. This latter category includes several kinds of empirical units. For example, Steffen et al. describe technological units, Pierce's units are functional, and Lambert's, Beck's and LeTourneau's chapters examine culture historical typological units. Finally, the volume compiles discussions that emphasize all three domains of archaeological variation: time, space, and material. Accordingly, we have organized the presentation of chapters by these domains: time (Beck, Reed and Stein, LeTourneau, Ramenofsky), space (Wandsnider, Hughes, Neff), and material (Steffen et al., Lambert, Pierce).

The relevance of other components discussed in this introduction is exemplified by issues addressed in the individual contributions. Those chapters that have a strong his-torical perspective (Lambert, LeTourneau, and Reed and Stein) focus on the importance of how units were constructed. The relationship between analytic and synthetic units is explored in chapters by LeTourneau, Pierce, and Steffen et al. Scale is a concept that is important in all of the chapters, and is discussed explicitly by Hughes, Neff, Ramenofsky, Steffen et al., and Wandsnider.

Finally, the use of reliability and validity as concepts for evaluating units is explicit in all the chapters, but there is considerable variation in emphasis among the different applications. Only Pierce, LeTourneau, and Neff evaluate both the reliability and validity of units. All other chapters evaluate only unit validity. Not surprisingly, there are shades of meaning in the application of this concept. The consideration of validity and archaeological sourcing by Neff and Hughes exhibits how validity can be defined and treated differently despite similarity in subject matter. In three chapters (Beck, Neff, and Pierce), the validity of units is assessed relative to explanatory theory, specifically Selectionism.[5] Finally, most of the chapters assess empirical validity, or the performance of units relative to a specific research goal. For example, whereas Lambert, and Reed and Stein, assess performance of units relative to the purpose for which the units were originally designed, Pierce and LeTourneau assess the performance of units relative to research purposes as they have changed historically.

In the end, then, the contributors of this volume present thoughtful analytic and descriptive discussions of the importance of units in their own research efforts. We are hopeful that their careful and systematic attention to measurement and their evaluation of the tools of observation and inference will stimulate others to consider the methodology of units within the context of their own research.

ACKNOWLEDGMENTS
This chapter has benefited greatly from discussions and critical readings by a large number of colleagues and students. We especially thank Bill Dancey, Phil LeTourneau, Steven

Mack, Chris Pierce, Gerry Raymond, Patrice Teltser, LuAnn Wandsnider, and the two outsider reviewers at the University of Utah Press. Jeff Grathwohl's encouragement to both elaborate and simplify the chapter was also extremely helpful. Finally, Robert Dunnell's vision regarding classificatory issues set this intellectual process in motion. We are grateful to him. Errors, omissions, and breaks in logic are our own doing.

Notes

1. G. A. Clark (1994:328–29) does not use the word "materialism" in his description of Upper Paleolithic types, but he makes exactly the same argument as presented here. According to Clark, lithic typologies have no "objective reality" (1994:328).

2. Validity assessment is typically broken down into different types. Carmines and Zeller (1979) recognize "criterion," "content," and "construct." Criterion validity measures the predictive power of the unit. Content validity addresses the completeness of the measurements. Construct validity focuses on the fit between unit construction and theory. Bernard (1994:38–39), however, recognizes only "face" and "criterion" validity. Face validity assesses the logical relationship between concept and unit. Criterion validity assesses the unit against a known standard. Bernard does not have a measure of the fit between unit and research structure. Hughes (this volume) offers a third breakdown of validity. His level one and level two validities are similar but not identical to our empirical and abstract validity.

3. Adams and Adams do not use the terms "validity" and "reliability" in their treatment of artifact typology, and they do not believe that units must have abstract validity. As they state, "While there must necessarily be some fundamental logic underlying our type concepts, if they work consistently for any purpose, it is often the case that we do not know what it is" (1991:74). It is clear that for Adams and Adams there is only empirical validity.

4. Dawkins and Hull have different definitions of "replicator," "interactor," and "vehicle." For an excellent review of the differences, see Brandon 1988 and Williams 1992. Williams's 1965 seminal book was a long argument against group selection, but with a different definition, the unit is again gaining currency among evolutionists.

5. We recognize the emphasis this places on Selectionism and acknowledge that the imbalance in part reflects our theoretical interests. More important, however, the emphasis is warranted given the nascent character of unit construction within Selectionism, as discussed in the historical analysis. In other theoretical frameworks (e.g., Behavioral Archaeology), these initial discussions of unit construction have already been undertaken.

Part II
Time

2

Projectile Point Types as Valid Chronological Units

CHARLOTTE BECK

Typological cross-dating has been used for decades in archaeology and is widely used today in cases where the application of chronometric methods is either impossible or inappropriate. Basic to the method are artifact types that are "temporally sensitive"; that is, they have historical significance (Krieger 1944) such that a particular type can be identified with a temporal period within a geographic area. Thus, assemblages can be compared with respect to these types and placed relative to one another in time.

Most commonly used in this approach are ceramic types, which are based on a large number of traits—primarily surface treatment and decoration—that are generally regarded as stylistic. For preceramic periods, however, or in areas such as the Great Basin, where ceramics were never widely used, other artifact categories have been employed for the construction of historical types; most prominent among these categories are projectile points.

In contrast to ceramic types, projectile point types are defined by a small number of traits, most of which are presumed to be functional (i.e., having to do with performance). Some researchers (e.g., Flenniken and Raymond 1986; Flenniken and Wilke 1989) have argued that projectile point types are not valid chronological units because, as a result of their performance, points can be broken and modified, altering their appearance and thereby precluding "correct" type assign-

ment. Nonetheless, at least gross temporal sequences can often be produced using projectile point types, no matter which region is considered. In eastern North America, for example, projectile point types can be identified with general periods, including early and late Archaic or early and late Woodland (e.g., Christenson 1986; Shott 1993). In the Great Basin, projectile point types, although often identified with temporal ranges encompassing thousands of years, consistently occur in the same temporal sequence from site to site within specific regions.

In this chapter the validity of projectile point types as chronological units is examined. The validity of a unit as a chronological indicator is ultimately a theoretical issue. Archaeologists have implicitly used style for many years to create chronological units (Dunnell 1978); but the question remains, is there an underlying theoretical basis for the argument that stylistic units are more appropriate for chronological purposes than are functional units? This issue is evaluated here with respect to Great Basin projectile point types. A distinction is made, however, between using a single type as an index fossil to locate an assemblage in time and a set of types used to order a group of assemblages in time. In the first case, all that is necessary is the knowledge that the type as defined can be identified with a limited temporal range within a particular area; it has historical significance in Krieger's terms (1944). To use a set of types to order a group of assemblages, however, those types must "behave historically"; that is, the frequency distributions of the types must be known, and those distributions must conform to what Ford (1952, 1962) referred to as a "battleship-shaped" curve. It is this latter use of chronological units that is of interest here.

Proceeding in several steps, there are three questions that must be answered. First, given the apparent historical behavior of the Great Basin projectile point types, are they, in fact, based entirely on functional traits or on a combination of both stylistic and functional ones? Second, which traits appear to be driving the historical behavior of the point types? Finally, if the traits that are responsible for this historical behavior are at least in part functional, does this mean that function can be used to construct chronological units? Before answering these questions, however, a more basic issue must be addressed: how stylistic and functional traits are distinguished from one another in the archaeological record.

STYLE AND FUNCTION

The concepts of style and function have been debated in archaeology for more than 50 years; most definitions offered have been in commonsense terms, generally equating function with use (e.g., Jelinek 1976; Sackett 1973, 1982) and style with decoration and group identity (e.g., Conkey 1990; Plog 1980, 1983; Wiessner 1983, 1990). Dunnell (1978, 1980), however, defines these concepts in evolutionary terms, where function is viewed as those variants that have detectable selective value and where style refers to those variants that are selectively neutral. A trait is deemed neutral if all variants of that trait have effectively equal fitness values (Neiman 1995; O'Brien and Holland 1990). A variant of a neutral trait may come under selection at any time if the selective environment changes such that fitness values among variants are no longer equal. Thus, identification of stylistic and functional traits is situational with respect to a fixed point in time and space.

The frequency of functional traits is controlled by natural selection and a set of external conditions (Dunnell 1978:199), while the frequency of stylistic traits, because they are selectively neutral, is controlled by random forces, including innovation, drift, and sorting (Dunnell 1978; Jones et al. 1995; Neiman 1995; O'Brien and Holland 1990). Because the frequencies of functional and stylistic traits are controlled by different mechanisms, they should have different temporal and spatial distributional patterns (Dunnell 1978). Although this statement makes perfect theoretical sense, in practice distinguishing the distributions of stylistic and functional traits is not so easily done (but see Allen 1996).

Using a biological analog, O'Brien and Holland (1990:52) model the temporal behavior of functional and stylistic traits, the former being determined by selection, and the latter by drift (Figure 2.1). Beginning at some frequency above zero, a variant that is under selection will increase in frequency at a steadily decelerating rate toward some arbitrary value. (The term "frequency" as used throughout this chapter refers to relative rather than actual frequency.) A variant not under selection (i.e., adaptively neutral) will, over the long run, drift randomly in frequency from generation to generation; ultimately its frequency will go either to zero or to 100 percent, eliminating the variant in the first instance, fixing it in the population in the second.

In actuality, however, this model is somewhat simplistic, as O'Brien and Holland state. Regarding functional variants, the actual pattern observed will depend upon the mode of selection. In evolutionary biology, a number of modes of selection have been defined, including directional, stabilizing, and diversifying selection (Dobzhansky 1982; O'Brien and Holland 1992). Directional selection focuses on a single trait (or trait complex), moving the frequency distribution in a specific direction. Stabilizing selection acts to reduce the frequency of any new

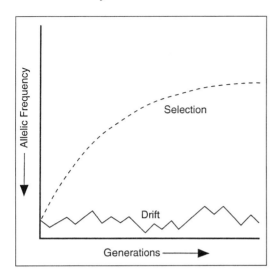

Figure 2.1. Hypothetical model of changes in trait variant frequency for traits under selection (functional) and those that are neutral (stylistic) (after O'Brien and Holland 1990).

variation that arises, creating a modal effect. Diversifying selection focuses on two or more trait variants, resulting in "balanced polymorphism." The frequency distributions across time resulting from these different modes should look somewhat different. Using a quantitative trait as an example, these patterns can be discussed in terms of the mean and variation about that mean. In the case of directional selection, the mean will shift over time in a particular direction, and in the case of stabilizing selection, the mean will remain effectively the same. In the case of diversifying selection, the mean will fluctuate, depending on the effects of the several traits being "balanced."

The temporal behavior of variants of stylistic traits is also more complex than O'Brien and Holland's model suggests. Although drift appears to be the primary mechanism responsible for temporal patterns of neutral variant distributions, Neiman (1995) shows that the introduction of random variation through innovation is an important factor in shaping these distributions. On the one hand, innovation introduces variation while, on the other, drift eliminates variation (Neiman 1995:14). Over time, however, the frequency distribu-

tions of neutral variants, despite short-term fluctuations, tend to be unimodal with the mode occurring near the center of the distribution. The tendency for style to behave in this way through time is what has made it so useful for chronological purposes (Dunnell 1978; Neiman 1995; Teltser 1995a).

Functional variants, however, can also be distributed unimodally through time. If a variant is under stabilizing selection, its frequency will increase to a point at which it becomes fixed in the population. Fixation in theory means that all other variants have been eliminated; but new variants are constantly being introduced through innovation. Thus, if the selective environment changes, another variant might come under selection, causing the frequency of the first to decrease. If the frequency of the first variant continues to decrease to zero and it then disappears, its distribution will appear the same as that of a stylistic variant.

Frequencies of both functional and stylistic variants may also be affected by other, unrelated factors, such as changes in population demographics (Jones et al. 1995). For instance, if a subpopulation carrying a neutral variant began to increase relative to other subpopulations, due to some factor under selection, the frequency of that variant would also increase relative to variants carried by other subpopulations. Such an increase might imply selection, but in reality would be a result of increased transmission within a larger population relative to other variants. This effect might be viewed as sorting (Abbott et al. 1996; Jones et al. 1995; Ramenofsky 1995), or the tendency for a neutral variant to be somehow linked with a variant that is under selection, making the temporal distribution of the neutral variant appear directional as well (see also Bettinger et al. 1996).

In short, functional traits are under selection and their temporal patterns will be determined by the mode in which selection is operating. Stylistic traits, on the other hand, are neutral, meaning the fitness of all variants is effectively the same. The frequency of functional traits is controlled by deterministic forces while that of stylistic traits is controlled by random forces. However, because a trait's status is situational, under conditions where the selective environment is rapidly changing, the temporal distributional pattern of any particular trait may be quite complex.

SPATIAL PATTERNS

The distribution of a trait in both time and space is in part a result of transmission (see Bettinger and Eerkins n.d.; Bettinger et al. 1996). Transmission refers to those processes of social learning by which certain traits are communicated between and among individuals (Boyd and Richerson 1985; Jones et al. 1995). The consequence of transmission in space is the diffusion of a trait or trait complex outward from the point of origin. This process has three effects. First, a trait, be it functional or stylistic, undergoing transmission will date earliest in its area of origin and successively later as it moves outward (Hagerstrand 1967). This effect, which was first described by Graebner (1905), was the basis of the age-area and culture-area concepts so prevalent in American archaeology during the early part of the twentieth century (see Kroeber 1931). Second, because all traits are not expected to arise in the same area, two traits diffusing from different areas of origin, but whose paths cross, may show an inverse temporal order once they have crossed, depending upon their locations of origin and their directions and rates of diffusion. Finally, several traits diffusing outward from the same location may or may not move at the same rate or even in the same direction. If clusters of traits are being transmitted together, it is the cluster that will have a distinctive temporal and spatial pattern; but if transmission is at the scale of the trait, each trait will have its own temporal and spatial pattern. Thus, transmission does not have to be at the same scale in every case; it may be at the scale of trait in one case and at the scale of trait cluster in another.

Because functional traits are tied to fitness, for a functional trait to be transmitted successfully to a new population that trait must enhance the fitness of the individuals in that new population as it does those in the

old. Transmission of a stylistic trait carries no such requirement, but may instead face demographic boundaries. That is, if two demographic groups come into contact, there is no assurance that a stylistic trait will be successfully transmitted across group boundaries, due to social factors that may be completely unrelated to the trait.

As in the case of temporal distributions, spatial distributions of functional and stylistic traits may often look quite similar. The relatively speedy diffusion of a trait (or trait complex) across space might suggest that trait is under selection, especially if replacement takes place (see Ramenofsky [1997] for a discussion of replacement). The bow and arrow, for example, diffused very quickly across the Great Basin, almost completely replacing the atlatl and dart in that region (Grayson 1993). However, rapid diffusion may also be the result of high population mobility in a region where there are few social boundaries and in which adaptation is fairly uniform.

The co-occurrence of several variants of a single trait from locality to locality might suggest trait neutrality (i.e., all variants have equal fitness values). But this is not necessarily the case. I have argued elsewhere (1995) for the slow dominance of corner-notching over side-notching in Great Basin projectile points, based on differences in their cost-benefit ratios. Because side-notched points often broke in a manner ending their use-lives, corner-notching began to "outcompete" side-notching. Corner-notching, however, never totally replaced side-notching, and these two hafting alternatives continued to co-occur through time; only their relative frequencies changed, with corner-notching increasing and side-notching decreasing.

PERFORMANCE CHARACTERISTICS

It is obvious from the discussion thus far that, taken alone, neither temporal nor spatial patterns are sufficient to distinguish stylistic from functional traits in the archaeological record. There is a third factor, however, that, when considered in conjunction with temporal and spatial patterns, may aid in solving this problem. A functional trait should have certain benefits that can be evaluated in terms of performance characteristics, defined by Schiffer and Skibo as "the behavioral capabilities that an artifact must possess in order to fulfill its functions in a specific activity" (1987:599). Schiffer and Skibo suggest that the performance characteristics of a knife for butchering, for example, are that it cuts cleanly, is easy to grasp, and does not wear out. Several researchers have conducted such performance studies (e.g., Allen 1996; Bleed and Bleed 1987; Braun 1983; Christenson 1986; Hally 1983; Klemptner and Johnson 1985, 1986; Odell and Cowan 1986; Schiffer 1988a, 1990a, 1990b; Schiffer and Skibo 1987; Schiffer et al. 1994; Titmus and Woods 1986), especially with respect to ceramics.

Because the status of a trait is context-specific and that status must be determined empirically (e.g., Meltzer 1981), performance studies can yield contextual information that, in concert with temporal and spatial distributional patterns, can be used to aid in distinguishing style from function archaeologically. Schiffer et al. (1994) recently found that surface treatments such as deep exterior texturing can increase thermal shock resistance. Some of these surface treatments, previously considered decorative traits, may, in fact, be functional. Schiffer et al. (1994: 210–11) strongly caution against drawing conclusions simply on this basis, because thermal shock resistance is also affected by other factors, including firing temperature, paste characteristics, and vessel shape, size, and wall thickness. Such studies, however, can isolate traits that affect certain aspects of performance and, using this information together with the temporal and spatial patterns of those traits, it may be possible to decipher whether they are functional or stylistic in a particular archaeological context.

Although there have been no detailed and systematic performance studies on projectile points as a whole, several limited experimental studies offer some general ideas with which to work. These studies suggest that the performance characteristics of a stone point used *exclusively* as a tip on an atlatl dart

might be balance and stability, impact resistance, and ability to penetrate the target (see Christenson 1986; Flenniken and Wilke 1989; Van Buren 1974). Stability and balance are a function of symmetry and weight (Christenson 1986); that is, if a point is symmetrical in both form and weight, then the balance should be good. The ability of a point to penetrate the intended target is a function of its cross-sectional area (Frison and Zeimens 1980) as well as the sharpness of its tip and blade edges (Frison 1973, 1976). Impact resistance is somewhat more complex; studies by Titmus and Woods (1986) and Flenniken and Wilke (1986) suggest that several factors may be important here, including raw material, thickness, and the location, size, and depth of notches used for hafting. As in the case of surface treatment on pottery, discussed above, these studies suggest, but are not conclusive, that all of these traits are functional because they appear to relate to the performance of the tool. But whether a trait is directly related to the performance of a tool is context specific, as are the temporal and spatial distributions of that trait. Thus, all three of these factors—time, space, and performance—must be considered within a particular context in order to determine the status of a trait.

In turning to an examination of the Great Basin projectile point types, I have two questions in mind. First, are there patterns in the temporal and spatial distributions of traits defining the Great Basin point types that may suggest whether these traits are functional or stylistic? Next, do specific traits appear to be driving the historical behavior of the individual types? If so, do these differ for specific types?

To seek answers, I begin by focusing on the data from a single site—Gatecliff Shelter (Thomas 1983)—where a long, well-dated cultural sequence exists.

ANALYSIS OF PROJECTILE POINT TRAITS AT GATECLIFF SHELTER

The traits examined here are those used by Thomas (1981) in his key to Great Basin projectile point types. Analysis focused on nine

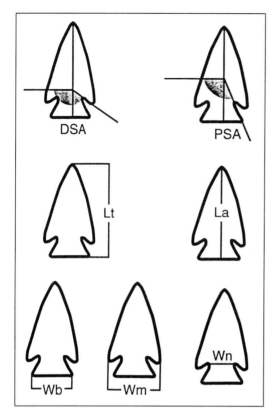

Figure 2.2. Seven of the nine projectile point traits defined by D. H. Thomas (1981) that are considered in the present analysis.

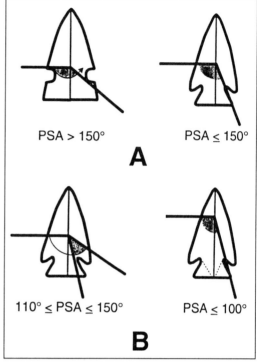

Figure 2.3. Schematic of the two qualitative traits conflated by proximal shoulder angle (using D. H. Thomas's 1981 metric designations). A. Type of haft: PSA > 150° = side-notched; PSA ≤ 150° = corner-notched. B. Shape of stem: 110° ≤ PSA ≤ 150° = expanding stem; PSA ≤ 100° = parallel/contracting stem.

metric traits (Figure 2.2): (1) several measures of size, including length, width, thickness, and weight; (2) proximal shoulder angle (PSA), which relates to the type of haft (corner-notched or side-notched) and, for corner-notched points, the shape of the stem (Figure 2.3); and (3) distal shoulder angle (DSA), a measure of blade extension.

First, the relation between the nine metric traits and time was investigated, to find which traits might show directional trends. The Gatecliff data are presented by Thomas (1983) in a set of 15 horizons, corresponding to the natural stratigraphy of the cave. Because each horizon does not represent the same length of time, mean dates were calculated here for horizons using the radiocarbon dates from each (Table 2.1).[1] Pearson's r cor-

relation coefficients were then calculated between these mean horizon dates and the means for each of the nine variables (Table 2.2).[2] Using p<.05 to indicate statistical significance (here, and throughout the rest of this analysis), only neck width ($r = .724$, $p = .027$) is significantly correlated with mean horizon date. PSA ($r = -.594$, $p = .091$) also shows a strong correlation with time (although not significant at the .05 level). These results suggest a directional trend over time in both neck width and PSA.

A factor that should be considered, however, is the change that occurred in projectile technology from the atlatl and dart to the bow and arrow. As stated earlier, given the speed with which the bow and arrow spread throughout the Great Basin and its almost to-

TABLE 2.1
Radiocarbon Dates and Calculated Means for Each Horizon at Gatecliff Shelter

Horizon	Radiocarbon Dates (B.P.)[a]	Mean Date (B.P.)
1	470±90	510
	550±90	
1/2	590±90	
	750±90	
2	—	750
3	1,000±90	1,000
4	2,020±90	1,845
4/5	1,670±80	
	1,739±90	
5	1,580±90	
	2,280±90	2,391
	2,760±60	
	2,945±45	
6	—	2,815
7	3,125±75	
	3,140±120	3,238
	3,295±55	
	3,390±45	
8	2,895±90	
	3,140±90	3,232
	3,660±55	
8/9	3,555±85	
9	3,315±65	
	3,340±80	3,344
	3,375±80	
10	3,975±65	4,038
	4,100±65	
11	4,140±70	4,140
12	5,000±80	
	5,200±120	5,150
	5,250±120	
13	—	5,055
14	4,140±125	
	4,850±95	4,960
	5,370±90	
	5,480±90	

[a]From Thomas (1983:42–52)

tal replacement of the atlatl and dart in that region, this new technology (including both behavioral and mechanical components [Schiffer and Skibo 1987]) was likely under strong selection. Thus, there is no reason to assume that the same set of constraints operating on the formal traits of the dart point tip were operating on the arrow point tip. It is more likely, given the discussion of functional and stylistic traits, that the traits being

TABLE 2.2
Correlation Coefficients for Nine Projectile Point
Attribute Means by Horizon Mean Date at Gatecliff Shelter

Variable		Pearson's r	Probability
Total Length	Lt	.308	.335
Medial Length	La	.269	.397
Maximum Width	Wm	.295	.327
Basal Width	Wb	.472	.103
Neck Width	Wn	.724	.027
Thickness	TH	.413	.161
Weight	WT	.470	.145
Proximal Shoulder Angle	PSA	−.594	.091
Distal Shoulder Angle	DSA	.109	.780

considered here have different temporal distributions relative to these two technologies. Thus, for this analysis the points from Gatecliff were separated into two size categories based on neck width, a variable used by a number of researchers as a dependable measure of projectile point size (e.g., Beck 1984; Christenson 1986; Corliss 1972; Fawcett and Kornfeld 1980; Patterson 1985). Correlation coefficients were recalculated between mean dates and the metric variables within these neck-width-size categories.

Table 2.3 shows correlation coefficients between the nine trait means and horizon mean dates within the two size groups defined by neck width. As expected, traits with significant correlations differ between these groups. For large points, both length measurements (Lt: $r = -.752, p = .012$; La: $r = -.718, p = .019$) and PSA ($r = -.788, p = .020$) show significant correlations with mean date. For small points thickness ($r = .682, p = .030$) is significantly correlated with horizon mean date and, once again, PSA ($r = -.604, p = .085$) shows a strong, although not quite significant, correlation.

Summarizing the results of the above analysis, when all Gatecliff points are considered, neck width shows a significant correlation with horizon mean date; further, PSA shows a strong, although not significant, correlation as well. These results indicate direc-

tional temporal trends in both variables. When large and small points are considered separately, temporal trends differ. For large points, PSA and both length measures show significant correlations; for small points, thickness is significantly correlated and PSA is strongly, but not quite significantly, correlated with horizon mean date. These results suggest that for dart points, PSA and length are under selection, and for arrow points, PSA and thickness are under selection.

The patterns of the remaining traits are much less distinctive. In all cases the mean fluctuates back and forth from horizon to horizon, a pattern suggesting drift. Such fluctuation could be misleading, however. For most functional traits there are ranges within which those traits may vary and still meet their performance requirements; that is, the values fluctuate within tolerance limits. These tolerance limits will vary depending on the performance requirements of the particular trait (or trait complex) under consideration. For instance, in trying to determine the optimal weight for an arrow point versus that for a dart point, several researchers (e.g., Browne 1938; Evans 1957; Fenenga 1953; Van Buren 1974) have found that each projectile technology will perform with points of a wide range of weights. The average weight by horizon for both large and small points in the Gatecliff assemblage is shown in Table

TABLE 2.3
Correlation Coefficients for Nine Projectile Point
Attribute Means by Horizon Mean Date within Two Size Groups
at Gatecliff Shelter

Variable	Large Points		Small Points	
	r	p	r	p
Lt	−.752	.012	.143	.694
La	−.718	.019	.058	.873
Wm	−.449	.166	−.266	.457
Wb	−.057	.869	−.413	.235
Wn	−.414	.307	.084	.817
TH	.158	.642	.682	.030
WT	−.401	.250	.157	.665
PSA	−.788	.020	−.604	.085
DSA	.261	.588	.085	.829

TABLE 2.4
Average Projectile Point Weight by Horizon
in the Gatecliff Assemblage

Horizon	Small	Large
1	0.60 g	4.60 g
2	1.87 g	—
3	1.52 g	3.20 g
4	2.43 g	4.39 g
5	1.92 g	3.84 g
6	1.40 g	4.21 g
7	1.70 g	3.11 g
8	1.84 g	3.42 g
9	1.40 g	4.09 g

2.4. Figure 2.4 presents a graphic representation of the changes in mean weight by horizon. As can be seen from Table 2.4, the ranges for small and large point weights do not overlap. In fact, a t-test shows a significant difference between the weights of small and large points (t = -17.962, df = 264.5, p = .000), suggesting that two different "optimal" ranges for projectile point weight do exist. However, the patterns of weight change through time in both cases (Figure 2.4), and strongly resemble the pattern of drift depicted in Figure 2.1, suggesting weight is a neutral trait. It is possible that both selection and drift are operating here. For each technological context there may be tolerance limits within which point weight can fluctuate randomly. Thus, the tolerance limits rather than the individual variates are under selection; the latter are controlled by drift, as indicated by the random fluctuation within the limits. If this is the case, then

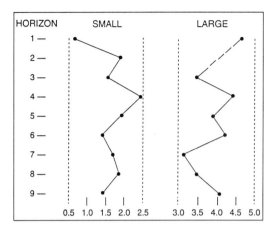

Figure 2.4. Graphic representation of the changes in mean projectile point weight (in grams) by horizon at Gatecliff Shelter.

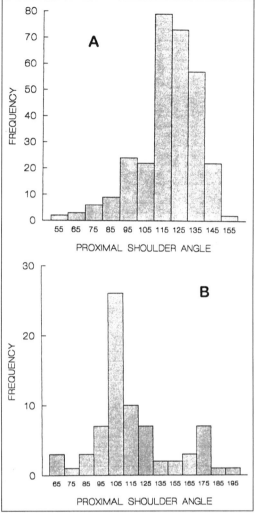

Figure 2.5. Bar graph of proximal shoulder angle (in 10-degree intervals) for (A) large points and (B) small points in the assemblage from Gatecliff Shelter.

weight is a functional trait. The limited experimental studies discussed earlier tend to confirm this conclusion, since weight is an important factor in balance and stability. The pattern described for weight is evident for all of the traits that show no directionality, suggesting that they too are functional traits. This suggestion, however, must be investigated through more detailed performance tests, designed to examine tolerance limits within particular contexts.

Focusing more closely on PSA, it is interesting to note that this trait appears to be under selection in both small and large points, with the mean increasing over time. An examination of PSA within the two size categories (Figure 2.5), however, shows that, although it is increasing over time in both, the range of values and shape of the distributions differ.[3] Most of the large points appear to be concentrated between 115° and 135° (Figure 2.5A). A weak break in the distribution is indicated at 105°, which is slightly above where Thomas (1981) places the division between the Gatecliff (parallel- and contracting-stemmed) and Elko (expanding-stemmed) types.

Figure 2.5B shows the distribution of PSA for small points. As this figure shows, the majority of small points are concentrated between 95° and 125°. A definite break in this distribution is indicated between 135° and 155°, also slightly above where Thomas (1981) places the division between Rosegate (corner-notched) and Desert Side-Notched (side-notched) types.

Could PSA, then, be at least partially responsible for the historical behavior of the Great Basin projectile point types? To investigate this possibility, PSA was partitioned into the divisions on the basis of the modality indicated in the histograms in Figure 2.5.

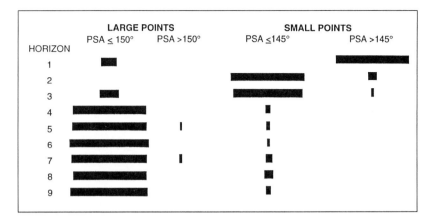

Figure 2.6. Relative frequencies of PSA partitioned into side-notched and corner-notched categories, based on the bar graphs in Figure 2.5.

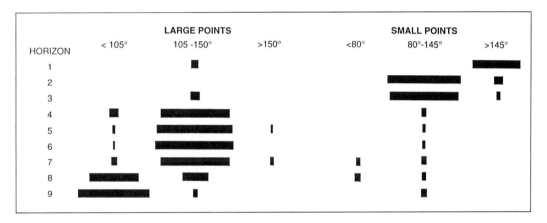

Figure 2.7. Relative frequencies of PSA further partitioned for corner-notched points into concave and straight/convex bases, based on the bar graphs in Figure 2.5.

As mentioned earlier, PSA actually conflates two nominal traits, the type of haft (corner-notched, side-notched) and, if the point is corner-notched, the shape of the stem (expanding, parallel/contracting). Thus, partitioning was done in two stages, beginning with the type of haft. Within each size category, PSA was partitioned into two groups, representing side-notched points and corner-notched points. Figure 2.6 shows the relative frequencies of these two groups by horizon. For small points, PSA partitioned in this way is distributed monotonically through time, the expected pattern of a historical trait. For large points, however, this is not the case.[3]

Next, PSA was partitioned further for corner-notched points. As can be seen in Figure 2.7, the distributions for small points remain the same, but those of large points are quite different; the latter are now distributed monotonically. The distributions in Figures 2.6 and 2.7 suggest that the combination of "type of haft" and "shape of stem" is largely responsible for the historical behavior of the large corner-notched types, but type of haft alone is responsible for the historical distribution of small point types.

These patterns can be investigated further through an examination of spatial distributions. That the historical behavior of large corner-notched point types appears to be determined by two traits while that of small point types seems to be determined by only one suggests a difference in the way traits are being transmitted. In the latter case, transmission appears to be at the scale of trait; in the former, of trait complex. If this is true, then in the case of small points the single trait of hafting should have a distinctive spatial distribution, but in the case of large points the variant combinations should have their own separate distributions.

Unfortunately, when describing projectile point assemblages other authors rarely report Thomas's metric traits (but see Elston and Budy 1989); most data are reported in type frequencies. Thus, the distributions of only those metric traits that can be translated into the nominal trait categories defining Great Basin point types can be examined. PSA has already been equated with the type of haft and the shape of the stem. One additional dimension can also be considered. To distinguish between concave- and straight/convex-based points within the Gatecliff and Elko Series (e.g., Elko Eared [concave-based] and Elko Corner-Notched [straight/convex-based]), Thomas (1981) calculates the basal indentation ratio (BIR), which is La/Lt. Because both La and Lt have strongly directional temporal distributions in the Gatecliff assemblage, it might be expected that BIR would also show such a distribution. This proves to be the case for large points; BIR shows a significant correlation with the horizon mean date for large points ($r = .185, p = .002$) but not for small points ($r = .111, p = .331$). Thus, the third dimension considered here is "base shape," whether it is concave or straight/convex.

Data from 19 archaeological sites across the Great Basin are used (Figure 2.8).[4] With the exception of the Skull Creek Dunes in the northwest and the Rose Spring site in the southwest, all have at least three radiocarbon dates, but 11 have nine or more dates. The data from these sites are variable in their quality due to several factors, including when and how the sites were excavated, differing formational histories, and quality and availability of datable materials. Thus, the focus

here is not on specific dates at individual localities but on general temporal and spatial trends.

BASIN-WIDE TRAIT PATTERNS
Regarding type of haft, Figure 2.9 shows the earliest date of occurrence of corner-notching and side-notching at each of the 19 sites. Both hafting techniques appear to be earliest in northwestern Utah, represented at Danger and Hogup Caves by 8,000 years ago. The distribution of dates suggests that corner-notching moves both westward and southward, followed by side-notching only slightly later, except in the extreme northwestern Basin at Connely Caves, where the two have widely different first appearances. What is striking, however, is that the early dates for these two hafting techniques occur only around the northern, eastern, and southeastern peripheries of the Great Basin. Neither corner-notching nor side-notching appear in the west/central or southwestern Basin earlier than 4500 B.P. A second pattern, however, is also evident in Figure 2.9. Once the projectile point record begins in the central and western Basin, side-notching is rare, represented only by a few specimens at South Fork Shelter, Newark Cave, and Amy's Shelter.

This pattern is consistent with arguments made recently by Grayson (1993), who reasserts a position reached by Baumhoff and Heizer (1965) three decades ago: that population in the Great Basin was severely diminished during the middle Holocene, ca. 7500–4500 B.P., a period of increased aridity. As Figure 2.9 shows, the early dates for the appearance of corner-notched and side-notched points occur at the end of the early Holocene or at the beginning of the middle Holocene. With the exception of those in the Bonneville Basin, which Grayson observes had water sources nearby, all of the sites with early occurrences of these points have a hiatus in occupation corresponding to much of the mid-Holocene. Reoccupation of these rock-shelters corresponds with the earliest occupation of rock-shelters in the central and western Great Basin.

Lower population density, however, does

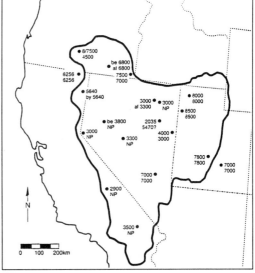

Figure 2.8. Location of the 19 Great Basin archaeological sites considered in the present analysis. 1. Connely Caves; 2. Skull Creek Dunes; 3. Dirty Shame Rockshelter; 4. Nightfire Island; 5. Surprise Valley (includes King's Dog, Rodriguez, and Menlo Baths); 6. South Fork Shelter; 7. James Creek Shelter; 8. Hogup Cave; 9. Danger Cave; 10. Newark Cave; 11. Amy's Shelter; 12. Gatecliff Shelter; 13. Hidden Cave; 14. Spooner Lake; 15. O'Malley Shelter; 16. Sudden Shelter; 17. Cowboy Cave; 18. Rose Spring; 19. Newberry Cave.

Figure 2.9. Earliest date (B.P.) of occurrence of corner-notching and side-notching for large points at the 19 Great Basin sites.

not explain the virtual absence of side-notching in the central/western Great Basin once people begin to move back into that area. I have argued elsewhere (1995) that corner-notching and side-notching represent two alternative hafting techniques (two alternative trait variants under selection). Corner-notching, however, proved to be slightly more effective than side-notching and came to dominate over time. Both appear about 8,000 years ago and, during the middle Holocene, where records exist, both are present. But the general trend is for the relative abundance of side-notching to decrease while that of corner-notching increases. Thus, when people began to move back into the central/western Basin at the end of the middle Holocene, corner-notching was the dominant form.

Because of the low population density and the virtual absence of archaeological deposits

in the central/western Basin during the middle Holocene as well as the very low frequency of side-notching in this area, the distinctions in patterning of projectile point traits are primarily along the periphery of this area, in the northern and eastern Great Basin.

As for the distribution of base shape (Figure 2.10), the two variants (concave, straight/convex) appear concurrently at each locality, except in the cases of Newark Cave in the east and O'Malley Shelter to the south. When considered in conjunction with type of haft, the distributions are remarkably similar to those in Figure 2.9. For side-notched points (Figure 2.11), both base-shape variants have the same spatial distribution, except at Skull Creek Dunes, South Fork Shelter, and Amy's Shelter, where one or the other variant is not present. There appears to be no

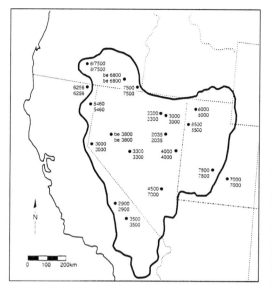

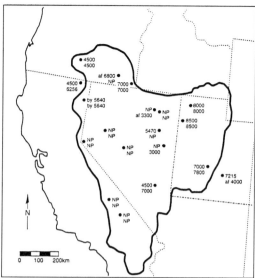

Figure 2.10. Earliest date (B.P.) of occurrence of concave and straight/convex bases for large points at the 19 Great Basin sites.

Figure 2.11. Earliest date (B.P.) of occurrence of large side-notched points with concave and straight/concave bases at the 19 Great Basin sites.

pattern, however, as to which variant is missing from these sites. There are also differences in timing, at Nightfire Island, O'Malley Shelter, and Cowboy Cave, but again, there is no pattern in these differences. Finally, there appear to be no patterns evident in the relative frequency distributions through time at any of the sites.

Interestingly, the duration of these two variant combinations (side-notched, concave base; side-notched, straight/convex base) differs at Nightfire Island and Cowboy Cave. At Nightfire Island, straight/convex bases are present throughout the entire sequence, whereas concave bases are present for a much shorter time. At Cowboy Cave there is no overlap in their distributions; concave bases are present from about 7215 B.P. until 6500 B.P., while straight/convex bases do not appear until 3635 B.P. The fact that both of these sites are outside the Basin proper may be important. Assemblages may reflect influences from adjacent areas as well as areas within the Basin. The Nightfire Island assemblage, for example, contains a range of nonshouldered points that have no counterparts in the Great Basin; points such as these, however, are quite

common in western Oregon and Washington. Thus, it is not surprising to find durational differences at these localities that are not reflected in Great Basin assemblages.

The distribution of corner-notching in combination with base shape (Figure 2.12) shows no differences from that of corner-notching alone (Figure 2.9), but when the third trait—stem shape—is added, different patterns begin to emerge. Base shape has little effect on the distribution of expanding-stemmed points (Figure 2.13). The most pronounced differences are at O'Malley Shelter, Sudden Shelter, and Cowboy Cave, all in the southeastern Basin, but these differences show no definite patterns. When base shape is considered for parallel/contracting-stemmed points, however, distributions differ (Figure 2.14). First, the straight/convex base is not present in most of the northern Basin; it is present at Nightfire Island, South Fork Shelter, and Danger Cave, but only in very low frequencies. Otherwise it is absent across this entire area. When both variants are present, they seem to appear concurrently, except at Sudden Shelter, where concave bases occur much earlier. When the distributions in Fig-

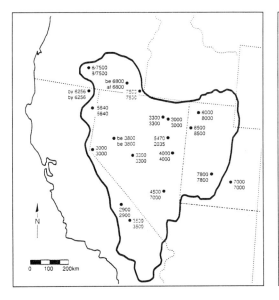

Figure 2.12 Earliest date (B.P.) of occurrence of large corner-notched points with concave and straight/convex bases at the 19 Great Basin sites.

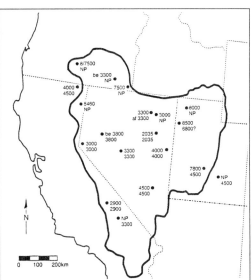

Figure 2.14. Earliest date (B.P.) of occurrence of large parallel/contracting-stemmed, corner-notched points with concave and straight/convex bases at the 19 Great Basin sites.

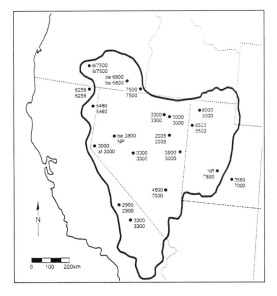

Figure 2.13. Earliest date (B.P.) of occurrence of large expanding-stemmed, corner-notched points with concave and straight/convex bases at the 19 Great Basin sites.

ure 2.13 are compared with those in Figure 2.14, temporal differences in the appearance of expanding and parallel/straight stems are also evident, primarily again in the southeastern Basin.

An examination of all four variant combinations for corner-notched points (stem shape and base shape) at each of the 19 localities, then, shows all are the same (except in the cases where parallel/contracting stems are not present) in the northern and central areas. But in the east and southeast, duration differs considerably. These four variant combinations have different relative distributions at each location, but there is no pattern to that difference.

In summary, for large points the distributions of side-notching and corner-notching are different, both spatially and temporally. Both appear earliest in northwestern Utah, diffusing fairly quickly to the west and south. Neither appear in the central and western Basin until after 4500 B.P. and, once they do appear, side-notching is rare. Although the duration of these two hafting alternatives is similar in most cases, the frequency of side-notching decreases over time relative to that of corner-notching in almost every case (Beck 1995).

When a second trait—base shape—is considered in conjunction with side-notching, the spatial and temporal distributions are virtually identical to those of side-notching considered in isolation. Both variants of base shape are present in nearly every case, with no apparent patterns in relative frequency distributions through time, suggesting that this trait is not under selection in this context and that it is also not contributing to the historical behavior of the side-notched types.

A consideration of base shape in conjunction with corner-notching yields similar results; when a third trait—stem shape—is added, however, distinct spatial and temporal distributions occur for certain variant combinations. Corner-notched points with expanding stems appear to be distributed slightly differently from those with parallel/contracting stems, especially when the latter are distinguished on the basis of base shape. Thus, for corner-notched points, there are three distinct distributions: corner-notched with expanding stems, corner-notched with parallel/contracting stems and concave bases, and corner-notched points with parallel/contracting stems and straight/ convex bases. In fact, these combinations correspond to the Elko Eared/Corner-Notched (expanding stems) (Figure 2.15A, B), Gatecliff Split-Stemmed (parallel/contracting stems, concave bases) (Figure 2.15C), and Gatecliff Contracting Stem (parallel/contracting stems, straight/ convex bases) (Figure 2.15D) types in Thomas's key (1981).

As for small points, Figure 2.16 shows the distribution of corner-notching and side-notching across the Basin. In every case, corner-notching occurs earlier than side-notching, between 3000 and 2500 B.P. at most locations. Side-notching appears at most localities between 1500 and 1000 B.P. There are, however, no pronounced directional patterns for either hafting technique as there were for large points. The lack of patterning in corner-notching is likely due to the rapid spread of the bow and arrow after its introduction. Thus, it is not corner-notching that is diffusing, but small size, as evidenced by neck width. Corner-notching is already the

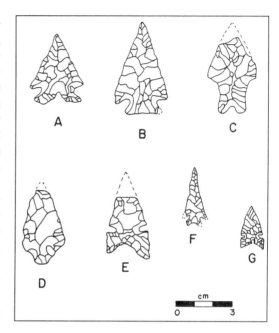

Figure 2.15. Examples of Great Basin projectile point types mentioned in the text. A. Elko Eared; B. Elko Corner-Notched; C. Gatecliff Split-Stemmed; D. Gatecliff Contracting Stem; E. Large side-notched; F. Rosegate; G. Desert Side-Notched. (A–C and E–F are from eastern Oregon; D is from eastern Nevada.)

dominant hafting technique when the bow and arrow is introduced; thus, arrow points are simply made in the "image" of dart points, just smaller.

The lack of patterning in side-notching may also be due to the rapid spread of a functional trait, this time an alternative hafting technique. It was argued earlier that corner-notching came to dominate over side-notching in dart points because corner-notching was a slightly more effective technique in that context. This may not be the case, however, when the projectile technology changes from atlatl and dart to bow and arrow. In fact, side-notching replaces corner-notching among arrow points not only in the Great Basin but also in eastern North America during late prehistoric times (see Shott 1993). In both areas, small triangular notched and unnotched forms replace corner-notched forms around 1500 to 1000 B.P., which may have to do with increasing the efficiency of the

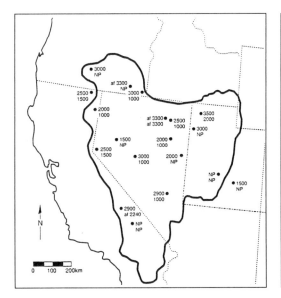

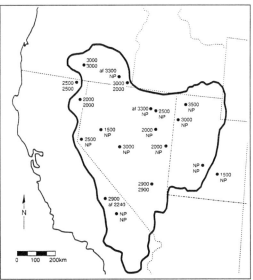

Figure 2.16. Earliest date (B.P.) of occurrence of side-notching and corner-notching for small points at the 19 Great Basin sites.

Figure 2.17. Earliest date (B.P.) of occurrence of expanding and parallel stems for small corner-notched points at the 19 Great Basin sites.

bow and arrow technology. This event remains to be demonstrated, however.

An additional factor that may have contributed to the rapid spread of side-notching is population size, which is believed to have been much larger in the late prehistoric than in previous periods (Grayson 1993). A larger population throughout the Basin would likely increase the rate of transmission, thus contributing to a more rapid rate of diffusion.

Because most published reports present type frequencies rather than frequencies of metric traits and because the corner-notched type descriptions do not distinguish base shape, it is possible to examine this variable only in a few cases. In the assemblages for which data are available, almost all corner-notched points have straight/convex bases. In side-notched points both variants are often present, but they have identical temporal distributions. Although their spatial distributions are not identical, no patterning is evident.

Information concerning stem shape is available, but as Figure 2.17 shows, only expanding stems are present at most sites. Par-

allel/contracting stems are present in the extreme north and south, suggesting this trait may be important on a local scale. However, when both are present, their temporal distributions are concurrent.

In summary, then, for small points type of haft seems to be the trait responsible for the historical behavior of types. Corner-notched types (Rose Spring, Eastgate Expanding Stem, which are included by Thomas in the Rosegate Series) (Figure 2.15F) appear earliest, followed by the side-notched type (Desert Side-Notched) (Figure 2.15G).

DISCUSSION AND CONCLUSION

Where does this leave us with respect to the validity of Great Basin projectile point types as chronological units? In order to address this problem I have proceeded in two steps, guided by three questions.

The first question relates to the selective status of the traits upon which the Great Basin projectile point types are based. Are they functional, stylistic, or a combination of both? Nine metric (as well as one ratio) traits were examined using the well-stratified and dated Gatecliff assemblage for directional trends through time. In an examination of the entire projectile point assemblage, only neck width and PSA showed directional trends, suggesting these traits are under selection and therefore functional. Two projectile technologies, however, atlatl and dart and bow and arrow, are represented in this assemblage. These two technologies are likely to have different performance requirements for point tips. Thus, dart and arrow points were separated on the basis of neck width, the only measure of size to show a directional trend. The spatial distribution of neck width also is suggestive of selection, as neck widths smaller than 9.0 mm spread relatively quickly across space.

For large points, Lt, La, PSA, and BIR have directional trends; for small points, PSA and thickness show such trends. Again, their strong directionality suggests that these traits are under selection within the contexts of either the atlatl and dart or bow and arrow technology. Limited performance studies add some degree of confirmation here. These studies suggest that the morphology of the hafting element (e.g., PSA) as well as thickness affect impact resistance and that thickness also affects penetration.

Spatial patterns tend to confirm that PSA is functional, and in two specific cases, basal indentation ratio is functional as well. Spatial patterns, however, suggest that in most cases BIR is not functional since both variants considered are present simultaneously at most localities throughout the Great Basin. Further, there are no distinctive temporal patterns in relative abundances of these variants at any locality. Thus, except in the case of large corner-notched, parallel/contracting-stemmed points, I consider this trait to be stylistic.

In cases where no directional trends are evident, mean values tend to fluctuate randomly through time, but all appear to fluctuate within limits. I have suggested that these limits are, in fact, tolerance limits within which a functional trait can vary and still meet its performance requirements. Thus, it is the tolerance limits that are under selection while the variants within these limits are random, controlled by drift.

In summary, then, I believe that all nine of the metric traits examined are indeed functional. However, I believe BIR to be stylistic, except in the specific case of large corner-notched, parallel/contracting-stemmed points.

The second question: which traits appear to be driving the historical behavior of the Great Basin projectile point types? A secondary question here concerns whether the same traits are responsible in all cases. The relative frequencies of side-notching and corner-notching—and for corner-notched points, the shape of the stem—all based on PSA, suggest that it is simply the position of the notch that is responsible for the historical behavior of small points and a combination of notching and stem shape in the case of large corner-notched points. The spatial distributions of the two traits—type of haft and stem shape—in isolation and in combination, largely confirm this suggestion. The addition of a third trait—base shape—suggests that this trait also contributes to the historical distribution of certain types. Table 2.5 shows the Great Basin projectile point types and the traits that seem to most strongly influence the temporal patterns of each. Type of haft (side-notched) alone is responsible for the historical behavior of large side-notched types. In the case of the Elko Eared and Elko Corner-Notched types, it is the combination of corner-notched haft and expanding stem shape that is important. Finally, a combination of three traits, type of haft (corner-notched), stem shape (parallel/contracting), and base shape (concave or straight/convex) determines the distributions of the Gatecliff Split-Stemmed and Gatecliff Contracting-Stemmed types.

In the case of small points, type of haft once again seems to be responsible for the historical behavior of the Rosegate and Desert Side-Notched types.

The fact that different trait complexes appear to be responsible for the historical behavior of individual types suggests that there are differences in the way traits are being transmitted. In the case of large side-notched and small points, transmission is in the form of a single trait, but for large corner-notched

TABLE 2.5
Great Basin Projectile Point Types and the Traits Responsible
for the Historical Behavior of Each

| Large | | Small | |
Type	Traits	Type	Traits
Large Side-Notched	Haft	Eastgate/Rose Spring[a]	Haft
Elko Eared Elko Corner-Notched	Haft, Stem Shape	Desert Side-Notched	Haft
Gatecliff Split Stem Gatecliff Contracting Stem	Haft, Stem Shape, Base Shape		

[a]Thomas (1981) combines the Rose Spring and Eastgate types into the Rosegate Series.

points, a complex of traits is undergoing transmission as a unit.

It appears, then, that the traits defining the Great Basin projectile point types are functional, the exception being BIR in most cases. Furthermore, even though these types distribute historically through time, different traits or trait combinations are contributing to that behavior across types.

The third question: are *both* stylistic and functional units valid for chronological purposes? My answer to this question is yes, but with qualification. As stated earlier, to use a set of types to order a group of assemblages, the frequency distributions of those types must be known, and those distributions must conform to Ford's (1952, 1962) "battleship-shaped" curve. Because of their neutrality, units defined by stylistic traits will fulfill this requirement. As shown, however, it is possible for units defined by functional traits to also fulfill this requirement.

The critical difference is in the predictability of these patterns. Because neutral traits are not subject to deterministic forces, such as selection, but only to random forces, such as drift, a prediction is possible that they will be distributed unimodally through time. But because functional traits *are* subject to deterministic forces, their behavior cannot be predicted. Thus, stylistic traits can be used inferentially to create chronological units, but

functional traits cannot. It must be demonstrated that a functional unit is distributed historically before it can be used for chronological purposes; the procedure for using function is by definition *post hoc*. Once this is done, however, a set of functional units can yield a chronological order just as a set of stylistic units can.

In conclusion, the Great Basin projectile point types have been examined in order to determine their validity as chronological units. It has been suggested that these types are constructed almost entirely on the basis of functional traits. It has also been suggested that, although both style and function can yield valid chronological units, the use of function is context-specific and requires demonstration on a case-by-case basis that the functional units are historically significant. The Great Basin projectile point types have passed the test of historical significance and thus remain the major tool for chronology in the Great Basin.

ACKNOWLEDGMENTS
I would like to thank Bob Bettinger, Bob Dunnell, Don Grayson, Tom Jones, Bob Leonard, Lee Lyman, Mike O'Brien, Ann Ramenofsky, Mike Schiffer, Mike Shott, Ana Steffen, Alan Sullivan, and Patrice Teltser for reading and commenting on various versions of this chapter. The issue of style and func-

tion and how they might be distinguished in the archaeological record is a problem that I have been trying to work through for some years and I am especially grateful to Ann Ramenofsky for her continual encouragement.

Notes

1. Average dates were calculated for horizons having more than one radiocarbon date. For those having only one date, that date was used as the mean. For those horizons having no radiocarbon dates (2, 5, 6, 13), estimates were calculated based on the dates bracketing those horizons.
2. Variable means were used in order to suppress within-horizon variation that might obscure between-horizon behavior.
3. As Figure 2.6 shows, there are very few occurrences of large side-notched points in the Gatecliff assemblage. Although their small number

affects the range of values for large points, it does not explain the lack of a monotonic distribution for these points.
4. Data for the 19 sites used were taken from the following sources: Aikens 1970: Hogup Cave; Aikens et al. 1977, Hanes 1977: Dirty Shame Rockshelter; Aikens et al. 1982, Wilde 1985: Skull Creek Dunes; Bedwell 1973: Connely Caves; C. A. Davis and Smith 1981: Newberry Cave; Elston 1971: Spooner Lake; Elston and Budy 1989: James Creek Shelter; Fowler 1968: Newark Cave; Fowler et al. 1973: O'Malley Shelter; Gruhn 1979: Amy's Shelter; Heizer et al 1968: South Fork Shelter; Holmer 1980, Jennings 1980: Cowboy Cave; Jennings 1957: Danger Cave; Jennings et al. 1980: Sudden Shelter; Lanning 1963: Rose Spring Site; O'-Connell 1971, 1975, O'Connell and Inoway 1994: Surprise Valley; Sampson 1985: Nightfire Island; Thomas 1983: Gatecliff Shelter; Thomas 1985: Hidden Cave.

3

Testing the Pecos Classification

Heidi E. Reed and John R. Stein

In August 1927, a conference was held at Pecos Pueblo in northern New Mexico. Among the 41 attendees were the majority of the most productive and most influential archaeologists of their generation working in the southwestern United States. The objectives of this conference were "to bring about contacts between workers in the Southwestern field; to discuss fundamental problems of Southwestern history, and to formulate plans for coordinated attack upon them; to pool knowledge of facts and techniques, and to lay foundations for a unified system of nomenclature" (Kidder 1927:489). Perhaps the most lasting product of this meeting is the combination of both a relative chronology and a classification of cultures that has become known as the Pecos Classification. Once proposed, the Pecos Classification immediately came to define the research direction in Southwestern archaeology. The Pecos Classification is still widely used by Southwestern archaeologists to designate a general time period and to refer to a suite of cultural materials and architecture belonging to a specific period. Current research is usually described and often conducted in the terms of this framework inherited from an earlier generation.

Preserving an intellectual link to a past generation of scholars is not necessarily bad. After all, the purpose of conducting research within a structured framework such as science is to allow each succeeding researcher to add to a growing body of knowledge. This growth would not be possible if ideas were discarded simply because they were old. It is important, however, to examine consciously the concepts that we inherit. These concepts have a tendency to structure the way we think and the potential to limit the questions that we ask or the possible explanations that we consider. This is especially true of ideas that are as basic as the subject matter of this volume: the units of study. There are an infinite number of criteria that may be used to partition the phenomenal world to form units for study. The criteria used are determined and justified implicitly or explicitly by the partitioner (Brew 1946a; Dunnell 1971; Sober 1984). A balance must be struck between the requirements of the specific research issues being addressed and the need for useful communication between researchers in order to avoid terminological chaos in the discipline.

There has been a great deal of discussion over the past several decades concerning how archaeological research might be made to conform better to the practice of science—or whether this is even desirable. Let us assume for the moment that the conduct of science is our goal. The units of study should therefore be relevant to the question being addressed and the theory being evaluated by the research. For example, evolutionary biology is a body of theory wherein genes are a potential unit of study. An evolutionary biologist interested in the manner of transmitting a specific behavior from one generation to another would postulate that genes might be an appropriate unit used in forming the hypothesis to be tested by the research. If no relationship could be found between the inheritance of genes and the transmission of the behavior, then the hypothesis that linked the gene and the behavior would be rejected. If, however, nothing could be found empirically that correlated to the unit "gene" as defined in the theory, then the theory itself may be called into question.

No formal statement of theory or the units of study derived from it is contained in Kidder's report of the Pecos Conference. However, much of the thinking concerning the nature and causes of cultural change can be surmised. In 1927, the entire Southwest was considered one culture area that followed one cultural developmental path (Kidder 1927). The unit of "culture" and the geographic area a culture occupies are, therefore, units in which the Pecos Classification was formed. Ascertaining the boundaries of the unit "culture area" became a research goal as a result of the conference. The Pecos developmental progress could be measured in terms of such things as specialization, development of the arts, and geographic expansion. Traits of this kind could be used to describe and identify developmental stages through which a culture passed.

"Stages" are another unit of study constructed by the creators of the Pecos Classification. Agricultural, sedentary, and large communities with permanent structures were viewed as advanced, whereas nonagricultural, mobile, small communities with ephemeral structures were considered more primitive. Cultures were believed to floresce and then degenerate. Either indigenous invention or the introduction of new technologies from outside (i.e., diffusion) were the causes of cultural change. The theory of the period linked time and cultural development; therefore, measuring cultural development allowed one to measure time.

Kidder (1927) makes it clear that the Pecos Classification was offered as an initial attempt to bring order and structure to the pool of observations available in 1927. Thus, the Pecos Classification may be considered a hypothetical construct derived from an implicit theory of cultural development. If viewed as a hypothesis, the classification and its underlying theory have consequences and implications that may be drawn out and tested. If the test implications are found to be false—that is, not to fit the evidence observable in the archaeological record—then the classification proposed at the Pecos Conference must be rejected as no longer useful. At the very least, the Pecos Classification could be found not to function well as a means to arrange archaeological materials chronologically. The Pecos Classification was proposed long before the discipline achieved its current level of maturity, hence it may seem unfair to apply the stringent evaluative criteria of reliability or validity. However, the problems engendered by using the Pecos Classification may be solved only by adopting the more conscientiously constructed methodology advocated here.

For our purpose, two tests that evaluate the performance of the Pecos Classification with respect to the empirical record were made. Because the Pecos Classification is based on an idea of progressive development from simple to complex, it predicted that the large masonry structures, such as Pueblo Bonito in Chaco Canyon in northwestern New Mexico and the cliff dwellings located in southern Colorado and northeastern Arizona, represent Pueblo III, or the Great Pueblo Period. The first test was to determine whether these large sites are, indeed, contemporary. The second test was to determine whether small-house ruins of this region, classed in the preceding stage (Pueblo II), are earlier temporally than Pueblo Bonito (Pueblo III). As we show, the Pecos Classification failed these and other tests posed since 1927. Despite this failure, the Pecos Classification is still used. Southwesternists need to reconsider whether these traditional units are still valid for conducting and presenting current research.

THE PRODUCTS OF THE PECOS CONFERENCE

The 1927 Southwestern Archaeological Conference, or the Pecos Conference, was hosted by A. V. Kidder at the end of the Phillips Academy of Andover's excavation field season at Pecos Pueblo in northern New Mexico. In his report on the conference, Kidder (1927:489) claims "entire unanimity in regard to the general nature of Southwestern culture-growth" and "practical unanimity as to the course of development." Kidder clarifies what is meant by "Southwestern culture-growth" and "course of development" by listing the material culture traits identified for the Southwest in their order of appearance, an accepted technique within the culture historical perspective. The course of development begins as "agriculture was taken up by a previously resident, long-headed, nomadic or semi-nomadic people, who did not practice skull-deformation, and who already made excellent coiled basketry, twined-woven bags, sandals, and used the atlatl; but whose dwellings were of perishable nature (Kidder 1927:489)." Thereafter,

> The *newly acquired art of agriculture led to a more settled life and to the development of more permanent houses.* For some time, however, pottery-making was unknown. At a later date pottery was introduced, or possibly independently invented, houses of the pit type were perfected, and became grouped into villages, and the bow-and-arrow began to supplant the atlatl. The long-headed race, however, still persisted. At a still later period there appeared certain important changes: skull-deformation was initiated . . . ; *dwellings emerged from the ground,* the rooms became rectangular, and were grouped more closely; structural rings (corrugations) were for the first time left unobliterated on cooking vessels. *From then on the development of the culture was rapid.* After a period of wide extension marked by small-village life, there was, perhaps a *decrease in amount of territory occupied, and surely a concentration of population in certain areas, to-*

> *gether with great architectural and ceramic achievement and strong regional specialization. Subsequently large areas were abandoned, there appears to have been a considerable shrinkage of population, and there was a definite cultural de-generation.* This period was brought to a close by the settlement of the Southwest by the Spanish about 1600. (1927:489-90; emphasis added)

The language of Kidder's report of this conference and other field reports by the participants reveals that the underlying theory of culture change prevalent at the time was one that presupposed a unified Southwestern culture that progressed to a climax and then naturally faded either to extinction or to replacement by another developmental wave. In the Pecos Conference report Kidder uses terms such as "Southwestern culture-growth," "course of development," and "degeneration." Developmental "stages" were proposed to describe a unilineal course for the entire Southwest as a unified culture area in which these people "passed from a simple hunting type to a relatively highly cultured group" (Roberts 1929). Intuitive measures for the degree of development implied are specialization; "development of the arts"; degree of complexity in, for example, ceramics; development of religion evidenced in presumed religious structures (kivas); and expansion. Advanced stages are characterized by agriculture, sedentary residence, masonry architecture, and large communities. A few years before the conference, Kidder wrote,

> Crude and primitive-looking remains, when compared with relics of an obviously more advanced type are usually, and doubtless often correctly, assumed to belong to an earlier period. *This method of chronological evaluation must, however, be very cautiously applied and should always have the support of corroborative evidence,* since in the history of the Southwest many cases of degeneration in culture and of irregularity in culture growth have occurred. (1962:160; emphasis added)

A subcommittee at the Pecos Conference

prepared a chronological tabulation of elements to be used by the group at large to define more precise culture stages and the list of diagnostic culture traits for each stage (see Appendix to this chapter). The chronology resulting from the discussions that followed should be familiar to any Southwestern archaeologist today. The chronological placement of the trait-defined stages is occasionally not only based on observed superposition of one suite of traits over another but also on judgments made concerning what is primitive versus more developed.

The Pecos Classification immediately influenced the direction and priorities of Southwestern research. With the classification as the ground plan, areas for further research were identified at the conference. These recommended areas for research were defined as geographic areas and chronological stages considered inadequately described. Plotting then-current research projects on a map of the Southwest illustrated to the participants that although "central" areas had adequate coverage, several "peripheral" areas required more investigation. Peripheral areas included southwestern Arizona, Sonora, Chihuahua, and eastern New Mexico. Within the central area, the Little Colorado area and Hopi country were designated as requiring more investigation. The rationale for labeling an area "central" versus "peripheral" was not stated in Kidder's report. The chronological stages Basket Maker I and II and Pueblo I and IV were not fully represented in the then-current research. Basket Maker I was merely postulated to have existed at the time of the conference, and an important direction of research was to find it definitively. Unfortunately, Basket Maker I has never been "found," and in current usage the sequence begins with Basket Maker II.

By the time of the Pecos Conference, there had been several decades of locating and describing prehistoric sites. Kidder and others felt that it was time to combine these data into a coherent whole in the form of a historical reconstruction, "but it must be remembered that such a reconstruction is merely a working hypothesis, designed to correlate our information, and to indicate more clearly the needs of future study. We must have no hesitation in abandoning our conclusions, partly or *in toto*, if contradictory evidence appears" (Kidder 1962:323). Such contradictory evidence has appeared. As more fieldwork was conducted in the 1930s, it became clear that the trait characteristics used to define the various stages were often found throughout several of the stages. For example, pit houses did not disappear at the end of Basket Maker III, and unit-type dwellings persisted well beyond Pueblo II. Many more contradictions became overwhelming with the advent of tree-ring dating.

THE DEVELOPMENT OF THE SOUTHWEST'S TREE-RING SEQUENCE

At the 1927 Pecos Conference, A. E. Douglass, an astronomer at the University of Arizona, presented a preliminary report on the progress of dating archaeological ruins by tree rings. Douglass had been working with tree rings from the Southwest for over a decade primarily to investigate past climate. Clark Wissler, of the American Museum of Natural History, was the first to ship archaeological specimens to Douglass asking whether tree rings might be useful for determining the relative ages of ruins. He specifically asked Douglass to determine the relative ages of two New Mexico sites, Pueblo Bonito and Aztec Ruin. From specimens provided by Wissler, Earl Morris, Neil Judd, and the American Museum, Douglass determined that Aztec was built 40 to 50 years after Pueblo Bonito and that five different Chaco Canyon ruins were built within 20 years of each other. Judd, inspired by this success, felt that exact dating might be possible. He suggested that one might start building a chronology from historic beams, such as those found at Hopi, and work backwards to the archaeological samples. He gained the National Geographic Society's sponsorship for "beam expeditions" to gather samples for Douglass to reconstruct this tree-ring chronology. Judd's specific motivation was to date Pueblo Bonito, the exemplar of Pueblo III, precisely.

The First Beam Expedition was in 1923.

One hundred samples were taken from Oraibi and other Hopi towns, Black Mesa, the Chinle area (including several from Citadel Ruin), Zuni, Chaco Canyon, several Rio Grande pueblos, Mesa Verde, and other parts of southern Colorado. Also, more than 100 samples were available from Wupatki in Arizona. Thus, by the end of 1927, a sequence termed the Citadel dating sequence (CD) had developed from those samples collected from Citadel Ruin, the small beams collected from Wupatki, and samples taken from the Tower in Mummy Cave (Canyon de Chelly, Arizona) and parts of Mesa Verde. In 1928, the CD was fitted to the end of the Relative Dating (RD) sequence developed from Morris's Aztec Ruins beams and those from Pueblo Bonito provided by the American Museum. Beams that allowed these two sequences to be joined came from Betatakin and Kiet Siel, two Arizona cliff houses (Haury and Hargrave 1931). At this point in the research, there was a continuous historical sequence extending back from recently felled trees to ca. A.D. 1400, but the RD/CD sequences were not yet connected to the historical sequence.

The Second Beam Expedition was launched in 1928 and again focused on Hopi villages. Hargrave, then a student of Bryan Cummings at the University of Arizona, collected the samples. From these samples the historical chronology was extended back to A.D. 1300 or more weakly to A.D. 1260, not far enough back to connect with the Bonito sequence. Hargrave suggested that the missing transitional period between the RD and the modern sequence appeared to coincide with the transition from polychrome red ceramics to the cream-colored wares. Based on this observation, the Third Beam Expedition (1929) targeted the area of Showlow and Pinedale, Arizona, where such pottery was plentiful. At Showlow, Hargrave, assisted by Emil Haury, found the beam that "closed" the gap. The gap was actually the period of the "great drought" of A.D. 1276 to 1325, an event that had caused the specimens for those years to be difficult to interpret.

Therefore, by 1929 (i.e., two years after

the first Pecos Conference and just before the second conference) the tree-ring record was complete from A.D. 700 to 1929. By the time of the second Pecos Conference in 1929, dates for a large number of sites throughout the Southwest were available. Furthermore, the period of cultural florescence, named the Great Pueblo Period or Pueblo III, was found to begin about A.D. 919, to climax in the late eleventh century, and to close with the great drought of A.D. 1276 to 1299 (Douglass 1935).

TEST #1: ARE LARGE SITES ASSIGNED TO PUEBLO III CONTEMPORANEOUS? With the tree-ring sequence complete, it became possible to address the question: Are Pueblo Bonito and the other Pueblo III ruins in Chaco Canyon contemporaneous with the cliff dwellings (e.g., Mummy Cave, Kiet Siel, Betatakin, and Cliff Palace)? According to the Pecos Classification, these sites should be contemporaneous. Evidence continued to be compiled throughout the 1930s as more tree-ring material was submitted to Douglass's laboratory. The cliff dwellings were constructed much later than Pueblo Bonito and the other large sites in Chaco Canyon. Table 3.1 lists the dates determined for seven of the large Chaco Canyon sites and six cliff dwellings in Arizona and Colorado, all of which were assigned to Pueblo III. Also included are additional Pueblo III sites dated during the 1930s. The dates range from the middle of the A.D. 800s to the late A.D. 1200s. For 14 out of 17 non–Chaco Canyon sites listed in Table 3.1, the earliest beams postdate the latest beams from Chaco Canyon.

The reaction to the evidence that sites assigned to the same period within the Pecos Classification showed widely varying construction dates was not to question the Pecos Classification, but to view Chaco Canyon's archaeology as an anomaly (i.e., cultural development in the canyon was accelerated for unknown reasons). Rather than interpreting the remains in the canyon, the largest and most elaborate assigned to Pueblo III, as the culmination of a long and progressive, region-wide evolution, the Chaco record was

TABLE 3.1
Tree-Ring Dates for Sites Assigned to Pueblo III

Sites	Dates	Location
Chaco Canyon Sites		
Pueblo Bonito	A.D. 838 to 1130[a]	Chaco Canyon
Chetro Ketl	A.D. 925 to 1116[a]	Chaco Canyon
Hungo Pavi	A.D. 924 to 1064[a]	Chaco Canyon
Peñasco Blanco	A.D. 898 to 1087[a]	Chaco Canyon
Pueblo Pintado	A.D. 1060[a]	Chaco Canyon
Una Vida	A.D. 847 to 1048[a]	Chaco Canyon
Pueblo del Arroyo	A.D. 1052 to 1101[a]	
Cliff Dwellings		
Betatakin	A.D. 1242 to 1277[b]	Tsegi area, AZ
Kiet Siel	early A.D. 1100s to late A.D. 1200s[b]	Tsegi area, AZ
Mummy Cave	A.D. 1253 to 1284[c]	Canyon de Chelly, AZ
Cliff Palace	A.D. 1175 to 1273[d]	Mesa Verde, CO
Balcony House	A.D. 1190 to 1272[d]	Mesa Verde, CO
Spruce Tree House	mid to late A.D. 1200s[d]	Mesa Verde, CO
Other Pueblo III Sites		
Aztec Ruins	A.D. 1110 to 1121[e]	La Plata District, northern NM
Wupatki	A.D. 1073 to 1205[e]	near Flagstaff, AZ
Citadel	A.D. 1192 to 1260[e]	near Flagstaff, AZ
Fewkes Ruin J	A.D. 1192[e]	near Flagstaff, AZ
Turkey Hill Pueblo	A.D. 1168 to 1278[e]	near Flagstaff, AZ
Elden Pueblo	A.D. 1162[e]	near Flagstaff, AZ
Loloma Ki	late A.D. 1200s[f]	Tsegi area, AZ
Bat Woman House	late A.D. 1200s[f]	Tsegi area, AZ
NA 2606	late A.D. 1200s[f]	Tsegi area, AZ
Calamity Cave	late A.D. 1200s[f]	Tsegi area, AZ
Lowry Ruin	late A.D. 1000s[g]	southwestern Colorado

[a]Data from Douglass (1938) and Senter (1938).

[b]Data from Douglass (1938) and McGregor (1934).

[c]Data from Douglass (1938) and Peterson (1935).

[d]Data from Douglass (1938), Getty (1935), and Peterson (1935).

[e]Data from Douglass (1938).

[f]Data from McGregor (1936).

[g]Data from Haury (1938) and Stallings (1937).

interpreted as an early and sudden eruption of high-culture centuries that foreshadowed later developments.

For example, in the Kayenta region of northeastern Arizona, evidence suggested that Pueblo II persisted until A.D. 1115 in the area of the San Francisco Mountains and Tsegi Canyon region (Hargrave 1933, 1935; McGregor 1932). At Chaco Canyon, Pueblo II appeared to be replaced by Pueblo III by A.D. 900. Being preternaturally advanced, Chaco Canyon was presumed to have spread its cultural, and perhaps political, dominance throughout the region. Somewhat colorfully, Florence Hawley (1937:118), described the process as the "influence from the center of highest culture virility carried out toward the peripheries." Moreover, the explanation for this sudden onset of high culture in Chaco Canyon that violated the expectations of researchers of the 1920s and 1930s is still being addressed today. Thus, we find a recent body of research intended to explain the "Chaco Phenomenon." The term "Chaco Phenomenon" was first coined by Cynthia Irwin-Williams (1972) when reporting on work at Salmon Ruin, a Pueblo III site on the San Juan River. Salmon Ruin is typically described as an "outlier" within a Chaco Canyon–centered "system." Further examples of this research focus may be found in Altschul (1978), Grebinger (1973, 1978), Judge (1979), Schelberg (1984), Sebastian (1992), and R. G. Vivian (1990).

TEST # 2: DO SMALL PUEBLO II SITES PREDATE LARGE PUEBLO III SITES?

The assumption of lineal development that determines the placement of a site in the Pecos chronology becomes even more questionable when considered in light of the presumed temporal sequence of small and large sites. The question here is whether smaller sites assigned to Pueblo II actually predate, and therefore prestage, the larger Pueblo III sites. Although dates from sites anywhere in the Anasazi area of the Southwest could be used, we once again examine the dates from sites within Chaco Canyon. Here, as elsewhere, sites assigned to Pueblo II co-occur

with or even postdate Pueblo III sites. The conflict with the expectations set by the Pecos Classification is more dramatic in Chaco Canyon where the small and large sites coexist.

The excavation of small unit-type houses assumed to be classified within Pueblo II began in Chaco Canyon in the 1930s. Beams from these structures were expected to be sufficiently earlier than A.D. 900 to allow time for Pueblo II to evolve into Pueblo III. This expectation proved false because both types of structures (small Pueblo II and large Pueblo III buildings) produced beams of a similar date. Tseh So (also known as Bc 50) was one of the three small-house sites excavated during the 1930s and had a superstructure that fit the Pueblo II type site description. One beam from Tseh So was dated to A.D. 922+ (Brand et al. 1937). Dates published for another small site in the canyon, Bc 51, were A.D. 1043 and A.D. 1077± (Kluckhohn and Reiter 1939). When compared with sites from Chaco Canyon assigned to Pueblo III (Table 3.1), there is clearly substantial overlap. The tree-ring dates for Pueblo Bonito range from A.D. 838 to 1130; those for Peñasco Blanco run from A.D. 898 to 1087.

Some archaeologists attempted to quibble with these dates for Bc 51, saying that the one room that contained the dated beam must have been rebuilt and reused at a later date. This argument, however, could not be supported. The ceramic type Sunset Red, dated by Colton and Hargrave (1937) from A.D. 1050 to 1200, was found on floor levels of four rooms and three kivas. The widespread and abundant occurrence of Sunset Red supported the conclusion that all or most of the entire building was of a later date than expected. Based on the excavation of small houses in Chaco Canyon, Hawley stated that masonry types and house types (small and large) were contemporaneous over large periods of their use (1937:115).

Again the Pecos Classification failed as a unit structure to accurately describe chronological stages. It is not possible reliably to arrange sites in a relative chronology using the stage descriptions found in the Pecos Classification. Sites that should be contemporaneous according to the Pecos Classification were not, and sites that should not be contemporaneous were. Nonetheless, the Pecos Classification was not rejected. Tenacious adherents continued to cite the unit-type dwelling described by Prudden (1903) as the type site for Pueblo II, although it was recognized, based on surface ceramic assemblages, that these same structures should be assigned to Pueblo III (Roberts 1935c:11 n.22).

Discrepancies between the prehistory described by the Pecos Classification and that evidenced by the archaeological record have influenced the direction of research. Decades have been spent attempting to explain how small houses (Pueblo II) and big houses (Pueblo III) could be contemporaneous and in the same area (e.g., Dutton 1938; Hawley 1937; Kluckhohn 1939) in clear contradiction of the Pecos Classification. Gordon Vivian and Tom Mathews (1973) suggested that the two house types represented two culture groups occupying the canyon during Pueblo III. Gwinn Vivian (1970) postulated that the two house types reflected two different systems of social organization—that is, the village (an amorphous organization) and the town (formal, planned, and large with greater architectural sophistication). Vivian associated towns with the water-control features that he identified on the north side of the canyon and that required centralized planning for use and maintenance. Many of the more recent discussions concerning the so-called dichotomy of site types in the canyon postulate social and political hierarchies, differential access to resources between elites and the common people, and the rise of social complexity (e.g., Altschul 1978; Grebinger 1973, 1978; Judge 1979; Schelberg 1984; Sebastian 1992; R. G. Vivian 1990).

INITIAL REACTIONS:
1930s AND 1940s

The lack of fit between chronological dates and the expectations embedded in the Pecos Classification was not confined to the Chaco archaeological record. As information from more excavations became available, it became harder to assign a site to one cultural stage. The criteria for assignment of a site to a stage were not sufficiently clear. The artifacts and architecture in the stage definitions were not exclusive to any one period. Often, important stage criteria were missing from a site. Even Roberts, who remained a staunch supporter of the Pecos Classification throughout his career and attempted to update the Pecos Classification criteria almost annually throughout the thirties (1929, 1930, 1931, 1932, 1935c, 1937), could not remove the overlap between the artifact groupings indicative of each stage. The stages were intended to represent culture complexes, but in practice, researchers began to assign sites to stages based on only one or two categories of artifacts such as architecture or pottery alone. For example, Hall (1933) and Hargrave (1935) were clear that it is the ceramics of a site that indicate to which period the site belongs. Hargrave's research design for the archaeological component of the Rainbow Bridge–Monument Valley Expedition of 1933 stated: "Of primary importance was the collection of surface sherds or fragments of broken pottery from which the position of the site in the chronological scale of the pueblo development and its relative time of occupation could be determined" (Hall 1933:24). Other researchers began to use tree-ring dates exclusively to assign sites to Pecos Classification stages (e.g., Baldwin 1939). Brew summarizes the situation admirably:

On the basis of evidence at hand a chronological scheme has been devised which is intended to show the development of the native agricultural civilization of the Colorado Plateau. . . . The criteria by which the various periods are defined are in many respects unsatisfactory for the purpose. . . . This situation arises partly from the lack of detailed stratigraphic evidence, partly from conflicting evidence in dated sites in different parts of the region, and partly from insufficient understanding of the nature and use of classification sytems. (1946a:40)

Thus, there was growing inconsistency in the means used to assign a site to a period (architecture, ceramics, tree rings, total culture complex). This problem arose primarily due to the ambiguities in the stage definitions.

With the knowledge gained during the 1930s and 1940s, it would appear problematic to augment the Pecos Classification by assigning actual dates to the stages. There is too much variation in the timing of the appearance of the traits used to identify the stages throughout the region to which it is applied. Furthermore, a clear method for applying the criteria to assign sites to stages as requested by Kluckhohn (1939) has never been formulated. Despite these shortcomings, the Pecos Classification continues in use today as both a chronological scheme and a classification of cultural development. Gladwin wrote, "It is true, of course, that every archaeologist at one time or another has shown the Pecos Classification to be all wrong, but after 16 years I find that those who make the loudest protests still use its terms when trying to define the period of a ruin" (1945:2). His statement still applies.

Others have objected to the continued use of the Pecos Classification before us. In his dilemma over how to classify the small sites in Chaco Canyon, Kluckhohn wrote:

> Probably the single fact of greatest general import which has emerged thus far from the Bc 50–51 excavations is that the various stages recognized by the Pecos classification (and very commonly referred to as "periods") do not, necessarily, represent separate and clear-cut time periods, *even in the same geographic locality*. Here it can hardly be merely a question of a brief overlap. Tree ring dates and pottery types both make it almost certain that cultures which most archaeologists would designate as Developmental and Great Pueblo existed for a considerable time within a very short distance of one another.
>
> In view of this fact (and other difficulties which have been mentioned) one is inclined to wonder whether the Pecos classification has not, after all, out-

lived its major usefulness.... A classification is useful so long as the facts fall without violence into it. So soon, however, as their greater bulk, greater complexity, or greater subtleties of discrimination make the classification a Procrustean bed into which the maimed and helpless facts are forced, the classification should be abandoned or radically modified. (1939: 159–60)

Kidder, when discussing the poor fit of the Rio Grande developmental sequence with the stage definitions and the dates being assigned to the Pecos Classification periods farther west, declared, "This well illustrates the fact that our investigation has now reached a point at which formal classifications such as the Pecos nomenclature are not only of lessening value, but are often, as in the present case, positively misleading" (Kidder and Shepard 1936: xviii n.3).

CONCLUSIONS

As we stated in our introduction, the concepts we inherit from a prior generation of scholars have a profound influence on the way we think and how we structure research. They potentially limit the questions that we ask or the possible explanations that we consider. For example, Chaco Canyon–centered research, if carried to an extreme, tends to place an inordinate emphasis on this one area as a "central place" and the rest of the Anasazi Southwest as "peripheral." This view is due largely to the observation that the canyon contains large buildings earlier than expected. However, this expectation derives from the Pecos Classification, a chronology that is demonstrably flawed. More balanced research not structured by units of cultural stages may allow the detection and exploration of more subtle differences in the timing and nature of changes in settlement and material culture throughout the region.

So why is the Pecos Classification still found in publications, professional discussions, and site documentation forms after nearly 70 years of thoroughly questioning its usefulness? Some researchers may still hold firm the position that progressive development from simple to complex, from ephemeral residences to substantial architecture, reflects the passage of time if only on a local level or intuitive basis. However, the real reason may lie in our desire to fit our observations and report our fieldwork within a framework that is easily communicated and accepted by peers even when the framework is somewhat flawed, incomplete, or vague. In fact, the vagueness of the Pecos Classification makes it more easily accepted. Most Southwesternists are comfortable speaking about their subject matter in general terms within the framework of the Pecos Classification, but become gradually less so as the topic turns specific. Disagreements arise when discussing specified circumstances and places, when determining exactly which ceramic types, sites, or dates fit the different periods in each locale. This is due to our preference for using generic language to express ideas rather than concentrating on developing units of measure of timing or "development" in terms that fit the research goals. If "development" is at issue, in what terms are we to measure development (e.g., architectural elaboration, ceramic style, agricultural intensification)? Can we expect these dimensions of change to covary? And if so, why? These research questions are typical of what is being addressed frequently today. However, these questions cannot be addressed in generic units of questionable empirical validity.

APPENDIX

The following outline lists the stages presented in the report of the Pecos Conference (Kidder 1927).

Basket Maker I or Early Basket Maker

No actual evidence had been found for this stage by 1927, but it was postulated to have existed since the subsequent stage was believed to be uniform and widespread. Thus, it was expected that additional field research would find either the native predecessor to Basket Maker II or the area from which Basket Maker culture was introduced into the Southwest (e.g., Gladwin and Gladwin 1934). Basket Maker I was described as "pre-agricultural, yet adumbrating later developments" (Kidder 1927:490).

Basket Maker II or simply Basket Maker

Basket Maker II was defined from the collections of McLoyd and Graham and John Wetherill as described by George Pepper (1902) and from cave burials (Guernsey and Kidder 1921; Kidder and Guernsey 1919; Morris 1927; Nusbaum 1922). Wetherill found Basket Maker remains below Cliff Dweller remains, so there was existing evidence that this stage predated those of masonry dwellings, although others had yet to confirm this stratigraphy (Kidder and Guernsey 1919). No residential Basket Maker II sites had been recovered by 1927. Basket Maker II was described as an "agricultural, atlatl-using, non-pottery-making stage" (Kidder 1927:490).

Basket Maker III, Late Basket Maker, or Post–Basket Maker

Kidder and Guernsey (1919) had found remains of this type under those of Cliff Dwellers in Fluteplayer Cave, so this stage also could be placed before the masonry building population at the time of the conference. The definition of Basket Maker III was based on the fieldwork of Kidder, Guernsey, Morris, and Roberts (Guernsey 1931; Guernsey and Kidder 1921; Kidder and Guernsey 1919; Morris 1919c, 1925, 1927, 1938; Roberts 1929). Basket Maker III was the "pit- or slab-house-building, pottery-making stage (the three Basket Maker stages were characterized by a long-headed population, which did not practice skull-deformation)" (Kidder 1927:490).

Pueblo I or Proto-Pueblo
This stage is roughly equivalent to the Pre-Pueblo stage described by Guernsey and Kidder (1921) and Morris (1921a). The relative placement of this stage in the chronology was not supported by stratigraphy. However, since Pueblo I represented the most rudimentary portion of the record in which masonry structures were constructed, it was felt that developmentally this was its most logical position in the chronology. Pueblo I was "the first stage during which cranial deformation was practiced, vessel neck corrugation was introduced, and villages composed of rectangular living-rooms of true masonry were developed" (Kidder 1927:490).

Pueblo II
This stage is defined based on the work of T. Mitchell Prudden (Prudden 1903, 1914, 1918; Roberts 1929), a medical doctor and avocational archaeologist. The placement of this stage in the chronology was not based on any observed superposition of site components. The definition is almost entirely based on architecture since very little excavation was done at the type sites and no artifact descriptions were available. Pueblo II was "marked by widespread geographical extension of life in small villages; corrugation, often of elaborate technique, extended over the whole surface of cooking vessels" (Kidder 1927:490).

Pueblo III or Great Period
The type sites of this stage were located in Chaco Canyon and the Mesa Verde area and included several large cliff dwellings in northeastern Arizona (Fewkes 1909, 1911a,

1911b; Hewett 1921a, 1921b, 1922; Judd 1922a, 1922b, 1923, 1924, 1925a, 1925b, 1926, 1927a, 1927b; Morley 1908; Morley and Kidder 1917; Morris 1919a, 1919b, 1921b, 1924, 1928a, 1928b; Pepper 1920). The placement in time of these sites was based mostly on assumptions about the trajectory of cultural development. However, some clues concerning their placement were developed through the ceramic stratigraphic sequences developed by Kidder (1917, 1962) and Nelson (1916) excavating at large sites in the Rio Grande vicinity. Both men had noticed that black-and-white ceramics appeared earlier in their stratigraphic sequences and that the Pueblo III sites were typified by similar black-and-white ceramics. The later ceramics in Kidder's and Nelson's sequences characterized the next stage (Pueblo IV). Pueblo III was "the stage of large communities, great development of the arts, and growth of intensive local specialization" (Kidder 1927:490).

Pueblo IV or Proto-Historic
Type sites for Pueblo IV were described by Fewkes (1898, 1904), Guthe (1917), Hewett (1909), Hodge (1918, 1922), Kidder (1962), and Nelson (1914, 1916). The relative placement of these sites was secured by Kidder's and Nelson's ceramic stratigraphy extended back through time from the historic period (Kidder 1962; N. C. Nelson 1916). Pueblo IV was "characterized by contraction of area occupied; by the gradual disappearance of corrugated wares; and, in general, by decline from the preceding cultural peak" (Kidder 1927:490).

Pueblo V or Historic
Pueblo V culminates the sequence and extends from A.D. 1600 to the present (Kidder 1927:490). No traits were specified for Pueblo V in the 1927 report of the Pecos Conference.

4

The "Folsom Problem"

Philippe D. LeTourneau

In 1926 and 1927, investigators with the Colorado Museum of Natural History discovered distinctive projectile points embedded in the ribs of extinct bison at Folsom, New Mexico. This find resolved the American Paleolithic controversy (Meltzer 1991a) and initiated the field of Paleo-Indian studies in American archaeology.[1] As the first Paleo-Indian archaeologists began to consider relationships among early projectile points, they encountered difficulties in organizing Folsom and other points that were spatially associated with them and/or that exhibited technological similarities to them; Howard used the phrase "the Folsom Problem" in 1935 to refer to this difficulty (1935a:110; see also Heizer 1940:79).[2]

By 1935, the Folsom point acted as two different kinds of units, a synthetic unit and an analytic unit, and continues to function in both roles today. The point was initially a unit at the scale of discrete object: it was defined and described in terms of attributes (Dunnell 1971:154–59). As the result of classification, the point became a classificatory, or synthetic, unit (Dunnell 1971:154–59). My evaluation in this chapter of the reliability of the point as a synthetic unit leads to the conclusion that Howard's Folsom problem has largely been resolved.

Another "Folsom problem" emerged when the scale of synthesis changed from discrete object to aggregate: the Folsom point assumed the role of analytic unit when ar-

chaeolgists began to use it to define a new, higher scale synthetic unit, that of Folsom culture. Archaeologists have used the Folsom point in its second role as an analytic unit in defining certain facts of the Folsom culture unit. My evaluation here of the reliability and validity of this use leads to the conclusion that the Folsom point analytic unit is reliable and/or valid for some uses but not for others.

THE FOLSOM POINT TYPE AS A SYNTHETIC UNIT

As noted above, the Folsom point is defined and described in terms of attributes and is thus a synthetic unit. It is like any other point type in this respect, but in North American archaeology no other field places greater emphasis on the study of projectile points than Paleo-Indian period research. This period is a continental, spatiotemporal construct that spans the latest Pleistocene and earliest Holocene of North America. Paleo-Indian sites are characterized by a narrow suite of material remains; organic preservation is often poor (Judge 1973:35; Shott 1990:4) and there are no ceramics, so artifact assemblages consist almost exclusively of flaked stone and a few rare bone items (e.g., Wilmsen and Roberts 1978:126–34). What stand out are extremely well-made, technologically distinctive projectile points that also happen to be the most temporally sensitive of Paleo-Indian artifacts (Frison 1991:125–37).

For these reasons, Paleo-Indian archaeologists have tended to focus their efforts on projectile points in an attempt to maximize the information obtained from them (see also Bamforth 1991a:309). Moreover, because of their role in resolving the American Paleolithic controversy and their status as the first and, for a time, only Paleo-Indian point type, Folsom points have received more unit construction attention than any other point type. The Folsom point type, therefore, provides an excellent case study of point types as synthetic units.

In the course of research on Folsom lithic procurement (LeTourneau n.d.) I began to consider some methodological issues basic to archaeology, one of which was how to identify the sites I would include in an analysis. The answer to that question seemed relatively straightforward: Folsom sites are identified by the presence of Folsom points. And what a Folsom point *is* also seemed obvious. After all, it is one of the best known and most easily identified point types (Agogino 1969:1117; Judge 1970:44). Most textbooks include at least one picture of the distinctive fluted point,[3] and many refer to the role that the Folsom Site played in resolving the American Paleolithic controversy (e.g., Ashmore and Sharer 1988:31; Fagan 1994:253; Hibben 1960:16; Thomas 1989:190; Willey and Sabloff 1980:121).

A review of the literature reveals two notable details pertinent to the question: What is a Folsom point? The first is a historical issue; the definition of a Folsom point has changed considerably since 1927. Many points, and therefore sites, identified as Folsom in the 1930s and 1940s are now assigned to Clovis, Cumberland, or some other Paleo-Indian type. The second detail is the substantial difference in the role of explicit unit construction and definition between the 1930s and 1940s and the present. During those early years of Paleo-Indian research, Folsom and other Paleo-Indian points were the subject of intense unit construction debate. The situation today is very different; there is a virtual absence of definitions of Folsom points in the current literature.

Before I proceed further, there are some terms important in the following discussion to be defined. Dunnell distinguishes between classification and grouping. Classification is restricted to arrangement in the ideational realm and "is defined as the creation of units of meaning by stipulating redundancies (classes)" (Dunnell 1971:44; see also Brew 1946b:46). Grouping "denotes arrangement in the phenomenological realm and [is] defined as the creation of units of things (groups)" (Dunnell 1971:44). Dunnell (1971: 15–18, 89, 199–201) also distinguishes among descriptions, extensional definitions, and intensional definitions, and provides the following discussion of each. "A description is a compilation of the variable attributes of an individual case or group of cases." An extensional definition is a definition by example and does not convey what a thing is; it "simply means that something is that something because it is, and nothing more." The necessary and sufficient conditions for membership in the group are often rendered by enumeration of the members of the already formed group. This kind of definition requires that readers already know what something (i.e., a Folsom point) is. Finally, extensional definitions are usually associated with grouping methods of arrangement.

Intensional definitions, in contrast, specify the necessary and sufficient conditions, the invariable attributes, for membership in a unit. Classification requires intensional definitions and, because classes are defined, they are constructs rather than empirical entities. Ramenofsky and Steffen (this volume) note that intensional definitions are imposed on phenomena.

For example, an extensional definition of a Folsom point would be one that lists as Folsom points those particular points from specific sites and might refer to a picture of a representative example of those points. Or it might list some of the attributes of a previously designated group of Folsom points. In any case, it does not say why a Folsom point is a Folsom point and cannot anticipate all future discoveries. In contrast, an intensional definition might state that fluting and thinness are invariable and thus are necessary and sufficient attributes of Folsom points. Any future finds with those attributes would be considered Folsom points, and any without those attributes would not be considered Folsom points. And a description of Folsom points within the unit so defined might include lithic material, color, or size.

HISTORY OF FOLSOM POINT SYNTHETIC UNIT CONSTRUCTION

I divide the history of Folsom Point synthetic unit construction along temporal and topical lines into six sections. The first section is the period ending with the Folsom Site discovery in 1927. The second section incorporates the Folsom Site discovery. The next three sections are delineated by major unit construction debates. The first debate concerned variation among Paleo-Indian points generally, and was known as the "Folsom-Yuma debate." The second debate concerned variation among fluted points; I refer to it as the "Folsom-Clovis debate." The third debate, the "Folsom-Midland debate," concerned variation among Folsom points. The resolution of each of the three debates resulted in a narrowing of the Folsom point synthetic unit. In the final section I discuss the current definition of the Folsom point synthetic unit.

Pre-Folsom Discovery (1870s–1927)

During the late 1800s, the first artifact unit structures were being developed as American archaeologists documented and described artifacts from various parts of the expanding American nation (Dunnell 1986b; Willey and Sabloff 1980:34). Unit structures for stone tools during this period were based on presumed objective criteria such as shape and size (e.g., Beauchamp 1897; Fowke 1896; Rau 1876; Wilson 1891, 1899), while technology was generally ignored and fluted points were rarely noted. There are several instances where fluted points were chosen for illustration by virtue of their size or shape, while their fluting was not mentioned (Fowke 1896:147; Holmes 1897:Plate 32; Moorehead 1910:71, 80). Similarly, Willis-

ton (1902, 1905) illustrated a fluted point associated with extinct bison at the site now known as 12 Mile Creek in Kansas, but did not mention the fact that the point was fluted (see also Rogers and Martin 1984). A few archaeologists illustrated and described fluted points, but mentioned the fluting as simply an interesting attribute (e.g., Beauchamp 1897: 21, Figures 13, 14; Brown 1926:138; Thruston 1890:231–32). All of these fluted points, except the 12 Mile Creek point, were from the eastern United States and would now be called Clovis or Cumberland.[4] Fluted points were actually common in private and public collections from the East, but were not considered remarkable because they were all surface finds and their age was unknown (Beauchamp 1897:21; Brown 1926: 138; Meltzer 1991b:27; Roberts 1935a:64).

Fluted points from the West were also known at this time, but not nearly as well as their eastern counterparts. Private collectors in Colorado had found fluted points in the early 1920s, many of which were later identified as Folsom (Cook 1931; Jenks 1937:45; Roberts 1935a:61, 1935b:2, 1939a:537). That eastern fluted points were better represented than western points is due in part to the former points' greater abundance and better exposure on the surface of plowed fields (Mason 1962:233–35).

Prior to the Folsom Site discovery in 1927, fluted points in general were known primarily from the eastern United States. The western points that would later be designated as Folsom were virtually unknown, and since almost all known fluted points were surface finds, they were, therefore, assumed to be unimportant.

Folsom

The discovery at Folsom, New Mexico, of the embedded fluted point greatly influenced the future of Paleo-Indian unit construction. By 1927, archaeologists' unit construction goals were only just beginning to change from simple objective description to spatiotemporal ordering and cultural-historical synthesis (Dunnell 1986b:190; Kidder 1927; Willey and Sabloff 1980:83–108). As archae-

TABLE 4.1
Summary Statistics for 16 Folsom Site Projectile Points

Measurement	n	Minimum	Maximum	Mean
Maximum Length[a] (mm)	4	33	57	43.0
Maximum Width (mm)	15	21	29	22.4
Maximum Thickness (mm)	14	3	5	3.9
Fluted Thickness (mm)	6	2	3	2.6
Percent Length Fluted	2	75	82	78.5
Percent Width Fluted	3	52	71	61.0

Note: Points were measured by Renaud (1931b:13–19).

[a]Two broken points measured 52 and 57 mm in length, so maximum complete length was even greater.

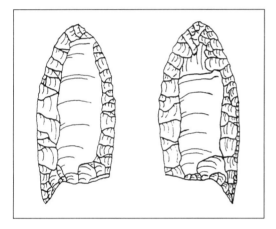

Figure 4.1. Folsom point (both faces), Folsom Site, Folsom, New Mexico. Actual size.

ologists began to consistently use the principles of superposition, stratigraphy, and seriation in their excavations and analyses (e.g., Kidder 1924; Nelson 1914; Petrie 1899), they realized that *ad hoc* artifact categories (types) often displayed predictably limited temporal distributions (Dunnell 1986b:190). The Folsom Site represented the first widely accepted association of Pleistocene mammals and human artifacts, thereby providing evidence of a previously unknown time depth to the human occupation of North America (Kidder 1936:144; Meltzer 1991a). By linking technologically distinctive points with extinct fauna in a deeply buried site, the Folsom Site provided a rough base upon which

archaeologists could begin building a cultural-historical synthesis.

The Folsom Site became the type site for the point style that would eventually bear that name (Howard 1935a:106). The fluted points from the Folsom Site immediately set the standard against which all future finds would be compared. The points were narrow, thin, well made, and distinguished by proportionally long and broad channel flake scars (Figure 4.1; see Table 4.1 for Renaud's summary statistics [1931b:13–19] for 16 points from the Folsom Site).

As archaeologists searched for additional evidence of early human occupation and began to document new projectile point finds, most of them from surface contexts, they quickly encountered problems in organizing the numerous finds that they felt were related in various ways to Folsom points. More specifically, they wondered which attributes of the Folsom Site points were relevant and whether, and how much, to expand the Folsom point type to include new finds. As new points were discovered, they were compared with the Folsom Site points and new groups were formed based on similarity of chosen attributes. The situation was confusing because archaeologists were entering new archaeological territory and lacked radiocarbon dating and modern knowledge of Pleistocene fauna and geology.

Three themes began to develop soon after the Folsom discovery, and these would continue to underlie the history of Folsom point synthetic unit construction. The first theme concerns the role of explicit definition in the process of unit construction. Folsom unit construction, like much of archaeological unit construction, has largely been implicit (see Dunnell 1971:139); this situation is problematic because it hinders evaluation of resulting units. The degree to which definition was explicit or implicit varied throughout the history of Folsom point synthetic unit construction. Varying degrees of explicitness also characterized the choice of defining attributes as well as the goals behind definition. In the 1920s and 1930s, Folsom unit construction was characterized by a lack of explicit definition. Intensional definitions (the necessary and sufficient conditions for membership) were rarely distinguished from descriptions. The result was a mixture of features that projectile points *must* display to belong to the Folsom point unit and features that projectile points *may* display to belong to it (after Dunnell 1971:139). Discussions of attributes were generally explicit; attributes deemed important included shape, quality of workmanship, size, presence of fluting, extent of fluting, and association with extinct fauna. But the goals of unit construction and, therefore, the reasons for choosing such attributes were not always explicitly stated, although it is frequently possible to identify those goals from a close reading of the literature.

The second theme concerns the goals of Folsom point synthetic unit construction. The primary goal of Paleo-Indian archaeologists (e.g., Howard 1936:402) was to construct units that demonstrated late-Pleistocene temporal patterning. Krieger later characterized such types as having "historical significance" (1944:272–73). A secondary, but still important, goal was to construct units that reflected culture. What was meant by culture was not always clear and thus neither were the criteria for choosing attributes.

The third theme concerns one of the ways in which archaeologists went about the work of unit construction: many of the major decisions regarding how to define the various Paleo-Indian types involved consensus.

Variation among Paleo-Indian Points (Folsom-Yuma)

In the search for additional evidence of human antiquity, archaeologists began to link unfluted points with the fluted points from the Folsom Site. Renaud (1932:5) named these unfluted Paleo-Indian points "Yuma" points after Yuma County, Colorado, where they were first found in blowouts during the dust-bowl days of the 1930s (Cook 1931; Renaud 1931b).[5] There were additional finds of both Folsom and Yuma points in blowouts in several places on the Great Plains (e.g., Barbour and Schultz 1936:442; Howard 1935a, 1935b:98, 1939; Roberts 1939b:106, 108). In general, these Yuma points varied widely in shape (stemmed and unstemmed), size, and technology (e.g., facial flaking patterns; see Figure 4.2). They bore certain technological similarities to the Folsom Site points, and many were associated with extinct fauna like those from the site, but they also exhibited some marked technological differences. The debate over how to organize the various Paleo-Indian points was known as the "Folsom-Yuma" debate; it was finally resolved by distinguishing between older fluted Folsom points and younger unfluted Yuma points.

For Figgins, the key criterion for identifying points that had a bearing on human antiquity in North America was their association with extinct bison. Thus, he grouped, as one unnamed type, points from two other sites—Lone Wolf Creek, Texas, and 12 Mile Creek, Kansas—with those from Folsom because all three sites contained extinct bison (1927:234). The Lone Wolf Creek points are now known as Plainview (Wormington 1957:110) and the 12 Mile Creek point is not available for study. Fluting was not one of Figgins's criteria, since the Lone Wolf Creek finds were unfluted. Figgins did not explicitly give a reason for constructing his units, but it seems clear that his goal was to organize Pleistocene projectile points. It also appears that he offered an intensional definition of his unnamed point type—the necessary and sufficient conditions for membership in his unit of unnamed points were simply that they be associated with extinct bison.

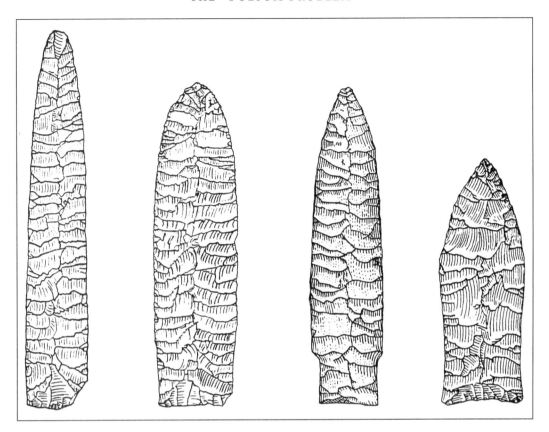

Figure 4.2. Yuma points (from left to right): Eden point, Blackwater Draw, Clovis, New Mexico; Portales point, Blackwater Draw, Clovis, New Mexico; Scottsbluff point, Scottsbluff Site, Scottsbluff, Nebraska; Plainview point, Plainview Site, Plainview, Texas (from Sellards 1952:71, 69, 64). All actual size.

Cook reported surface associations in Yuma County, Colorado, of fluted "Folsom type points," "modifications of the typical [fluted] Folsom points," and unfluted points (1931:103). He linked all three based on overall technological similarities and on horizontal spatial proximity. Cook's goal, again, was to construct units that related to the Pleistocene human presence in North America. His intensional definition for the unit Folsom point was any point that was technologically similar to those from the Folsom Site, although "technologically similar" was not a clear attribute.

Others believed that technological similarities between the fluted and unfluted points alone were sufficient to indicate a close relationship (e.g., Barbour and Schultz 1936; Jenks 1934:205, 1935:9, 1937:46). Barbour and Schultz (1936:444) noted that unifacially fluted Folsom points in Nebraska showed flaking on the *unfluted* faces that was typical of Yuma points from the same sites. Cotter (1937b:29, 30) added stratigraphic relationships, similar geographic distributions, as well as association with similar extinct fauna as grounds for including the unfluted Yuma points in a Folsom industry. Although these researchers did not explicitly state their unit construction goals, it appears that they, too, were interested in establishing a chronological framework.

Others, including Renaud, Figgins, Howard, and Roberts, criticized what they viewed as excessive lumping. Renaud was interested in the organization of artifacts generally (1931a, 1935, 1940, 1941, 1945). In presenting the first systematic attempt to organize Folsom points and the various points associated with them (1931b, 1932, 1934, 1937), he included "flaked points of different appearance, shape, technique, or quality, from those usually found in collections of Indian artifacts" (1931b:6).

Renaud argued for differences between the Folsom and Yuma types as seen in his definitions and use of the different names:

These pieces and fragments with long and broad lengthwise groove, more or less fine marginal retouching between the edges and the lateral ridges, concave base with often long and sharp base points, are really the only ones that could be called "Folsom points," stricto sensu, that is to say points of the same shape and technique as those actually found at Folsom and likely made by the same ancient people, representing the same culture and probably belonging to the same age. . . . What constitutes a Folsom point properly so-called, is the actual grouping and co-existence of those typologic and technique elements in one piece. . . . We are logically warranted in calling "Folsom point," by extension of meaning, artifacts found elsewhere which conform closely to the Folsom type (1931b:12–15)

This designation is a mix of description and definition, although it is possible to extract an intensional definition for Folsom point from it: long and broad groove (flute), fine lateral retouch, and concave base; the presence of basal ears was variable. By 1937, Renaud's necessary and sufficient conditions for Folsom point had changed somewhat to fluted, and not stemmed or barbed; basal shape and fineness of pressure flaking were variable attributes (1937:74). And now his Yuma Points invariably exhibited pressure flaking and stemmed hafting elements; their outlines were variable (parallel, convex, or subtriangular) as were their base shapes (parallel, concave, or convex) (1937:75). While his definitions were not explicit, Renaud's unit construction goals were. He sought to identify Pleistocene-age points and point

types made by specific cultural groups (Renaud 1931b:12–15, 1934, 1937:76). His criteria for attribute selection are not as clear, however.

Renaud also argued for a close relationship between the two types. Using the term "Folsom-Yuma" to describe the aggregate of fluted and unfluted points (1934), he noted that all of the non-Folsom points in his study shared at least one of the Folsom Point characteristics (i.e., unusually fine pressure flaking; marginal retouch; lateral margin grinding; parallel, oblique, narrow, and ribbonlike flaking; as well as blade and base shapes) (1931b, 1932:10). Fluting was the only really distinctive characteristic separating the two. Based on the similarities between the two types, Renaud proposed a progressive technomorphological evolution from the simpler, unfluted Yumas to the more complex, fluted Folsoms (with fluting becoming proportionally longer and wider) (1931b:11–12, 1932:13, 1934:2–9, 1940:152–53, 1945:3). Noting similar facial flaking on Yumas and on the unfluted faces of unifacially fluted Folsoms, Renaud concluded that Folsom points were simply fluted Yuma points (see also Barbour and Schultz 1932b:286; Jenks 1937:44; Schultz and Eiseley 1935:308–9, 1936:522).

Figgins (1934:2) had obviously modified his earlier 1927 position when he argued that "there is no material similarity in form and detail between Folsom and Yuma artifacts," but his goal was still to identify Pleistocene projectile points. He discounted surface associations as having no bearing on their relative ages and rejected Renaud's Yuma-to-Folsom evolutionary scheme. In his first discussion of the two types, Figgins (1934:3–4) does not present necessary and sufficient conditions for membership in either type. Instead, he uses words like "best," "sometimes," and "practically all" to describe attributes for each type. These words indicate that the attributes are variable. Figgins was equally unclear in his later discussion of the two types:

On the one hand, so wide a range of variation might be attributed to the Yuma types that it would be quite impossible to apply a reasonable set of characters through which all could be identified. On the other hand, the characteristics of Folsom artifacts could be circumscribed to a degree that would prohibit allowance for the normal factors which entered into their production: the uses for which they were designed, individual preference and skill of the worker, and the nature of the materials at hand. . . . There is need for more clearly defined distinctions between Folsom and Yuma artifacts; for more liberal interpretations of Folsom characters, and, in the total absence of evidence to show that Yuma artifacts are culturally related to Folsom types, that variation in the former be confined within reasonable limitations. . . . Therefore, we are no more justified in restricting Folsom artifacts to the types with fluted sides, and circumscribing their limits of distribution, provided other characters are in evidence, than we are in demanding diagonal side chipping for the identity of all Yuma types. (1935:2–3)

Interestingly, Figgins was clear in stating that fluting was not a necessary Folsom point attribute.

Howard and Roberts were much clearer in their definitions and both argued that only attributes of the original Folsom Site points should be used in defining the point type. Howard's invariable Folsom point attributes were leaf shape, fluting, fine retouch, and a concave base with earlike projections (1935a:105). He was clear that these were invariable attributes when he stated that "this covers the true Folsom point, and any others that may have all these characteristics should qualify as such no matter where they are found" (1935a:112). His definition for the Yuma point is not as clear, since he defines it only as having a different shape, hafting element, and cross section than the Folsom point (1936:403, also 1935a:112). Roberts's definition duplicated Howard's except that he added thin cross section and omitted base shape as invariable attributes (*Literary Digest* 1934a; Roberts 1935b:7, 17).

A group of archaeologists (including Cotter, Gladwin, Renaud, and Wormington) ad-dressed the unit construction problems at a Philadelphia conference on "Early Man" in 1937 and formalized the fluted Folsom versus unfluted Yuma dichotomy. This conference marked the first public instance of the use of consensus in Folsom unit construction. Gladwin, as the group's chair, gave the following definitions. Folsom is "a leaf-shaped blade. It has a varying base, neither barbed nor stemmed. It is fluted on one or both sides, wholly or partially. It is pressure-flaked from both sides" (Howard 1938:444). Yuma is "triangular. It runs from triangular, through parallel sides, to leaf-shaped. Its base is either straight or convex or concave. It is frequently stemmed, but when stemmed, has parallel sides—the sides of the stem are parallel. It is never fluted. It is pressure-flaked from both sides, the flakes being parallel" (Howard 1938:444). The unit construction goals and unit structure were not explicitly stated, but attributes were.

In terms of goals, it is interesting that Gladwin felt the unit structure was "generic and . . . not related to chronology or to distribution" (Howard 1938:444), despite the fact that chronology had been the major goal of unit construction thus far in the Folsom-Yuma debate. The only necessary and sufficient conditions for Folsom point unit membership in the 1937 definition were that they be leaf-shaped, fluted, and pressure-flaked; those for Yuma Point unit membership were that they be unfluted and possess parallel flaking.

Many archaeologists followed the Philadelphia decision (see Heizer 1940:79), but definitional problems continued and became the focus of a second conference in Santa Fe in 1941 (Howard 1943a; Hurst 1941). It was agreed there that Yuma points were unfluted, and that Folsom points were one of several fluted point types. By this time, in situ Yuma finds had been documented at the Finley and Scottsbluff Sites, so specific Yuma types were formally recognized (i.e., the Eden and Scottsbluff types). Meanwhile, excavations at Lindenmeier were providing evidence that at least some Yuma points were stratigraphically higher, and thus younger, than Folsom points (Roberts 1937d:74, 1941:82, 1945:407).

Despite these general agreements, a widely acceptable resolution was not achieved until the 1950s and 1960s, when the stratigraphic position of Yuma points above Folsom points was confirmed at several sites (Agogino and Frankforter 1960; Forbis and Sperry 1952; Irwin-Williams et al. 1973; Roberts 1951:21; Sellards 1952:72–74). Thus, resolution of the Folsom-Yuma debate was achieved by dividing the types along temporal lines.

In sum, although unit construction goals were often not explicitly discussed, the Folsom-Yuma debate was marked by unit construction aimed primarily at identifying units that would date to the late Pleistocene. A secondary goal was to identify cultural groups via projectile point types. Attributes tended to be explicitly discussed, but description was often confused with definition. I have characterized the definitions of the Folsom-Yuma debate as intensional ones, but extensional ones also played a role. Although differentiating between the two types of definition is not always a straightforward task, it seems clear that many of the definitions originated as extensional ones. This was the case since archaeologists were working with and established their definitions based on groups of actual artifacts (i.e., those from the Folsom Site). But, once they delineated the necessary and sufficient conditions for membership in the unit called "Folsom point," and used those definitions to organize future finds, they were clearly using intensional definitions.

Variation among Fluted Points (Folsom-Clovis)

The Folsom-Yuma debate was not the only debate during the 1930s and 1940s over how to organize Paleo-Indian projectile points. A simultaneous discussion concerned the meaning of the variation among fluted points. Sellards (1952) eventually named as Clovis the larger fluted form that possessed proportionally shorter and narrower flutes than Folsom points. Because the fluting of the Folsom Site points was so distinctive, all

fluted points were initially called Folsom points with the result that "Folsom" points were documented from all over the United States.[6] The Folsom-Clovis debate, like the Folsom-Yuma debate, focused primarily on the temporal placement of various projectile point types and was finally resolved in the 1950s by designating the earlier Plains fluted points as Clovis types and the later ones as Folsom types, by restricting the term "Folsom" to the Plains and adjacent areas, and by using "Clovis" to refer to most of the far western and eastern fluted points. Intensional definitions and their attributes were generally explicit and were restricted to attributes of fluted points.

Beginning in the 1930s, a number of researchers recognized major differences among fluted points (see Figure 4.3; compare with Figure 4.1). For example, Figgins (1931, 1933), in announcing the Angus and Dent Sites (both fluted point–mammoth associations), called the points Folsom points, but noted cruder fluting and secondary flaking than on the smaller points from the original Folsom Site. Studer called the fluted points found with mammoth bones at Miami, Texas, Folsom, although he noted that these points had relatively shorter fluting than those from the Folsom Site (*Science News Letter* 1935:92).

Others, like Howard and Roberts, also recognized differences among fluted points from other parts of the country, and thought they were significant enough to warrant a name other than Folsom. Their reasons for distinguishing among the types were generally not explicit, but, given their chronological goals in the Folsom-Yuma debate, it is likely that these archaeologists still sought to construct temporally sensitive units. Researchers distinguished between the Folsom Site points and larger, cruder points with proportionally shorter flutes (e.g., Howard 1935a:106–9; Roberts 1932:145). Howard coined the names "Generalized Folsom" (Howard 1932:12) and "Folsom-like" (Howard 1935a:69) for the latter points and reserved the name "True Folsom" for the points at the Folsom Site and those that

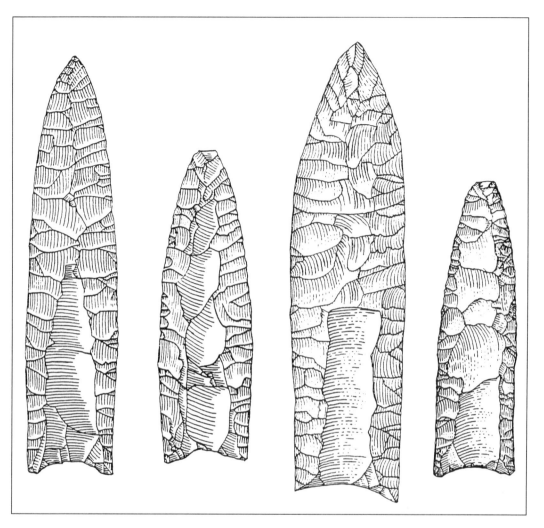

Figure 4.3. Clovis points (from left to right): Blackwater Draw, Clovis, New Mexico; Blackwater Draw, Clovis, New Mexico; unnamed site in Ohio; McLean site, Taylor County, Texas (from Sellards 1952:35, 41, 39). All actual size.

exhibited all the characteristics of the type-site points (Howard 1935a:109). Roberts (1935b:7) used the term "Folsomoid" for the Dent Site points because they bore "certain characteristics of the true Folsom type, yet [were] not definitely assignable to that class." For the same reasons, he also assigned a fluted point from Burnet Cave, New Mexico, to the Folsomlike/Folsomoid category, but thought it still belonged to a "basic Folsom type" (Roberts 1939b:537). As seen above, an intensional definition of "True Folsom" points for Howard and Roberts was that

they be small and well made with proportionally long flutes.

Bryan and Ray (1940:48) noted that the Dent Site points had been called Folsomoid, but because of their "similarities" to the Lindenmeier Site points thought the points from both sites were probably contemporaneous. In 1936, Shetrone (1936:241, 243) proposed that all fluted points be grouped under the term "fluted blades" to reflect their apparent common cultural derivation. But he also argued that points from different regions or even individual sites be distinguished by specific names, such as Folsom Variant, Lindenmeier Variant, Ohio Fluted, etc.

Although Figgins (1935:4) recognized a great deal of variation among fluted points, he rejected the use of terms such as "Folsomlike" and felt that all fluted points should be called Folsom (also Figgins 1934). While fluting was not a necessary Folsom attribute, it was a sufficient one.

Renaud called attention to the differences in fluting in his evolutionary scheme (discussed in the Folsom-Yuma section). He felt that fluting progressed from shorter, cruder flutes (on types others called Folsomoid and Folsomlike) to the proportionally longer and broader flutes on the Folsom Site points (Renaud 1945:4). Although Figgins had earlier rejected Renaud's scheme for an evolution of Yuma points into Folsom points, he agreed with Renaud on the evolution of cruder Folsom points into finer Folsom points as exhibited in fluting (Figgins 1935:3).

Patterning in geographic distributions and faunal associations was noticed as well. The larger Folsomlike points were found all over North America, and when found with faunal remains, often the remains were of mammoths (Cotter 1937b; Howard 1934:13–14, 1935a:119, 1936:403, 1943a:233; Roberts 1935b:8, 1937b:161, 1939a:543–45). "True Folsom" points were found with extinct bison, but not with mammoths, and were restricted to the Plains and Rockies. Absolute dates and stratigraphic relationships were still missing, so the temporal relationship between mammoth and bison was still unknown. However, Howard (1936:405) suggested that the wider distribution of the Folsomlike points might indicate an earlier age for them.

Consensus and personal opinion also played a role in the Folsom-Clovis debate. Howard (1932:14) brought his fluted point from Burnet Cave, New Mexico, to an archaeology conference in Santa Fe in 1932, where everyone who saw it agreed that it was "similar to the Folsom type." Kelly had his find of a fluted point in Georgia "authenticated as a true Southeastern type Folsom" (1938:7). Haag showed some fluted points from the Parrish Site in Kentucky to a group of archaeologists that included Figgins and Cotter who pronounced them "similar in many respects to western Folsom-Yuma" (Haag 1942:218). At the 1937 Philadelphia conference, it was decided (as mentioned above) to simply call all fluted points Folsom (Howard 1938:444). Cotter (1939:152–53) supported this decision and thus called the Burnet Cave fluted point "Folsom" (see also Fischel 1939:235). Roberts (1937b:161, 1939a:543) preferred Shetrone's idea of using site-specific types like Folsom-Folsom and Lindenmeier-Folsom, but accepted the Santa Fe decision (Roberts 1938:173).

Tentative evidence for stratigraphic relationships among fluted points, as well as for faunal association patterning, began to trickle in from Blackwater Draw (Cotter 1937a, 1938). At that site, Cotter demonstrated a possible relationship between larger Folsomlike points and mammoths in depositional units stratigraphically below smaller, finer "True Folsom" points associated with bison. At the 1941 Santa Fe conference, the participants adopted Shetrone's idea and formalized the observed differences in the fluted points (Howard 1943a:227; Hurst 1941). Thus, the smaller, finer points were called Folsom, and the larger ones, previously called Folsomlike, were named after their sites or geographic foci (e.g., Clovis Fluted and Ohio Fluted). They did not adopt Shetrone's suggestion that Folsom points from different sites be given regional names, however. These decisions were widely accepted (see Howard 1943a:233; Krieger 1946:10), although Roberts (1945:404–5) continued to assign all fluted points to the "Folsom Complex" and J. Clarence Simpson (1948) identified Folsomlike points in Florida.

Evans (1951) and Sellards (1952) synthesized the stratigraphic, faunal, and technological evidence from their 1949–50 excavations at Blackwater Draw (also Hester 1972:39–41; Sellards and Evans 1960) and codified the distinction between Clovis and Folsom points. Thus, we now use the term "Clovis" to refer to the larger points with proportionally smaller flutes that are found with extinct mammoths and bison. Folsom points are found with bison but not with mammoths; and at sites where both types are found in place (e.g., Blackwater Draw), Folsom points are stratified above Clovis points. Finally, radiocarbon dates for Clovis points are consistently older than those for Folsom points (Haynes 1992; Haynes et al. 1992).

This division applies primarily to sites in the Plains where both Clovis and Folsom points occur. The new term "Clovis" was applied to virtually all fluted points in the eastern and far western United States (Glennan 1971; Irwin 1971:50; Mason 1962:230–34, 246). Clovis points from excavated sites are still rare in these latter areas and even more rare are Clovis points found associated with radiometric dates or fauna; the few dated sites are roughly contemporaneous with Folsom sites on the Plains (Haynes et al. 1984).

In sum, unit construction during the Folsom-Clovis debate was much like that during the Folsom-Yuma debate: chronology was the primary goal (although identification of cultural groups was a secondary goal), proposed definitions were actually a mix of intensional definitions and descriptions, and definitions consisted of explicit attributes.

Variation among Folsom Points (Folsom-Midland)

Soon after resolution of the Folsom-Clovis debate came the discovery in 1953 of human bones in close proximity to Folsom points at Scharbauer Ranch, near Midland, Texas (Wendorf et al. 1955). Scientific attention focused not only on the skeleton but also on the nearby surface artifacts. These artifacts included fluted Folsom points as well as *unfluted* points that were virtually identical to the Folsom points in terms of shape, size, and technology. These unfluted points were soon named Midland points (see below). This situation brought to the fore another issue that had been only peripherally discussed prior to 1953 and that has since come to be known as the Folsom-Midland debate. Since 1927, archaeologists had noted variation in *fluting* of the "classic" or "True Folsom" points (e.g.,

Barbour and Schultz 1936:444; Howard 1936:403; Renaud 1937:77; Wormington 1944:7). A mix of bifacially fluted, unifacially fluted, and/or unfluted points was found in seemingly clear stratigraphic association at excavated sites like Lindenmeier (Roberts 1935b:17–18; Wilmsen and Roberts 1978:175), Blackwater Draw (Howard 1943a:232–33; Hester 1972:124), and Folsom (Howard 1935a: 112; Rovner and Agogino 1967:132) (see Figure 4.4). The primary unit construction goal of this debate was to establish the temporal relationship among these late Pleistocene projectile points. This debate is ongoing because, unlike the Folsom-Yuma and Folsom-Clovis debates, a temporal relationship between the Folsom and Midland point types has not been firmly established. Besides temporal goals, unit construction has addressed issues of cultural identity more explicitly than in other debates.

It was generally agreed that the *unifacially* fluted points qualified as Folsom (although Roberts [*Literary Digest* 1934a] cautioned against including these points in the Folsom type). Roberts also felt that an *unfluted* point excavated with fluted Folsom points at Lindenmeier could not "be considered a Folsom point (Roberts 1935b:18). Wormington (1939:23, 28–32) termed the *unfluted* points "Indeterminate Yuma" points at first, but at the 1941 Santa Fe conference it was decided that they should be included in the Folsom type (Howard 1943a:232–33). Recall that Renaud (1937:81) considered Folsom and Yuma points to be closely related based in part on refits of channel flakes onto fluted Folsom points; some of his Yuma points may have been these "unfluted Folsom points." But the large numbers of unfluted Folsom points at Scharbauer Ranch (Wendorf et al. 1955:65) and at other sites on the southern Plains, including some sites without fluted Folsom points, caused many to reconsider the issue.

In fact, Wendorf and Krieger eventually believed a new type, "Midland," was in order. Their extensional definition for the Scharbauer Midland points was that they were "thin specimens of about the same

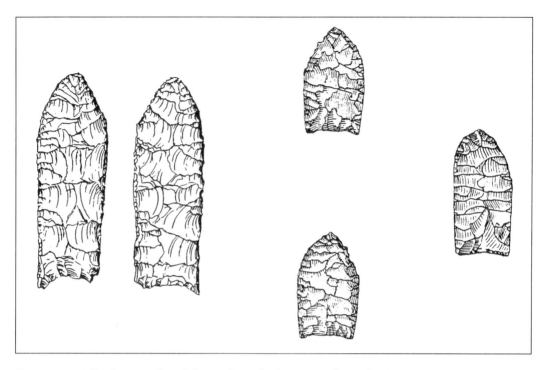

Figure 4.4. Midland points (from left to right): Scharbauer Ranch, Midland County, Texas (both faces); Blackwater Draw, Clovis, New Mexico (both faces); Blackwater Draw, Clovis, New Mexico (Wendorf et al. 1955:44; Sellards 1952:56). All actual size.

shape and dimensions [as fluted Folsom points] which were fluted on but one side or unfluted" (Wendorf and Krieger 1959:67) (see Figure 4.4); Folsom points for them were thus always bifacially fluted. Wormington (1957:263) modified Wendorf and Krieger's definition into an intensional one, but restricted the term "Midland" to *unfluted* specimens only and defined Folsom points as fluted on one or both faces. For Wormington the necessary and sufficient conditions for membership in the unit Folsom point were that a point be fluted (on one or both faces), pressure-flaked, thin, roughly leaf-shaped, have a concave base, and exhibit excellent workmanship (1957:27). Variable attributes were length, presence of basal ears, presence of basal nipple, presence of basal and lateral margin grinding, and length of fluting. The necessary and sufficient conditions for membership in the unit Midland point were that a point be unfluted, pressure-flaked, thin, roughly leaf-shaped, have a concave base,

and exhibit excellent workmanship (Wormington 1957:263). Most archaeologists now agree with these definitions (e.g., Boldurian 1990:68; Bradley 1982:203; Broilo 1971:31; Judge 1973:174; Rovner and Agogino 1967: 132). Others have proposed their own definitions (e.g., Judge 1970:44; Mason 1962: 231), but still distinguish between the two types on the basis of fluting.

Currently, the temporal relationship between the unfluted Midland and fluted Folsom points remains ambiguous. On the one hand, stratigraphic relationships between them at excavated sites have not provided conclusive evidence for or against their contemporaneity (Martinez 1991:3; Sellet and Frison 1994). On the other hand, the frequent co-occurrence of the two point types in surface contexts and the overall technological similarity between them has led archaeologists to reaffirm the 1941 decision to consider unfluted Midland and fluted Folsom points contemporaneous technological variants of a single (Folsom) type (e.g., Agogino 1969; Amick 1994:100; Bamforth 1991a:313–14; Boldurian 1990:75; Hofman et al. 1990: 240–46; Rovner and Agogino 1967; Sollberger 1985:46).

The assumption of contemporaneity has led to discussions that focus on the technological and economic reasons for the variation between Midland and Folsom points. Some have argued that Midland points are simply Folsom points that were too thin to flute (Howard 1943a:232–33; Rovner and Agogino 1967:133; Wendorf and Krieger 1959:67; Wormington 1957:34, 41). More recent studies have shown that at least some Midland points were thick enough to flute (as thick as Folsom points prior to fluting) (Frison and Bradley 1980:80; Hofman et al. 1990:243), leading Judge to suggest that the difference in fluting is due to raw material and other technological variables (1970:44–49). Bamforth has noted that unfluted points are common at Folsom camp and small kill sites, while they are virtually absent at large communal kill sites (1991a:313–14). He argues that the distribution reflects a situation where the most skilled knappers manufactured fluted projectile points in preparation for communal kills, while hunters of all skill levels manufactured their own points (mainly unfluted) for normal hunting. Hofman has hypothesized that Midland points represent an attempt to conserve lithic raw material because fluting is a riskier thinning technique than simple lateral flaking (Hofman 1991: 345, 1992:212). The expectation that Folsom points should be found closer to raw material sources and Midland points farther away has not been confirmed with data from the southern Plains (Hofman 1991:345; Martinez 1991), but data from a broader geographic area (including the Basin and Range of New Mexico) have supported Hofman's expectation (Amick 1994:342). Hofman (1991:345) has suggested that the unexpectedly common occurrence of Midland points close to sources might reflect a situation of hunters leaving for a planned trip of such long duration in a known lithic-poor area that their next visit to a source might be months in the future.

Cultural, or social, causes have also been suggested to account for the differences between Folsom and Midland points. A few archaeologists have proposed that the two types represent different cultural groups, based in part on the existence of sites with only Midland points (e.g., Blaine 1968; Irwin 1971:47–52; Smith 1970).

Like the previous debates, the Folsom-Midland debate has been guided by the primary goal of establishing the temporal relationship between the two point types. While this relationship is not yet firmly established, most archaeologists have at least tentatively decided that the two types are contemporaneous. This goal has been explicit. Definitions have been both extensional and intensional and have been explicit. The debate now focuses on a single attribute: the presence or absence of fluting.

Folsom Point Synthetic Unit as Currently Defined

Paleo-Indian archaeologists sought to construct units (point types) using attributes that would enable them to construct a chronological framework. The Folsom point synthetic unit was initially limited to the points from the Folsom Site. The definition of the unit widened after the initial Folsom Site find to include most late Pleistocene points as archaeologists rushed to document other examples of early human occupation in North America. The unit ultimately narrowed through a series of debates during the 1930s, 1940s, and 1950s that split off Yuma and Clovis points as separate temporal types. Currently, absolute and relative dating indicate that Folsom points are younger than fluted Clovis points and older than most of the unfluted Yuma points (although fluting did carry on in a limited way in post-Folsom times. See Agogino 1970; Barbour and Schultz 1932a; Bell and Van Royen 1934:54, Figure 4; Jenks 1935:10; Meserve and Barbour 1932; Schultz 1932:273). Midland points were originally separated out as Yuma points, but are now generally considered to be contemporaneous technological variants of Folsom points. The geographic distribution of Folsom points has seen a reduction from an almost continent-wide range to one that spans the middle of the continent and is centered on the Plains, Rocky Mountains, and parts of the Southwest (Jodry 1987).

The current definition of the Folsom point synthetic unit has not changed since Wormington defined it in 1957. Interestingly, archaeologists have virtually ceased to discuss what they mean by "Folsom point," much less provide explicit definitions (e.g., Amick 1994; Bradley 1982:203; Frison 1991; Frison and Bradley 1980:80; Hester 1972; Hofman 1989; Largent et al. 1991:323; LeTourneau 1992a, 1992b; Sellards 1952). Even Sellards (1952), credited with formalizing the differentiation between Clovis and Folsom, did not provide a definition for Folsom points; he simply defined the Llano (Clovis) complex based on points associated with mammoth bones and thus defined Folsom by exclusion. Other than extensional definitions of site-specific assemblages (Hester 1972:124; Sellards 1952), Wormington's Folsom point definition (1957:27) is one of the last explicit, intensional definitions to be published and is heavily cited today (e.g., Boldurian 1990:68; Bradley 1982:203; Judge 1973:174; Rovner and Agogino 1967:132).

Within the current definition of the Folsom point synthetic unit there is variation in size, shape, fluting, and quality of workmanship (see Figure 4.5). This variation is seen in point assemblages from both excavated and/or dated sites (Hester 1972; Howard 1935a:Plate 33; Schultz 1943:240, 147; Wilmsen and Roberts 1978; Wormington 1957:20) and has been the subject of discussion, most of which has been aimed at further splitting of the unit (e.g., Roberts 1935b:15, 1936:18; Wormington 1957:34). Proponents of further splitting feel that technological and morphological differences reflect functional (Wormington 1957:34), temporal (Galloway and Agogino 1961:205–6), or cultural differences (Krone 1975, 1978; Van Buren 1974:3; Wilmsen and Roberts 1978:179). Opponents of further splitting suggest that much of the variation is due simply to manufacturing or use damage (e.g., Tunnell 1977:143).

RELIABILITY OF THE FOLSOM POINT AS A SYNTHETIC UNIT

Is the Folsom point, as currently defined, a reliable synthetic unit? Here I use reliability to mean consistency in identification (Carmines and Zeller 1979:11; Nance 1987:246; Spector 1981:12). In other words, when one researcher uses the term "Folsom point," do others generally know what he/she means? The answer is a qualified "yes." As discussed above, Folsom point is no longer explicitly defined because there is informal agreement among Paleo-Indian archaeologists as to what a Folsom point is (see also Holliday and Anderson 1993:80). The combination of distinctive technology and morphology make the Folsom point one of the most reliable types in North America. The lack of definitions, I think, reflects a consensus that the Folsom point is a reliable synthetic unit.

But even if the Folsom point is a reliable synthetic unit, the lack of explicit definition is still troubling. The question may be asked how Paleo-Indian archaeologists can communicate without explicitly defining the types that are so important to their work. The lack of explicit definitions at least potentially impedes communication among researchers by restricting understanding of what is meant by the type to an experienced few. This situation is characterized by a lack of explicit definitions and descriptions in the current literature. At best, there is only a drawing of a "typical example" or a vague statement that "these points are within the range of variability of Folsom points." At worst, there is a simple statement that "these are Folsom points." This situation makes communication, and especially evaluation, difficult. It requires that readers guess what the author means. A further problem derives from the fact that informal agreement as to definitions implies informal agreement as to goals as well. Explicit goals are necessary for intensional definitions. Wormington's intensional definition (1957) works generally for communication and for marking time, but may not perform well for other goals. So, while the Folsom point is a generally reliable synthetic unit, it still behooves us to follow Brew's advice to "always remember to advise the reader thoroughly of the concepts we are using" (1946b:65).

THE FOLSOM POINT AS AN ANALYTIC UNIT

The Folsom point changes from a synthetic to an analytic unit when the research focus changes from Folsom point to Folsom culture. In this role the point becomes a defining attribute of the culture and, in fact, is the single most important attribute of the larger unit. Given this importance, it is appropriate to evaluate the performance of the Folsom point as an analytic unit (for the remainder of this chapter I consider the Folsom point only as currently defined).

Folsom sites are identified primarily by the presence of Folsom points; but in common usage, "Folsom site" means more than simply a site with Folsom points. It means that the site is referable to the Folsom culture. "Folsom culture" is a construct comprising such concepts as settlement, subsistence, and spatiotemporal range. There are problems with using the Folsom point to define the culture, and I consider these problems below.

The construction of the unit Folsom culture has been quite simple: it has formed by accretional growth directed by the presence of Folsom points. Every time a Folsom point has been found, associated artifacts and faunal remains have been included in an effort to flesh out the picture of Folsom culture. The specifics of this process have had some

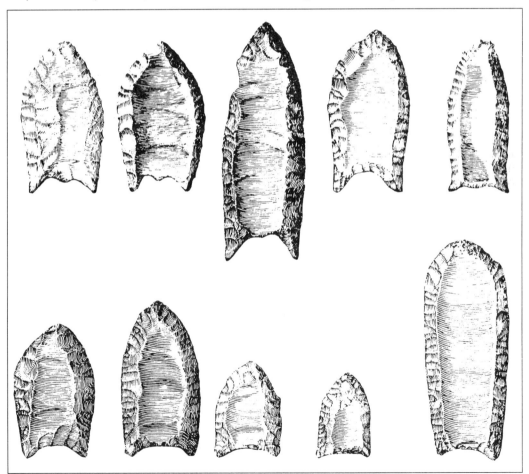

Figure 4.5. Folsom points, Lindenmeier Site, Larimer County, Colorado (Wilmsen and Roberts 1978:114). All actual size.

significant results for the current character of the unit Folsom culture.

The question, then, is whether the Folsom point is reliable and/or valid as an analytic unit for defining the unit Folsom culture. Reliability, as already defined, is consistency or replicability in measurement. Validity addresses whether the unit measures what it was designed to measure (Carmines and Zeller 1979:12; Nance 1987:246; Spector 1981:14). If the Folsom point is not reliable and/or valid as an analytic unit, then the validity of the unit Folsom culture suffers. This discussion is limited to three facets of the Folsom culture: chronology, subsistence, and culture.

CHRONOLOGY

Because establishing a chronological framework has been, and remains, the primary goal of Paleo-Indian archaeologists, the performance of the Folsom point as an analytic unit in measuring time is important. In terms of reliability, the issue is whether Folsom points consistently provide the same temporal resolution. It appears that they do, but the evidence is extremely limited.

Two sorts of information help evaluate the temporal sensitivity of Folsom points. First is radiocarbon dating. Seven sites with Folsom points have been dated by the radiocarbon method; the mean dates span a 700-year period from approximately 10,900 to 10,200 years B.P.[7] This then is the Folsom period. The only problem is that a sample size of seven dated sites is a very small fraction (less than 1 percent) of the 1,000 or more known Folsom sites.[8] At the same time, a 700-year duration at a temporal distance of 10,000 years is relatively short. Consequently, the association between Folsom points and radiocarbon dates is reliable. Second are faunal associations. When Folsom points are associated with faunal remains, bones of extinct *Bison antiquus* are invariably present; this association supports a late Pleistocene date for these otherwise undated Folsom point sites. It thus appears that the Folsom point is a reliable analytic unit for measuring time at a scale of at least the terminal Pleistocene

epoch and possibly at a scale of approximately 700 years.

It is also appropriate to consider whether the point is a valid temporal marker. Is the point an appropriate device for measuring chronology? If the goal is to identify sites from the last several hundred years of the Pleistocene, then it is partially valid. Just as the presence of Folsom points means that the occupation falls within the dated Folsom period, their absence does not mean that the occupation does not fall within that period. By maintaining a narrow focus on projectile points, Paleo-Indian archaeologists implicitly ignore sites on the Plains occupied between 10,900 and 10,200 years B.P. that do not have Folsom points. The presence of Folsom points is sufficient for dating a site to the Folsom period, but the assumption that it is also necessary for doing so is not valid. Although the exclusive identification of Folsom points with a 700-year time period is too narrow, finding other temporal measures is more difficult. Other than Folsom points and the byproducts of their manufacture, there are no currently known artifacts (or attributes) that perform the role of temporal marker as well (see also Amick 1994:100; Roberts 1945:404).

Despite the problem of exclusive linkage between the Folsom point analytic unit and the period, the unit is demonstrably both reliable and valid in its role as an analytic unit for measuring chronology. The primary reason for its reliability as a synthetic unit is its narrow expression of technomorphological attributes (primarily fluting). These same characteristics are clearly restricted to the late Pleistocene and thus also work for chronological control. The unit would not work as well if this equation of fluting and late Pleistocene was not so strong. Today the primary use of the Folsom point analytic unit is still to establish chronology (e.g., Amick 1994:10).

SUBSISTENCE

Since only about 30 (or 3 percent) of the 1,000+ Folsom sites contain faunal remains, Folsom points cannot be considered reliable for measuring subsistence. All 30 faunal sites contain bison bones, but 15 (50 percent) also contain bones of genera other than bison. These remains include at least 26 mammalian genera and at least 14 species of birds, reptiles, and fish (Amick 1994:231). Thus, Folsom points are not reliable for measuring subsistence because they are not consistently found with potential subsistence remains.

Folsom points are not valid measures of subsistence because their use introduces significant biases. The initial Folsom point finds were at sites with extinct bison on the Plains; indeed, most of the first Folsom point sites were found *because* of the presence of bison bones (Meltzer 1993:293–94). The immediate inference from this pattern was that Folsom point users were bison-hunting specialists (e.g., Figgins 1934; Roberts 1939a:541), and additional point finds did not change it since they were either associated with bison bones or were not associated with any faunal remains at all. This view became well entrenched in the literature (e.g., Harrington 1938a; Howard 1943b:258; Mason 1962: 229; Roberts 1939a:541; Sellards 1952:47).

Munson (1990:262) goes so far as to state that Folsom point manufacture is more than just a technique; rather "it is part of a cultural tradition that includes a specific technology and a particular environmental-subsistence adaptation." Based primarily on the presence of Folsom points in "Prairie Peninsula states" in the upper Mississippi River drainage, Munson argues that a grassland environment with bison was present and that Folsom people hunted those bison. Yet he does not identify bison remains at any of these sites, and the nearest Folsom bison kills are approximately 1,200 kilometers west of his easternmost Folsom point sites (see Amick [1994:9–10] for a similar critique). Simpson (1948:14), writing on Folsomlike points found associated with megafaunal remains in Florida river beds, similarly concluded that the points were, like their Plains counterparts, used for hunting Plains-type game animals.

Focusing only on sites with Folsom points

and then attempting to address questions concerning subsistence automatically truncates the possible variation within that domain and then systematically biases the results of investigation. If Folsom points were used for hunting and if hunting was not the sole subsistence activity of Folsom point users, then there should be a range of sites with nonhunting functions in which Folsom points are absent.

As noted above, Folsom points are associated with genera other than bison. There is some evidence that humans introduced and/ or modified at least some of these bones (e.g., Amick 1994:231–44; Johnson 1987: 124), although the overall subsistence role of the nonbison genera at these sites is not clear. Bison would certainly have been a good food source, and the geographic distribution of Folsom points lies almost completely within that of *Bison antiquus* remains (Kurtén and Anderson 1980:338; McDonald 1981: 76–95). As for the interpretation that Folsom points were used strictly for bison hunting, blood residue analysis suggests that they were used for hunting and/or processing rabbit, bear, and pronghorn in addition to bison (Amick 1994:248; Hyland and Anderson 1990:109).

There is still virtually no evidence for plant use during the period, but this can be assumed to reflect preservational biases rather than an actual lack of plant use. Bison bone from both surface and excavated Folsom sites is often in poor condition (e.g., Ingbar 1992:175; Jodry and Stanford 1992:109; Zeimens 1982:215). Given that bison bones are larger and denser than other likely organic remains (Amick 1994:231), and given that denser bones are less susceptible to the effects of weathering and postdepositional modification (Lyman 1984), it is probable that a wide range of subsistence remains has been eliminated from the archaeological record.

Meltzer (1993:298–301) has noted that only 8 percent (n = 16) of North American ethnographic groups included in Murdock's Ethnographic Atlas (1967) were specialized hunters. All of these groups inhabited restricted environmental settings, and all but two inhabited the Plains. But even these 14 groups were "not entirely specialized" (Meltzer 1993:300) since, although bison was their main source of food and clothing, the groups also ate a wide variety of smaller mammals, birds, plants, and berries (Driver 1969:57; Ewers 1955:121–22; Meltzer 1993:300).

There are two reasons to question the likelihood that Folsom groups were as specialized as the ethnographic Plains groups. First, all of the ethnographic groups used horses for hunting bison (Bamforth 1988:97; Murdock 1967). Acquisition of the horse greatly improved hunting success and enabled the transport of much larger food stores (Driver 1969:57; Ewers 1955:302–5; Jablow 1951: 10–20), so Plains groups may have relied less on bison prior to the introduction of the horse. There is clear evidence for differences between Paleo-Indian (including Folsom) and later Plains groups in terms of bison procurement. Compared with later Plains groups, Paleo-Indian groups killed bison in different seasons (Frison 1982a; Todd 1987: 259, 1991), Folsom groups killed fewer bison in a kill event (Meltzer 1993:302), and Paleo-Indian groups processed and used the bison they killed differently (Frison 1982a). Second, although late Pleistocene environmental reconstructions differ in many specific aspects, they do agree that the environment during the last thousand years of the Pleistocene on the Plains and Prairies was significantly different from today and that there are no modern analogs for those environments (Bamforth 1988:134–49; Bryant and Shafer 1977; Ferring 1990:254; Graham 1986a: 134–41, 1986b:311–13, 1987:38–43; Jodry and Stanford 1992:101–5). Meltzer (1993: 302) has suggested that perhaps bison populations were much smaller in the late Pleistocene and may not have provided the abundant source of food that they did in the Holocene.

The archaeological, ethnographic, and paleoenvironmental evidence does not support the scenario that Folsom point users subsisted entirely on bison, or even solely on hunting, although bison probably did provide a significant source of food. That scenario formed largely due to biases inherent in the use of Folsom points to measure subsistence. The Folsom point is neither reliable nor valid in its role as an analytic unit for addressing questions of subsistence.

CULTURE

A third facet of the Folsom Culture package is "culture" itself. As discussed above, the construction of units that had some undefined cultural meaning was a secondary goal of Paleo-Indian archaeologists. There are problems that derive from equating the Folsom point analytic unit with the concept of culture, whether that concept is used in Binford's sense of "man's extrasomatic means of adaptation" (1962:217–18, 1965:205) or in the more traditional sense of shared ideas (Kroeber and Kluckhohn 1952:50–54). Historically, the term "Folsom culture" has been used as an umbrella concept for all facets of the Folsom culture package. As noted earlier, Figgins (1933:5) and Cook (1928:39, 1931:103) used the term "Folsom Culture" to refer to a broader context for the Folsom points. Figgins (1934:5) pushed this equation the farthest by arguing that the extinction of Pleistocene bison resulted in the extinction of "Folsom man himself"; he cited as evidence the absence of any associations of Folsom points with modern bison. Roberts (1937c:67) preferred the term "Folsom Complex" for Folsom points and other artifacts from Lindenmeier, but attributed the complex to "Folsom Man." And Renaud (1931b: 12) felt that the term "Folsom point" should be reserved for those points "likely made by the same ancient people." Other archaeologists equating Folsom points with Folsom culture in this sense include Agogino (1969:1118), Fischel (1939:240), and Harrington (1938a).

Although use of the term "Folsom culture" has generally been discontinued, I think the concept still exists in other guises. Many still tend to think of Paleo-Indian point types as reflecting cultural identity, expect them to have spatiotemporal distributions discrete from each other, and are surprised when these distributions overlap (see also Amick 1994:11; Sellet and Frison 1994:8). In this context, the Folsom-Midland debate has recently become part of a larger debate concerning the relationship of those point types with the Goshen and Plainview types. On the basis of geochronology, radiocarbon dates, and technological similarities, Haynes (1991b) recently concluded that the spatiotemporal and technological relationship of the four point types is not as discrete as traditionally thought. And Sellet and Frison (1994:8) have shown in their reevaluation of the stratigraphy at the Hell Gap site (long viewed as the master sequence of spatiotemporally discrete Plains Paleo-Indian point types), that several different point types are found in association with each other. They conclude that many of the current point types probably each represent several different cultures (Sellet and Frison 1994:5).

Several authors have warned against equating a point type with a culture (e.g., Binford 1994; Binford and Sabloff 1982; Brew 1946b; Dunnell 1971; Sellet and Frison 1994:8). Binford and Sabloff (1982) note that this assumption follows Krieger's definition (1944) that types are based on shared similarities and are presumed to represent periods of cultural cohesion, but "culture," as used in the previous examples, is not defined. The concept is vague at best, and as Brew (1946b:57) warns, "is an epistemological solecism which can and has warped our studies." If the concept is vague and not defined, then the Folsom Point analytic unit cannot be a valid measure of it. Furthermore, just as it is not valid to assume that a single artifact class reflects all aspects of subsistence or a cohesive subsistence system, so too is it not valid to assume that a single artifact fully reflects a cohesive culture.

Folsom points appear to have a restricted spatiotemporal distribution. But given this, is it appropriate to interpret this distribution as a reflection of cultural identity? If so, does it mean that all Folsom point users roaming the Plains, Rockies, and Southwest belonged to one large social, family, linguistic, or ethnic group? It is unlikely that any cohesive cultural group actually occupied the whole of the Folsom point geographic distribution during the late Pleistocene. The term "Folsom culture" appears to be used mainly as a shorthand for some undefined concept that needs to be explicitly discussed. Thus, the Folsom point analytic unit is not valid for measuring culture.

In sum, the Folsom point has limited reliability and validity in its use as an analytic unit to define the unit Folsom culture. It appears to be reliable and valid for measuring chronology, but there is simply not enough empirical evidence to be able to fully evaluate its performance. The Folsom point unit is not particularly reliable or valid for measuring subsistence. And it is not valid for identifying the culture facet of the Folsom culture unit.

DISCUSSION

In this chapter, I have shown how the Folsom point acts as two different kinds of units: first as a synthetic unit and second as an analytic unit. The Folsom point synthetic unit was constructed through a series of debates aimed primarily at constructing units capable of establishing a chronological framework. It was the fact that the Folsom point both demonstrated historical significance (Krieger 1960) and exhibited such a narrow range of technological and morphological variation that cemented its existence as a synthetic unit. It thus appears that Howard's "Folsom Problem" (1935a:110) has been solved. Although problems do exist with its use as a synthetic unit, the Folsom point is generally reliable as such.

There are mixed results for the Folsom point's performance as an analytic unit in constructing the unit Folsom culture. It seems to be reliable and partially valid in its role as an analytic unit for measuring chronology, but is not particularly reliable or valid for measuring subsistence. It is also not valid for measuring culture. Thus, the validity of the larger unit Folsom culture suffers as well. Because the Folsom point is so reliable as a synthetic unit and is reliable and valid in its role as a temporal marker, archaeologists have come to think of it as valid for a variety of other questions. This confidence in the Folsom point type is not well founded.

Paleo-Indian archaeologists are fortunate to have technologically distinctive projectile points that are so reliable as synthetic units (see also Shott 1989:292). This distinctiveness makes the Folsom point a fairly consistent synthetic unit, although archaeologists must continue to explicitly define it. And the Folsom point analytic unit seems to measure time fairly well. The real problem lies in using these types as the primary means of delimiting inquiry into topics such as subsistence or settlement. The Folsom point analytic unit should not be considered validated by the reliable performance of the Folsom point synthetic unit.

Paleo-Indian point types are the principal means by which we currently are able to identify late Pleistocene and early Holocene occupation. But until solid research can ground further interpretation, we can feel limited confidence only in the use of the Folsom point as a synthetic unit and as an analytic unit for establishing chronological control.

ACKNOWLEDGMENTS
I thank first and foremost the co-editors of this volume, Ann Ramenofsky and Ana Steffen, for their extraordinary support and excellent comments. I also thank Tom Jones, Bruce Huckell, Dave Meltzer, Bob Leonard, Tony Baker, Jan Cummings, and Janna Rolland for commenting on earlier versions. I presented parts of this chapter in symposia at the 1994 Plains Conference and the 1995 annual meeting of the Society for American Archaeology; I thank the symposium organizers—Dan Amick (1994), Ann Ramenofsky, and Ana Steffen (1995)—for including me.

Notes

1. Roberts (1940) introduced the term "Paleo-Indian" for archaeological remains associated with extinct fauna. Prior to 1940, and for some time afterward, "Early Man" was the favored term for those remains (e.g., Bushnell 1941; Forbis and Sperry 1952; Howard 1935a). Although I use the term "Paleo-Indian" in my historical discussion, the projectile points I discuss were referred to as Early Man points at the time. Holliday and Anderson (1993:79) present a brief history of the use of the term "Paleo-Indian."

2. Howard (1943b) and Roberts (1935a:21, 1937b:153, 1939a:531) also used the phrase "the Folsom Problem," but in a different sense to emphasize the knowledge gap that the newly demonstrated time depth for the human presence in North America presented for culture-history synthesis.

3. "Fluting" is the name given to the technique by which Folsom and Clovis points (as we know them today) were thinned by the removal of long flakes from the base of the points toward the tip. The flakes removed are known as channel flakes (Tunnell 1977). The distinction between fluting and basal thinning techniques is made on the length, width, and number of flakes that have been removed from the base of the point. Bruce Bradley defines flutes "as any basal thinning flake(s) that have traveled past the area of the hafting element" (1993:254, citing a 1988 personal communication with J. B. Sollberger). Fluting saw only a relatively brief span of use (ending with Folsom) and is a hallmark of late Pleistocene lithic technology in North America.

4. The 12 Mile Creek point is currently missing and it is not known what type of fluted point it would now be called (Hofman 1994; Howard 1935a:144; Rogers and Martin 1984).

5. The term "Yuma" is no longer used (Wormington 1948:12, 1950), since that type has been divided into several individual types such as Scottsbluff, Eden, and Agate Basin.

6. See Bushnell (1935, 1940, 1941), Haag (1942:217–21), Kelly (1938:7), *Literary Digest* (1934b), McCary (1951:15–16), and Shetrone (1936) on Folsom points in the Eastern Woodlands. See Amsden (1937:86), Campbell and Campbell (1940), Crouse (1954), Davis (1963:205–6), M.R. Harrington (1938a, 1938b), and Heizer (1938) on Folsom points in the Far West. See Thompson (1948) on Folsom points in the Arctic, and see Figgins (1931, 1933) and Howard (1932) on Folsom points from the Rockies and the Plains. None of these fluted points would now be called Folsom.

7. I include only those seven sites with radiocarbon dates on charcoal that was firmly associated with Folsom artifacts. Those sites are Agate Basin (two Folsom components), Blackwater Draw (multiple Folsom components), Carter/Kerr-McGee, Folsom, Hanson (two Folsom components), Lindenmeier (multiple Folsom components), and Lubbock Lake (multiple Folsom components). Dates are those listed in vari-

ous reports (see below). The 10,900–10,200 time span is based on the mean dates; it does not include standard deviations. Dated charcoal from many of these sites is from Folsom artifact–containing strata that were deposited over long periods of time (possibly hundreds of years) and contain multiple Folsom components; the dates should therefore be interpreted as dating the strata and not necessarily the specific Folsom components. Charcoal dates indirectly associated with Folsom components generally confirm this time span. A redeposited charcoal sample from a Folsom point–bearing stratum at Indian Creek (Downstream Locality), for example, gives a maximum age of 10,980 ± 110 for the Folsom points there. And an average of three dates from a stratum overlying the Folsom level at Bonfire Shelter gives a minimum age of 10,080 ± 100. References for the sites are Agate Basin (Frison 1982b), Blackwater Draw (Hester 1972), Bonfire Shelter (Dibble 1968, 1970; Haynes et al. 1984:189), Carter/Kerr-McGee (Frison 1984), Folsom (Haynes et al. 1992), Hanson (Frison and Bradley 1980; Ingbar 1992), Indian Creek (Davis and Greiser 1992), Lindenmeier (Haynes et al. 1992; Wilmsen and Roberts 1978:39-40), Lubbock Lake (Johnson and Holliday 1987:10–12; Holliday and Allen 1987:27–29).

8. I have compiled a database of approximately 1,000 published and unpublished Folsom sites. Most of these sites are located on the southern Plains and in the Southwest because my research has focused on those areas (n.d.). The total number of Folsom sites is likely far greater than 1,000. By "Folsom site" I mean sites with Folsom points and/or Folsom point preforms and/or channel flakes. In this total I include isolated finds (which I define as single, spatially isolated Folsom points, preforms, or channel flakes) because they are a significant part of the archaeological record. I have excluded from this total all early reports of sites with points originally identified as Folsom but have since been reassigned to other Paleo-Indian types, such as Clovis, Eastern Fluted, etc.

5

The Illusion of Time

ANN F. RAMENOFSKY

The distinction between past, present and future is only an illusion, even if a stubborn one.

Albert Einstein

All archaeologists agree that time is of fundamental importance in our discipline. The great temporal depth of the human record is a strong selling point, drawing students into our introductory classes. In terms of research, the time depth affords us a unique path into the study of change and development. Time, however, is an abstraction (Spaulding 1960; but see Stahl 1992). Because there is no physical entity that is *time*, archaeological research frequently begins with measuring the temporal dimension.

Chronologies are the archaeological units that slice up time, making the concept into usable, archaeological products. As Renfrew put it: "Without a reliable chronology, the past is chaotic: there is no way of relating or ordering people, events and cultures into the coherent narrative the prehistorian seeks to construct" (1973:20). Constructing chronologies was the heart of culture history and marked the beginning of the development of archaeological science. With the recognition of deep time for human existence (Daniel 1976; Grayson 1983; Meltzer 1983), archaeologists turned their research efforts to the division of the temporal continuum.

The contributions and development of culture history have been analyzed from different perspectives (e.g., Adams and Adams 1992; Daniel 1976; Dunnell 1986a, 1986b; Trigger 1989; Willey and Sabloff 1993), and I will not duplicate those efforts in this chapter. As suggested by such phrases as "the con-

trol of time" or "establishing time," methodological distinctions between time and chronology have become blurred. This blurring of the concept and the measurement tool, of time and chronology, is the stimulus for this chapter.

Because chronologies are tools, their performance must be evaluated in terms of either reliability or validity or both (see chapter 1 for definitions). Reliability and validity assessment of chronologies are part of our methodological arsenal. An assessment of the reliability of chronological units focuses on the empirical aspects of chronological efforts. Cross-dating is a reliability assessment employed to extend chronologies spatially. Multiple lines of evidence, including temporal markers, or calendrical dates, are compared with established temporal markers to place a newly excavated deposit into the appropriate framework. Using multiple criteria to make a temporal assignment increases precision and accuracy. If multiple indicators suggest the same temporal placement, then we are more confident that the assignment is correct. In addition, discussions of reliability appear frequently in archaeological literature. Refining the precision of the radiocarbon curve through correlation of radiocarbon dates with dendrodates of bristlecone pines (e.g., Browman 1981; Renfrew 1973: 72–83; Stuiver 1982; Stuiver and Kra 1986; Watkins 1975) or having several laboratories independently assess the authenticity of the

Shroud of Turin (Dale 1987; Gove 1987) are examples.

To evaluate the validity of chronological units, in contrast, means analyzing the fit between units and temporal research goals. Assessment of empirical validity examines the performance of chronological units for temporal goals. Whenever the meaning of temporal units is questioned, however, issues of abstract validity are being raised (see chapter 1 for definitions of empirical and abstract validity). The classic debates that questioned artifacts as temporal types, for example, the Ford and Spaulding debate (Ford 1954a, 1954b, 1954c, 1961; Hill and Evans 1972; Spaulding 1953a, 1953b, 1954) or the Thomas and Flenniken debate (Bettinger et al. 1991; Flenniken and Raymond 1986; Flenniken and Wilke 1989; Thomas 1981, 1986; Wilke and Flenniken 1991) are examples of assessing the validity of one type of chronological unit.

The focus of this chapter is on the abstract validity of chronological units, and I discuss the importance of conceptual fit between goals and temporal units and offer some examples of performance in particular contexts. Focusing on abstract validity implies that I am most concerned with whether temporal divisions work in a specified context. Do the chronological divisions allow us to investigate the problem of interest? Because of the variation in research questions, there can be no universal, or perfectly valid, chronology. Chronological units are task-specific tools and, conceivably, there are as many chronologies as there are research questions.

As mentioned above, validity assessment has historically punctuated discussions of artifact types as temporal markers. Chronological structures, however, have not been comparably scrutinized.[1] There has not been much discussion of whether there is a conceptual fit between chronological units and temporal research goals. The absence of debate regarding the validity of chronological units is a function of two factors. On the one hand, the events described by cultural historical sequences are correct. There can be no debate regarding the development of agriculture; it is a more recent development than

broad-scale foraging. On the other hand, because culture historical sequences are correct, we have assumed that the units describing the sequences are real and have been discovered. Quite simply, we have conflated temporal orders with the units that measure the sequences. The result is that the validity of the units has not been questioned. (Wills 1990:328 for a similar point.)

Essentialism in chronological research assumes that chronological units are real and discoverable; I do not adopt that ontology here. Instead, ontological materialism, or population thinking, guides my discussion of time and chronology (Mayr 1994; Sober 1980; see also chapter 1). Adopting a materialist ontology in the context of chronological units means that there are no natural, temporal divisions. Time is not packaged, but rather infinitely divisible. Consequently, chronologies cannot be discovered. Temporal indicators may be recovered from archaeological deposits, and estimates of duration may be derived from these materials. This sort of activity does not mean that we discover time. In addition, chronological units that bound time may be convenient, obvious, or intuitively satisfying. They do not, however, occur at natural joints. There are no joints in nature. Chronological units are conceptual, defined, and imposed on the continuum of time.

Because it is easy to confuse the continuum of time with the units that measure time, an explicit discussion of the differences between them is required. So, I begin by briefly considering the properties of time in theoretical physics and contrast those properties with archaeological time. This contrast underscores the conceptual nature of time. The research goals in physics and archaeology are fundamentally different, resulting in different conceptions and measurement of time. I then discuss the properties of chronology and conclude with describing why archaeologists have confused the discovery of time with the construction of chronology.

PROPERTIES OF TIME

Archaeology is a historical science. Our perception of time as linear—"time's arrow"

(Gould 1987)—grew out of the constructions of time in other earth sciences, geology and paleontology (Daniel 1976; Grayson 1983). Yet, within archaeology, we have no theory of time. Physics, by contrast, is largely an ahistorical science with a grand theory of time that is powerful and counterintuitive to the measurement and use of time in any historical science. In theoretical physics, time is a process that is always occurring. The measurement of this process at the scale of universe is dependent on space, and neither space nor time are linear. Both are warped by the presence of mass. Thus, time is nonlinear and constitutes the fourth dimension of physical measurement.

The revolution in the theory of time began with Newtonian mechanics and culminated with the theoretical work of Einstein, Bohr, and Hawking (Chaisson 1981, 1988; Davies 1995; Einstein 1961; Hawking 1988; Pais 1982, 1994). One implication of Newton's law of gravity was the destruction of the concept of absolute rest. Because rest must occur somewhere, the loss of absolute rest also meant the loss of absolute space. From Newton forward, space became relative to the position of the observer (Hawking 1988). In other words, moving through space in a rocket at a uniform speed and direction is relative to the rocket. It is simply not possible to move through space absolutely.

Newtonian time, however, was quintessentially mathematical and absolute. Newton defined time as continuous flux, independent of any other force. Other physical processes occurred within the backdrop of time. Time was the stage, universal and unaffected by those processes. Because there was only one universal time in the Newtonian cosmology, past, present, and future were logical constructs (Davies 1995). In essence, everyone had to agree on what had happened five years ago and what might happen five years into the future.

Although Newton's conception of time as absolute was shown to be erroneous by the late nineteenth century (Chaisson 1981, 1988; Davies 1995; Hawking 1988), it was Einstein who turned Newtonian time on its head. In Einstein's cosmology, time is flexible and relative. Einstein began with the fundamental postulate that the laws of science are universal (Chaisson 1988; Einstein 1961; Hawking 1988). To that, he added the relativity of space and the constancy of the speed of light, 300,000 km per second, derived from electromagnetic theory. In that theory, it had been shown that light moves at the same speed regardless of whether an observer is moving or standing still. The speed of light, not time, is unaffected by where we are or how fast we travel. Into this mix, he added an elastic time that changed according to speed, mass, and location.

Einstein's demonstration of the relativity of time is of less importance than discussing the counterintuitive implications of the theory. First, time is not linear, but is deformed by both speed and mass (Chaisson 1988; Davies 1995; Einstein 1961). As the mass of objects increases, or as speed increases, the warp of time becomes more extreme. The reverse is also true. As mass or speed decreases, time stretches. For instance, in the absence of influencing bodies, highly charged subatomic particles have great speed and decay in a few millionths of a second. As those particles move toward the earth, however, speed decreases, and decay times stretch sufficiently to register their presence in our atmosphere.

A second remarkable consequence of Einstein's relativity is that space and time are twins. Rather than "space" and "time," only one term, "space-time," is appropriate at the scale of the universe. Time is the fourth dimension making location an unimaginable manifold, composed of X, Y, Z, and time. As an object approaches the speed of light, we cannot ask where something is without also asking when it occurred. Moreover, the answer to that question changes according to the reference frame of the observer. As a result, every time we look through a telescope at a distant galaxy, we are simultaneously looking out into space and back into time. But, the cosmic events viewed will be different if the viewings are separated by only a few earth minutes or through a telescope at another location. In other words, the manifold of the observer affects the observed "there and then" of cosmic events.

The differences in observers' space-time is made real through the simple example of a set of twins, Kate and Emma, and space travel. Kate takes off from earth in a spaceship, and Emma stays put. Viewed from earth, Kate's time in the spaceship seems to slow. From the ship, however, Emma's time seems slower. Yet, upon return, the times of the two twins are again in sync, and Emma has aged more than Kate. Kate's space travel was not perfectly uniform; acceleration and mass changed throughout the journey. These changes stretched time. As measured in earth years, the duration of Kate's journey was shorter than the number of years Emma experienced on earth (Davies 1995).

Finally, because mass and speed change the shape of space-time, the shortest distance between two points is not a straight line, but a bending arc, or geodesic (Chaisson 1981, 1988; Hawking 1988). In the space travel example, then, the shortest distance between earth and Kate's destination is not a straight line, but a curve. Were a spaceship able to travel in a straight line from earth (which it can not), the trip would take longer to reach the destination than a curved trajectory (Davies 1995).

Time in physics, then, is neither linear nor absolute. Time is relative, elastic, and deformed by mass and speed. At the scale of universe, the shortest distance between two points is curved, and the measurement of time at the scale of the universe is a manifold, composed of X, Y, Z, and time. Finally, perceptions of time change according to the reference frame of the observer.

In archaeology, by contrast, the definition and perception of time is necessarily tied to the scale and nature of our research field: the archaeological record of the planet. I define time as a continuous variable that is constantly elapsing (see Spaulding [1960] for a similar definition of time). Because time is continuous, it is infinitely divisible. There are no seams in the continuum of time. In addition, time is constantly passing away.

We implicitly recognize both the continuous nature and passing away of time. We can, for instance, divide the temporal dimension into millennia, centuries, decades, years, months, days, or minutes. Speaking of one century as opposed to 52,560,000 minutes is more convenient, but there is nothing inherently better or more correct about centuries than about minutes. Centuries and minutes are equally reliable measurements of time. Even if we are not aware of the passage of time, we routinely use the consequence of that passage in research. Because time elapses, it has direction, and is conceived as linear. Earth time, then, is an arrow where past, present, and future are logical constructs. Time lines, as well as the ordinal comparisons of earlier and later or younger and older, indicate both the direction and linear nature of archaeological time.

The contrast between warped time at the scale of universe and earth time as linear has two significant implications for archaeological perception and analysis of time. First, time is neither absolute nor a discoverable entity. Time passes, but even the perception of that passage is contingent on the location of the observer. Consequently, we cannot discover time because there is nothing to discover. Second, the archaeological conception of time as linear is appropriate for the scale of our research endeavor. At the scale of the planet, we perceive the temporal process as linear, and our measurements of that process are more or less successful in the context of our research setting. Only when the scale of the temporal process changes from earth to universe does linear time become nonlinear, requiring a different conceptualization, description, and measurement.

We have long recognized the abstract nature of earth time, and built that recognition into our framework for analyzing the concept. As Spaulding (1960) stated some 35 years ago, of the three variables in archaeological research—time, space, and form—time is the only one that cannot be observed directly. It must be inferred from space and form. This inference, itself, is a complex process that requires distinguishing between the causal processes or events that incorporate time into the archaeological record versus the goal of the temporal estimate. Dean's 1978 phrases of *target event* and *dated event* cleanly capture this distinction (but see also Binford 1968b:249; Dunnell 1981; Dunnell and Readhead 1988).

The *dated event* refers to those events that incorporate time into the archaeological record, and these obviously vary in duration and complexity. Earth-building processes are causal for incorporating time into strata. For trees or bivalves, growth rings are annual. Thermoluminescence signals are more complex, caused by a suite of factors, including the instability of radioactive ions, the crystalline structure of materials, and heat. The *target event* describes the archaeological event of interest (e.g., the construction of a room, abandonment of a settlement, or the last time a ceramic was fired.) As Dean (1978:228) has pointed out, there is no necessary agreement between the dated and the target events. Stratigraphy can be reversed; beams can be recycled; old carbon can be transported and redeposited into younger sediments.

In summary, regardless of disciplinary boundaries, time is recognized as a physical process that has no physical existence. Whether in a spaceship or driving in a car, we can not touch, smell, or taste time. It is conceptual. Here, however, commonalities between physics and archaeology end. Einstein's time is a "flexiband" where distinctions of past, present, and future no longer make sense. Archaeological time is closer conceptually to Newtonian time. Time is continuous, linear and nonreversible. We experience time as constantly becoming older or as slipping away. Because time has direction, distinguishing past from future is possible. The discipline of archaeology is one obvious consequence of that separation. Because time is abstract, we extract chunks of time from space and form. Processes by which time is incorporated into the archaeological record are distinct from the ability to measure those processes or the goals of the measurement.

PROPERTIES OF CHRONOLOGY

Chronologies are the measurement tools of time in archaeology and all other earth sciences. "Continually elapsing" defines what time is, but it is difficult to use this definition in the doing of archaeology. By dividing time into units, archaeologists are converting the lapsing nature of time into a product that measures the temporal dimension.

The construction of chronologies is a methodological endeavor and, I contend, materialism is the ontology that drives that construction effort. As a consequence, chronological units are neither real nor discoverable. They are conceptual and imposed on the temporal dimension. Because they are imposed, chronological divisions are arbitrary (Brew 1946b; Hull 1970:47), and there are an infinite number of divisions. Arbitrary does not imply mindlessness, or lack of rigor. Use of the term, in fact, emphasizes that chronological research must be deliberate and thoughtful because there is no "correct" separation. Choosing a different set of defining criteria results in a different division of the temporal continuum and a different structuring of archaeological materials.

The composition and number of units that slice up the temporal continuum vary. Just as there is no universal chronology, the analytic units employed to build chronologies vary. Single traits—for example, projectile points, isotopic estimates, or even the size of boreholes of kaolin pipes (Binford 1961; Harrington 1954)—may be adequate units in some settings. In contrast, the analytic units of cultural historical phases or traditions are complex and include single traits—ceramics, for example—as well as trait aggregates—burial type and position, grave furniture, and architecture, for example.

Viewing chronological units as constructed has implications for the creation process itself. Because the number of divisions of time is infinite, there must be some logic driving the selection of units and the creation of one as opposed to another set of units. Here validity assessment becomes an explicit concern. Chronologies are units that cannot be constructed in isolation, or independently, of a temporal goal. Chronological units are a kind of description of time, but description in the absence of research goal is meaningless. Without the logical connection between goal and units, there is no basis for saying that one chronological division is superior to another (Hull 1970:32; Lewontin 1974). To assess the abstract validity of chronological units is to examine the fit between temporal goals and chronology.

Archaeological research on the timing and magnitude of introduced infectious diseases to American Indians demonstrates how chronological structures change with changing temporal goals (e.g., Campbell 1990; Perttula 1992; Ramenofsky 1987; Smith 1987; Snow 1995). Although 1492 marks the beginning of sustained European presence in the Americas, Europeans spread through the continents in waves. Consequently, the beginning of the post-European period varies regionally. Prior to the mid-1980s, trade goods, derived largely from burial contexts, and/or historical documents were the units employed to indicate the beginning of historical periods by region (e.g., Brain 1980; Quimby 1966). The possibility that infectious diseases diffused independently of, and possibly earlier than, trade goods had significant implications. The beginning of post-European chronologies might be masking the timing of significant post-European, demographic shifts in native populations. Existing chronologies did not fit the context of the disease problem. Clearly, to assess the timing and consequences of disease outbreaks and native population change at regional scales required new temporal units.

Finally, the nature of the research dictates the degree of temporal resolution required by a chronology. Relative and absolute dates are deeply entrenched archaeological terms that describe differences in temporal resolution, but these terms are ambiguous (Colman et al. 1987). First, because all divisions of the temporal dimension are estimates, the distinction between relative and absolute is false. Relative and absolute estimates of time differ only in terms of resolution. (Absolute dates are more exact [i.e., measured more minutely] than relative dates.) Second, despite the difference in resolution, absolute and relative dates are both unique solutions. Third, the terms describe both the methods for deriving a temporal estimate—for example, "stratigraphy is a relative dating method"—and the temporal resolution of the estimate, a relative date (Colman et al. 1987).

To avoid the ambiguities and to emphasize that the key chronological issue is the scale of measurement, I employ several terms. "Estimate" describes the product of temporal measurement. "Ordinal" and "interval" refers to types of estimates; the scale of measurement of relative estimates is ordinal; that of an absolute estimate is interval. When used as an adjective, the term "dating" describes methods used to produce the estimates. (Blackwell and Schwarcz 1993; Colman 1986; Colman et al. 1987).

An ordinal dating method creates ranks that have duration and direction. A stratigraphic layer in a profile has a beginning, middle, and end, but we don't know how much time is incorporated in that layer or whether two layers in stratigraphic sequence have equal durations. Ordinal scale chronologies require a minimum of two events. One event is ranked older than the other. The temporal distance between ranks is unknown (Spaulding 1960). The lack of specificity in duration of chronological units means that the resolution of relative chronologies is fairly coarse-grained, or crude.

Although coarse-grained, ordinal scale units are reliable. Evidence of this reliability is embodied in the nineteenth-century concept of *fossile directeur*. Because of the repeated stratigraphic demonstration that certain forms occurred in sequence, the forms themselves became robust measurements of the temporal dimension (Sackett 1981). The occurrence of these forms in any deposit was sufficient to establish its temporal rank. In the twentieth century, cultural historians excelled in developing ordinal chronologies through seriation and the stylistic analysis of

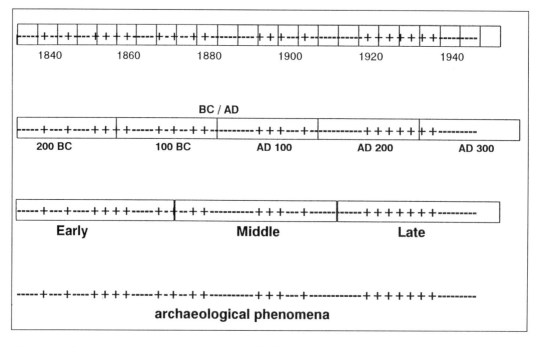

Figure 5.1. Archaeological phenomena across ordinal and interval time scales.

artifacts (e.g., Ford 1961; Krieger 1944; Dunnell 1986a, 1986b; Teltser 1995a).

In interval measurement, numbers are attached to ordinal direction, and the distance between numbers is equal. Thus, the difference between 3 and 4 is exactly the same as that between 103 and 104. In contrast to ratio scale measurement, however, the placement of zero in interval measurement is arbitrary. Calendars are interval scale units because there is no absolute zero. The zero in the Jewish calendar is the "origin of creation"; the birth of Christ marks the difference between B.C. and A.D. in the Christian calendar; for B.P. dating, all estimates are subtracted from A.D. 1950.

The difference in resolution between ordinal and interval chronologies is important and a function of the specificity of numbers. Numbers create the divisions between units in interval scale chronologies, and the resulting units are typically finer-grained than ordinal scale estimates. Because the information content of interval scale is greater, interval scale chronologies can always be downsized, converted into an ordinal scale. The reverse, however, is impossible. Without numbers, ordinal designations cannot be upgraded.

The gain in exactness afforded by interval-scale temporal units is both attractive and desirable. What archaeologist, after all, wouldn't prefer the fine-grained resolution of a dendronchronology to an imprecise periodization of I, II, III, etc. At the same time, we have confused the exactness of interval scale measurements with the assessment of accuracy and validity. In fact, we have equated the high resolution of interval estimates of time with both accuracy and validity, assuming that the more precise estimate has no systematic bias and is, therefore, valid. This equation is simply erroneous. Time is a continuous variable, which means that there are an infinite number of "unique solutions," not just one. Figure 5.1 demonstrates how moving up the measurement scale from ordinal to interval creates more temporal divisions. Yet, the interval scale is continuous. To change interval estimates from centuries to years means that a single point along a number line balloons into an interval.

My point here: the temporal resolution that is required varies by research goal (Bernard 1994). Thus, an estimate may be sufficiently precise for one purpose and imprecise for another. Exactness, however, does not guarantee that an estimate is free of systematic error nor that the estimate will work for the purpose at hand. Resolution, accuracy, and validity address different aspects of measurement, but validity is the engine that drives the selection of units.

The conflation of resolution, accuracy, and validity is demonstrated by the continuing and seemingly irreconcilable debate regarding the temporal estimates of the earliest cultural deposits at Meadowcroft Rockshelter (Adovasio et al. 1975, 1980, 1990, 1992; Haynes 1980, 1991a; Mead 1980; Tankersley and Munson 1992). There are 11 stratigraphic units in the rockshelter; each stratigraphic unit is associated with radiometric estimates. Moreover, the stratigraphic sequence and radiometric estimates are largely in agreement. As of 1990, of the 52 estimates for the entire sequence, only 4 were reversed.

Because Meadowcroft Rockshelter is south of the glacial margin, the validity issue driving the debate is the timing of human entry into the Americas. The stakes on this issue are high. Six late-Pleistocene estimates with strong cultural associations are the sticking points in this debate. The estimates occur in the middle of Stratum IIa, and all of them are older than 12,800 B.C. If the radiometric estimates are accepted, then the implication is clear: humans were south of the glacial margin prior to the Two Creeks interval. Breaking the "Clovis barrier" (Meltzer 1995:33), however, is not a simple matter. The criteria for accepting a deposit as late Pleistocene are stringent and well known: artifacts in undisturbed geological deposits with indisputable radiometric estimates of age. Multiple criteria increase the probability that the deposit falls into the appropriate temporal interval.

The initial and continuing criticisms of the earliest, culturally affiliated estimates focus on the accuracy of interval estimates. Haynes (1980, 1991a) and Tankersley and Munson (1992) have raised the possibility of particulate and soluble contaminants as sources of error. Haynes (1980) has even suggested methods that could be employed to evaluate the problem of systematic bias. Mead's comments (1980) have focused on the required redundancy of pre-Clovis deposits. The lithic, flora, and faunal assemblages from Stratum IIa are Holocene in character. A late-Pleistocene deposit should have, at least, one or two distinct elements. As Haynes (1980:583) has said: "The only data indicative of a Pleistocene age for Stratum IIa are the radiocarbon analyses...."

Adovasio et al. (1975, 1992) have responded by creating more interval estimates of the entire sequence. Since 1975, the number of radiometric estimates for the rockshelter has increased from 17 to 52 (Adovasio et al. 1975, 1990, 1992). Adovasio et al. have argued that ordinal and interval estimates of time are in agreement. Because, with four exceptions, interval estimates get older with depth, Adovasio et al. have argued that "the entire Meadowcroft sequence is internally consistent" (1992:330). They have also queried why the problem of contamination is raised only in Stratum IIa. If contamination is a source of systematic bias, it should affect the entire sequence.

Although this overview does not do justice to the intricacies of the debate, it is sufficient to show the conflation of resolution with accuracy in the context of a well-known research problem. The principals in this debate are using different types of assessment and, as a result, are talking past each other. There can be no consensus in this situation. Because the validity issue in the Meadowcroft case is clear-cut, the conflation of resolution and accuracy is transparent. Questions regarding the accuracy of radiometric estimates in Stratum IIa cannot be answered by repeated demonstration that the ordinal position of the stratum is correct. Moreover, more or finer chronological divisions of the temporal scale do not correct the disparity between the late-Pleistocene estimates and Holocene character of the assemblages. The data from Meadowcroft Rockshelter simply do not fit the units required to measure "early" in North America.

As demonstrated in the Meadowcroft example, it is very easy to confuse resolution, accuracy, and validity. Resolution and accuracy address the empirical aspects of measurements. Although interval estimates are more exact than ordinal estimates, greater precision is not always necessary. Only specified research goals can inform on the degree of resolution required. Moreover, a precise estimate need not be accurate. The control of resolution is a research issue; the control of systematic bias is a statistical and research issue. Finally, the nature of the research framework determines the type of chronological division required. Interval estimates are not inherently superior and will not resolve all issues. For some types of questions, an ordinal division of the temporal continuum may be perfectly adequate. For other types of research, however, such as the "Clovis First or Second" controversy, nothing short of interval scale estimates from contaminant free—"sealed"—contexts will suffice.

In summary, then, chronologies slice up time and in so doing make the abstract process into archaeological products. This slicing of time is a deliberate research activity meaning that chronological units are constructed in accord with temporal research goals. The units are not discovered. Traits used to build chronologies are temporally sensitive, and the resulting orders and the degree of temporal resolution are contingent on what we want to know. Because all measurements of time are estimates and because these estimates differ in resolution, I suggest using ordinal and interval as descriptions of temporal estimates. As argued, we have confused precision of interval measures with accuracy and validity. There is a tendency to seek interval estimates without evaluating whether such estimates are necessary or appropriate for the research. Even, as in the Meadowcroft case, when the validity issue is clear, resolution and accuracy can become conflated. But finer temporal resolution and control of systematic bias does not address whether the units work in context. Because time is ab-stract, chronological units must fit within the reference frame of the observer.

CONFUSING TIME AND CHRONOLOGY

At the beginning of this chapter, I stated that as a discipline we have confused the abstract dimension of time with our measurement tools of that dimension. In the discussion that followed, I separated time from chronology, and the explicit separation of time and chronology demonstrated the logical and analytic independence of the two research endeavors. Temporal research need not be directed toward developing chronologies, and constructing chronological units depends on the research frame of the archaeologist. Despite the independence, the confusion of the two concepts cuts through all aspects of archaeological practice. There are two reasons for this situation. First is the difference between common sense and science. Second is the ontological position of essentialism.

The weight of natural, or common sense, notions of time makes it easy to confuse the abstract process with chronological units (See Dunnell [1982] and Wolpert [1992] for distinctions between common sense and science). Time is a lived experience in our daily lives. In Judeo-Christian tradition, time is linear (Gould 1987). We are always growing older, and our daily experiences occur in a temporal envelope. Clocks and calendars make time something tangible, and our reliance on these tools results in thinking that the tool is equivalent to the abstract process. We bring this deeply enculturated notion and life-long experience of time to bear on chronological issues in archaeology. We know what time is, and because we know, we confuse chronologies, the measurement tools of time, with time itself.

As I have tried to emphasize, however, time in physics is unquestionably counterintuitive. There is nothing common sense about the relativity, or warping, of spacetime. Moreover, time is continuous and infinitely divisible. Because time is infinite, we must build the metaphorical equivalent to clocks to divide time appropriately. Chronological units are those tools. Making unit construction dependent on the research goals may be the simplest way to separate natural from scientific thinking and time from chronology.

The ontological position of essentialism (Hull 1967; Mayr 1994; Sober 1980) also accounts for archaeological confusion between time and chronology. Essentialism is a metaphysically complex ontology, but three aspects are particularly important. In essentialism, the world is ordered into natural packages, the packages are discoverable, and identifying membership within a package is explanatory.

These assumptions affect how we conceive of time and how we create chronological units. Viewing time as packaged and discoverable makes twins of time and chronology. The discovery of one is the discovery of the other. We have assumed that the conversion of luminescence curves, or rates of isotopic disintegration, into temporal estimates is discovering natural packages. Moreover, interval scale packages are finer-grained than ordinal scale estimates and are, therefore, preferable.

Describing how the explanatory assumption affects the confusion between time and chronology is more problematical largely because "explanation" is such a loaded word in archaeology. In this context, however, explanations address "why" questions. To say that X site belongs to Y period tells us what X is and why it is that way. Essentialism in temporal measurement and chronological construction is best demonstrated through culture historical units and artifacts that define those units. This statement is true regardless of regional sequence selected. Essentialist assumptions are present in both Kidder's Pecos classification (1924) and Griffin's Eastern Woods-lands sequence (1967).

Culture historical units are empirical generalizations derived from stylistic analyses of artifacts, stratigraphy, and seriations. Once established, the units are often accepted as natural, and traits that define those units are tangible evidence of the reality. A particular kind of logical and explanatory circularity

results. The recovery of glaze-on-red ceramics for a new location, for instance, is sufficient to identify that place as within the Pueblo IV period. The trait not only extends the temporal package to that location but also justifies the existing division. Were we to ask why this location is identified as Pueblo IV, the answer would be that, during Pueblo IV, people made glaze-on-red ceramics.

That units are real is epitomized by what I describe as chronological redefinition. Instead of questioning whether the "in-use" temporal divisions work within the confines of proposed research, existing divisions are maintained and redefined in the context of current research interests. The changing definition of "Mississippian" (see Griffin [1985] for discussion) is a succinct example of chronological redefinition.

Mississippian began as a geographic division, conceived as the archaeological equivalent to an ethnological culture area (Holmes 1903, 1914). In the Midwestern Taxonomic System, Mississippian was a pattern (Deuel 1937; McKern 1939). Because McKern's divisions were inherently temporal, Willey and Phillips redefined the unit as a tradition (Griffin 1952a; Willey and Phillips 1958). This unit designation lasted roughly until Smith (1978) defined Mississippian as a kind of adaptation. Even, within the redefinition, the temporal boundaries summarized by Griffin (1952c) survived. More recently still, Mississippian has been redefined as a sociopolitical structure (e.g., Pauketat 1994), characterized by the exchange of prestige items.

Given that we are still using culture historical units, it would seem that in terms of temporal measurement, culture historians found natural archaeological packages. This conclusion is reinforced by recent historical treatment of culture history. Dunnell (1986a, 1986b) has stressed that culture historians were doing good science and were methodologically skilled in their chronological analyses of artifacts. Methodological skill does not mean, however, that the units were natural or real. Mississippian is later than Woodland and Pueblo IV is later than Pueblo

III because time has direction. Whether Mississippian is the only, or most appropriate, unit is a different question that requires an assessment of validity.

The nature of research determines whether existing divisions of time are appropriate. Research justifies our division of time, and there is no other justification. In the Mississippian example, unit redefinition may be useful in some settings but, as suggested by such phrases as "Emergent" or "Incipient" Mississippian (Hall 1991; Smith 1989), this is not always the case. Using the term "emergent" or "incipient" indicates that the unit of interest here is not time or traits, but culture. Moreover, the terms themselves suggest that there is intellectual interest in finding the origin of a cultural unit. Given this goal, it is possible that a different temporal division that incorporated both the origin and growth of "Mississippian" culture would be more appropriate.

Rather than assuming or forcing research into an existing temporal framework, validity assessment requires us to question whether existing units are the only, or most appropriate, divisions of time. We are each observers, and our research frames vary. If existing temporal units fit within our research goals, then analysis within that framework is appropriate. If existing units do not divide time appropriately, then, as Brew argued for artifact classifications generally: "We need more rather than fewer classifications, different classifications, always new classifications to meet new needs (1946b:65).

CONCLUSION

Because archaeology is a historical science, time is a major dimension of variation that must be considered. Unlike space, however, time is not observable, and this obvious fact has implications for the measurement and division of time. I have stressed that, although

chronological units are the tools by which we divide time, chronological divisions are not natural. The infinity of time means that chronological units can and should be more variable than they are. Knowing that time could be divided differently, however, does not tell us how to create a different division. Here, validity assessment is useful. We can begin by asking how close existing temporal units fit with our research goals as well as whether new temporal units are any more appropriate.

In the end, then, rather than assuming that time and chronology are closed issues, that we have successfully divided time for all time, I am suggesting that the temporal box be opened each time research begins. If the research process structures our thoughts and divisions of time, I am quite sure that our knowledge of the past will change in significant and unexpected ways.

ACKNOWLEDGMENTS
The ideas expressed in this chapter have been brewing in my head for a long time. Delving into the literature on time in physics was both challenging and difficult, but served to make clear some of our fundamental temporal concepts in archaeology. I benefited enormously from the help and insight of colleagues. I would especially like to thank my co-editor, Anastasia Steffen, Fraser Neiman, James Feathers, and Charlotte Beck. Errors and confusions are mine.

Note
1. The clearest examples of change in chronological structures occurred when culture historians were building their units. The Willey and Phillips system (1958) replaced that of McKern (1939); Phillips's Lower Valley phases replaced those of Phillips, Ford, and Griffin (Phillips 1970; Phillips, Ford, and Griffin 1951). The Gladwins disagreed with the Pecos classification, but it survived despite that disagreement (Gladwin and Gladwin 1934; Kidder [1924] 1962).

Part III
Space

6

Regional Scale Processes and Archaeological Landscape Units

LuAnn Wandsnider

The landscape is a palimpsest on to which each generation inscribes its own impressions and removes some of the marks of earlier generations. Constructions of one age are often overlain, modified or erased by the work of another. The present patchwork of settlement . . . has evolved as a result of thousands of years of human endeavor, producing a landscape which possesses not only a beauty associated with long and slow development, but an inexhaustible store of information about the many kinds of human activities in the past.

Aston and Rowley (1974:14)

Archaeological landscapes, as described above, are formed through the actions of people working at various spatial scales and tempos and with varying degrees of integration and coordination. In equal measure, the character of the archaeological landscape is due to a suite of natural processes that also operate at a variety of spatial scales and at a range of rates (Foley 1981a; Schiffer 1987; Wandsnider 1995). On the stage of the atmosphere-lithosphere interface, people, their artifacts, and other natural clasts participate in many simultaneous ballets, some of them elaborate and sweeping, others isolated and abrupt. The archaeological landscape, a patterned and convoluted surface, is created as a result of these multiple dances.

Our continuing challenge as archaeologists is to infer process from pattern (Binford 1981; Orton 1982). Thus, on the basis of the patterning evident in the archaeological landscape, our goal is to distinguish, from among the many simultaneous dances that have occurred, those specific dances of interest to a particular research question. Having identified a specific dance, a second goal is to ask how and why that dance occurred as it

did. As elaborated below, the first goal is a matter of identifying that a specific spatial process has occurred. The second goal concerns adducing the prehistoric condition of what McGlade (1995) calls "the socionatural system," a system composed of intimately coupled human and natural agents and processes. The condition or configuration of the socionatural system is associated with a specific suite of spatial processes and is knowable by identifying those processes.

Like all units, those used to document and interpret the archaeological landscape are dictated by our ideas about past human-land conditions and past processes that contributed to those landscapes. Several other factors influence unit design, however (Figure 6.1). Given our ideas about the past, we ideally proceed to develop field and analytic instruments that will allow us to evaluate those ideas. Thus, the bodies of knowledge we rely on to sustain inferences about the archaeological landscape also influence unit selection and design as do the technical limits of available instrumentation. A fourth factor is that of the empirical reality of the archaeological record, which constrains the ques-

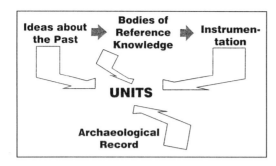

Figure 6.1. Unit design model.

the nature of the relationships between the spatial and temporal scale of the target process, the spatial scale of the resulting pattern and pattern components, and the appropriate scale of measurement. Critical to understanding these relationships are the concepts of unit and scale, which I take up below.

tions that can be entertained and, hence, the design and use of appropriate units.

As sketched in Figure 6.1, the first three (ideas, bodies of reference knowledge, and instrumentation) are related to the activities of the archaeologist and are separate from the fourth, the archaeological phenomenon that is the focus of that activity. In practice, there seems to be a great deal of independent development within each of these domains. Hence, it is useful to consider unit design and implementation as they relate to each of these four factors.

This chapter elaborates on the four elements of unit design that attend documenting and analyzing archaeological deposits in a landscape context. It begins with a general discussion of measurement issues as they pertain to condition, process, and pattern in two-dimensional space. This discussion is followed by an analysis of unit design in light of four governing factors: anticipated past processes, nature of the archaeological landscape, bodies of reference knowledge, and instrumentation. The end result is a general recipe for designing units useful in archaeological landscape studies.

MEASURING PATTERN TO INFER PROCESS AND CONDITION

A number of disciplines (e.g., astronomy, ecology, geography, and geology as well as archaeology) are routinely confronted with the problem of inferring a specific process from an observed pattern as seen in two- or three-dimensional space. In each of these disciplines, there is a growing appreciation for

UNITS

In discussing archaeological landscapes, several kinds of units are commonly manipulated. They relate to two different domains, the formal and the spatial, and also to the role played by the unit in description, analysis, and synthesis. Examples of formal units of description include artifact and site attributes, which may be dimensional, functional, morphological, and so forth. Units of provenience commonly are constructed at the scale of artifacts or sites; tracts of land of varying dimensions, as discussed below, also sometimes served as the spatial unit of documentation and analysis.

With respect to the interpretation process, the hierarchical relationship between units of observation (i.e., basal analytic units), analysis, and synthesis is widely appreciated (e.g., Chang 1968; Dunnell 1971; Schiffer 1988b). Interpretation may involve a series of steps in which analytic units are constructed and manipulated to describe the operation of a landscape process over increasingly larger areas. For example, in the siteless studies of hunter-gatherer land use carried out during the 1970s, artifacts served as both the formal and spatial units of documentation (e.g., Bettinger 1976, 1977; Thomas 1971, 1973). These units were synthesized to describe artifact ratios or densities for individual parcels of land. In turn, these synthetic land-use units served as the units of analysis when hunter-gatherer land use over larger stretches of land (i.e., biomes) was considered.

SCALE

Scale is another word with multiple meanings (Ramenofsky and Steffen, this volume; Schneider 1994; Stein 1993). I define scale as the size, extent, or duration of a phenomenon. For example, Dunnell (1971: 145–209) uses the word "scale" to refer to entities that are less inclusive (e.g., attributes) or more inclusive (e.g., site occupations).

Similarly, both Crumley and Marquardt (Crumley 1979; Marquardt and Crumley 1987) use "scale" to refer to the range, or maximal spatial extent, of a phenomenon. They introduce the notion of *effective scale*, meaning both the range at which archaeologists repeatedly detect interpretable patterning and the range over which a particular process characteristically operated. They underscore that, for reasons of limited time and resources, archaeologists may have access to only a small portion of the total area encompassed by, for example, the political, trading, or subsistence system responsible for regional patterning.

In a recent treatment of the archaeological landscape that is wholly concerned with the relationship between scale and function, Ebert (1992) focused on the effective scales of different hunter-gatherer activities which contribute materials to that landscape. He used ethnographic literature and formation process research to develop a theoretical understanding of these effective scales. He then examined the multiscale patterning in the spatial distribution of functional units across the landscape, seeking empirical expression of those effective scales.

In her review of the concept of scale as utilized in archaeological, geological, and geoarchaeological contexts, Stein (1993) paid attention to issues of scale that pertain especially to the *measurement* of archaeological phenomena. Thus, she concentrated on the maximal range over which observations are to be made as well as observation resolution or the frequency of observation. This latter aspect of measurement, observation resolution, is critical because it corresponds to the minimal size of measurement units. Stein also noted that such observations can be made both spatially and temporally and that issues of scale come into play both when designing data collection and when carrying out data analysis.

Schneider (1994) presented an insightful discussion of scale as it relates to ecological processes. Like Stein, he found it useful to discuss scale in terms of observation, or measurement, and similarly recognized the dimensions of range and resolution. He extended the discussion of scale beyond space and time to include matter and energy. Schneider offered no empirical rules for determining the appropriate resolution of measurement, but suggested that it may be possible theoretically to estimate measurement resolution on the basis of necessary matter and energy flows between biological entities or across trophic levels (1994:122–23). He introduced the concept of *scope* as the ratio between the observed maximal extent of a phenomenon and the resolution at which it is monitored and suggested that biological phenomena may have a characteristic measurement scope. For example, the scope of the metabolic rate of mammals is around 10 and is allometrically related to body mass. Finally, he noted that, practically, the range and resolution at which we can measure a phenomenon is set by our instrumentation capabilities, which, as Stein (1993:3) noted, have become increasingly wide-ranging and precise.

In terms of processes that contribute to the archaeological landscape, Dewar and McBride (1992) identified a hierarchy of processes with spatial and temporal ranges that are often but not necessarily linked (Figure 6.2). For example, individual activities engaged in by individuals often occur for short durations (minutes, hours) in limited areas (square meters, hectares). Annual hunter-gatherer settlement processes occur seasonally and may take place over tens to hundreds of square kilometers. Ecological processes (e.g., soil exhaustion; species rebound) may be recognizable over the span of human years and over large areas (tens to thousands of square kilometers). Finally, evolutionary processes, resulting in the differential persistence of genotypes, occur at the scale of human generations and large regions.

Figure 6.2 underscores that linkages exist between the processes that typically occur at various effective spatial and temporal scales,

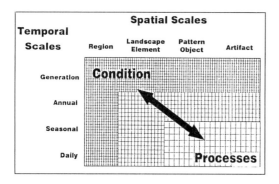

Figure 6.2. Formation processes by spatial and temporal scales. Smaller scale processes may contribute to larger scale phenomenon, and larger scale processes may initiate smaller scale processes.

as discussed by landscape ecologists (Forman and Godron 1986; Naveh and Leiberman 1994; see also McGlade 1995 and Schneider 1994). Thus, the cumulative effect of small-scale activities (e.g., dam building) will ultimately have a very wide spatial impact in a relatively short time. And, the large-scale clear-cutting of an area propagates other processes, such as rilling and downcutting, that operate at smaller spatial and temporal scales. In this sense, the operation of processes at one scale can be said to give rise to conditions perceived at a larger scale, and larger scale conditions set the stage for processes occurring at smaller scales. Clearly, to portray accurately and reliably any of these conditions and processes requires attention to the duration and areal extent of those observations; the spatial or temporal frequency with which observations are made is also important.

Archaeological Landscapes, Units, and Scale

The above discussion of units and scale considered phenomenon both in the systemic and archaeological contexts. Since archaeological landscapes are, of course, archaeological phenomena, the emphasis shifts here to the measurements made of archaeological phenomena to learn about systemic domain processes and conditions. In this area, the literature on spatial processes (Getis and Boots

1978), image processing (Gonzalez and Wintz 1987), and pattern theory (Grenander 1996) is useful.

All processes involve the transformation of energy, matter, or species from one to another pattern. A *spatial process* is specifically concerned with the spatial domain and refers to a sequence of transformational episodes by which new spatial patterns in, for example, artifacts, clasts, or sites, are created (Getis and Boots 1978). Spatial processes operate under specific *conditions* or within particular *environments* that differentially constrain or support the operation of a process. A *pattern* is an arrangement of biomass or matter that is created as a result of the operation of the spatial process (Getis and Boots 1978). Following Grenander (1996:68–69), *pattern object* refers to those critical elements in a pattern that allow us to distinguish among patterns (and, therefore, the relevant generating processes).

Consider, for example, the settlement process described by the Central Place Theorem, in which a settlement hierarchy develops on a landscape as people operate to minimize transportation costs of items with different costs and use frequencies (Hodder and Orton 1976:54–85). The condition under which such a hierarchy may develop is that of the ideal featureless and frictionless plain. In this case, the resulting pattern is the settlement hierarchy, with many smaller settlements dispersed about fewer, larger settlements offering more commodities and services. Individual settlements with specific sizes are the pattern objects. It is the arrangement of these settlements, or pattern objects, with respect to one another that creates a pattern identifiable as a settlement hierarchy.

As another example, take Binford's seated worker model (1978). In this case, the process of ongoing site maintenance by workers seated around a hearth results in a distinctive artifact distribution, with small artifacts inadvertently or consciously dropped in the work area near the hearth and larger artifacts tossed to a peripheral location. The conditions under which such a process occurs are those promoting site maintenance, such as the intensive or continued occupation of a re-stricted space. The resulting pattern includes a zone of large artifacts encircling a central zone containing small artifacts. The pattern objects include each zone and perhaps a fea-ture to which the drop zone is tethered. Again, the presence and arrangement of the pattern objects allow the recognition of the larger pattern which, in turn, supports the in-ference that ongoing site maintenance has oc-curred. Other examples of spatial processes that operate to create spatial patterns come from ecology (e.g., Grieg-Smith 1983) and geology (e.g., Schumm 1991).

Given the operation of such processes con-strained by various conditions and the devel-opment of patterned deposits, how should those deposits be measured? The Whittaker-Shannon Sampling Theorem states that to differentiate a phenomenon with a minimum spatial extent α, the sampling frequency of at least one half must be used (Carr 1987:267; Gonzalez and Wintz 1987:94; Hodder and Orton 1976:30–37; A. Rogers 1982). From this theorem follow both the appropriate ob-servation resolution and range. Spatial reso-lution depends on the size of the pattern ob-jects. If settlements are the target pattern objects, then a sampling frequency of one half the size of the smallest settlement would be necessary. If toss or drop zones are the tar-get pattern object, then a sampling resolution of one half their smallest size would be re-quired. Indeed, an even finer observation res-olution may be necessary since each of these pattern objects (i.e., settlements and drop zones) are entities that are derived through analysis, synthesis, and inference rather than observation.

As already noted, researchers have long recognized the hierarchical ordering of ob-servation, analysis, and synthesis (e.g., dis-cussion in Chang 1968). Dunnell (1971: 145–209) explicitly described this relation-ship in terms of analytic and synthetic units. Synthetic units, in this case, settlement pat-terns and drop-toss zones, are synthesized from smaller analytic units, such as settle-ments, for the one, and artifacts and features, for the other. These synthetic units may

themselves serve as analytic units if a phe-nomenon of greater duration or spatial ex-tent is to be synthesized.

The maximal extent of observation fol-lows from the Whittaker-Shannon Sampling Theorem as well. To recognize the larger pat-tern, a total sampling region that is at least two times that of the maximal extent of the spatial pattern would be ideal.

In sum, units employed in the documenta-tion and analysis of archaeological land-scapes have formal, spatial, and temporal di-mensions, all of which are deliberately selected to serve specific analytic and syn-thetic goals. The scale of processes that we suspect may have contributed to the archaeo-logical landscape relates directly to unit se-lection: the resolution we hope to achieve in our measurements sets the maximal size of our spatial units of observation. As well, the technical resolution of our measurement tools places a lower limit on the size of the unit of observation, as discussed below.

Dunnell (1971:147) sees the selection of scale and units as a research choice. Schneider (1994), however, suggested that the necessary relationships in energy and matter transfer between components in biological and eco-logical systems set minimal limits on units to be used in measuring those phenomena. The units that best allow for discrimination of past processes can be estimated on the basis of a theoretical understanding of those rela-tionships. At present, we have a theoretical understanding for some but not all of the processes that contribute to archaeological landscapes. This understanding, accumu-lated over the last several decades and attrib-utable to the focused research on archaeolog-ical formation processes (Schiffer 1987), also aids in the design of units of observation (see below).

Absent from the above has been an ex-plicit discussion of the role played in unit de-sign by the bodies of reference knowledge we use to make inferences from archaeological observations. For example, if we wish to in-fer age from archaeological deposits using a seriated ceramic sequence, then the formal units of the ceramic chronology (e.g., design elements on rim sherds) must also be used in making archaeological observations. Essentially, this issue is also one of instrumentation, that is, designing our units of observation to be minimally concordant with the interpretative devices that are required to translate observations on the static archaeological deposits to the dynamic systemic world. In the interpretation of archaeological landscapes, such middle-range bodies of reference knowledge are critical to all treatments, as discussed below.

In the following sections, archaeological landscapes and unit design are considered with respect to each of these four areas: prevailing ideas about prehistoric conditions and processes, the formation and nature of the archaeological landscape, bodies of reference knowledge, and available instrumentation. Archaeological landscapes are, by definition, spatially extensive entities. For this reason, archaeological survey is the primary method used to document them. Thus, the discussion of archaeological landscapes below necessarily relies on pedestrian surface survey, both design and results.[1]

IDEAS ABOUT THE PAST AND ARCHAEOLOGICAL LANDSCAPE UNITS

Prior to the 1950s, only a few archaeologists had approached the regional archaeological landscape in a systematic way (e.g., Braidwood 1937; Thomas 1985 [1894]). With Gordon Willey's work in the Virú Valley of Peru, a golden age of archaeological landscape studies dawned and continues today. According to Willey (1953:xviii), it was Julian Steward who prompted him to address the nonmaterial and organizational aspects of prehistoric societies through the study of settlement patterns. Willey's success and the appearance of an increasingly rich geographical literature on locational analyses prompted several generations of archaeologists to bring their ideas about settlements and settlement patterns to the archaeological record (Parsons 1972). Three general phases of settlement studies are evident and, in each of these, there is self-conscious examination of and

discernible refinement in the observational (i.e., field) and analytic units employed. Table 6.1 highlights this history in terms of condition, process, and unit construction.

Early treatments of the archaeological landscape focused on settlement patterns with the end of gaining information about a variety of geographical processes. In studying these processes, archaeologists relied on various spatial units, such as architecture, settlements (composed of architectural elements), and macropatterns (composed of settlements); in turn, these spatial patterns were taken to reflect, in some way, the political, economic, and other processes by which they were generated (contributors to Chang 1968 and to Ucko et al. 1972). The distribution of the analytic units of settlements was critical in many of these exercises. Willey (1968:216) identified two problems in isolating "settlements" to use in this synthetic undertaking. He acknowledged the difficulty of proceeding from units of observation (i.e., architectural structures and features) to sites as spatial analytic units. He also recognized that it was up to the archaeologist to demonstrate that a site could be interpreted as a settlement (i.e., the material reflection of a community).

A later iteration of settlement pattern studies in the Basin of Mexico (Sanders et al. 1979), Mesopotamia (Adams 1981), and other parts of the world focused expressly on recognizing sites ranked by size, which were interpreted as settlement hierarchies that developed in response to the economical flow of goods between centers. In these studies, the archaeological landscape was documented in terms of sites, for which size and density attributes were recorded, as well as the presence of architectural elements. Relying on ethnoarchaeological studies, Sanders and colleagues (1979:38–39) developed a convention for estimating human population sizes from sherd densities. For the Uruk countryside, Adams depended on site size alone. In each of these cases, the researchers (Adams 1981:43–51) recognized the same set of bedevilments as had Willey: that is, the large and unwarrantable inferential leaps they made as they moved from survey obser-

TABLE 6.1
Summary of Approaches to Archaeological Landscapes

Type of Study	Past Condition	Regional Scale Culture Formation Process	Unit of Documentation (Basal Analytic Unit)		Secondary Analytic Unit/Synthetic Unit	Examples	Comment
			Formal	Spatial			
Settlement Survey, 1950–1980	Social environment	Settlement	site attributes	site	settlement	Willey 1953; Sanders et al. 1979; Adams 1981	biome is tertiary analytic unit
Siteless Survey, 1970s	Antiquity of land use mode	Land use	artifact attributes	artifact	artifact ratios and densities/survey unit	Thomas (1971, 1973); Bettinger (1976, 1977)	settlements recognized as anomalous with respect to densities observed in field tracts
Greek Siteless Survey, 1980s	Control of agricultural production	Settlement dispersion/aggregation	artifact attributes	artifact	settlements and artifact densities by field tract	Cherry et al. 1991	
Historical Ecology, 1980s	Mode of production	Land use	site, scatter	site, scatter	site, scatter by time period and physiological features	Marquardt et al. 1987	archaeology presented but not really used to explore historical interpretations
Place-Use Studies, 1980–1990s	Land-use organization	Place-use history	artifact attributes	artifact, site	places	contributors to Rossignol and Wandsnider 1992	place use by landscape element supports description of land-use organization for segments of time

vations to their analytic units of settlements. They also acknowledged a whole host of other issues (see below). After fully disclosing these caveats, they forged ahead with their interpretations of settlement patterns.

More recent settlement pattern research evinces goals similar to those of the early studies. Researchers employ settlement distributions as a cue to other properties of prehistoric societies. In contrast to the early studies, nonsite field methods have been implemented to address the definitional problem of site as unit. For example, in Greece during the late 1970s and early 1980s, several programs (Bintliff and Snodgrass 1985, 1988; Cherry et al. 1991) carried out intensive surveys to document the advent of nucleated versus dispersed settlement patterns at Boeotia (Bintliff and Snodgrass 1985, 1988), Keos, in the Cycladic Islands (Cherry et al. 1991), and, more recently, Nemea (Athanassopoulos 1993; Cherry et al. 1988). In turn, they related these settlement patterns to larger political and agricultural production conditions that prevailed through time. These regional studies, again, rely on settlements as the fundamental analytic units.

Cherry and colleagues (1991:12–54; see also Cherry et al. 1988) explicitly detailed the analytic journey they made in traveling from units of observation—artifacts and sites—to settlements, their units of analysis. In northern Keos, they first documented the archaeological landscape in terms of artifact types (formal units of observation) as observed within the spatial units of surveyed agricultural fields and also sites identified in the field on the basis of exposed architecture or obviously high artifact densities. In addition to field-designated sites, they arbitrarily and explicitly defined other sites on the basis of anomalous high artifact densities. They reviewed several explanations for the existence of relatively rare, high-density peaks of sherds and other artifacts, and concluded that such locations most likely represent settlements. Synthesizing the distribution of these settlements, they recognized alternating nucleated and dispersed settlement patterns for different time periods. Nucleated settle-

ment patterns were taken as evidence for greater control of the populace by elites; dispersed settlement patterns suggested to them that individuals were able to maximize agriculture production in an environment less controlled by elites.

In carrying out settlement pattern archaeology of any variety, there are a number of interrelated problems that pertain to unit reliability and validity, some of which were identified very early on by Willey and others (Taylor 1972). The first one concerns the spatial unit of analysis usually employed in these studies (i.e., the site). Numerous authors (e.g., Cherry 1983; Cherry et al. 1988, 1991; Dunnell 1992b; Dunnell and Dancey 1983; Ebert 1992) have pointed to the difficulty of reliably constructing sites as units of analysis. Dunnell (1992b), Dancey (1973), and Ebert (1992) contend that because of how archaeological landscape deposits form (see below), sites are inherently unreliable units of observation and analysis. As noted above for several Grecian projects, Cherry and other colleagues recognized some of the liabilities of sites as units, especially the subjective manner in which sites are usually defined in the field. They, therefore, elected to define sites *post hoc* as density peaks on an otherwise continuous density surface. Thus, for them, the problem of unit reliability was effectively defined away.

The second problem deals with the validity of the formal unit employed in settlement analyses of the archaeological landscape (i.e., the settlement). Teltser (1997) recently examined how archaeological sites are inferred to represent settlements, the material reflection of coherent communities of people. As she demonstrates, the definitions for the three units—site, settlement, and community—each rely on the other in a teleological fashion. No independent definitional or explicit inferential criteria exist. Settlement pattern analyses that rely on these flawed units of settlements, thus, are themselves likewise flawed.

A final problem appears in the literature as the "contemporaneity problem" (Schacht 1984) and is concerned with the validity of settlements as temporal units of analysis. As recently articulated by Dewar: "Any analysis of intersite spacing, aggregation, or interaction that proceeds from a map of all of the components of a phase *assumes that all sites are contemporary*" (1992:605; emphasis in original). Again, because of how deposits form over the span of a specified period of time, this assumption cannot be warranted. Dewar (1992) suggested dealing with this problem by estimating the number of simultaneous occupations in a phase, given phase length and the presence at a site of phase indicators between phases. Others, Crumley and colleagues (1987), for example, perhaps anticipating this problem, chose to view distributions of Iron Age, Roman, and remains of other ages with respect to enduring elements of the landscape, such as faults and exposures, rather than with respect to each other. Certainly in this latter analysis, the authors are well aware of the likely incompleteness of their archaeological document (*sensu* Wandsnider and Camilli 1992) because of differential visibility and destruction.

Settlement pattern archaeologists have approached the archaeological landscape with ideas about what could be learned of past social organization from reconstructed community composition, location, and relation. These ideas depend on the definition and analysis of units like sites and settlements. Settlement pattern studies continue to be reported (e.g., contributors to Fish and Kowalewski 1989 and to Allen et al. 1989; Falconer and Savage 1995), with varying attention paid to the issues of the validity and reliability of settlements. Meanwhile other archaeologists, some of them explicitly concerned with these unit liabilities, have addressed the archaeological landscape using units influenced, I suggest below, by an increasingly explicit understanding of how the archaeological landscape is formed.

THE NATURE OF THE ARCHAEOLOGICAL LANDSCAPE AND UNITS

"Methodological double bind" describes the eternal purgatory of scientists: To measure something, we must first know what it is like;

but, to know what it is like, we must first measure it. There is no escape from this double bind; indeed, the process of science is precisely concerned with posing our ideas about the world against our measurements of it, prompting a continuing evolution of both ideas and measurements. Certainly, our knowledge of the phenomenon of archaeological landscape has grown markedly because of earlier attempts to measure it. In turn, this knowledge has helped in the design of analytic and synthetic units.

While archaeologists working on archaeological landscapes attributable to "complex societies" grappled with defining, analyzing, and interpreting sites and settlements, archaeologists confronted with "hunter-gatherer" archaeological landscapes chose other units and analytic protocols. In part, this divergence in method is due to the clear invalidity of settlement pattern units for landscapes of this sort. For parts of the world, similar to the North American Great Basin, the rich ethnographic record depicted the compositional fluidity and very short duration of social units such as communities. Archaeological sites formed under such situations, thus, were likely created through the actions of people participating in a succession of communities, rather than just the one as assumed by most settlement pattern analyses. That chronologically heterogeneous artifacts are often recovered at hunter-gatherer archaeological sites provided empirical support for this understanding.

Also, throughout the 1970s and 1980s, archaeologists accumulated a rich corpus of knowledge about the cultural and noncultural formation of archaeological landscapes (e.g., Ebert 1992; Foley 1981a, 1981c; Schiffer 1987). Yellen's work with the San (1997) and Binford's work with Nunamiut Eskimo (1979a, 1980) provided additional information about how humans distributed themselves on the landscape and created patterned deposits.

These two factors are responsible, I think, for the very different set of approaches to hunter-gatherer archaeological landscapes that began to appear in the early 1970s. Certainly, the ideas held by the researchers about the past were reflected in unit design and implementation, but, increasingly, those units were formationally informed. This section highlights aspects of the formation process literature as it pertains to the study of archaeological landscapes. Recent insights from the discipline of landscape ecology are also pertinent here.

The Nature of the Archaeological Landscape

As a result of knowledge on formation processes gained by archaeologists during the 1970s and 1980s, we can appreciate that archaeological landscapes are both cultural and geological phenomena, with clear consequences for the temporal properties of such surface deposits. For example, we understand that if the cultural deposition rate is faster than the natural deposition rate, a palimpsest deposit, like that described above by Aston and Rowley, will result (Binford 1980, 1981; Ferring 1986). Conversely, if the natural deposition rate exceeds the rate of cultural deposition, then burial and fine-grain deposits result. In fact, most landscapes exhibit a mosaic of temporal planes because deposition and erosion are spatially localized rather than regional (Bettis and Benn 1989).

An important distinction follows from this largely geological observation: an archaeological landscape cares not who or what contributes to its form or character. That is, archaeological landscapes are rarely if ever the product of actors participating in a single cultural system. Rather, they form through the actions of multiple actors participating in multiple reproductive, social, economic, and political systems that operate at a variety of temporal and spatial scales that are differentially coherent and integrated. For example, Foley's pioneering nonsite work in the Amboseli (1981c) recognized the contribution of contemporary Maasai herdsmen as well as Stone Age hunter-gatherers. Similarly, a modern agropastoral landscape in south-central India, where I have conducted ethnoarchaeological work, receives input from a number of agents whom anthropologists

usually consider separate cultural groups. Near Hospet, the state of Karnataka has created a reserve forest, which attracts local farmers who graze their animals here. Non-local pastoralists (speaking the language native to their birthplace, 250 km to the west) move into the reserve forest on a seasonal basis seeking forage for their animals, thereby creating substantial encampments. When these camps are abandoned, the local farmers pick through the remains for still serviceable tools and recycle scrub brush—used for corrals by the pastoralists—into fencing designed to keep animals out of agricultural fields. Encampment areas may be preferentially tilled because they are already well fertilized by the urine and dung of the vacated sheep. These various actors have little direct contact with each other except through the local city market. Nevertheless, they all contribute to the character of the archaeological landscape currently being formed in this area.

Thus, we cannot assume that landscape deposits inform on only one cultural group. For this reason, the archaeological landscape is better attributed to a socionatural system (McGlade 1995:114), with irreducibly linked cultural and natural components.

Conceiving of the archaeological landscape as an artifact of the socionatural system (also called "the human-land system" by landscape ecologists [Forman and Godron 1986; Naveh and Lieberman 1994]) leads to a series of provocative insights that cannot be examined here (but see McGlade 1995:125). For now, I note only that the configuration of the socionatural system will differentially affect the nature and rate of energy and matter flow on and between various adjoining parts of the landscape (Figure 6.3).

Figure 6.3 abstracts two different conditions of the socionatural system along the Tungabhadra River in south-central India. One condition (to the left in Figure 6.3) pertains to the massive irrigation system developed and maintained by the Vijayanagara polity and the temple during the Vijayanagara Period (A.D. 1336–1560) (Morrison 1995; Morrison and Sinopoli 1992; Sinopoli

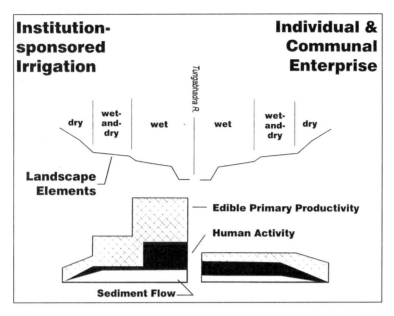

Figure 6.3. Model of productivity, human activity, sediment features, and monuments.

and Morrison 1995); an even more extensive irrigation system is in place today, supported by the modern Indian state. The second condition (to the right in Figure 6.3) is dominated by dry-land agriculture with a very localized irrigation component, and appears to have obtained before the Vijayanagara Period and during the British occupation (A.D. 1576–1947) of the Indian subcontinent (Stein 1983, 1992). Under each of these two different conditions, the suites of cultural and natural processes that operated were very different and had very different consequences for the archaeological landscape.

Figure 6.3 also distinguishes between portions of the landscape useful for wet agriculture, dry agriculture, and wet-and-dry agriculture. Each of these areas was differentially attractive to people involved in dry- or wet-land agriculture and was differentially impacted by agricultural activities transacted during the Vijayanagara and modern periods, on one hand, and the British period, on the other. Landscape ecologists refer to these different portions of the landscape as *landscape elements* (Forman and Godron 1986:9–12); landscape elements describe a spatial unit

that hosts a self-contained ecosystem (which may be defined at any one of a variety of scales). Landscape elements are characterized by the resident amount and distribution of energy, materials, and species.

The important point here is that by (1) partitioning the landscape into landscape elements that are sensitive to the prehistoric processes and conditions we hope to understand and (2) examining archaeological materials with respect to these landscape elements, archaeologists are in a good position to see the effects of the operation of a particular socionatural system. Indeed, as described below, exactly this strategy, selecting specific landscape elements as a secondary or tertiary spatial unit of analysis (to which the basal observational units are synthesized), has been implicitly and explicitly implemented by archaeologists.

FORMATIONALLY INFORMED
ARCHAEOLOGICAL LANDSCAPE UNITS

As understanding of archaeological landscape formation developed, archaeologists explored ideas about the past that were explicitly consistent with that understanding. Several early efforts include those by Thomas (1971, 1973), Bettinger (1976, 1977), and Dancey (1973) in the American West to examine prehistoric land use with respect to features of the landscape, such as landforms or stands of pinyon trees, that could be warranted as enduring (see also Jones 1984; Ebert 1992). Both Thomas and Bettinger were explicitly concerned with attempting to evaluate the null hypothesis that ethnographically documented Shoshone land use continued into the prehistoric past. In each of these cases, artifacts are the primary spatial unit of documentation and artifact attributes are the formal unit of documentation (see Table 6.1). Thomas and Bettinger each summarized land use in terms of artifact densities and ratios by land parcel. Having created these synthetic units, they then used them analytically to describe prehistoric land use at the scale of biome.

Archaeologists working with "complex society" landscapes, which they recognize to be heavily impacted by a host of depositional and erosional processes, exhibit yet other goals, but rely on similar units and strategies. Colleagues of Marquardt and Crumley (1987), for example, considered both low- and high-density archaeological materials on the Burgundy landscape in France to determine which segments of the landscape were used during the Iron Age, Roman period, and so forth. In the American Southwest, S. K. Fish and colleagues (1990) considered the spatial and temporal distribution of gravel features across the Tucson basin, which they interpreted in terms of a gravel-mulch agricultural technology. The study of the complex Vijayanagara landscape in southern India by Morrison and Sinopoli likewise focused on the age and distribution of investments in dry-land (terracing) and wetland (reservoirs, canals) agricultural features. This construction sequence was interpreted in terms of economic organization (Morrison and Sinopoli 1992) and agricultural intensification (Morrison 1995).

In each of these cases, the archaeologists relied on changes through time in the configuration of features and architecture on specific landscape elements to argue for a change in the condition that controls the spatial process. Thus, both Marquardt, Crumley, and colleagues (1987) and S. K. Fish and colleagues (1990) pointed to subsistence changes that brought into use landscape elements that had been underused or used less intensively. Morrison and Sinopoli similarly recognized change in the distribution and nature of land modification, which appears increasingly through time on landscape elements that are marginal (even with respect to dry-land agriculture), to argue for intensified agricultural practices during the Vijayanagara period.

Other recent treatments of the archaeological landscape are explicitly the result of formation process research and are concerned with place-use history (Camilli et al. 1988; Lycett 1995; contributors to Rossignol and Wandsnider 1992; Sullivan 1992; Wandsnider and Camilli 1996; Wandsnider 1997) (Table 6.1). Places are points on the landscape where humans paused to carry out some activity (Binford 1982a:5). Some places were used repeatedly, others not. Some were used by only one social group, others by many. Some places were targeted for use again and again; others received serendipitous use. Archaeologists concerned with reading the configuration of place use through time rely on small spatial units of observation (e.g., artifacts, sites) and small formal units (i.e., artifact attributes). These units, in turn, are manipulated in a variety of ways to support interpretation of place use along a variety of dimensions. For example, Dewar and McBride (1992) and Wandsnider and Camilli (1996) explored distinctive spatial patterning in artifact attributes that, they argued, developed as a result of different place-use trajectories. Jones and Beck (1992) and Sullivan (1992) relied on the observed range of chronologically sensitive artifacts to determine place-use history. Changes in place-use histories, then, serve as evidence for a change in the human-land configuration and subsistence organization against a framework of landscape elements with different qualities (e.g., contributors to Rossignol and Wandsnider 1992).

Each of the above analyses expressly avoids using settlements as analytic units (although sites—dense clusters of artifacts—are sometimes used). Rather, researchers have shifted their analyses to smaller scale phenomenon, artifact and feature attributes, which are synthesized into other units, corresponding in scale to landscape elements that describe land use and place use. In turn, the values for these land- or place-use units indicate that specific human-land configurations or conditions existed in the past.

Schneider (1994) argued that biologists can design better measurement units in light of their increased understanding of biological phenomenon. I am making a similar case here. Because of the several decades of formation process research, we have a much better understanding of the phenomena we are trying to measure. In turn, this knowledge has helped us to design units and implement analytic protocols that are concordant with, and take advantage of, this knowledge. We can never escape the methodological double bind that makes it difficult to describe the elephant until we know that the elephant has two ears, a tail, a trunk, and a very large body mass. Nevertheless, by understanding that successful terrestrial mammals have organs that perform various grasping, hearing, and smelling functions and by understanding the relationship between forage quality, predator intensities, and body size, we can begin to develop a series of units that will help us to recognize and distinguish elephants from oranges and automobiles.

BODIES OF REFERENCE KNOWLEDGE AND UNITS

Through the efforts of Binford (1981) and others, it is widely appreciated that our interpretations of the past are only as good as the bodies of reference knowledge we use to bridge the archaeological and systemic domains (O'Connell 1995; Trigger 1995). Such bodies of reference knowledge may be theoretically based, like that describing the behavior of clasts or artifacts on a slope or the mechanics of artifact fracture caused by trampling. They may have a theoretical basis, but be highly contingent on other factors. The formation of site structure as a consequence of differentially implemented, site maintenance behaviors appears to be of this sort (Wandsnider 1996), as does the treatment of carcasses with respect to butchering and transportation (Hudson 1993). These bodies of reference knowledge may be a series of independent observations yet to be theoretically coordinated (hence, the term "bodies of reference knowledge," rather than "middle-range theory" [Binford 1981] or "reconstructive theory" [Schiffer 1988b]). The artifact density convention explicitly articulated by archaeologists working in Greece to infer settlements is an example of an empirically rather than theoretically based body of reference knowledge.

Bodies of reference knowledge are constructed in terms of units and specify the relationship among those units. For these bodies of reference knowledge to be useful, the archaeological record also must be documented with units of the same or finer resolution.

Thus, Cherry and colleagues (see above) argued that to recognize the anomalously high artifact densities they defined as settlements, systematic observations on artifact density must be made. Their field protocol was accordingly designed to capture density information.

Similarly, an embryonic understanding of human ecology undergirds the work of the early nonsite archaeologists (i.e., Bettinger and D. H. Thomas). Their choice of biome-based landscape elements as synthetic units within which to summarize human-land use comes from this body of reference knowledge. Marquardt, Crumley, and colleagues instead relied on landscape elements based on enduring geological features. They inventoried the changing prehistoric use of the landscape during Iron Age and Roman times with respect to these elements.

Recent analyses of place use by Jones and Beck (1992) relied on the relative dating technique of obsidian hydration. The sensitivity of this dating technique depends, in turn, on a body of reference knowledge that explains how obsidian hydration occurs and why different glasses hydrate at different rates. This geochemical theory dictates that the units of archaeological observation useful for assessing chronology must incorporate the dimensions of obsidian source as well as context. Another attempt at constructing place-use histories (Wandsnider 1996) referred to Schiffer's waste-stream theory (1987, 1988b), which makes claims about the differential depositional histories of small and large objects in maintained and unmaintained spaces. Archaeological observations manipulatable within this theory must therefore include artifact size and the local "intrasite" location of the artifacts.

Using archaeological phenomena to evaluate our ideas about the past necessarily involves reference to bodies of knowledge that are theoretically (or conventionally) more secure than the relationship under study (Binford 1981). These bodies of knowledge implicate the form of the archaeological observational language, with further implications for the instruments that are taken into the field, as described in the following section.

INSTRUMENTATION AND UNITS

Archaeologists have long been concerned with past relationships between technology and ideas as mediated by intent and innovation. Did, for example, prehistoric people develop ceramic pottery to meet certain cooking demands or did the availability of ceramic technology permit past people to experiment with cooking (Brown 1989)? This same question can be posed about the process of science in general. In the case of the study of archaeological landscapes, the answer seems to be both that technology has permitted finer resolution in observation and that the need for instruments that can produce higher resolution observations has driven the development in this area.

The instruments used to document archaeological landscapes are various and include survey protocols (e.g., transect intervals, survey unit size and location, etc.), mapping instruments, and chronological indicators. I recognize three major technological elaborations that especially impacted the choice of the spatial and temporal units used to measure and analyze archaeological landscape deposits.

Improved sampling methods, precipitated by Binford's discussion (1964) of sampling issues, was one such elaboration of instrumentation. During the mid-1960s and through the 1970s, research on the fundamental issues of measurement accuracy and reliability in archaeological survey was carried out (e.g., Flannery 1976; Mueller 1975; Sanders et al. 1979; Schiffer et al. 1978). The resolution of these issues was critical to the design and conduct of settlement pattern studies, and it is not surprising that research on archaeological sampling issues and studies of this sort proceeded hand in hand. It could be argued that, ultimately, this refinement of method prompted other research into the nature of the archaeological record, already discussed above.

The computer revolution is a second technological advancement with dramatic impact on the documentation and analysis of archaeological landscapes. The advent of integrated circuit technology and increasing miniaturization of computing capability has had two ramifications. First, over the last decade and a half, microcomputer and microwave technology has been built into mapping equipment so that it is now possible to obtain high-quality, low-cost maps using widely available EDM (electronic distance measuring) technology. Previously, the majority of a project budget might be directed to producing high resolution maps. Similarly, until recently, individual artifact mapping was rarely undertaken because of the high time investment it required (e.g., Dancey 1973; Davis 1975). Today, the EDM mapping of architectural elements (e.g., Sabloff and Tourtellot 1991) and artifacts is a common means of documenting the archaeological landscape (Camilli et al. 1988; Ebert 1992). Certainly, the relative ease with which high-resolution spatial data can be obtained has made it easier to entertain questions of place use that rely on the synthesis of such artifact data (e.g., Camilli et al. 1988; Lycett 1995). As well, questions that rely on multiscalar data are readily addressed (e.g., Ebert 1992). The availability of low-cost global-positioning system (GPS) technology promises to deliver similar dividends to archaeologists operating at the regional scale.

A second ramification is that during the last ten years we have witnessed the increasing availability of powerful desktop computers with the concomitant development of powerful low-cost graphical, image processing, and geographical information system (GIS) software. Such software has greatly enhanced our ability to synthesize and manipulate spatial data. Today, GIS technology is increasingly used to investigate a variety of prehistoric settlement and other geographic processes (e.g., contributors to Allen et al. 1990). Because of the issues of site and settlement validity already mentioned, such applications must be viewed with a healthy dose of skepticism. The results of sophisticated treatments that rely on inaccurately or unreliably measured archaeological observations are meaningless, and so are the treatments that make use of crippled analytic units like settlements. However, where archaeological landscapes are analyzed in terms of smaller scale units (i.e., artifacts and feature attributes), I anticipate that such technologies will prove most useful.

Finally, another technological elaboration is currently under way. Archaeologists (e.g., contributors to Beck 1994; Jones and Beck 1992) have recognized the need for high-resolution chronological indicators that perform well, especially in surface contexts. As a result of this perceived need, much research is being conducted to develop other techniques for telling time using surficial artifacts and ecofacts. Over the next several years, this continuing research will greatly improve our ability to "parse" (Sullivan 1992) palimpsest deposits, thereby facilitating those treatments of the archaeological landscape concerned with land use or the evolution of the human-land relationship.

RESEARCHING ARCHAEOLOGICAL LANDSCAPES

Gordon Willey's pioneering research in the Virú Valley almost 50 years ago has led to a dramatic evolution in our ideas about the past, our knowledge of archaeological landscape formation, the sophistication of our interpretative tools, and available measurement technology. The units that have been employed to document and analyze archaeological landscapes are a reflection of these individual developments.

Given the preceding sketch of archaeological landscape studies, can we discern any principles useful for designing valid and reliable units of observation and analysis? I offer the following series of questions as a preliminary guide to unit design:

1. What is the general nature of the prehistoric socionatural system condition to be investigated? Examples: subsistence reorganization (Bettinger 1976, 1977; Thomas 1971, 1973), agricultural intensification (Fish et al. 1990; Morrison and Sinopoli 1992; Morrison 1995).

2. What are the processes (natural and cultural) propagated by that condition?

a. What are the processes that create distinctive pattern objects? What is the scale of those objects?

– spatial unit of observation should be one quarter to one half the size of the pattern object.

b. What are the effective spatial scales of the processes?

– project area should be at least twice as large as spatial extent of the effective scale of the target process.

c. Collaborate with archaeogeomorphologist (Linse 1993) to recognize and monitor contributing surface processes?

3. What is the availability and nature of the bodies of reference knowledge that sustain valid and reliable inferences about archaeological phenomena?

a. Which basal spatial and formal analytic units (i.e., units of archaeological observation) are required by the interpretative tools?

– recruit and elaborate on available technology and protocols.

b. Define landscape elements to serve as units of synthesis.

This unit design distillation seems to represent as well many recent and not-so-recent approaches to the archaeological landscape. Of course, productive archaeological landscape studies depend on other conceptual (McGlade 1995) and methodological (Linse 1993; contributors to Rossignol and Wandsnider 1992; Schiffer 1987) issues beyond unit design. Nevertheless, as evolution continues in our ideas about the past, the understanding of the archaeological landscape, relevant bodies of reference knowledge, and available instrumentation, we can expect continued innovation in archaeological landscape studies.

ACKNOWLEDGMENTS

This chapter has benefited greatly from discussions on the issues of unit definition with Ann Ramenofsky and ongoing discussions about archaeological landscapes with Effie Athanassopoulos, John Swigert, and Patrice Teltser. I am also grateful to the volume editors, Ann and Ana, for this opportunity to think about archaeological landscape units. I thank these individuals and take responsibility for lingering inconsistencies in my thoughts and deeds.

Note

1. Other recent treatments of archaeological landscapes include those contributed to Yamin and Bescherer Metheny (1995) and to Lock and Stančič (1995). The first volume focuses on using landscape modifications and features in historical contexts across the eastern United States to comment on text-derived interpretations. The second volume has a similar theme of landscape features and monuments as a reflection of ideology, and showcases geographical information system (GIS) tools useful for extracting such information. In each volume, there is little explicit discussion of unit design, which likely reflects the admittedly embryonic nature of such studies (Bescherer Metheny et al. 1995:6; Trigger 1995).

7

On Reliability, Validity, and Scale in Obsidian Sourcing Research

Richard E. Hughes

Just as radiocarbon dating revolutionized archaeology in the early 1950s, so it seemed that the introduction and widespread application of other physical-science measurement techniques into archaeology coincident with the coming of the New Archeology in the late 1960s would herald the transformation of archaeology into a truly scientific enterprise. In those days, as Patty Jo Watson put it:

> it seemed that with sufficient ingenuity, an emphasis on deductive inference, and use of new-fangled equipment and techniques (computers, magnetometers, trace-element analysis, flotation devices, pollen spectra) wielded by interdisciplinary teams (geoarchaeologists, zooarchaeologists, archaeobotanists), we could say something interesting, significant, and true about any part of the archaeological record to which we turned our attention. (1986:440)

One of those new-fangled techniques, obsidian source analysis, was first applied to archaeological problems in the Mediterranean (Cann and Renfrew 1964), and immediately caught fire elsewhere in the world where glassy volcanic rocks occurred (e.g., Green et al. 1967; Weaver and Stross 1965). In the following decade, sourcing studies were practiced widely in archaeology, culminating in some important publications (e.g., Earle and Ericson 1977; Taylor 1976) that remain influential today. These and more recent suc-

cesses notwithstanding, the downside of this otherwise happy interdisciplinary collaboration was that archaeologists (often untrained in geology or geochemistry) and geochemists and geologists (often with only vague, stereotypical views of archaeology) sometimes talked past one another, in part because of differences in conceptual language and observational frames of reference. Some of these misunderstandings have had interpretive consequences important in sourcing research. While we have come a long way in the past two decades, there is still much to be learned and appreciated about these cross-disciplinary differences and the ways in which historical factors have conditioned collaborative research. In the pages that follow, I discuss some of the ways in which these factors have influenced obsidian sourcing studies, emphasizing the special articulation of geological, geochemical, and archaeological domains in such research. Although the examples are drawn largely from X-ray fluorescence (XRF) studies in North America and Mesoamerica, the issues apply to other instrumental techniques and are relevant elsewhere in the world.

WHAT IS A SOURCE? GEOLOGICAL, GEOCHEMICAL, AND ARCHAEOLOGICAL CONSIDERATIONS

There is perhaps no better place to begin than with the term "source," which has long been employed in geology to specify the point source of origin for a material type. Ericson et al. (1976:218) defined an obsidian source as "a single volcanic event such as an obsidian-perlite dome, flow, aerial bomb scatter or sedimentary stratum containing obsidian." The problem with this definition, from the standpoint of geochemistry, is that (1) sedimentary strata may, depending on local geologic factors, contain obsidians of different chemical types that may themselves be redistributed far from their original eruptive home(s), and (2) it fails to consider that the geologic processes involved in the formation of obsidians in ash-flow sheets may result in the distribution of multiple *primary sources* across vast geographic space (see Hughes and Smith 1993:85–89; Ross and Smith 1961; Smith 1960). With respect to the first point, field observation may be insufficient to determine the number of chemical types occurring in such redeposited contexts; resolution of this issue falls within the geochemical domain. From the standpoint of archaeology, what matters is whether such redeposited occurrences of obsidian were used prehistorically as quarries for raw material. If archaeological evidence shows that they were used, the areal extent of redeposition must be taken into consideration. Some dome and flow obsidians, particularly "young" ones, have been redeposited only a few kilometers; other, "older" glasses may be redeposited tens to hundreds of kilometers from the original source (see, e.g., Hughes and Smith 1993; Sappington 1984; Shackley 1992). In light of these foregoing considerations, the areal correlate of what a source actually "is" may be more difficult to determine in practice than once believed; at a minimum such definitions must be informed by knowledge of the genesis of the obsidian (whether of dome and flow or ash-flow tuff origin), by familiarity with where obsidian occurs in secondary contexts (including where it might be scavenged from older archaeological sites and reused), and by its geochemistry.

The definition of a source (quoted above) refers primarily to an event, with spatial and genetic implications, but such a definition is not well suited to geochemically based obsidian provenance studies because it can convey a misleading geographic exactitude (see Neff, this volume, for a different discussion of source). Obsidian sources are defined, geochemically speaking, on the basis of chemical composition—not spatial distribution. From a geochemical standpoint, it doesn't matter whether an obsidian source is 1/10th of a kilometer in areal extent or 10,000 km²; what matters is whether the occurrence(s) share(s) a distinctive chemical signature. If significant chemical contrasts are identified, obsidian outcrops located in the same mountain range or volcanic field can be segregated from one another; conversely, if chemical identity is present, obsidians occurring in mountain ranges many miles apart may be combined into a single geochemical unit. Because obsidian sourcing studies rely almost exclusively on geochemistry, the chemical bias of this work has encouraged the use of an alternative term, "chemical group" (also referred to as "chemical type" and/or "geochemical variety"), for describing sources (cf. Jack and Heizer 1968). Use of the term "chemical group" emphasizes geochemical distinctiveness, leaving the spatial dimension to be revised as new distributional information accumulates.

THE BAD NEWS

This distinction between the colloquial use of the term "source" and the use of the term "chemical group" is more than semantic. A source traditionally denotes a *spatial* unit while chemical group is a *geochemical* unit. Both incorporate, by implication, elements of one another: chemical coherence is implied but not explicitly required in the use of "source," whereas some element of spatial circumscription is implied, although not explicitly required, by the use of "chemical group." Importantly, the subtle differences provide the basis for communication difficulties between geochemists and archaeologists. For example, archaeologists have samples geochemically characterized ("sourced") because they want to know where the obsidian came from so that questions regarding past trade/exchange and/or group mobility may be addressed. Leaving aside for the moment difficulties inherent in independently monitoring these latter issues (see below), the "answer" archaeologists get back from the lab isn't always what they expect.

When source analysis is performed by a laboratory, data often are reported to archaeologists in table and graph form, listing artifact-to-chemical type (or source) attribution. Implicit in a geologically informed chemical analysis is the understanding that the term "source" has come to be taken as a shorthand for chemical type and that chemical types may have dramatically different spatial correlates. This may become particularly troublesome archaeologically when obsidians have been redeposited from upland outcrops into streams and incorporated into river gravels, making—in effect—both the primary and secondary occurrences a "source" in a geochemical sense. Archaeological research questions, however, are sometimes phrased at a scale that may be at odds with the spatial resolution that can be provided by chemical analysis.

For example, let's say you've excavated at Snakebite pueblo—located on the Rio Grande in northern New Mexico—and you want to have the obsidian you found there analyzed to get independent evidence to support your hypothesis that Snakebite wasn't occupied year-round, but was just one seasonal stopover for groups moving through the area. You want to know the source of the obsidian, in part, because you think it is likely that the obsidian could have been obtained on brief fall trips into the Jemez Mountains at the same time of the year as the flora and fauna excavated from the site indicate. You have the analysis done, but what you get back from the lab doesn't do much for you. The analyst tells you that your sample contains 30 pieces of glass of the Obsidian Ridge chemical type, but also mentions in passing that there are several places in the lower, mid, and upper reaches of the Jemez where this glass can be obtained. You begin to squirm as the lab person goes on to point out that obsidian of this chemical type has been redeposited and that nodules and pebbles of Obsidian Ridge glass occur in the Rio Grande gravels that could have been picked up and used any time of the year! Your impulse to lash out at this person is fueled by the realization that you'll have to rephrase and rethink the way obsidian data relate to your research question.

This (partly) fictional case illustrates how different analytical frames of reference, with their attendant expectations and assumptions, affect interdisciplinary understandings between archaeologists and geochemists. When the spatial units held by archaeologists are only partly congruent with units geochemically defined, some archaeological research questions (like the hypothetical one played out above) may not be addressed meaningfully with geochemical data. There is an interesting irony here. In the context of this example, geochemical (sourcing) data do not *sensu strictu* "measure what they are designed to measure" (Spector 1981:14) in *archaeological* terms, although they most certainly do measure what they're supposed to in *geochemical* terms. This disjunction is but one example of a more widespread interdisciplinary malaise echoing the earlier plea of W. W. Taylor (1957) for mutual problem-oriented understandings between specialists and archaeologists (for more recent emphasis see Bishop 1992; DeAtley and Bishop 1991; Dunnell 1993; Renfrew 1982).

At a coarse scale, however, the lack of exact geographic congruence between "source" and "geochemical group" can carry a less severe interpretive liability. If one wishes to investigate the time/space distribution of glass of the Obsidian Cliff chemical type in Hopewell archaeological sites in the Scioto River Valley in southern Ohio, it hardly matters that obsidian of this geochemical variety also occurs at the Crystal Spring flow, a scant three kilometers north of Obsidian Cliff in Yellowstone National Park. At the scale of this research problem, it is probably sufficient to know that obsidian of this geochemical type occurs about 1,500 airline miles west-northwest of the Scioto Valley.

To this point, I've tried to emphasize, as others have noted (e.g., Harbottle 1982a), that sources and geochemical groups, despite the fact that they are sometimes mistakenly assumed to be isomorphic, are different analytical units which, depending on geologic circumstances and the degree of resolution (coarse versus fine) required by specific research questions, may or may not be relevant to addressing test implications generated from archaeological hypotheses.

THE GOOD NEWS

But, there are situations in which the unit disjunction between archaeology and geochemistry may open unanticipated and exciting new opportunities for archaeologists to ask more finely grained questions about obsidian use and distribution, in addition to helping expose and render understandable some of the largely unanticipated shortcomings of previous approaches.

To provide some background: In the early days of obsidian sourcing research, entire areas (i.e., mountain ranges, volcanic fields) were often lumped together and referred to generically as "sources" by specialists. This practice resulted largely from the nature of the field sampling method itself, not from the geochemistry. Most geologic samples were few in number, taken on-the-fly from easily accessible areas (often by those unfamiliar with local geology), then handed off to geochemical specialists for analysis. While this reconnaissance phase of sourcing work had the important result of identifying many of the major obsidian chemical types that are still being referred to today, because the sampling method employed was rarely thorough, significant chemical variability among obsidians *within* mountain ranges and volcanic fields often went unrecognized. More recent systematic collection and geochemical analysis of geologic obsidian samples from areas in California (e.g., Bacon et al. 1981; Hughes 1986, 1988b, 1989, 1994a; Jackson 1989; Metz and Mahood 1991) and Mesoamerica (e.g., Harris 1986; Mahood 1981, 1988), for example, has revealed significant chemical variability within areas once considered a single geologic source.

With this in mind, consider the following example. In 1972 a small number of obsidian samples taken from road cuts in and around the Casa Diablo area in east-central California were used to define the Casa Diablo obsidian source. Artifacts analyzed from archaeological sites throughout central California and the western Great Basin were matched to the "fingerprint" of Casa Diablo glass on the basis of Rb/Sr/Zr relative intensity data determined by XRF analysis. However, a significant number of artifacts had fingerprints superficially similar to, yet subtly variant from, the dominant "fingerprint" of Casa Diablo obsidian. Although early geologic mapping in the area (Bailey 1974) had revealed a sequence of distinct eruptive units (some of which contained artifact-quality obsidian), little was made of this archaeologically until some years later when more detailed reconnaissance, collection, and chemical analysis was undertaken pursuant to the U.S. Forest Service's mandate to address management of lithic resources on their lands. The results of this recent study (Hughes 1994a) showed that not just one, but two chemically different varieties of obsidian occurred in the Casa Diablo area: one (named Lookout Mountain) at the northern side of the caldera, the other (named Sawmill Ridge) venting in areas to the south. Subsequent inspection of quantitative geochemical analyses, coupled with quantitative reanalysis of specimens earlier subjected only to semiquantitative analysis, indicates that these obsidians have rather different *distributional* histories and potentially different use-life histories as well.

The importance of this example isn't only that it shows fine-scale chemical distinctions can be made with improved instrumentation, although that's certainly true. I find it equally interesting to reflect on how this situation came about in the first place. To understand it, we need to consider some historical developments in sourcing research.

In the early days of XRF obsidian sourcing studies, normalized plots of the relative intensities of three elements (usually rubidium [Rb], strontium [Sr], and zirconium [Zr]) on ternary diagrams worked well to identify and separate different chemical varieties of obsidian in both North America and Mesoamerica when compositions were comparatively distinct (see, e.g., Jack 1971, 1976; Jack and Carmichael 1969; Jack and Heizer 1968; Jackson 1974).[1] But three problems would emerge: the first was that as the inventory of artifact-quality geologic obsidians increased, the Rb/Sr/Zr distinctions once apparent between sources frequently became fuzzy. As a consequence of improved inventory, a unit of measurement that appeared perfectly appropriate to the goals of research at one scale became inappropriate as the scale of research was enlarged. It was *reliable* (i.e., the relative intensity ratios were always the same), but increasingly problematic as new sources were discovered in adjacent regions that yielded the same or overlapping Rb/Sr/Zr ratios (Hughes 1984). The second problem was that if element intensities all varied in the same direction, identical Rb/Sr/Zr ratios would result despite the fact that the absolute concentration of each element might vary significantly. If these intensity ratios alone were relied upon, obsidians that were chemically different from one another might be lumped together if they shared the same relative proportions of Rb, Sr and Zr. Third, relative intensity plots for Rb/Sr/Zr showed poor agreement with ternary diagram plots determined from quantitative data on the same samples (Hughes 1984), making it difficult to compare semiquantitative and quantitative data directly. In certain circumstances, the acknowledged pitfalls of this approach could be avoided when ratios of other elements (e.g., iron versus manganese; Jack 1976) were employed in concert with Rb/Sr/Zr ternary plots.

Use of relative intensity units also was legitimized by the assumption that sources (as they were understood in light of extant sampling "strategies," sketched above) were homogeneous units. While it is certainly true that obsidians formed in domes and flows are often remarkably homogeneous because they represent the quenched, solid phase of pristine magma, in other cases sequential tapping of laterally zoned magma chambers, com-bined with roof and wall rock contamination of erupting magma, can yield obsidians of quite different chemical types within the same volcanic field (Hughes and Smith 1993). Although these chemical differences are detectable quantitatively, past sampling strategies, in concert with the measurement units in which *artifact* data were expressed, had an impact on whether intra- or inter-source variation was even recognized in early XRF work. As a consequence of improved sampling and quantitative analysis, some of yesterday's sources have become today's *source areas*, effectively transforming the relations between chemical units and geologic space, complicating the utility of some older analyses and, in turn, altering the kinds of archaeological research questions susceptible to resolution by geochemical techniques.

In this case, technological limitations and concerns with artifact conservation encouraged the use of particular kinds of measurement units to assign artifacts to source, and the assumptions about homogeneity of those units were compromised both by the nature of the sampling and by the limitations of the measurement units to provide the fine-scale resolution required to recognize geochemical variability. The ability to generate quantitative data nondestructively by energy dispersive XRF ushered in a new era in obsidian sourcing studies, which helped overcome some of the unavoidable weaknesses of previous work.

ON RELIABILITY AND VALIDITY

The preceding discussion illustrates how the unit source can have variable meanings geologically and archaeologically depending on the geologic processes that created and dispersed the glasses, the measurement units employed to characterize them, and the variable scales at which archaeological research questions are situated. Further consideration of geological, geochemical, and archaeological factors involves the concepts of *reliability* and *validity*, reliability involving mainly issues of measurement and instrumentation, and validity combining measurement issues with noninstrumental purpose.[2]

Reliability concerns "the extent to which [the] measuring procedures yield the same results on repeated trials" (Carmines and Zeller 1979:11). In geochemistry, reliability involves consideration of both precision and accuracy—precision directing attention to repeatability and stability of measurement, and accuracy concerning the degree to which measurements conform to "correct" values (e.g., those recommended for international reference standards). As Peck (1964:54) pointed out, "although precise results are not necessarily accurate, lack of precision is a good indication of inaccuracy." Recognizing this, obsidian analysts have long been concerned with both issues (see, e.g., Asaro et al. 1978; Giauque et al. 1993; Hughes 1984, 1986; Stross et al. 1983); only the highlights will be mentioned here. Needless to say, interlaboratory calibration and comparison of results both turn on issues of precision and accuracy.

The most widely recognized method for assessing precision involves repeated measurement on in-house standards or international rock standards (see Flanagan [1986] for a historical perspective). I routinely conduct and report analyses (e.g., Hughes 1986:Table 2, 1988a:Table I, 1988b:Table I) of obsidian, and other, internationally recognized standards to monitor both machine precision and accuracy (see also Nelson 1984; Shackley 1991, 1992); neutron activation analyses (NAA) of obsidian are calibrated employing both in-house pottery (Perlman and Asaro 1969) and USGS reference standards (Glascock and Anderson 1993; Harbottle 1982b). Precision is most easily assessed and monitored if a standard measurement-unit convention is employed. As Harbottle (1982a:26) put it: "There is nothing more frustrating than to discover that another research group has studied materials similar to yours, but reported their results in units that cannot be translated into simple concentrations." Although recognized for some time that reporting measurements in internationally recognized units (i.e., parts-per-million [ppm] and weight percent composition) is prerequisite to

any serious interlaboratory comparison (Bieber et al. 1976; Harbottle 1982a), some researchers (e.g., Godfrey-Smith and Haywood 1984; Kunselman 1994), despite generally good agreement with concentration measurements reported by others (e.g., Kunselman 1991:Table 2), continue to report analyses in machine-specific units. This form of reporting greatly limits the usefulness of their data beyond the confines of their own labs (e.g., James et al. 1996). It is surprising that archaeologists continue to accept data reported in machine-specific units. If archaeologists had received results from radiocarbon laboratories expressed in decay counts (rather than such counts transformed into estimates of elapsed time), radiocarbon dating almost certainly would not have the influence in archaeology that it presently enjoys. But perhaps archaeologists tolerate this in obsidian studies because it doesn't appear to make any difference (i.e., whether expressed in ppm or relative intensity ratios); what matters is the source, not the precision, accuracy, or comparability of the data used to infer it. It is less easy to account for this tolerance among specialists.

The accuracy of an analysis is most readily evaluated by comparing the result obtained with the values recommended or certified by internationally recognized bodies (such as the U.S. Geological Survey, Geostandards International Working Group, Geological Survey of Japan, etc.). In practice, accuracy is affected by several factors (see, e.g., Baedecker and McKown 1987:H9–H13; Johnson and King 1987:F4) that need to be considered by every analyst.

Generally speaking, reliability in obsidian sourcing research can be measured by the extent to which (1) the measurements obtained correspond, within specified limits of analytical uncertainty, to values recommended for international rock standards and (2) the values subsequently obtained agree with values determined using the same, or different, instrumentation at another laboratory. Some interlaboratory comparisons for elements measured in common by neutron activation and XRF show excellent agreement (e.g., Giauque et al. 1993:Tables 6 and 7; Hughes 1984:Table 3, 1988b:Table II), but it is clear that difficulties still remain. The exemplary attempt by Stross et al. (1983:Appendix B) at interlaboratory calibration of some Meso-american obsidian data illustrates some of the difficulties still to be anticipated in such reconciliation efforts (cf. R. Macdonald et al. 1992:3; Mahood 1988:Table 1 n.).

VALIDITY

Validity can be considered at two levels in obsidian sourcing research. In its most basic expression (level one) validity concerns the extent to which measurement units are suited to goals of research (i.e., are the units *themselves* valid measures for identifying distinct geochemical varieties of obsidian and for matching artifacts to them?), whereas at a deeper level (level two) it concerns the degree to which geochemical data serve archaeological ends.

Validity: Level One

As discussed earlier, the validity of units historically employed to identify sources and match their chemical profiles with artifacts has changed, partly because the inventory of sources has increased, partly because of improved instrumentation, and partly because of increased sophistication resulting from interdisciplinary cooperation. I discussed some of these issues with respect to early XRF studies employing ratio level measurement (see above), and it is also important to acknowledge that neutron activation studies relying solely on element ratios (e.g., sodium/manganese; see Hatch et al. 1990) suffer some of the same interpretive liabilities as those done by XRF (see Hughes 1992a; Stross et al. 1976).

Despite an increase in the number of known geologic sources of obsidian, in some geographic areas it is valid to employ relative intensity unit measurements to characterize obsidians that contain unusually high or low concentrations of certain elements (e.g., yttrium and niobium in Big Southern Butte, Idaho, obsidian [Macdonald et al. 1992:Appendix I; Nelson 1984:Table 5], rubidium

and tin in Macusani glass from Peru [Macdonald et al. 1992:Appendix IV]). When such unique compositions are encountered, the intensity ratio plot (on a ternary diagram, for example) is often so distinctive that quantitative data are not required to make valid artifact-to-chemical type (source) ascription. This does not, however, eliminate the problem of interlaboratory comparison of machine-specific results (discussed above).

Validity: Level Two

The second operational level of validity of significance to archaeology concerns the degree to which the results of obsidian sourcing studies constitute a valid measure for what archaeologists purport to use them for: as proxies for prehistoric trade, exchange, territoriality, and/or mobility. Countless archaeologists have either commented about or agonized over the difficulty of distinguishing trade/exchange from mobility archaeologically, and no immediate solution to this problem can be posed here. It is perhaps worthwhile, nonetheless, to consider some of the reasons this difficulty has emerged, because such consideration may reveal why we hold the assumptions we do and how they have been influenced and shaped by the archaeological units constructed to investigate the past.

Archaeologists who have *studied obsidian trade* have been hopeful that chemical differences in obsidians from various sources might enable them to identify with certainty the original place from which imported obsidian found in archaeological sites was obtained. (Heizer et al. 1965:94; emphasis added)

Tracing the varieties of obsidian from their sources to the villages where they turn up in manufactured objects, we can reconstruct the trade routes of that early time in man's economic and social history. (Dixon et al. 1968:45)

As uncontroversial as these statements appear, they illustrate a subtle, fundamentally important problem. To paraphrase Binford (1989:3), archaeologists do not study trade;

they study artifacts. And, from knowledge about the geologic and geochemical contexts in which those artifactual materials occur, they then make inferences about how artifacts made from those materials found their way into an archaeological site. Trade, like exchange and mobility, is an activity inferred to link, in behavioral terms, spatially disjunct locations of artifacts with geologic/geochemical points of origin. Yet in the early literature on obsidian sourcing, it was too little appreciated that what we really get from sourcing studies is a measure of the physical displacement of materials, not direct evidence for trade, exchange, direct procurement, or mobility.

The conflation of distribution with process occurred early on in the collaborations between geochemists and archaeologists. In one of the earliest sourcing studies in California, Jack and Carmichael (1969:24) wrote that their initial interest in archaeology was stimulated by R. F. Heizer, then a colleague in the Anthropology Department at Berkeley, who "proposed to the authors that the identification of the source of material used to make the weapon points would be interesting and possibly informative." In this brief study, they presented their results in terms of matches between the Rb/Sr/Zr trace-element proportions of source samples and artifacts, concluding that their study "produced data to support other anthropological evidence of Indian trade across the Sierra Nevada." At a superficial level, this appeared to make good sense; after all, the obsidian source materials identified in the artifact samples were located well over a hundred miles from the archaeological sites where they were recovered, and there was evidence for trans-Sierran obsidian procurement (trading) treks in the California ethnographic literature. Because of the distance involved and the ethnographic examples, it must have seemed preposterous to entertain the notion that the obsidian could have made its way there by any other means.

Because the linkage between distance and trade was so fundamentally shaped and reinforced by received tradition, it was probably difficult, if not impossible, to escape phrasing and thinking about problems in these conventional classificatory units (see Dunnell 1982). In California, the Direct Historical Approach, supplemented by local ethnographic analogy, provided the methodological rationale for writing linguistic prehistory (Hughes 1992b) just as it influenced studies of trade/exchange (Hughes 1994c).[3] Historic period peoples were conjoined with prehistoric populations on the basis of continuities; discontinuities, or abrupt changes in archaeological assemblages, were typically interpreted as signaling population replacements rather than changes in settlement-subsistence practices (Hughes 1994b). Only recently has it been acknowledged that the ethnographic landscape in California may bear only a faint resemblance to those of prehistory and that the effects of recently introduced European diseases likely altered not only population densities but also social organization, religion, and social boundaries as well as native oral tradition (see Heizer 1975, 1978). The implications of this awakening present a daunting challenge to archaeology generally and to obsidian sourcing studies in particular.

The conceptual unit "trade" was borrowed from ethnography and applied to archaeology, but the transposition proved unexpectedly troublesome because unlike other inferential activities—for example, hunting, about which more secure inferences could be made (from arrow points imbedded in and butchering marks found on animal bones)—there was no explicit description of what "trade" should look like when it was "encountered" archaeologically. There were numerous descriptions in the ethnographic literature of when, where, and how trade took place, but no signatures that could readily be discerned archaeologically. Without a secure empirical referent, geographic distance and common sense were invoked: the farther away an artifact was recovered from its source of origin, the more likely it got there by trade (cf. Basgall 1979).

There is perhaps no better illustration of this reasoning than that provided by Robert Heizer in his discussion of nonlocal materials encountered in central California Early Horizon sites:

> Since the Windmiller facies settlements lie on the stoneless alluvial plain, it is certain that the wide variety of lithic materials found in these settlements (in addition to obsidian) was brought in from outside. Some of the stone probably derives from the Sierra region to the east and some probably comes from the Coast Range region which borders the Great Valley on the west. It is thus apparent either that the Early Sacramento people were extensive foragers or that they had trade relations with Sierran and Coast Range groups who could supply these varieties of stone. It is impossible at present to decide which of these two explanations would best account for the presence of foreign lithic materials; on purely speculative grounds, I incline to the theory of trade relations. (1949:34)

With benefit of chemical determinations, he later made his reasoning more explicit:

> The valley Windmiller people were securing obsidian (either as raw material, preforms, blanks, or finished implements) from two main zones: (1) three trans-Sierran obsidian flows situated at a distance of 150 miles to the east, and (2) two continuous obsidian deposits in Napa County in the Coast Ranges lying 65 miles to the west. These distances are fairly considerable, and judging from ethnographic analogy of recent California Indians, it is more probable that the obsidian from the several sources reached the Windmiller people through intergroup trade than by actual treks to the several obsidian localities to the west and east. (1974:195)

Conclusions derived from Mesoamerican obsidian studies were equally affected by distance-based considerations. As Heizer et al. (1965:96) put it when considering Mesoamerican obsidian sourcing results: "Since the La Venta site is three hundred miles distant from Pachuca we have clear evidence of long distance trade." Jack and Heizer added:

Initial work on Mesoamerican obsidians by Weaver and Stross (1965) was successful in demonstrating that obsidian from Pachuca (i.e., Cerro de Navajas, Hidalgo) was traded as far south as the La Venta site in the state of Tabasco . . . but the archaeological sample was collected from the surface and could not be dated. [Subsequent] excavations at La Venta in 1967–1968 . . . produced 12 small obsidian blades . . . recovered from Middle Pre-Classic deposits. Since three of these are of Type A obsidian from Pachuca, *we can be certain of the fact* that obsidian from the Mexican highland was being traded to southeastern Mexico in the Middle Pre-Classic. (1968:89; emphasis added)

In retrospect, adoption of distance-driven assumptions was ironic, because ethnographies throughout North America provided many examples of both long-distance trading expeditions *and* long-distance direct-procurement forays. Nonetheless, distance to source, coupled with local ethnographic analogy and/or historical accounts, were the two principal factors invoked to justify archaeological portraits of prehistoric trade in North America.

DISCUSSION

Since trade, exchange, direct procurement, and/or mobility cannot be distinguished using obsidian sourcing information *alone*, it should be clear that geochemical data (the foundation for sourcing studies) are not direct evidence for prehistoric trade/exchange. This follows if we grant that geochemical data are directly relevant only to identification of chemical varieties of obsidian and that inferences about distribution mechanisms are essentially nongeochemical in nature. It is axiomatic in archaeology that sourcing studies are conducted to inform on such nongeochemical topics, yet they do not speak directly to these issues.

Geochemical data provide archaeology with quantifiable and comparable measures of chemical properties that inform directly on the *distribution of materials in space* and, in concert with other dating techniques, *time*. Distributionally focused studies that employed fine-grained chronological controls have already revealed diachronic and synchronic variability and patterning unmatched by, and directly at variance with, locally known ethnographic accounts.

Geological and geochemical issues aside, it is important to acknowledge that much of what archaeologists have inferred about prehistoric trade from sourcing studies has been accommodated to, and linked with, ethnographic models rooted in historical circumstances unlike those that may have existed in the past. Trade and direct procurement, as employed ethnographically, describe transmission mechanisms observed in a wide variety of historic settings among peoples who experienced, to varying degrees, post-Contact alteration in lifeways. The ethnographic landscape—the prototype for analogic reasoning—was the result of the transformation of a host of unique environmental and cultural factors, many of which probably gave rise to sociocultural expressions unlike any that preceded them. It is easy to imagine how differences in social organization and population density, for example, operating within different lithic resource environments, might encourage any number of different access opportunities. In some circumstances, trade/exchange might be the best solution; in others, requirements might be met through shifts in residential mobility; in others, a shifting combination of the two. In the example cited above by Heizer, 65 miles might seem a long way to travel to get obsidian in a densely populated area of ethnographic central California, but that travel distance would by no means be considered extreme under conditions of lower population density, such as throughout much of the Great Basin and the American Southwest.

Confounding implications of different procurement alternatives have been implicit in trade/exchange studies from their very inception. Archaeologists interested in trade were well aware of these alternatives, but rather than ask how different kinds of acquisition, conveyance, and consumption patterns might be reflected archaeologically (as

Meltzer [1989] has recently attempted), they most often used ethnographic descriptions of trade/exchange and direct procurement as templates against which archaeological data were compared. This predilection may have been the result of the long-standing view that the general outline of prehistory was already known in North America (see Fredrickson [1994:92] for discussion) and that the job of the archaeologist was principally to fill in the blanks connecting the ethnographic inhabitants to their assumed prehistoric forebears. To the extent that this view was perceived to be true archaeologically, sourcing studies had a warrant to commingle ethnographic groups and late prehistoric obsidian artifacts (cf. Jack 1976:186–87).

The point is that, holding the geologic and geochemical landscape constant, if we believe transmission modes and physical access mechanisms are strongly influenced by population density and if we believe introduced diseases and widespread social disintegration following therefrom (Dunnell 1991; Ramenofsky 1987) profoundly changed the preContact social organizational landscapes, then we cannot realistically expect the ethnographic record to serve in any but the most general sense as a source of knowledge about trade, direct access, and mobility patterns that preceded it.

CONCLUDING COMMENTS AND OBSERVATIONS

In the context of the broader archaeological goals of obsidian sourcing research, it is probably apparent that one of the areas we need to address is inference justification. This is hardly news, but it commands a special place in sourcing research as soon as the focus shifts *from* strict chemical identification *to* considerations of how the obsidian got where it was finally recovered archaeologically.

In composing this chapter, I have tried to illustrate some of the ways that geological, geochemical, and archaeological factors entwine in sourcing studies, underscoring the variable contexts in which issues of reliability and validity come to the fore and how different analytical frames of reference can sometimes dramatically affect archaeological conclusions. In this regard, it is important to emphasize that, despite their central role today in some archaeological research programs, sourcing studies were not initially driven by archaeological problems and that, in the early days of such research, archaeologists were almost exclusively awed consumers of data provided by geochemists and geologists. As one archaeologist put it:

> Archaeologists are notorious gadgeteers, seizing avidly on the latest fads and tools that offer hope of lending precision to an inherently ambiguous business. Because of this, I would feel distinctly uneasy if archaeometry were being practiced by archaeologists. Mercifully, most of my colleagues in archaeology have eschewed taking archaeometric matters into their own hands, preferring instead to enlist specialist aid when needs have been perceived. (Hole 1982:80)

While one would hope that increased cross-disciplinary collaboration and training over the past decade have altered this perception, implicit in this view is the belief that archaeologists had little to contribute to an enterprise that was essentially the province of the physical sciences. Although this perception is still largely true with respect to instrumentation (an issue of reliability, as discussed above), it is not true in the context of the broader archaeological goals of sourcing studies (validity) which conjoin geology, geochemistry, and archaeology. Understanding the geological distributions and physical characteristics of obsidian is of paramount importance archaeologically, yet these properties may be highly variable from a chemical standpoint and, depending on whether they are, they carry different implications for how archaeological research questions are framed. Geochemistry informs archaeology by providing an understanding of the positioning of chemical units in geologic space; such analysis is vital to determining whether single or multiple chemical types are present at particular places in the geological landscape. Yet chemistry-based analyses, by themselves, help us apprehend only a part of the variability we are interested in as archaeologists. Moreover, a geologically uninformed (or analytically flawed) chemical analysis can result in a perfect match to an obsidian of absolutely no consequence archaeologically.

I have found discussions with geologists and chemists about these issues to be extremely stimulating and informative, and believe that such cross-disciplinary dialogue has helped us immeasurably to expose and critically evaluate what we think we know. Notwithstanding the appreciation of mutualism and the variable impacts on archaeological interpretation that follow therefrom, the long-term payoffs to archaeology will accrue in an environment where archaeologists also confront the anthropological framework within which their own research historically has been cast.

ACKNOWLEDGMENTS
I thank the volume editors for various suggestions that improved the organization and content of this chapter. Jeanette Blomberg, David Fredrickson, Barbara Luedtke, and Robert L. Smith also made insightful and helpful comments on various drafts of the manuscript.

Notes

1. It is important to recognize that prior to the advent of energy dispersive XRF, XRF analysts had the ability to generate quantitative data, but most analyses of archaeological artifacts were done semiquantitatively because generating quantitative data required powdering (grinding up) a portion of the sample for analysis (see, e.g., Nelson et al. 1978; Nelson and Holmes 1979:68). Generating quantitative data was not only time-consuming but it also destroyed all, or a large part, of an artifact. In view of these limiting factors, semiquantitative data, usually presented on ternary diagrams, were considered an appropriate proxy for quantitative data when artifacts were analyzed (see Jack 1976:186–87).

2. The interested reader should consult Nance (1987) and Bernard (1994:38–40) for extended discussions of the concept of reliability in archaeology as well as for considerations of dif-

ferent operation levels of validity. Kaplan (1964:198–206) also provides a useful discussion of these issues.

3. Methodological problems with the use of ethnographic analogy and the Direct Historical Approach in archaeology have been recognized and debated elsewhere for some time (see, e.g., Binford 1967; Gould and Watson 1982; Ramenofsky 1987; Upham 1987; Wobst 1978; Wylie 1985).

8

Units in Chemistry-Based Ceramic Provenance Investigations

HECTOR NEFF

In thinking about units and measurement scales in ceramic provenance research, it occurred to me that a chapter on the subject might take one of two complementary but quite distinct approaches. One would be to analyze and critique how units have been defined and used in the past; it might be called the "critical approach." Certainly it should be possible to find weaknesses in previous provenance investigations—we all learn how to find fault with previous work in graduate school. But there is also a second approach, in which emphasis is placed on constructive suggestions about how to make interesting and useful archaeological measurements; this second one might be called "constructive" as opposed to "critical."

On the whole, I do not believe that chemistry-based archaeological sourcing is a hopelessly misguided enterprise in need of fundamental rethinking before anything approaching *Science* can be achieved. Instead, I take the more modest view that sourcing can be put on slightly firmer methodological ground by considering explicitly what it is we are trying to measure when we characterize artifacts and how we go about aligning the compositional data with the measurement dimensions in which we are really interested. Toward this end, I endeavor in this chapter to make some constructive suggestions about how to use chemical characterization of ceramics to make interesting and useful measurements of archaeological phenomena.

THEORY AND METHOD IN CERAMIC SOURCING

I am concerned here mainly with issues of validity and reliability in chemistry-based ceramic provenance investigations. But before turning to these methodological issues, let me briefly describe my theoretical rationale.

I assert that a focus on sourcing is warranted because it describes what is perhaps the most salient human phenotypic characteristic observable in the archaeological record: namely, the propensity to move objects through space. Remains of processed or consumed food, building material, lithic tool material, ceramics, and virtually all other constituents of the archaeological record have all been displaced over some distance by humans. The universality of the human propensity to move objects through space implies that it must initially have been fixed by selection and that its various manifestations must be at least partly under the control of selection. The high archaeological visibility of this propensity implies that we can study its evolution in past human populations. First, however, we need a way to describe this universal, highly visible human propensity for moving things around, and that is where sourcing comes in: in principle, sourcing provides a means to monitor how humans moved materials through space from a location of natural occurrence or manufacture to a location of consumption or final discard.

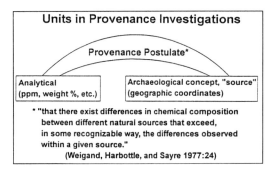

Units in Provenance Investigations

Provenance Postulate*

Analytical
(ppm, weight %, etc.)

Archaeological concept, "source"
(geographic coordinates)

* "that there exist differences in chemical composition
between different natural sources that exceed,
in some recognizable way, the differences observed
within a given source."
(Weigand, Harbottle, and Sayre 1977:24)

Figure 8.1. Units in provenance investigations.

I leave further theoretical justification of the concept of "source" and move to a discussion of methodological issues in ceramic sourcing. The key point to keep in mind is that the theoretical concept of interest here is "source," defined as a location or set of locations in geographic space. "Sourcing" a pot entails determining for the materials used to make that pot a point or zone of origin (i.e., specific coordinates or a range of likely coordinates). Identifying "source" in this way enables us to monitor the past movement of ceramics through space, which we strongly suspect is a human phenotypic trait controlled by selection.

To use chemical characterization to monitor our theoretical concept, "source," we need to construct a bridge between units measured in two distinct domains (Figure 8.1). One domain is that of the individual analyzed specimen, in which the units are imposed by the analytical technique: that is, weight percent or parts per million (ppm) of the various measured elements or oxides. The other domain is geographic space, in terms of which "source" may be described. The units in this second domain are conventional geographic coordinates (e.g., latitude and longitude, UTM coordinates, etc.). The assumption that a bridge between these two domains exists is the foundation for all chemical sourcing and has been formalized as the "Provenance Postulate" (Weigand et al. 1977:24).[1] The fundamental methodological challenge in provenance research, therefore, does not concern the definition of measurement units (for these are unambiguously

defined by the analytical technique and by the definition of "source" as a location in geographic space). Instead, the fundamental challenge in provenance research is to align geographic coordinate units with the multidimensional space defined by measured elemental concentration units.

To reiterate, the measuring instrument here is compositional characterization. The instrument is a *reliable* indicator of geographic space if specimens from a given "source" consistently yield measurements that assign them to the same "source." The instrument is a *valid* indicator to the extent that composition really does measure "source" as a location in geographic space and not some other concept. Following Carmines and Zeller (1979), reliability is a matter of random error (or slop or noise), whereas validity is a matter of nonrandom or systematic error that impedes measurement of the focal theoretical concept.

PROCESSES THAT COMPROMISE THE RELIABILITY AND VALIDITY OF CERAMIC SOURCING

As indicated above, I find no fundamental flaws in ceramic sourcing methods that might serve as take-off points for a scathing critique. In fact, in the very first publication of a neutron activation analysis (NAA) study of archaeological ceramics is an exceptionally concise statement about processes that might affect the reliability and validity of a ceramic provenance investigation:

> Among the possible difficulties and interferences which may come into attempts to apply the method [NAA for provenance determination] one may note the following: lack of sufficient uniformity of clays in a given region or of sufficient differences between those from different regions of interest; differences in fabrication affecting the impurity pattern; effects of weathering. The effects of these must be assessed by further experiment. (Sayre and Dodson 1957:40)

One can elaborate on this statement, as I do here, but the fact is that the basic principles of ceramic sourcing articulated in this pas-

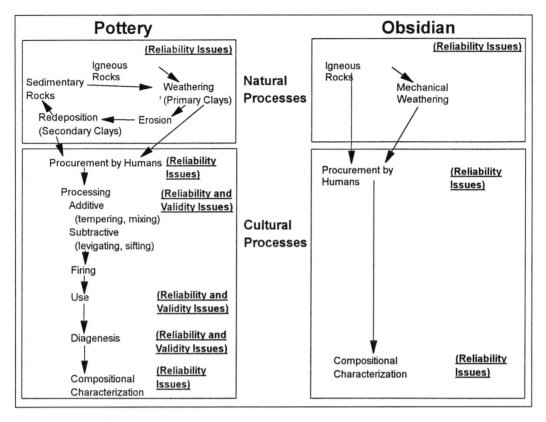

Figure 8.2. How the life histories of ceramics and obsidian affect reliability and validity in provenance investigations.

sage have proved highly durable and have guided an abundance of productive research over the past 40 years.

To elaborate on Sayre's and Dodson's formulation, it is useful to consider the "life history" of ceramic materials and to contrast them with the "life history" of tools made of lithic material, such as obsidian (Figure 8.2; see Hughes, this volume, for a more detailed consideration of obsidian). To use compositional characterization to measure "source," one has to be concerned about effects that may compromise reliability and validity of our measuring instrument throughout the materials' life history.

In the case of obsidian, reliability of chemical characterization as a monitor of "source" may be compromised by natural variation within sources and analytical error (which create outliers whose affiliation with a source

may not be clear)[2]; by natural dispersion of chemically uniform obsidian over wide areas through eruptive or weathering processes (e.g., Hughes, this volume); or by vagaries in human procurement. But the fundamental linkage between artifact composition and source material composition cannot be questioned seriously. Obsidian does not undergo chemical alteration that would affect provenance investigations either during tool manufacture or during weathering, so the validity of chemical characterization of an individual specimen is simply not an issue in obsidian provenance research.

The situation is much more complicated for ceramics. First, natural geological formation processes include both mechanical and chemical weathering, and raw argillaceous sediments might have gone through several weathering cycles before being procured for use in ceramics. Natural chemical variation, even within small areas, can thus be quite high in clays. These natural formation processes also make clays widely available, so humans don't have to keep going back to the same clay pit time after time, but instead can get clay from a different pit every time they replenish their raw materials. These steps in the life history of a ceramic compromise the reliability of chemical characterization as a measure of source. That is, they introduce the potential for random error in source assignment.[3]

After their procurement by humans, ceramic materials, unlike lithics, go through processes that can change their chemical composition. Clay may be refined (Blackman 1992; Kilikoglou et al. 1988) or nonplastic material may be added as temper (Arnold et al. 1991; Bishop et al. 1982; Rice 1978), and both practices modify the clay's original chemical composition. Conceivably, such practices might either create subgroup patterning unrelated to clay source (Bishop and Neff 1989; Neff, Bishop, and Arnold 1988, 1990) or destroy an existing clay source distinction (Neff, Bishop, and Sayre 1988, 1989).[4] After manufacture, use and diagenetic processes in the burial environment may further alter elemental concentrations (Franklin and Vitali 1985), enriching some elements (Dunnell and Hunt 1990; Garcia Heras 1993; Lemoine and Picon 1982; Picon 1985, 1987; Walter and Besnus 1989) and diluting others (Cogswell et al. 1993; Myers et al. 1992). In the end, the bulk chemical composition of an archaeological ceramic expresses chemical contributions from all particle-size ranges and mineralogical phases actually present in the ceramic fabric, without regard to when those particles or phases came to reside in the fabric (Bishop et al. 1982:294).

Whereas the nature of variation within and among sources primarily affects the *reliability* of compositional characterization as a measure of geographic space, the possibility of compositional change during manufacture, use, and burial affects *both* validity and reliability. Conceivably, in an extreme case, the

compositional profile of a ceramic might be dominated by signals from paste processing and/or postmanufacturing changes to such an extent that the resemblance of the ceramic to its source clays is completely unrecoverable. In such a case, compositional characterization becomes a completely invalid measure of source and measures some other concept instead. One might imagine, for example, that a ceramic made from calcareous clay tempered with a large proportion of crushed volcanic rock and left in a highly acidic burial environment for several thousand years would be chemically very different from the original source clay. Supplementary analyses, either by relatively simple techniques, such as low-power microscopic examination or more powerful mineralogical or microchemical characterization techniques, are the primary means for identifying extreme effects of paste preparation, use, and diagenesis.

A SYSTEMATIC APPROACH TO CERAMIC PROVENANCE INVESTIGATION

Ceramic provenance investigations usually involve comparison of individual specimens of known derivation to groups of unknown specimens whose geographic provenance is sought. This is the reverse of the approach taken in most lithic provenance studies, in which source (quarry) materials are sampled and characterized, and the unknown individual specimens are then compared to the known groups. This difference in research strategy is a consequence of the ubiquity of ceramic raw materials.[5]

The basic strategy of ceramic provenance research can be implemented by means of the following steps: (1) sample ceramics (unknowns) for which sources are sought along with raw materials of known geographic derivation; (2) analyze the knowns and unknowns; (3) based on the raw material sample, evaluate the potential reliability and validity of chemistry-based sourcing in the sampled region; (4) divide the sample of unknowns into compositionally homogeneous groups, which, based on the provenance postulate, are assumed to derive from a single

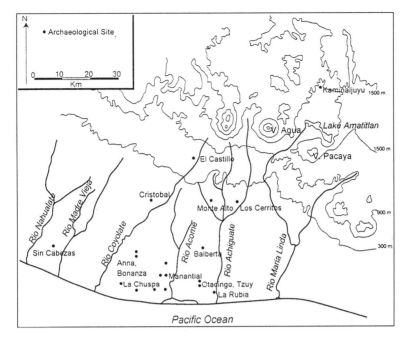

Figure 8.3. Map of southern Guatemala showing sites where Achiguate tradition domestic vessels have been found.

source or a geographically restricted range of sources; (5) identify and compensate for effects that might compromise the validity of compositional characterization as a measure of source for the various compositional groups; (6) compare the knowns (raw material samples) to the unknown groups in order to assign geographic coordinates (sources) or ranges of coordinates (source zones) to the unknowns.

AN EXAMPLE OF PROVENANCE INVESTIGATION

A systematic approach to ceramic sourcing may be illustrated by some relatively large, volcanic ash-tempered vessels that are found in Terminal Formative (0–A.D. 200) through Middle Classic (A.D. 400–A.D. 700) contexts on the Guatemalan central Pacific coast and in the adjacent central Guatemalan highlands. As part of an ongoing ceramic sourcing project in coastal Guatemala, my colleagues and I have sampled and analyzed 92 of these vessels by NAA. The sites from which ceramics were sampled are shown in Figure 8.3.

As detailed elsewhere (Neff et al. 1992), we have also analyzed raw argillaceous sediments and potential tempering materials, including sands and volcanic ash, from across the region shown in Figure 8.3. The raw material data show several consistent geographic trends, such as the east-west trend in values of principal component 1 of the raw-materials data set (Figure 8.4). The existence of consistent geographic trends in raw materials implies that composition provides a *valid* monitor of source, at least in the absence of the ceramic life-history effects discussed above. Judging from experiments in which individual raw material samples are treated as unknowns, composition seems also to be a fairly *reliable* measure of source; that is, actual provenances tend to fall within zones of likely provenance calculated from the compositional data (Figure 8.5; also see Neff 1995a).

Subgroup patterning in the Achiguate tradition data set is relatively weak, so one reasonable approach is to seek a source zone for the whole collection. There is, however, some tendency for distinct decorative variants to segre-

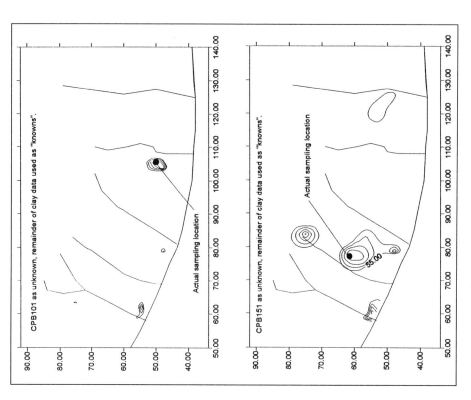

Figure 8.5. Tests of reliability with the coastal Guatemalan raw materials. Peaks on the surface show the locations of highest probability for the raw material sample whose location is shown (the raw material sample of interest is removed from the data set).

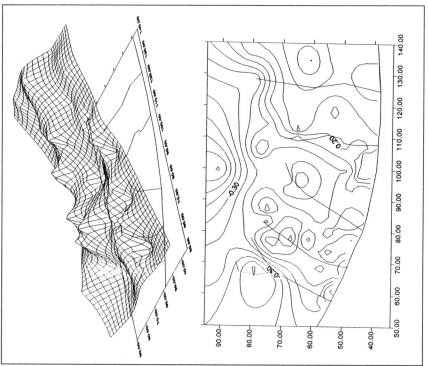

Figure 8.4. Geographic trend in raw material compositions in Pacific coastal Guatemala (principal component 1 of the raw clay data). Geographic trends establish the validity of chemical characterization for sourcing, providing ceramic compositions reflect raw clay properties.

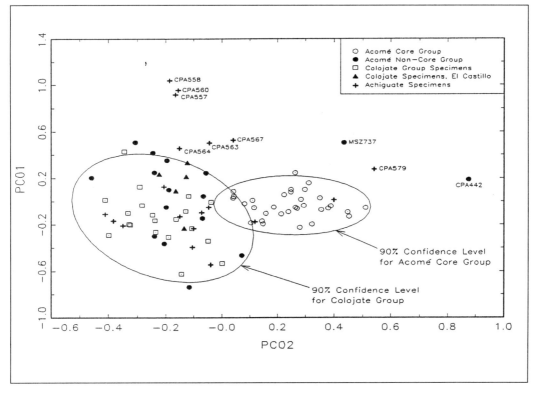

Figure 8.6. Achiguate tradition ceramics projected onto the first two components of the 92-specimen data set. Two compositional subgroups that are more homogeneous than the total group are enclosed by 90 percent confidence ellipses.

gate compositionally, as illustrated in Figure 8.6. The possibility that these compositionally more uniform subgroups may represent distinct source zones must also be examined. In addition, there are some obvious outliers that may represent yet additional sources.

The *validity* of composition as a measure of source for the Achiguate tradition vessels might be compromised by the presence of volcanic ash temper, which is easily identified in the pastes with low-power magnification. Validity would be compromised to the extent that compositional similarity among the analyzed specimens reflects volcanic ash content more than it reflects common origin of the raw clays. To compensate for the presence of volcanic ash, compositional characteristics of the known clays can be recalculated to express the presence of the ash before comparing them to the unknown ceramics. Estimated tempering proportions were around 40 percent, so that is the factor used to recalculate

the raw clay compositions. The volcanic ash concentrations used to correct the raw clays were obtained from a volcanic ash deposit on the upper edge of the coastal plain.

After correcting the compositions to allow for the presence of volcanic ash temper, the raw clays were compared to various subgroups of Achiguate tradition ceramics using multivariate probability statistics based on Mahalanobis distance (see Beier and Mommsen 1994; Bieber et al. 1976; Bishop and Neff 1989; Harbottle 1976; Leese and Main 1994; Sayre 1975). Probabilities calculated for clays sampled at different x-y coordinates provide the basis for estimating a probability surface on which high probability plateaus are most likely to contain the sources of raw materials used for the unknown ceramic groups.

Results of comparing the (tempered) raw materials to the various Achiguate subgroups are shown in the next series of figures. Figure

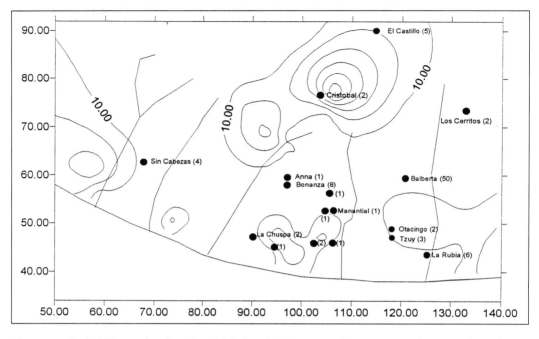

Figure 8.7. Probability surface based on Mahalanobis distances of 162 "tempered" pastes from the total Achiguate group centroid ("tempered" paste compositions reflect 40 percent mixtures of volcanic ash CPD018A with 60 percent of each of the 162 raw clays). Numbers in parentheses next to each site indicate number of analyzed specimens from each site in the total Achiguate group.

8.7 shows results for the total 92-specimen data set, Figure 8.8 shows results for the Acomé subgroup, and Figure 8.9 shows results for the Colojate subgroup. In all cases, the piedmont zone along the upper Coyolate River is a zone of peak probability (Figure 8.10). Therefore, we conclude that the vast majority of Achiguate domestic ware in our sample probably was produced from raw materials procured within this zone. Substantively, what makes this interesting is that many of the sampled vessels come from coastal-plain sites outside the identified production zone and that implied transport distances are on the order of 10 to 50 km.

Results for the outliers are informative as well. Although most appear to come from the same piedmont production zone as the main reference groups, some show an extremely flat probability surface configured differently from the main groups (Figure 8.11). The latter specimens may represent production outside of the region sampled in our raw materials survey.

The study area of the example discussed

here is distinguished by gradual trends in raw material composition and few geographically discrete, chemically distinct, raw material sources (e.g., Figure 8.4; see Neff et al. 1992 and Neff 1995a). These conditions are less than ideal for sourcing, which is most easily accomplished where natural sources are both discrete spatially and distinct chemically. But the absence of geological/geochemical contrasts highlights the need for an explicit approach to the problem of aligning units of compositional space with units of geographic space. Indeed, the dangers of failing to take an explicit approach are well illustrated by previous compositional investigation of Achiguate tradition domestic ware. Without a sample of raw materials and with only a limited sample of Achiguate tradition ceramics, it was possible to suggest that Acomé vessels may have been made in the highlands around Kaminaljuyu (see Figure 8.10) and exported to the Pacific coast and piedmont (Neff, Bishop, and Bove 1989). Now, based on the sampling of coastal raw materials, modeling the effect of paste preparation (i.e.,

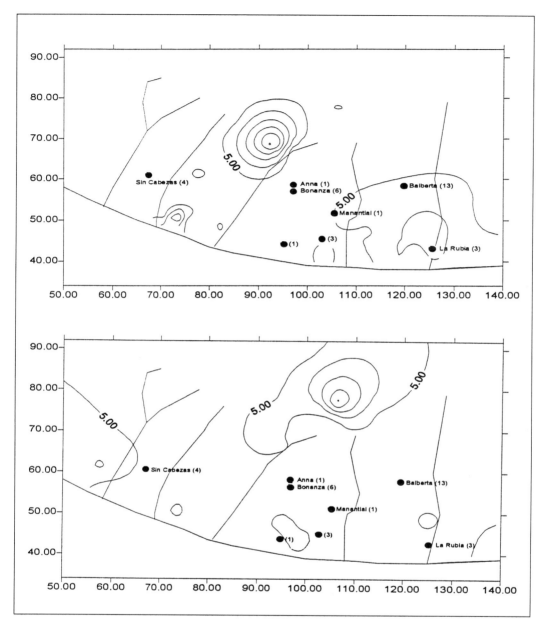

Figure 8.8. Top: Probability surface based on Mahalanobis distances of 162 "tempered" pastes from the Acomé core group centroid; due to the small size of the core group, a number of elements were omitted for this analysis (see text). Bottom: Probability surface based on Mahalanobis distances of 162 "tempered" pastes from the Acomé core group centroid, using the variance-covariance matrix of the total Achiguate group for the calculation of Mahalanobis distances. Numbers in parentheses next to each site indicate number of analyzed specimens from each site.

addition of volcanic ash temper), and comparing raw materials of known provenance to subgroups representing both common and extreme (outlier) compositional profiles found in Achiguate tradition domestic ware,

it is clear that most vessels in this category fall within the range of chemical variation of raw materials found on the Pacific piedmont along the Coyolate, Acomé, and Achiguate Rivers (Figure 8.10).

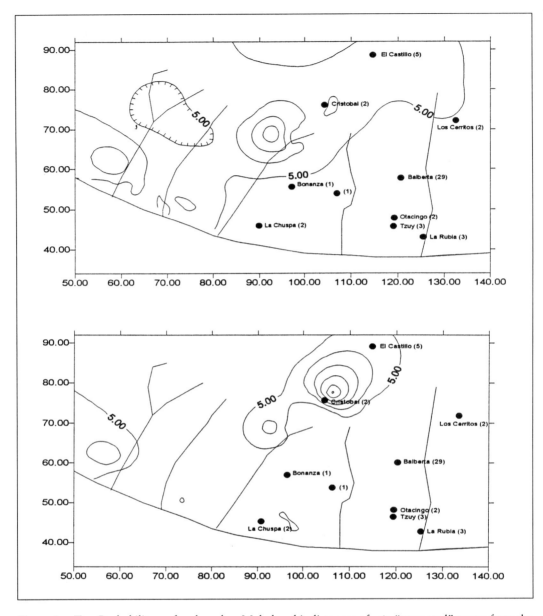

Figure 8.9. Top: Probability surface based on Mahalanobis distances of 162 "tempered" pastes from the Colojate core group centroid (includes Colojate specimens plus specimens of types Achiguate and Acomé that match the Colojate profile). Bottom: Probability surface based on Mahalanobis distances of 162 "tempered" pastes from the Colojate core group centroid, using the variance-covariance matrix of the total Achiguate group in the calculation of Mahalanobis distances. Numbers in parentheses next to each site indicate number of analyzed specimens from each site.

CONCLUSION

A wide range of past human activities involved movement of objects through space, and these activities become susceptible to scientific investigation if sources of artifact raw materials can be identified. Over the past 30 years, chemical characterization has been promoted as a means for identifying sources. Unfortunately, chemical characterization data are expressed in units of elemental con-

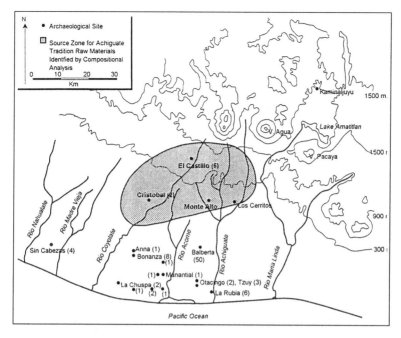

Figure 8.10. Best-bet production zone for Achiguate domestic ware vessels, based on provenance assessment of numerous subgroups and individual specimens.

centration, whereas source locations must be described in terms of geographic coordinate units. This means that the basic methodological task in provenance research is to construct a bridge between the analytical units actually measured and the geographic coordinate units that can be used to describe source locations.

If raw material composition varies predictably through geographic space, then the elemental concentration space produced by chemical characterization can be aligned with geographic space. As with any measuring instrument, the use of chemical characterization to measure geographic space can be evaluated in terms of validity and reliability (Carmines and Zeller 1979). Reliability is compromised by analytical error, within-source variation, and other random sources of error. Validity is compromised by systematic effects, such as changes in ceramic composition during and after manufacture. In ceramic provenance investigations, reliability and validity can be improved through better

raw material sampling, more sophisticated quantitative analysis of the data, and supplementing bulk chemical characterization with microscopic, mineralogical, and microchemical analysis.

Many of the foregoing points have been made before. As demonstrated by the paper by Sayre and Dodson (1957) cited earlier, ceramic provenance researchers have been concerned with validity and reliability assessment for at least the past 40 years. There may be some value, however, in revisiting these issues periodically to see how the basic methodological principles fare and how they can be refined or modified in light of new technical developments and recent case studies.

The main recommendation I would make at the present time is that provenance researchers need to be more explicit and more systematic in their approach to sourcing. What we are trying to measure is a clear, simple archaeological concept: ceramic raw material source. But we measure this concept in-

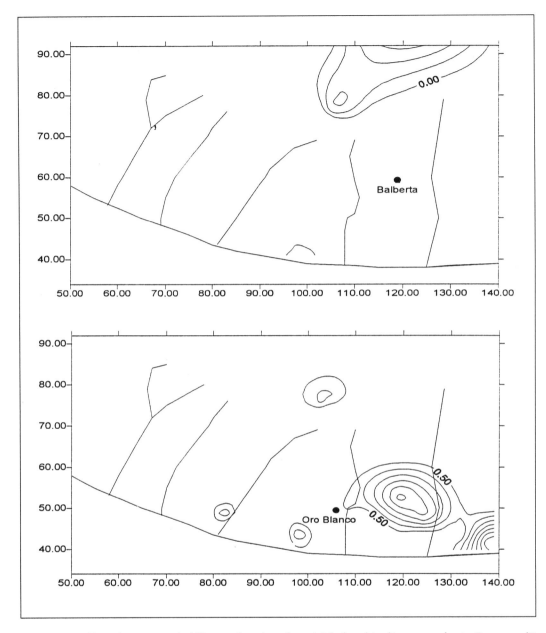

Figure 8.11. Top: Average probability surface based on Mahalanobis distances of 162 "tempered" pastes from Acomé outlier CPA442; the variance-covariance matrix of the total Achiguate group is used in the calculation of Mahalanobis distance. Bottom: Average probability surface based on Mahalanobis distances of 162 "tempered" pastes from Acomé outlier MSZ373; the variance-covariance matrix of the total Achiguate group is used in the calculation of Mahalanobis distance. The overall flatness of both surfaces suggests strongly that these two outlying specimens are derived from somewhere other than the main production zone shown for Achiguate ware vessels.

directly by chemically characterizing the archaeological ceramics of interest. Because our measurements are indirect, we need to evaluate carefully how well the units of the first domain (geographic coordinates) relate to the units of the second domain (ppm, weight percent, etc.). Explicit consideration of these issues in turn highlights the importance of systematic raw material sampling, modeling effects of paste preparation and diagenesis, and developing appropriate techniques of quantitative compositional data analysis.

ACKNOWLEDGMENTS

I am extremely grateful to the National Science Foundation for funding the research discussed above (BNS89-11580 and BNS91-02016). None of the results presented in the example application would have been available without the collaboration of Fred Bove, who initiated provenance research with coastal Guatemalan pottery a decade and a half ago. Among the other individuals who contributed time and effort to the project are Barbara Arroyo, Mike Glascock, Cynthia Hays, Carlos Herman, Enrique Linares, Brenda Lou, Sonia Medrano, Sergio Rodas, and Claudia Wolley. Ann Ramenofsky, Anastasia Steffen, and Alan Sullivan contributed valuable comments on earlier drafts of this chapter. Perhaps my biggest debts are to Ron Bishop, Jim Blackman, Gar Harbottle, and Ed Sayre, who have contributed far more than I to the development of sourcing methods. I assume full responsibility and apologize for any distortions of their ideas that might have crept into this chapter.

Notes

1. Weigand et al. (1977) call this the "provenience postulate." I substitute the alternative spelling "provenance" for "provenience" in order to eliminate confusion that may arise from using the same word to refer to the two distinct concepts, "source" and "archaeological context."

2. While recognizing the potential for these effects to compromise the reliability of obsidian sourcing, it is important to point out that extreme chemical homogeneity within obsidian sources coupled with huge differences between sources make obsidian the epitome of a sourceable material according to the criteria specified by the provenance postulate. As a result, many chemical characterization techniques (e.g., XRF, NAA, and others) have proved capable of differentiating among obsidian sources with a near-100 percent success rate.

3. These natural processes create considerably more compositional variation in clays than in obsidian, so sourcing is expected to be considerably less reliable for ceramics, even before considering the additional effects of manufacture and postdepositional alteration. As mentioned previously, however (note 2), obsidian represents a special, extreme case of reliability in sourcing. Other lithic materials, including chert (Luedtke 1979), turquoise (Weigand et al. 1977), jadeite rock (Lange 1993), and steatite (Truncer 1995), meet the characteristics of a sourceable material (spelled out by the provenance postulate), only much more approximately, and sourcing results are coincidentally much less clear-cut than with obsidian.

4. Firing has been considered a further possible source of chemical change during manufacture, but recent experiments (Cogswell et al. 1996) have failed to identify any changes in concentration of a large number of elements determined by neutron activation analysis through a range of firing temperatures up to 1,100 degrees C.

5. There are obvious exceptions to this generalization about the contrast between ceramic and lithic sourcing. Most obviously, if ceramic workshops have been located, characterization of wasters from the workshops yields a series of known groups to which unknowns may be compared (e.g., Mommsen et al. 1992).

Part IV
Material

9

A View to the Core
Technological Units and Debitage Analysis

ANASTASIA STEFFEN, ELIZABETH J. SKINNER, AND PETER W. AINSWORTH

In this chapter we examine available techniques for the analysis of debitage, the waste products generated during the manufacture of flaked stone artifacts. It is our observation that much of the difficulty in understanding debitage literature derives from the form and structure of the units of analysis. Our goal is to distill and make explicit the underlying organization of debitage analyses. To this end, we focus on the units of observation and inference employed in some of the most widely known and popularly used debitage analysis techniques in North America.

Two themes guide the discussion that follows. The first theme is that lithic debitage analysis necessarily falls under the study of reductive technology. The chapter, then, begins with general discussions of flaked stone as a reductive technology and of units in lithic technology. This examination of the relationship between core reduction and basic descriptive units is designed to provide a foundation for the subsequent evaluation of debitage analyses. The second theme is that the validity of analytical techniques is significantly influenced not only by the content but also by the structure of the units employed. The units created to record observations about debitage have important consequences not only for the character of the data generated but also for research outcomes and, sometimes, for the formulation of future research questions. To identify how this interplay is expressed, we examine the intrinsic unit structure of some of the available debitage analysis techniques and evaluate the validity of the techniques in light of unit structure. We have not attempted a review of all techniques, nor a comprehensive guide to the debitage analysis literature (for a recent review, see Shott 1994). Rather, our aim is to provide guideposts so that individual researchers can select techniques that are adequate, appropriate, and feasible for their research. In essence, we examine the method behind the techniques, a necessary first step in evaluation.

FLAKED STONE TECHNOLOGY AS REDUCTIVE TECHNOLOGY

We define technology as "the methods and materials used to manufacture a product." The concept of technology can be broken down into three subdivisions: reductive, additive, and altered. In a reductive technology, products are manufactured solely through the removal or subtraction of material. In contrast, additive and altered technologies include the manufacture of materials through the appending, joining, combining, or compositional alteration of like and unlike materials. Ceramic technology is an obvious example of an additive/altered technology, and lithic technology is an obvious example of a reductive technology (except for lithic heat treatment, which is an altered technology).

In a reductive technology only a single

kind of material is manipulated at a time—in fact, only a single item or mass is manipulated. Furthermore, the only manipulation is the removal of material from that mass (i.e., the core). Finally, the manipulation of that mass is simple in mechanical terms: fracture is the single mechanical process involved. Examples of fracture include flaking, pecking, grinding, abrading, and polishing, with each distinguished by the decrease, respectively, in the size of the fracture. This discussion focuses on the manufacture of stone artifacts through the control of relatively large fractures (i.e., "flaking"). Therefore, we use the term "lithic technology" to refer specifically to flaked stone technology.

Identifying a technology as reductive has several implications for the archaeological units we create to investigate that technology. Given that the archaeological record is dominated by bits and fragments, the units created for objects are frequently constructed to investigate the whole by examining the pieces.[1] In a reductive technology, what does the artifact as a basic archaeological unit represent about some larger whole? What information on technology is contained in the artifact, and how does this compare with artifacts of an additive or altered technology?

Consider the differences between a ceramic sherd and a lithic flake. A sherd is a broken piece of a final product (e.g., a vessel), and as an object, the sherd is created by breakage, or failure, after the completion of manufacture. While a sherd contains information on the materials and manipulations used in manufacture, it represents the final product. In contrast, a flake is rarely a portion of some other final product. As an object, a flake is created as part of the manufacture, not the fragmentation, of a product. The flake itself may serve as a final product, but does not necessarily contain any information about any other product. Thus, the larger whole that a flake represents is not a product, but the manufacture process itself. A flake contains a unique record of the process of manufacture employed in its creation. This remarkably detailed record of the lithic manufacture process is abundant and

ubiquitous, and there is no similar artifactual record in ceramic assemblages (except in very rare cases).

It is the simplicity of manufacture that gives debitage assemblages such information potential: reductive technologies leave a record of the manufacturing process on the pieces removed. A flake, unless substantially modified after detachment, retains information on the portion of the core from which it was removed, at the point when it was removed. This information includes not only the morphology of the core prior to removal but also the manipulation that resulted in fracture and detachment. In contrast, the core contains a record of its own final morphology and a record of the final series of removals from the it. The core and removals together contain a complete record of the reduction events.

The simplicity of reductive manufacture has an even more basic implication: reduction determines almost all empirical aspects of these artifacts. Even if pertinent research goals are not explicitly technological, it is hardly possible to describe a piece of debitage without some reference to results of reduction. Indeed, we rely on the redundant characteristics of conchoidal fracture to identify a flake as an artifact rather than merely as a rock. Most dimensions of morphological variation in a piece of debitage describe the consequences of the reductive method of manufacture. These dimensions include the host of "flake characteristics," such as interior versus exterior surfaces, relative thickness or width, platform, terminus, waves of force, flake scars, cortex, etc., as well as the more fundamental measurements of size, shape, and weight. It follows from the identification of flaked stone technology as reductive technology that technological considerations be integral to virtually all of the units we use to describe lithic artifacts. Similar technological observations should be made on all items in the assemblage if a goal is to generate technological data. Consistency in analysis should also extend throughout the unit structures discussed in this chapter. Thus, debitage units should accord with lithic technology units, which, in turn, should be consistent with units of a reductive technology. Viewing flaked stone technology in terms of reductive technology provides an important perspective for understanding and improving the internal coherence among the units we use to describe lithic artifacts.

UNITS IN LITHIC TECHNOLOGY

While particular research questions pursued vary widely, all lithic analyses investigate variation in reduction. That is, unless only raw material characteristics are described, all technological inferences pursued about lithic artifacts will be built on descriptions of reductive variation. Thus, the broad goal of lithic technology research is to make inferences about the kinds of manufacture that produce lithic assemblages and to investigate and/or explain the variation observed in and among lithic assemblages.

Basic observational units designed to measure this variation should be created in terms of reduction. First, they should adhere to guidelines for unambiguous archaeological unit construction. That is, they need to be clearly defined, mutually exclusive, and employ only criteria that can be directly observed. Second, these descriptive units should be explicit technological units. Since nearly all of the relevant variation is a result of reduction, the adequacy of lithic technology descriptions will depend on how well the observational units accord with basic tenets of reductive technology.

Basic units are best defined with simple terminology (i.e., encompassing the fullest range of variation while incorporating the fewest number of assumptions). The key *technological* distinction in lithic artifacts is between cores and removals. We define a *core* as a nucleus from which material has been removed. *Removals* are defined as pieces that have been removed from a core and that themselves show no evidence of further postdetachment reduction.[2] These two categories are mutually exclusive and encompass the entirety of material resulting from reduction. At the minimum, there are two pieces that compose a lithic manufacture as-

semblage: a core and a removal. And at a maximum, regardless of how large, complex, and variable a reductive manufacture assemblage may be, these two units describe the entirety of lithic materials represented with the same amount of sufficiency as when the assemblage contains only the two pieces, core and removal. Distinguishing further technological variation will proceed from specific research goals.

It is our perception that lithic technology studies do not usually investigate the full range of reduction variation. Many North American debitage analyses are driven by implicit emphases. In particular, there is a research focus on biface production that has influenced not only the direction of research but also the basic units used. This narrowing of the range of core reduction variation to be investigated may be a reasonable and appropriate research strategy, but should be a methodological decision that is explicit in the design of research.

This "biface bias" has developed as a result of several factors. Paleo-Indian studies have been especially influential because the Paleo-Indian archaeological record, with its remarkable, finely executed bifacial forms, captured the fascination of North American archaeologists early on (e.g., Roberts 1935b, 1937b). Later, these bifaces served as a powerful stimulus for the growth of flintknapping both as avocation and as research strategy (see Johnson 1978; also Flenniken 1984). For chronological goals, Clovis and Folsom bifaces have served as exceptional temporal markers for Paleo-Indian (see LeTourneau, this volume), and have thus become paragons in the typological dominance of bifacial forms over nonbifacial lithic materials employed in the construction of culture historical sequences throughout North American prehistory.

Lithic research in the 1970s and 1980s focused on processual questions that led to the creation of production trajectory and reduction sequence models (e.g., Bradley 1975; Callahan 1979; Collins 1975; Flenniken and Ozbun 1988; Muto 1971; Young and Bonnichsen 1985). These models were fre-

		FUNCTION / USE	
		Product (tool)	**By-product** (non-tool)
T E C H N O L O G Y	**Core**	*biface projectile point*	*blade core*
	Removal	*utilized flake*	*waste flake*

Figure 9.1. Intersection of technological units and functional units; entries in each cell are examples.

quently, although not exclusively (e.g., Bordes and Crabtree 1969; Crabtree 1968; Sheets 1975), focused on biface production. Bifacial reduction is heavily represented in the lithic experimentation that developed subsequent to this production modeling (Magne 1985:25). Finally, biface production is central to much of the research concerned with the organization of technology (see review article by Nelson 1991). This research, inspired in large part by the concepts of expedient and curated technologies proposed by Binford (1977, 1979b), but now substantially augmented and transformed, is currently one of the most popular for lithic studies as applied to well-defined research goals (e.g., Bamforth 1991b; Bleed 1986; Jeske 1992; Kelly 1988; Parry and Kelly 1987; and most recently, an entire edited volume [Carr 1994]).

The problem we see with the research emphasis on bifaces is that it has contributed to a conflation of technology and function in the construction and use of basic lithic units. A ubiquitous example can be seen in the conventional usage of the terms "core" and "tool," especially when used in the context of distinguishing between "core reduction" and "tool production." These seemingly neutral phrases are rich in information content, as a simple breakdown of the phrases demonstrates. First, reduction is contrasted to production—a distinction that makes little sense in a reductive technology. Second, core

is distinguished from tool—a contrast that is not technological, but rather pertains to artifact use.

Our concern with these phrases is more than semantic: the basic terminology employed in archaeological lithic studies specifies our most fundamental units, and ultimately can influence our approaches to research. What on the surface is little more than a naming convention actually belies a set of units constructed without accord to reductive technology. When the phrases "core reduction" and "tool production" are used in contrast to each other, they effectively serve to specify the range of reduction variation that will be considered in a study and to what detail the variation will be examined. That is, tool production is the focus—where "tool" actually means biface. All other variation in reduction is subsumed under the "other" category called core reduction. That is, while a category called core reduction should encompass all variation in lithic manufacture, in this dichotomy, tool production is highlighted and all other kinds of reduction are treated as generic.

Deciding whether to call a biface a core or a tool should be a methodological problem solved by selecting or creating units relevant to the specified research goals.[3] As defined above, the central technological distinction is between cores and removals. In contrast, research goals that are functional require units that are defined in terms of use, not manufacture, because the basic question is whether an item was used as a tool. Therefore, the key *functional* distinction is between product and by-product. *By-products* are items that have no evidence of postmanufacture manipulation (use); *products* are items that do. These categories are mutually exclusive, defined wholly in terms of use, and include only properties that are empirically observable. Intent, manufacturing goals, and object form are not necessary criteria.

Figure 9.1 shows these units (core and removal, product and by-product) as dimensions of variability. Clearly, core and tool are units derived from different research domains. Cores can be by-products or products; by-products can be cores or removals. To assume otherwise is to conflate technological with functional research goals. Further, this blurring of functional and technological units betrays a tendency to conceive of artifact description in terms of the products of manufacture rather than the process of manufacture—a perspective appropriate for an additive technology but not for a reductive technology. The biface bias is the archetype of this prejudice.

UNITS IN DEBITAGE ANALYSIS

In this section we incorporate the perspective on lithic technology as reductive technology to describe the unit structure of some of the most popular and widely known debitage analysis techniques used in North America. Deciding which technique or techniques to use requires evaluating the validity and reliability of a technique as well as considering pragmatic factors such as time and labor efficiency. How well a technique performs within each of these areas of consideration depends in large part on how the observational (analytic) units are structured. Thus, we provide the following descriptions of unit structure, with a focus on scale, as important background for understanding the strengths and weaknesses of the techniques as research tools.

We have grouped debitage analysis techniques into three categories according to the scale of observation employed. From least to most inclusive, these three categories are attribute, item, and aggregate. Scale has two important properties: inclusiveness and resolution (see chapter 1). Inclusiveness pertains to the scope or range of phenomena for which units are constructed (Dunnell 1971:145–47), and resolution pertains to the specificity obtained. The relationship between these properties is inverse; as inclusiveness increases, resolution decreases. Inclusiveness determines the breadth of information possible at a given scale, while resolution determines the amount or detail of that information (Figure 9.2). Thus, simply identifying the scale of the units used in a given debitage analysis technique will provide a good deal of information on the form of the data that will be produced.

The use of scale-defined categories is familiar in debitage analysis literature. Our categories are similar, for example, to Ahler's distinction between individual flake and flake aggregate analyses (e.g., 1989b:86–87) and Shott's distinction (1994) between formal and mass analyses (the latter term coined originally in Ahler 1972 [as cited in Ahler 1989b:95]). Here, however, we specify three rather than two scales; our two lower scales, attribute and item, subdivide their single lower scale.

The three categories—attribute, item, and aggregate—serve to organize the descriptions that follow. We explore the role of scale in determining the kind of information gathered using these observational units. We also make note of the implications of scale for several practical considerations (Table 9.1). These are identified as difficulty, expediency, reliability, flexibility, and "generalizability" (Amick et al. 1989:4).

ATTRIBUTE ANALYSES

In attribute analysis, the analytic units are the individual attributes (properties and variables) of removals recorded for each specimen. These techniques record observations at the lowest scale of inclusiveness. The attributes selected can number 1 to n, and usually include some combination of variables and properties of raw material, flake mor-

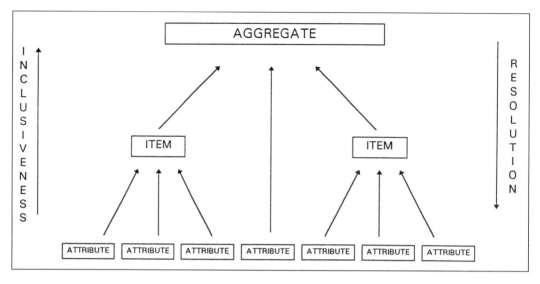

Figure 9.2. Scales of observation used in debitage analyses.

phology, and size. A range of continuous and categorical measurements (i.e., nominal, ordinal, interval, and ratio) may be employed.

Attribute scale analyses were instrumental in the early development of systematic debitage analysis in the 1970s. These early efforts (e.g., Knudson 1973; Phagan 1976; Wilmsen 1970) were exploratory and creative, producing lengthy attribute inventories. The goal was exhaustively to identify attributes that could potentially measure relationships between the control of fracture and patterning in characteristics observable on flakes. The subsequent development of attribute analysis has tended toward refining rather than augmenting early attribute lists, with a pronounced trend toward reducing the number of attributes recorded.

As with all techniques we consider, the inclusiveness and resolution of attribute analysis play a significant role in determining the kind of information created. Because the units in attribute analyses are defined at the least inclusive scale, the resolution of information is extremely high; the observations recorded provide the most detailed information of all the analysis techniques. Usually, the data are generated in a form that maintains a link between specimen and observations, which allows any combination or re-

combination of attributes to be examined by specimen. Thus, attribute analyses are capable of recording large amounts of information (depending on the number of attributes included) and are highly flexible because, through the selection of individual attributes, they can be precisely tailored to research goals.

This flexibility has certain practical implications as well (see Table 9.1). The independence of attributes allows attribute analyses to be highly generalizable; once generated, data can be used for purposes beyond those defined for the original analysis. These strengths of attribute analysis are also its greatest weakness, especially in practical terms: recording high resolution information results in a technique that is time-consuming and labor-intensive. The difficulty of application (i.e., the degree of familiarity with debitage morphology required to make accurate observations) varies with the actual attributes selected. Once again the flexibility of the technique serves the analyst: it is possible for inexperienced analysts to include only those attributes with which they are familiar.

ITEM (FLAKE) TYPOLOGIES

Techniques at the item level of observation record information in a single observational

TABLE 9.1

Practical Considerations of Debitage Analyses at Differing Scales

INCLUSIVENESS ←→ RESOLUTION

| | Attribute Analysis | Technological Types | Flake Typologies | Cortical Categories | Mass Analysis |
	Multiple Attributes[a]		Flake Completeness		Size Grading
DIFFICULTY: making observations —Expertise required	Variable	High	Low	Low	Low
EXPEDIENCY: creating data —Rapidity of observation	Low	Medium	Medium	Medium	High
RELIABILITY: assessing data —Replicability of observations	Variable	Low	Medium	Medium	High
FLEXIBILITY: manipulating data —Resolution/Amount of information	High	Medium	Medium	Low	Low
GENERALIZABILITY: obtaining data —Broadness of utility	High	Medium	Medium	Medium	Medium

[a] Number and kind of attributes significantly affect difficulty, expediency, and reliability.

step. The analytic units are item categories, usually "characteristic flakes," or individual specimens with specified groups of distinctive attributes. In contrast to attribute analyses, item (flake) typologies record attribute clusters not by attribute but as they co-occur by item.

We recognize three main kinds of item (flake) typologies: cortical categories, technological types, and flake-completeness categories. *Cortical categories* are the simplest: only a single attribute, dorsal cortex coverage, is observed or measured for sorting items into ordinal categories. The historical popularity of cortex categories is likely due to the ease of application (given that only one observation is required) as well as to historical precedence (it is one of the oldest of all debitage units, originally introduced by White in 1963, and subsequently subject to numerous reinterpretations [see discussion by Sullivan and Rozen 1985:755–57]). Because these are essentially single-attribute categories, we do not discuss cortical categories in any further detail.

Technological types are much more complex than cortical categories: they combine multiple observations and require considerable familiarity with debitage morphology. They are most often used by analysts with direct training in the technique. Flenniken's types (1981; Flenniken and Ozbun 1988) focus on variation in flake morphology that is indicative of removal during various portions of modeled reduction trajectories. This focus on sequential variation is readily apparent in the names used for the categories: primary and secondary decortication flakes, early bifacial thinning, late bifacial thinning, edge preparation flakes, and so forth. Another example of a technological typology is provided by Ahler (1986, 1989a; also described in detail by Root [1992]). These types focus on different kinds of reduction, again evident in the type names: bipolar flakes, bifacial thinning flakes, hard hammer flakes, freehand flakes, and so forth.

Finally, the third kind of flake typology is *flake-completeness* as introduced by Sullivan and Rozen (1985). Their categories—complete flakes, broken flakes, flake fragments, and debris—are based not on technologically defined attributes but rather on attributes designed to measure flake breakage. Sullivan and Rozen explicitly designed this new kind of flake typology as an alternative to cortical categories and technological flake types. As is discussed later, the introduction of this typology, as well as the explicitness with which it addressed unit concerns, touched off debates and stimulated research that explored many of the implications of unit structure in debitage analysis addressed here.

To summarize the item-scale units, flake types are constructed at the middle level of inclusiveness and resolution. Compared to attribute analyses, detail is diminished because information is recorded as grouped rather than as individual attributes. Typically, the amount of information is lessened as well because fewer observations are made per item; cortical categories are at the extreme low end with only one attribute recorded, the flake-completeness types are intermediate, and the technological types are at the high end. When flake typologies are used as a sorting procedure, and information is not recorded by individual (i.e., numbered) specimen, it becomes impossible to manipulate information except by frequency of flake type.

However, the use of item-scale and combined-attribute observations affords significant practical advantages. Most important, it is possible to record a relatively large amount of technological information in a manner that is, potentially, much more rapid than for attribute analysis. Using flake types can be so efficient that they are well suited to in-field analyses. However, determining whether this gain in efficiency is worth the loss in resolution of information requires a consideration of validity, not simply practicality.

AGGREGATE (MASS) ANALYSES

Techniques at the highest scale of inclusiveness are those that record observations on entire aggregates of debitage. Information is recorded for groups of debitage rather than for individual items. Thus, unlike techniques at the two lower scales, mass analyses record attributes of an aggregate rather than attributes of an item (flake). Aggregate analyses vary in complexity. Ahler's work (e.g., 1986, 1989a, 1989b) represents both the most complex and the most comprehensive application of mass analysis, while Patterson's work (e.g., 1990) exemplifies a less complicated formulation. Despite differences, the sorting of debitage aggregates by size-grade is common to all aggregate analyses. The analytic units are frequency counts of items by size-grade and summary weights of the size-graded subaggregates. Given the high level of inclusiveness, the resolution is necessarily low: the information obtained includes only a small number of attributes, such as count or weight by subaggregate.

The great advantage of an analytic unit defined at the highest level of inclusiveness is that it enables extremely rapid artifact processing. Where only size is recorded, entire assemblages can be processed in a single step. Further refining of the information obtained—for example, by separating debitage by raw material—adds to the time required. Because the main observations are made by using an external instrument (e.g., graded sieves, balance) rather than human perception, the technique requires almost no expertise, employs unit definitions that are explicitly defined and standardized, and therefore is presumed to be highly reliable. Clearly, however, the amount of information recorded is reduced to only a few attributes. In contrast to attribute analyses and flake typologies, there is no direct observation of flake morphology.

To summarize the three scales of debitage analysis, attribute analyses record the most information and are the most flexible because information is contained in packages that can be recombined and manipulated most readily. However, recording all this information is costly in terms of time and labor. Item (flake) types occupy an intermediate position of information content, time required, and flexibility of data manipulation. Aggregate (mass) analyses are the most rapid for processing debitage, but the amount of information obtained is quite small.

Describing the scale of observations used in the various techniques makes clear the determining role that inclusiveness and resolution play in the form of information recorded. In practical terms, these aspects of unit structure are responsible for the inverse relationship between speed of data recording and the amount of information recorded. The balance between speed and information is, of course, what is described by the term "efficiency." However, it is important to distinguish between efficiency in practical terms and the adequacy of analysis for specified research goals. For determining the validity of a technique for producing sufficient and relevant data, there is no *a priori* "most efficient" technique. The assessment of validity, or research performance, requires a more complex evaluation.

EVALUATING DEBITAGE ANALYSIS TECHNIQUES

In describing the unit structure of the various techniques, we examined how structure determines the form of information obtained. An evaluation of the utility and adequacy of a technique for specified research applications builds on these descriptions and entails considering how inferences can be constructed using the information gathered. In unit terms, creating inferences involves constructing synthetic units. Just as the structure of analytic units determines the kind of information, the structure of synthetic units constrains the kind of inferences possible.

For the remainder of this chapter, we explore how the relationship between analytic and synthetic units affects the validity of the debitage analysis techniques. For each of the debitage analysis categories, we discuss how analytic unit structure affects validity and examine implications of how synthetic units are constructed from analytic units. We begin with a brief summary of the role of units and the terms of unit evaluation.

ANALYTIC AND SYNTHETIC UNITS

Analytic units are the observational units used to describe empirical properties being measured. Synthetic units organize these analytic observations into inferential aggregates. Thus, "analytic" and "synthetic" describe two different roles that units play in a research design. Several relationships exist between analytic and synthetic units (see Dunnell 1971; also chapter 1). First, analytic units are used for observation, while synthetic units are used in inference. Second, when strictly defined, there is a hierarchical relationship: synthetic units are constructed at a higher scale of inclusiveness than the analytic units from which they are formed. Third, the role of a given unit is relative: the same unit may be analytic in one study while synthetic in another. Problems arise when this swapping of roles occurs in the same analysis.

VALIDITY AND RELIABILITY
Validity and reliability describe two distinct realms of unit evaluation. Validity concerns the relevance of units to the goals of research, while reliability describes the consistency and replicability of measurement (Amick et al. 1989; Carmines and Zeller 1979). The focus of our discussion is entirely on validity.[4] The contrast with reliability, however, is a useful illustration of validity. Reliability describes the redundancy of actual measures or observations, whereas validity describes the degree to which those measures are relevant. Reliability concerns the performance of an instrument in repeated trials, under varying conditions, or with different investigators. Validity addresses the selection of the instrument, and the units that compose it, for specified research goals.

The broad perspective of core reduction, as outlined above, provides the context in which we evaluate the validity of debitage analysis techniques. To restate, the primary purpose of a debitage analysis technique is to describe variation in debitage that was produced by variation in core reduction. Here we consider validity by evaluating how well a debitage analysis technique describes reductive variation. Given the descriptions of unit structure provided earlier, we assess the effect of that analytic structure for the construction and performance of synthetic, or inferential, units.

For example, debitage analyses historically have been dominated by the investigation of three sources of variation in reduction: force application (e.g., hard versus soft hammer, percussion versus pressure), reduction stage or intensity, and technique or kind of core reduction (e.g., bifacial, bipolar, blade, and generalized core reduction). Our discussion of validity pertains to all of these research goals: we examine how the organization of observational units facilitates the empirical description of debitage used for making inferences about these sources of core reduction variation.

Throughout the development of research in lithic technology, experimentation has been the most important means for establishing validity. First, experimentation provides an invaluable opportunity for observing descriptive aspects of debitage that later are codified as analytic units. This productive relationship between experimentation and unit creation is possible in part because of the relative simplicity of reductive technology and the constancy of fracture mechanics.

Experimentation is also used to test the validity of specific techniques.[5] This second use of experimentation has more potential for problems because it involves synthetic units of inference in addition to analytic units of description. The difficulties associated with this complex use of experimentation are well illustrated in debitage attribute analyses, to be taken up in the next section. Thus, we turn now to the evaluation of specific techniques, beginning at the highest resolution.

ATTRIBUTE ANALYSES
The central validity concern for attribute analyses is the selection of attributes to record. Indeed, this is the most fundamental concern for all debitage analyses. In spite of, or perhaps as a result of, the many studies conducted at this scale of observation, there is no consensus on which flake attributes are presumed relevant for describing variation in reduction or on which attributes have been demonstrated to perform well (Ahler 1989b; Shott 1994). As noted above, experimentation has played an important role in the de-

velopment of attribute analysis, where the primary means for "discovering" and testing for relevancy has been through the use of controlled and replicative experimentation. Controlled experimentation has tended to focus on the relevance of single or few attributes of debitage morphology (e.g., Dibble and Whittaker 1981; Speth 1981), while replicative experimentation has frequently examined numerous attributes, including both morphology and size attributes (e.g., Amick et al. 1988; Baumler and Downum 1989; Henry et al. 1976; Ingbar et al. 1989; Magne 1985; Magne and Pokotylo 1981; Tomka 1989).

Given the potential for generating overwhelmingly large and complex data sets when multiple attributes are used, it makes sense that multivariate statistical analyses were introduced early in the development of attribute analysis (e.g., Burton 1980; Chandler and Ware 1976), and have become increasingly common (e.g., Amick et al. 1988; Odell 1989; Root 1992). In brief, the statistical techniques are used to group relevant attributes or to discriminate relevant from ineffectual or redundant attributes. Although these studies have obtained mixed results for creating effective attribute clusters, they have provided a mass of individual observations that are useful as a basis for the selection of attributes. Thus, experimentation has succeeded in contributing to the most important challenge for attribute-scale analyses: deciding what aspects of debitage variation to describe.

The use of multivariate grouping procedures and experimental replication to validate analysis techniques illustrates a complex unit problem. When experimentally replicated debitage is used, the aggregates of debitage represent some specified "bounding," or subset, of reductive variation that is focused by research interest. For example, the debitage aggregate could represent all of the debitage produced during some defined stage of reduction or the debitage produced from the reduction of a core from beginning to end. For the sake of simplicity, we call these replication aggregates "reduction sets." The

problem lies not in using the experimental reduction set as a unit within which variation is examined, but in employing it as a conceptual or statistical "control unit." Multivariate classification procedures, such as discriminant analysis, require that unknown items be compared to a group of known items that was used to create the statistical definitions for group membership; when applied in experimental debitage analysis, the reduction set (or sets) serves as that "known." We are concerned with the validity of units constructed in this manner. The use of reduction sets as control groups effectively specifies that the bounded group designated as the control (e.g., all of the debitage produced during a bifacial reduction stage) is the targeted synthetic unit. That is, if we construct or evaluate our descriptive units by comparison to experimental assemblages, then we are implicitly designating these reduction subsets—and unmixed assemblages—as our desired synthetic (inferential, interpretive) unit.

We emphasize that our concern is not with the sufficiency of the reduction set as a behavioral analog nor with its equivalence to archaeological assemblages subject to formation processes unrelated to manufacture (e.g., Ingbar et al. 1989). Rather, the use of the reduction set as a synthetic unit presumes that our unit design specifies *that aggregate* as the scale of our synthetic unit. The eventual goal of experimental analyses is to make inferences about archaeological deposits, and it is unclear how this unit structure can be valid, given the technological mixing contained in most archaeological assemblages. The mixing is not a problem to be overcome. Rather, technological mixing within assemblages is an intrinsic part of the archaeological record—our units should reflect this.

The issues of how experimental debitage units should be constructed and used and how technological mixing within assemblages should be viewed in the design of research are relevant not only in attribute analyses but also for experimental debitage studies defined at all scales of observation. These concerns are highlighted in attribute analyses because the use of statistical procedures lends an air of objectivity to the process and also because attribute analyses are often used to inform or test debitage analysis techniques at the higher scales of item and aggregate.

Technological Flake Types

Two of the most frequent criticisms of technological typologies are (1) they are subjective and unstandardized, and (2) they suffer from inferential biases (see discussion in Sullivan and Rozen 1985; also Ahler 1989b; Ingbar et al. 1989). Both of these problems stem directly from the unit structure. Thus, considering units identifies the source of the problems and also suggests potential remedies. In the first case, the cause is the form and definition of the analytic units; in the second case, the difficulties arise due to overlap between analytic and synthetic units. We take up each problem in turn.

Flake types are the analytic units used in technological flake typologies. Usually these units were created subjectively from the recognition (i.e., discovery) of patterned variation in debitage observed from replication experimentation (e.g., Flenniken 1981). The primary goal of unit description was to capture the important characteristics for group membership—creating precise definitions was less important because training rather than documentation served as the primary means for sharing type identification. Thus, at their worst, flake types are ambiguously defined. They are polythetic empirical groupings that highlight modal tendencies rather than rigorously specifying the criteria of group membership.

Fortunately, this problem can be easily corrected: all that is required is improvement in how the units are defined. Technological types should be constructed using explicit and standardized definitions that systematically and comprehensively specify the attributes that belong with each unit. The types need to be mutually exclusive with regard to the combination of attributes necessary for membership, yet still be free to vary for other attributes. While experience will always be important for effective identification of attributes, explicit definition will make the data produced from typological analyses more generalizable. Recent work with technological types demonstrates this kind of improvement in the clarity and adequacy of type definition, as exemplified by Root's type definitions and lucid discussion of technological typology (1992:80–89).

The second problem area concerns how the flake types are used in inference. Specifically, analytic units and synthetic units become merged, creating bias in data collection as well as interpretation. Here it is useful to consider some of Sullivan's and Rozen's criticisms (1985) of traditional typologies by restating their arguments in terms of unit structure.

First, Sullivan and Rozen argue that analytic units for describing variation in debitage "should not be linked *a priori* to specific conclusions about lithic technology" (1985: 758). In other words, units in debitage *analysis* should describe variation in core reduction without automatically synthesizing the implications of that description. Second, they propose that inferences about technological origins of debitage should be made at the scale of assemblage rather than individual item. When considered in terms of unit structure, the latter point argues that where analytic units are defined at the lower scale of item, the synthetic units should be constructed at the higher scale of aggregate. In other words, when the relationship between analytic and synthetic units becomes blurred both in definition and in scale, technological typologies are then structured so that the unit of inference is employed as the unit of observation (Shott 1994:77). The technological type "biface thinning flake" serves as an example. Clearly, the name of the unit identifies the kind of core reduction that produced the removal. If the research goal of the analysis includes identifying whether bifacial reduction took place, then typing a specimen also answers the technological question being asked.

The potential for circularity in logic

(Teltser 1991:366) undermines the descriptive capacity of technological types and contributes significantly to their interpretive "subjectivity."[6] Thus, technological types may not be valid descriptive units if applied to debitage derived from kinds of core reduction that are outside of the range considered when the types were originally constructed. For example, the performance of most technological typologies for describing removals generated during bipolar reduction must be questioned if this kind of reduction was not originally considered.

The solution to the conflation of observation and inference in technological typology may not be easily obtained. Much of the inferential power of technological types is achieved as a result of their subjective derivation, which plays a significant role in the "directness" of their link to technological variation (Ahler 1989b:87; Root 1992:88). Despite the existence of methodological problems, technological types do seem to have validity for identifying distinctive patterns of attributes that correspond with the differences in reduction targeted in specific research studies (e.g., Hayden and Hutchings 1989; Magne 1985). Experimental research, especially if broadened to include a wider range of core reduction variation, is one obvious avenue for evaluating the type definitions and refining the selection of attributes included in those definitions.

Flake-Completeness Typology
Sullivan's and Rozen's flake typology (1985) was constructed explicitly to overcome problem areas identified for technological and cortical types. The flake-completeness typology offered certain improvements in unit structure and content: explicit and non-polythetic analytic unit definitions, a simple and unambiguous specification of criteria for sorting debitage (including only criteria that describe morphological attributes relating to flake breakage), and the specification of the scale of both the analytic and synthetic units. Their typology made an important contribution to the development of debitage analysis: their proposal brought unit

concerns to the forefront of debitage analysis and stimulated a wave of evaluation. Indeed, no other debitage analysis technique has received such swift and focused response. Their typology was immediately questioned on theoretical and inferential grounds (Amick and Mauldin, eds. 1989; Ensor and Roemer 1989), and has been subjected to a number of experimental applications (e.g., Baumler and Downum 1989; Bradbury and Carr 1995; Ingbar et al. 1989; Kuijt et al. 1995; Mauldin and Amick 1989; Prentiss and Romanski 1989; Tomka 1989; many of these experimental studies appear together in an edited volume [Amick and Mauldin, eds. 1989] that was compiled largely in response to Sullivan's and Rozen's proposal of the typology).

This outpouring of critical and constructive response to the flake-completeness typology explored or directly challenged the validity of the technique for describing debitage variation relevant to core reduction variation. The intensity of the response was due to the lack of empirically grounded, warranting arguments for validity in Sullivan's and Rozen's original presentation. In other words, Sullivan and Rozen did not satisfactorily explain why their breakage categories should bear any relationship to the reduction variation they targeted (i.e., a comparison of core reduction and tool production). The sparse attribute descriptions included in their category definitions further exacerbated the problem.

Despite these criticisms, Sullivan and Rozen accomplished an important part of their purpose in proposing an alternative to the traditional typologies: they offered a typology that was significantly better organized and rigorous in structure. The unit structure of the flake-completeness typology is explicit and employs an internally coherent set of criteria that are mutually exclusive and encompass the full range of expressed variation within the dimensions employed. The specification of the criteria is explicit, and thus designed to facilitate objectivity and standardization among researchers. Furthermore, their identification of the scalar relationship between the analytic and synthetic units and the specification of synthetic units at the scale of assemblage are thoughtful contributions.[7]

To return to a comparison with the other item (flake) types, it appears that the flake-completeness typology, in solving many of the concerns raised for traditional typologies, abandoned many of the strengths of technological typology. Overall, technological typologies were explicitly derived from and supported by empirical observation of debitage variation based on experimental replication and fracture mechanics research. In contrast, the flake-completeness typology was introduced with little prior external validation. Interestingly, the experimentation generated in response to the typology has provided a base of empirical evaluation that, now, approaches or exceeds other techniques.

An obvious way to maximize the benefits of each kind of typology is to combine the explicitness and strict adherence to observation contained in the structure of flake-completeness typology with the technological content and multidimensional approach of technological typology. Much of the ease, and part of the "objectivity," of Sullivan's and Rozen's typology results from the paucity of information recorded during the sorting process. In this regard, their approach yields little more information than do the cortical categories. The decision whether to employ their typology as it was originally formulated must take into consideration this limited information potential.

AGGREGATE (MASS) ANALYSES

The two most significant concerns about the validity of aggregate-scale analyses have been identified and discussed by Ahler (1989b: 87–93). The first is the "potential lack of clear linkage between the data sets or variables recorded and behavioral variation in the archaeological record" (1989b:88–89). The second pertains to the validity of applying the technique to mixed assemblages. Clearly, the first concern is the issue central to the validity of all debitage analyses. Ahler has em-

phasized it for mass analysis because the relationship of the attributes measured in mass analysis to the subsequent construction of synthetic units is neither intuitively apparent nor derived from the more customary item- and attribute-scale observations. The explicit discussion that Ahler offers for developing an "explanation for why mass analysis or aggregate analysis *works*" (1989b:89, emphasis in original) contributes substantially to establishing abstract and empirical validity for this technique.

To paraphrase Ahler's points, the general ideas used to support the validity of mass analyses consider how the nature of reductive technology pertains to size and weight as technological units and how variation in reduction (specifically, load application) can be inferred from relatively simple combinations of measurements (of size and shape) undertaken on debitage aggregates. Clearly, these arguments for the validity of the units derive explicitly from a view of lithic technology as reductive technology. Evaluating whether the particulars of these arguments are sufficiently tested or supported by the empirical observations generated can be undertaken by examining the data that he presents (as well as others, e.g., Baumler and Downum 1989; Patterson 1982, 1990; Root 1992; Stahle and Dunn 1982; see also Shott [1994] for a lengthy discussion of specific aggregate analyses).

The second validity concern, the performance of the technique for examining mixed assemblages, is considered by Ahler to be "relatively unique to the aggregate approach" (1989b:89). We do not agree, for we consider the problem of mixed assemblages to be of similar import for all the analyses undertaken at all scales. What is unique is the relationship of aggregate-scale analytic units to aggregate-scale synthetic units: they are constructed at the same scale, and no hierarchical relationship pertains. An important result of constructing units at this high scale of inclusiveness is that it has required researchers to more carefully consider the implications of assemblage as the inferential unit. As discussed above for attribute analyses, use of experimental reduction sets as analogs for archaeological assemblages is problematic when attempting to establish the validity of debitage analysis techniques; these problems are simply more obvious for aggregate-scale analyses.

CONCLUSIONS

Our goal has been to clarify the organization of debitage analysis to enable an evaluation of the techniques for determining appropriateness for technological research goals further specified in individual research programs. Both validity and practicality are relevant concerns for selecting a technique best suited to the application. Our discussion should make it plain why there is no best technique, since these decisions must incorporate a variety of considerations.

If there were no practical concerns, then detailed attribute analyses would offer the greatest potential for information recovery since all other techniques use units that can be formed from attribute-scale descriptions. Probably some combination of the techniques will characterize the most productive and practical approach for each research application.

We initially identified two themes, the relevance of reductive technology to unit construction, and the influence of unit structure in the validity of debitage analysis techniques. We examined the latter theme by describing the unit structure and then by demonstrating the role of that structure in key issues of validity for each set of techniques. Two issues emerge as central to validity for all of the analysis techniques we have discussed. These issues are (1) the selection of specific analytic units for describing relevant variation in debitage and (2) the construction of synthetic units to accord with the inferences sought for archaeological debitage assemblages. The former concerns observations at the finest resolution, the latter concerns inferences at the largest scale of application.

Improving the techniques will require continued attention to the two validity issues stated above. In pursuing this goal, we are well served continually to reconsider debitage analysis in terms of reductive technology. Thinking of stone tool production as core reduction suggests novel possibilities for reformulating our analytic and synthetic units. For example, the problems of using assemblage as a synthetic unit when applied to archaeological debitage assemblages that are technologically mixed may be reduced if we consider the core rather than the assemblage as a synthetic unit. Instead of treating assemblages as samples of the debitage aggregates produced by complete reduction trajectories or as imperfect proxies of lithic final products (tools), we might consider individual pieces of debitage as representatives of the core at the point in reduction when the removal occurred. This approach requires only a subtle shift in attention, but may have substantial consequences for how we construct units for debitage analysis. From this perspective, debitage represents the manufacture process by representing the state of the core. Our inferences about variation in reduction would focus more directly on variation in how cores were reduced. Likewise, focusing more directly on how cores are reduced rephrases reductive variation as core variation, and the range of variation in core reduction examined in debitage analysis would automatically broaden.

This could likewise improve our use of experimentation. For example, with this view to the core, the unit of comparison in experimental replication studies shifts from idealized debitage assemblages to individual removals, each one representing differing core states during a known process, or trajectory, of reduction. The mixing of archaeological debitage assemblages would pose less of an obstacle to inference.

These suggestions serve two purposes. The first is to demonstrate that the available debitage analysis techniques do not represent the totality of possible descriptive techniques and analytic approaches. The units used in lithic analysis need not be viewed as static. The second is to illustrate that reconsidering debitage analysis from the most inclusive perspective of reductive technology not only serves as a check on the internal coherence of basic units but also affords creative potential for constructing new units.

Four major concepts were introduced in this chapter. The first is that the entirety of material resulting from lithic reduction is composed of cores and removals. The second is that a core and its removals together contain a complete record of the reduction event. The third is that the construction of technological units must be research driven. The fourth is that all units in lithic technology describe variation in core reduction. If these four concepts are adopted by lithic analysts, we can begin to develop a universally understood body of basic knowledge that will allow us to move forward.

ACKNOWLEDGMENTS

We would like to thank several people for providing comments and important suggestions on earlier drafts of the chapter: William Dancey, John Fagan, Bruce Huckell, Robert Jackson, Phil LeTourneau, Steven Mack, Kristen Martine, Gerry Raymond, Mark Slaughter, Alan Sullivan, and David Vaughan. In particular, we thank Ann Ramenofsky; her assistance and patience cannot be overstated.

Notes

1. Schiffer discusses the relationship between fragments and wholes with regard to formation processes. In describing his Completeness and Fragmentation Indices (1983:686–89), his comparison of stone artifacts to ceramic and glass artifacts clearly exemplifies how the kind of technology is relevant for archaeological measurement.
2. It is common to further partition removals by whether they bear sufficient measurable attributes deemed relevant in a debitage analysis (i.e., "flakes" do, whereas shatter, angular debris, and chunks do not).
3. Kelly (1988) offers a similar discussion. However, he is concerned with the different "roles" of a biface in the organization of technology, whereas we are discussing categories for biface in the organization of research methodology.
4. Although not considered here, reliability studies are well represented in the lithic analysis literature (e.g., Beck and Jones 1989; Fish 1978; Larralde 1984; Nance 1987; see Shott's discussion [1994:74–75] of measurement error).
5. The use of experimentation for evaluating validity may account for a terminological incongruity: in the debitage literature, the term "reliability" is frequently used to mean what we consider to be validity. For example, it is common in the literature to indicate that a technique is "reliable" for diagnosing the presence of bipolar reduction or that platform lipping is a "reliable" attribute for determining that a soft hammer was used. However, as the terms are defined in this volume, the above are examples of validity, not reliability. Experimentation may be an origin of this blending of reliability and validity, because when a technique is "tested" for accuracy, successful outcomes can be readily conceived of as evidence for the "reliability" of the technique. However, unless the test measures only replicability, the term "reliability" is likely being used in a colloquial sense rather than the more restricted definition employed here. Also, reliability is sometimes used in a similar sense in certain statistical applications, such as multivariate discrimination and clustering routines. This may have contributed to the use of the term in lithic analyses, especially given the association of such statistics and experimental debitage studies.
6. This is, in part, the point that Sullivan and Rozen (1985) were making in their call for "interpretation-free" categories.
7. Nonetheless, certain misunderstandings and disagreements have arisen concerning their treatment of analytic and synthetic units. We believe that much of the debate surrounding inference and methodology contained in the 1989 comments and response articles (Amick and Mauldin 1989; Ensor and Roemer 1989; Rozen and Sullivan 1989; Rozen and Sullivan 1989b) is largely a complex miscommunication among the authors concerning different understandings of the construction of synthetic versus analytic units.

10

Ceramic Wares and Types Assessing
H. S. Colton's Ceramic Concepts

RUTH E. LAMBERT

Beginning in the early part of this century, Harold Colton investigated Northern Arizona prehistory using ceramic materials (Colton 1932; M. R. F. Colton and Colton 1918). Colton believed that ceramic materials could provide important information on culture history because this class of materials was relatively indestructible and ubiquitous in the Flagstaff area. When these materials were sorted into types and wares, information about temporal and spatial aspects of prehistory could be obtained (Colton and Hargrave 1937). According to Colton, the distinguishing features of *types* included clay manipulation, surface color, temper composition, paint materials, and style of design (when present). Similar types were then grouped together into a larger unit, *ware*. Colton believed that ceramic types were temporal, but wares were spatial. A ware was the product of a cultural group and the distribution of a ware indicated the area occupied by the group (Colton 1939b). For the most part, Colton's definitions of ceramic types and wares remain in place today and they have formed the foundation of much of Northern Arizona and Flagstaff area archaeology.

In this chapter, I am concerned with the validity of one of Colton's ceramic wares, Prescott Gray Ware, and its occurrence in the Flagstaff area. Prescott Gray Ware is separated into four types, Prescott Gray, Prescott Black-on-gray, Aquarius Orange, and Aquarius Black-on-orange. Although sourcing studies have not been conducted, the tempering material of Prescott Gray Ware does not occur in the Flagstaff area. The nonlocal temper and distinctive designs of two of the four types have resulted in general agreement that Prescott Gray wares are intrusive. The majority of the Prescott ceramics vessels in the Flagstaff area are plain jars rather than decorated bowls, and this fact contradicts Colton's ideas about the kinds of nonlocal ceramics that should be present. In short, there is a contradiction between the belief that Prescott Gray Ware types in the Flagstaff area are intrusive and the form and size of the Prescott Gray ceramics that are present.

Archaeologists have consistently demonstrated that Colton's ceramic types vary spatially and temporally, which suggests varied utility of the types for certain kinds of research (e.g., Downum 1988; Stanislawski 1990). Here, I do not debate the concept of ceramic type per se. Rather, I investigate the validity of the Prescott Gray Ware ceramic types to measure differences in ceramic production using Colton's type attributes.

For the purposes of measurement, Carmines and Zeller define validity (1979: 12–13) as the ability to measure the intended quality. If the validity of Prescott Gray Ware types is problematic, research results based on these types is suspect. These ware and type designations present a particularly difficult case, a situation that was clearly recognized by Colton very early (1958:1). Recently, these typological problems were raised by archaeologists working in the Prescott area. Their concerns stimulated a ceramic conference, where the existing ceramic scheme of Prescott Gray Ware types was debated. The intent of this chapter is to revisit Colton's concept of types and their distribution as applied to Prescott Gray Ware in the Flagstaff area and to suggest a method to render type assessments more useful.

This investigation of the Prescott Gray Ware types is part of a larger ongoing study that addresses synchronic settlement distributions and site use in the Citadel District of Wupatki National Monument. Research questions in that study focus on the context and use of Prescott Gray Ware vessels, given their transport distance, the high frequencies present at a few sites, the predominance of jar forms, and the apparent inferiority of vessel construction and design relative to other ceramic types produced at that time. All of these observations have fostered hypotheses that the vessel contents may have been the object of attention rather than the container (King 1949; Peter Pilles, personal communication 1992).

In order to address questions of vessel use, information about ceramic frequency distributions by provenience, ceramic type, and vessel form must be collected. A first step for acquiring that data involves sorting sherds by ceramic types in order to assess the ceramic materials. Colton's types were formulated using specific criteria (Colton and Hargrave 1937:2–3), with the purpose of identifying and organizing certain ceramic attributes that could indicate prehistoric interactions and help reconstruct Flagstaff area culture history. With the types as the starting point, the key question is whether there is a fit between Colton's conceptual framework for wares and types and the nature of the Prescott Gray Ware types in the Flagstaff area.

I begin this chapter with a description of Colton's definitions of ceramic wares and types and the concepts related to their spatial distribution. Then, I evaluate Colton's descriptions and expectations for spatial distribution of the four Prescott Gray Ware types

using survey and excavation data from a portion of Wupatki National Monument in the Flagstaff area.

HISTORY OF COLTON'S CERAMIC CONCEPTS

In 1937, the Museum of Northern Arizona published the *Handbook of Northern Arizona Pottery Wares* (Colton and Hargrave 1937). The handbook was a response to a growing demand to organize Northern Arizona ceramic information so that an area chronology and a synthesis of the cultural phenomena could be formulated.

In 1922, Colton had argued that ceramics provided a good medium for the reconstruction of prehistory because their remains were ubiquitous in the Flagstaff area, were relatively indestructible, and the decorated vessels appeared to change through time. According to Colton (1939b, 1953), ceramic analyses must include assessments of the construction materials, the techniques of manufacture, and the characteristics of cultural contact. Among others, these factors produce the ceramic variation of the archaeological record that is used to interpret the culture history of the area under investigation.

Colton's 1953 work emphasized the technological aspect of ceramics: the materials and techniques of manufacture. He argued that individuals opportunistically and frequently procured materials available in their local area. In ceramic manufacture, basic materials such as clay, tempers, and paint pigments would be locally extracted.

Manufacturing techniques include the procedures of vessel manufacture, firing, and surface treatment (Colton and Hargrave 1937). Colton (1953) argued that these techniques were responses to the materials used and that they would vary with materials. Because techniques were responsive to materials, knowledge and skills associated with useful procedures were passed from one generation to another. Therefore, manufacturing techniques and materials should indicate a locus of ceramic production where a particular group of individuals shared technical knowledge and resources.

TABLE 10.1
Attributes of Colton's Functional Ceramic Categories

Attribute	Utility Types	Table Types
Use	Cooking/storage	Serving
Appearance	Plain	Decorated
Size	Larger	Smaller
Wall Thickness	Thicker	Thinner
Distribution	Local	Nonlocal, Local

To Colton, analyses of ceramics from archaeological contexts also allowed the identification of characteristics of contact between culture groups (Colton and Hargrave 1937:xi–xii). These characteristics include ceramic attributes, such as vessel form, method of ornamentation, and styles of design that can reflect group interaction through trade relations, migrations, and/or vogue ("trends of the times"). Colton (1935:4) argued that these attributes were temporally sensitive and that their presence could be interpreted in a manner similar to index fossils in geology.

Colton believed these general concepts applied to the manufacture of all ceramics. He also suggested (1939b, 1953) different uses for ceramics and asserted that two related but different ceramics environments existed, each informing on different aspects of the culture history of an area. Colton (1939b) argued for the existence of small discrete geographical areas where pottery was manufactured from locally procured clay and temper resources.

In this area, individuals would be expected to manufacture two categories of ceramics: "table types" and "utility types" (Colton and Hargrave 1937:27–28). Table types were nonculinary, decorated, thin-walled, small vessels (Table 10.1). Utility types were used for cooking or storing of water or foodstuffs and tended to be large and undecorated. Colton stated that all groups made both categories of ceramics and that utility types would not be traded between groups because each pottery-producing group would have its own utility type (Colton and Hargrave 1937:27–28). As such, utility types should be indigenous to the region where they are found. In contrast, table types tended to be small and to circulate widely through processes of trade or migration of individuals, and the composition of the clay or temper of these vessels may not be local to the area where they are recovered.[1]

Colton (1939b, 1946, 1968) hypothesized identifiable foci for the manufacture and distribution of table and utility types using frequency counts supported by independent sourcing data. He asserted that the locus of manufacture occurred where the frequency of utility types was the greatest and where the same materials were present in both table and utility type vessels. In peripheral areas, the frequency of utility types should decline with distance from the core; however, table types need not follow this falloff pattern due to exchange or other factors. Therefore, in areas away from the core manufacturing area, the distribution of table and utility types should be different from each other. Colton (1953) noted that manufacturing locations are identifiable through laboratory studies based on spectroscopic or petrographic tests for the sourcing of paste and temper (Fowler 1935:109–11). Sourcing studies and dendrochronological information could provide information on the distribution of decorated ceramics through time.

COLTON'S CERAMIC TYPES AND WARES
With these guiding concepts and the purpose of culture history reconstruction within the Flagstaff area, definitions of ceramic types, wares, and series were formulated (Colton and Hargrave 1937) (see Appendix, this chapter).

Although some of the biologically based taxonomy initially formulated for area ceramics (Hargrave 1932) was retained, the ceramic classificatory framework was reformulated into an inductive hierarchical structure designed to provide information on the ceramic ware (Colton and Hargrave 1937; Downum 1988). The ware became the important designation because its presence indicated the cultural area of the group and its relations with other groups (Colton 1939b). To arrive at the definition of a ware, pottery types were first defined on the basis of shared technical attributes that satisfied certain necessary conditions; vessels of a particular type were alike in all criteria defined by Colton, except possibly vessel form (Colton and Hargrave 1937:2–3). A number of ceramic types with a majority of the observable technical attributes were then grouped together into a ware. Thus, all members of a ceramic type shared the same attributes. Member types of a ware shared a majority, but not necessary all, of the technical attributes.

The "series" classification was developed as a nexus between ware and type (Colton and Hargrave 1937) because the conceptual framework required spatial and temporal information for the description and explanation of the culture history of a group. The series designation linked historically related pottery types of the same ware to a geographical location. As a consequence, the series evidenced continuities of ceramic manufacture and design through time for that group. While environmental changes could result in some modifications in basic materials and techniques of manufacture, continuities should be discernable within the ceramic series.

Colton's (1946) classic example is the change to ash temper in the Rio de Flag ceramic series following the eruptions of Sunset Crater. Prior to these eruptions, ceramic types contain little, if any, ash temper. However, following these eruptions, the dominant type, Sunset Red, is ash-tempered. Recent sourcing of the ash temper corroborates Colton's assertion of continuities within the series. While other preexisting ash sources are also present, the ash temper following the eruption of Sunset Crater is from that eruption (Boston 1995).

HISTORY OF PRESCOTT GRAY WARE

Prescott Gray Ware was first identified in the Verde area of central Arizona by Winifred and Harold Gladwin (1930a). Shortly afterward, excavations were conducted in the Prescott and Verde Valley areas and these reports elaborated on the initial description of the ware (Caywood and Spicer 1935; Spicer and Caywood 1936). The Prescott Gray Ware types were first named by Caywood and Spicer (1935) and included Verde Black-on-gray, Verde Black-on-brown, and Verde Polychrome. These types were included in then current ceramic descriptions (Colton and Hargrave 1937:184–87). Colton (1939a:16–18) later identified additional types within the ware, Aquarius Orange and Aquarius Black-on-orange, during fieldwork in Northwestern Arizona. These types were included within Prescott Gray Ware based on their co-occurrence with Verde Gray and Verde Black-on-gray. Later, Colton (1958) consolidated Prescott Gray Ware into four types: Verde Gray, Verde Black-on-gray, Aquarius Orange, and Aquarius Black-on-orange. He stated that the main types were Verde Gray and Aquarius Orange and that the differences between these types were probably due to uncontrolled firing practices. Due to confusion over nomenclature, Verde Gray and Verde Black-on-gray were renamed Prescott Gray and Prescott Black-on-gray during a ceramic conference in 1969 (Peter Pilles, personal communication 1993).

Prescott Gray Ware has been identified in a broad area extending from the San Francisco Mountains west to the Hualapai Mountains near Kingman, Arizona, and south to the Yarnell area south of the Bradshaw Mountains in central Arizona (Figure 10.1). General dates associated with the ware, using relative ceramic chronometric dating, are ca. A.D. 1150 to 1400 (Colton 1958). The type sites for the ware in the Prescott area are hilltop pueblos of 20 to 30 rooms and include King's Ruin (Spicer and

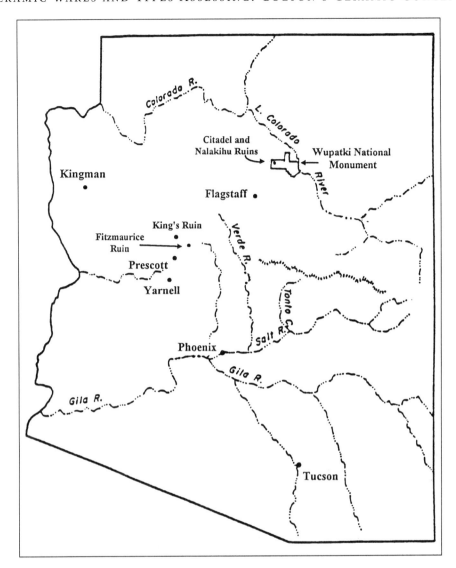

Figure 10.1. Arizona, showing locations of Prescott area sites, Wupatki National Monument, and Citadel and Nalakihu ruins.

Caywood 1936) and Fitzmaurice Ruin (Barnett 1974; Spicer and Caywood 1936).

DESCRIPTION OF PRESCOTT GRAY WARE
The ware is described as paddle and anvil construction with gray paste fired in an oxidizing atmosphere (Caywood and Spicer 1935:41–42; Spicer and Caywood 1936: 28–41). The paste contains inclusions of quartz, sand, and mica fragments that constitute at least 50 percent. The core texture is coarse, irregular, and crumbly, and the muscovite mica flakes are visible on both surfaces. The surface colors can vary from gray to brown to orange, and the firing atmosphere appears to be relatively uncontrolled to produce the variation in the surface color. Surface finishes exhibit smoothing; bowls have smooth interior surfaces while jars are often rough on both the interior and the exterior. No slips are present. Paint pigments are described as organic. Subsequent testing has confirmed most of the original observations (Frampton and Gratz 1978a:55). More re-

cently, some temper variation in the types has been identified and it has been suggested (Frampton and Gratz 1978a) that the two varieties, micaceous and sandy, may relate to either functional use or the specific area of manufacture (Euler and Dobyns 1962).

The primary vessel forms include jars and bowls; dippers and scoops are infrequently encountered (Colton 1958). Jars from Prescott area sites tend to be globular with short necks and narrow mouths, and are often called ollas (Barnett 1970, 1973, 1974, 1978; Caywood and Spicer 1935). The morphology of the jars varies. One form has short necks and globular bodies, with horizontal dimensions greater than vertical dimensions. The second variant is elongated with longer necks and bodies, with horizontal and vertical measurements approximately equal. Jar rims are generally rounded and everted.

Bowls are deep with rounded bottoms and direct round rims. Of the 108 bowls assessed at one excavated site (Spicer and Caywood 1936:35), the average diameter was ca. 10.5 inches and the depth ca. 6.5 inches. In the Prescott area, bowls are most frequently encountered in burials and they constitute the majority of whole vessels in these assemblages (Barnett 1978; Spicer and Caywood 1936). However, the frequencies from the complete ceramic assemblage from individual sites in the Prescott area indicate that the majority of the sherds are from jars (Frampton and Gratz 1978a, 1978b).

Black painted designs occur on bowl interiors (Barnett 1970; Frampton and Gratz 1978a, 1978b), which tend to be executed on crudely finished surfaces with thin, runny paint and poor brushwork. Design layouts are irregular with combinations of diverse elements and asymmetrical schemes. Although painted designs appear on jar bodies in broad and often widely spaced geometrical motifs that incorporate large unpainted areas (Barnett 1978:45–48), jar designs are more frequently limited to the exterior and interior necks (Barnett 1970; Spicer and Caywood 1936). These appear as trailing lines and crude geometric designs that extend into the

interior of the vessel and often terminate as drips and splashes of paint. Rare examples have been recovered that indicate entire interior jar surfaces were painted with irregular crudely executed motifs (Barnett 1978:48, Figure 44C; Spicer and Caywood 1936:Plate XL). Analyses from an excavated assemblage (Frampton and Gratz 1978a, 1978b) indicated that jars tended to be decorated at the rim, especially if decorations occurred on the vessel body.[2]

Survey work of the 1920s and 1930s identified Prescott Gray Ware at a few sites in the Wupatki and Deadman's Wash areas northeast of Flagstaff (Colton 1946), with surface sherds apparently from large crudely painted or plain jars. During excavations in the 1930s, Prescott Gray Ware was identified in the Wupatki area at the site of Nalakihu where it constituted about 27 percent (n = 4,861) of all ceramics recovered (Colton 1946; King 1949:111). The presence of substantial quantities of this ware northeast of Flagstaff was difficult to explain based on Colton's expectations for ceramic distributions. Because the ware was thought to originate in the Prescott "heartland" (Gladwin and Gladwin 1930a; Spicer and Caywood 1936), Colton suggested (1939b) that its presence was a result of Prescott area migrants who had established a colony at Nalakihu in Wupatki. This explanation was cited frequently in area publications to account for the presence of the ceramic intrusives (Caywood and Spicer 1935; Colton 1939a, 1939b, 1958; Colton and Hargrave 1937; Spicer and Caywood 1936).

Since the 1930s, Prescott Gray Ware has been identified in small quantities at a few other sites in the vicinity of Wupatki (Colton 1946; Smith 1952; United States Department of Agriculture, Coconino National Forest Site Files). Recent investigations by Wilcox in small Cohonina sites in the Kaibab National Forest to the west of the San Francisco Peaks also have yielded occasional sherds of the ware, indicating very low frequencies over a broad area (David Wilcox, personal communication 1992). However, the largest concentrations of the ware seem to occur in the Deadman's Wash and Wupatki areas located to the northeast of Flagstaff where frequencies can range from 20 to 27 percent of the ceramic assemblage (Colton 1946; King 1949).

The most recent field research in the area is the National Park Service's Wupatki Archaeological Inventory Survey Project (Anderson 1990), which identified 2,397 prehistoric sites within the Monument (Figure 10.2). During the survey, data were recorded on the frequency and distribution of Prescott Gray Ware ceramics. The survey indicated that Prescott Gray Ware was present at 12.5 percent (n = 299) of the sites within the monument. On 294 of those sites, Prescott Gray Ware composed 20 percent or less of the total ceramic assemblage. At four sites (1.3 percent of all sites with Prescott Gray Ware), however, 20 to 40 percent of the ceramic assemblage was Prescott Gray Ware; frequencies reached 49 percent on one site. The locations of sites with Prescott Gray Ware seem to be concentrated either in the western areas of the monument or in the vicinity of Deadman's Wash (Anderson 1990; Downum and Sullivan 1990).

To summarize, the Gladwins first identified Prescott Gray Ware in the Verde Valley area of Arizona. By 1958, Colton had consolidated Prescott Gray Ware into four types, two decorated and two undecorated. Bowls and jars were the most common forms. Colton also identified the ware in the Flagstaff area; it was especially abundant in the vicinity of Wupatki National Monument.

Colton's ceramic structure was hierarchical, and included type, ware, and series. Decorated wares were identified as table wares and were expected to be traded beyond the area of manufacture. Undecorated wares were utility wares and were asserted to be spatially confined to the region of manufacture.

The nature of the Prescott Gray Ware assemblages in the Flagstaff area does not appear to conform to Colton's assumptions for ceramic distributions of wares and types. Be-cause the ceramic sherd assemblages from Wupatki indicate that the majority of the vessels are large, plain storage jars (utility types), Colton's assertions regarding the dichotomous distribution between utility and table types is called into question. The evaluation of the validity of Prescott type distinctions is a first step in exploring the apparent contradictions.

ANALYSIS OF PRESCOTT GRAY WARE CERAMICS

Colton's conceptual framework, his unit structure of type and ware, and the specific separation of Prescott Gray Ware into four types, serve as my point of departure for analyzing the validity of the distinctions. Because table wares are decorated, they should be circulated beyond the area of manufacture. Thus, in the Flagstaff area, decorated types of Prescott Gray Ware should predominate. Second, because the distance between the area of origin and Flagstaff is greater than 90 miles, the decorated vessels should be small. Finally, the small vessels should be bowls because bowls should be nestable for transport (Whittlesey 1974).

Clearly, these expectations refer to whole vessels, but the bulk of the archaeological record is composed of sherds, not vessels. There are only three reconstructed whole vessels of Prescott Gray Ware from the Wupatki area, and a sample of three is simply too small from which to draw any firm conclusions. In this study, the sherd is the relevant analytic unit. Focusing the analysis at the scale of sherd requires specification so that the subsequent analysis is meaningful.

Sherds are separated by vessel type, jar and bowl, and by vessel part, rim and body. Two criteria are used to separate bowls and jars: the relative smoothing of surfaces and the presence and location of decoration. As noted above, bowl sherds tend to have relatively smoother surfaces on the interior, while jar sherds are often rough on both the interior and exterior surfaces. Designs are confined to bowl interiors; designs on jars occur most frequently on the exterior, and on interior neck surfaces. Rim sherds are particularly impor-

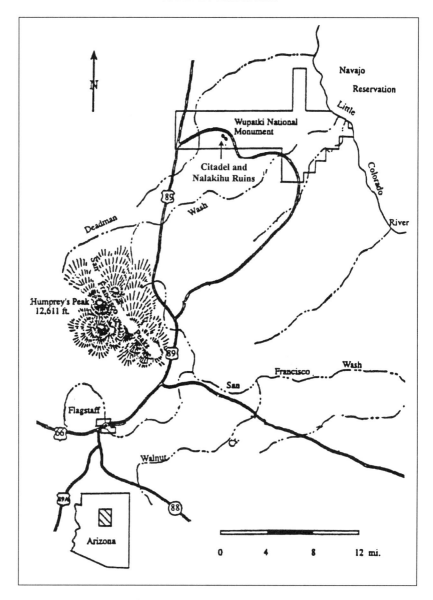

Figure 10.2. Location of Wupatki National Monument and Citadel and Nalak-ihu ruins.

tant in this analysis not only because jar designs are often limited to the rim portion of vessels but also because rims can suggest vessel type. At the same time, counting only rim sherds can result in overrepresentation of bowls relative to jars because bowls tend to have more rim area relative to their size than do jars. To maximize available information on Prescott Gray Ware ceramics in the Flagstaff area and to control for such record formation processes as preservation and breakage rates, I estimate the relationship between decorated and undecorated bowls and jars through a ratio of rim to body part.

In essence, then, if Colton's ideas about the distribution of table and utility wares are correct, in the Flagstaff area, there should be more decorated than undecorated sherds, and more bowl than jar sherds. Sherds of small decorated bowls (e.g., Prescott Black-on-gray and Aquarius Black-on-orange) should be most abundant. Moreover, the ratio of rim to body sherds for jars should be less than the ratio for bowls. Any other outcome would contradict Colton's assumptions about the type of ware that ought to circulate beyond the area of manufacture.

This analysis of Prescott Gray Ware types is conducted at three progressively finer scales; a literature review of Prescott Gray Ware in the Flagstaff area, an analysis of data from the 1990 survey in a portion of the Citadel District of Wupatki National Monument, and an evaluation of excavated material from the Nalakihu site within the Citadel District. Although it would be convenient to use the same information in all evaluations, such an approach is not possible. Information on Prescott Gray Ware was collected at different times, with different research designs, and analyzed using different protocols. Because of these differences, information cannot be combined into one data base. Regardless of outcome, the three separate evaluations will strengthen the general conclusions regarding the validity of the Colton's concepts and Prescott Gray Ware types.

LITERATURE REVIEW

An examination of the literature suggests there are contradictions to the expectations of the frequency and nature of Prescott Gray sherds in the Flagstaff area. The Prescott Gray Ware paste and temper of granite and muscovite mica are distinctive and readily discernable in cross section and on surfaces. Because the temper materials do not occur in the Flagstaff area and because they display morphological similarities to temper materials from the greater Prescott area, it is likely that the ceramics were imported to the Flagstaff area. This inference is supported by the rarity of the Prescott Gray Ware ceramics in the region. The ware generally occurs in trace amounts, if at all. However, at a few sites in the Flagstaff area (n = > 15) it is found in frequencies of 10 to 40 percent of the ceramic assemblages (Colton 1946; Downum and Sullivan 1990; King 1949).

Because it appears that Prescott Gray

Ware is intrusive in the Flagstaff area, the majority of ceramics encountered should be decorated (Colton 1939b, 1953). However, an initial assessment of available surface and excavation data (Anderson 1990; Colton 1946; King 1949) indicates that ceramic assemblages consist primarily of plain sherds from large globular jars. Thus, the distribution of the vessel size, form, and design of Prescott Gray Wares in the Wupatki area seems to contradict Colton's assumptions regarding the kind of ceramic that should be imported. Plain wares should not be found outside the area of their manufacture; small decorated vessels should circulate to other areas.

ANALYSIS OF SURVEY DATA

Survey data were obtained from the Wupatki Archaeological Inventory Survey Project (Anderson 1990), and the study area used in this analysis represents a subset of that project area. The study area is an arbitrarily defined locale of approximately 2.5 miles that surrounds the Citadel Ruin in the Citadel District of the National Monument. A total of 258 prehistoric sites were located within the study area, representing approximately 10.8 percent of the total known prehistoric sites (n = 2,397) within the monument. The sites range in size from 1 to 30 rooms and, based on ceramic assemblages, are believed to date from ca. A.D. 1130 to 1220.

Of the 258 survey sites in the Citadel study area, 41 (16 percent) yielded Prescott Gray Ware. This proportion is slightly higher than that for the monument as a whole, where Prescott Gray Ware is present at 299 sites (12.5 percent). However, with only a few exceptions, Prescott Gray Ware has been found at sites in the western area of the monument adjacent to the study area (Christian Downum, personal communication 1993). Consequently, the occurrences of Prescott Gray Ware are spatially concentrated in the vicinity of the Citadel study area. An assessment of the surface survey data for the Prescott Gray Ware types within the Citadel area indicates that Prescott Gray is the most abundant type, followed by Prescott Black-on-gray, Aquarius Orange, and Aquarius

TABLE 10.2
Prescott Gray Ware at 41 Sites in the Citadel Area

Ceramic Type	Frequency of Occurrence	Sherd Frequency	Percent	Frequency Range
Prescott Gray	31	77	62.6	1–33
Prescott Black-on-gray	8	34	27.6	1–19
Aquarius Orange	5	8	6.5	1–4
Aquarius Orange-on-gray	3	4	3.3	1–2
Total	47	123	100.0	

Black-on-orange. Table 10.2 details the ceramic sherd frequencies, the number of observations, and the range of frequencies observed for each type.

Based on this information, some general inferences are possible. For all survey sites, plain types (Prescott Gray and Aquarius Orange) outnumber the decorated types by ratios of at least 2:1. In addition, plain types occur at more locations than decorated types (36 versus 11 locations), indicating that they are more common.

This information supports observations made by other archaeologists (Anderson 1990; Colton 1946; King 1949). Once again, the nature of the Prescott Gray Ware types is different from Colton's original assertions for ceramic distributions of plain and decorated types. In the Citadel area, at least, plain Prescott types occur in more locations and in greater frequencies at those locations than decorated Prescott types do.

ANALYSIS OF NALAKIHU MATERIAL

In 1933 and 1934, Nalakihu Pueblo was excavated by the Museum of Northern Arizona (King 1949). The pueblo is located at the base of a prominent mesa where the Citadel Ruin is situated (Figure 10.2). The area around the Citadel has a high site density (ca. 60 sites/acre), and is believed to have been a major prehistoric settlement locale (Downum and Sullivan 1990).

Nalakihu was originally excavated so monument tourists could visit a restored prehistoric village (King 1949). Consequently, the entire 10-room pueblo and a number of extramural pit features were excavated. During the excavations a substantial quantity of Prescott Gray Ware was encountered, prompting speculations that Prescott migrants had established an outpost at Wupatki (Colton 1939b, 1946; King 1949; Spicer and Caywood 1936). Although Prescott ceramic information from Nalakihu was initially reported as all Prescott Black-on-gray (King 1949), analyses of sherd collections by ceramic type and vessel form indicate that all Prescott types were present (Museum of Northern Arizona, Ceramic Collections).

Of the total sherd assemblage (n = 4,681), 27 percent (n = 1,279) were Prescott Gray Ware (King 1949:111). Within the Prescott assemblage, 291 sherds were attributed to three reconstructed jars from the site, and the remainder (n = 988) were from other vessels. This total is reduced by 152 jar body sherds that could not be assigned to one of the four Prescott types, and I have excluded them from further consideration. As shown in Table 10.3, the remaining 836 sherds and the 291 sherds from the reconstructed vessels (n = 1,127) were sorted into Prescott Gray, Prescott Black-on-gray, Aquarius Orange, and Aquarius Black-on-orange by Museum of Northern Arizona personnel prior to this study. In the Prescott assemblage, Prescott Gray is the most abundant, followed by Prescott Black-on-gray, Aquarius Orange, and Aquarius Black-on-orange.

TABLE 10.3
Ceramic Vessel Form Data from Nalakihu Excavations

Ceramic Types	Bowl		Jar		Total	% Total
	Body	Rim	Body	Rim		
Plain Types						
Prescott Gray	0	0	412	4	416	36.9
Aquarius Orange	0	0	295	1	296	26.3
Total	0	0	707	5	712	63.2
Decorated Types						
Prescott Black-on-gray	12	11	270	39	332	29.4
Aquarius Black-on-orange	0	0	82	1	83	7.4
Total	12	11	352	40	415	36.8
Grand Total	12	11	1059	45	1127	100.0

TABLE 10.4
Summary Data for Ceramic Sherds from Nalakihu Excavations: Vessel Form

Vessel Form	Number of Sherds	Percent of Total
Bowl	23	2
Jar	1104	98
Total	1127	100

Regarding vessel form, Table 10.4 indicates that jar sherds constitute 98 percent of the total; bowl sherds compose 2 percent. Moreover, a further breakdown by type (see Table 10.3) indicates that 100 percent of all Prescott Gray, Aquarius Orange, and Black-on-orange sherds are jars; thus, all of the bowl sherds are Prescott Black-on-gray.

As in the other two analyses, these data are in conflict with Colton's ideas regarding the distribution and form of ceramic types. The ceramic frequencies (Table 10.3) indicate that the two plain types constitute 63.2 percent of all sherds; decorated types make up 36.8 percent. Vessel form is predominately jars: 98 percent jar sherds as compared with 2 percent for bowl sherds. The three reconstructible vessels from the site are all large Prescott Black-on-gray storage jars (Museum of Northern Arizona, Nalakihu Site File). Only a few whole vessels have been found in the Flagstaff area, necessitating ves-

sel size estimates from sherds using sherd wall thickness as a proxy measurement. The comparison of wall thickness of the reconstructible vessels with sherd samples from the Prescott Gray Ware assemblage suggests the other jars on the site were also large. Thus, the Prescott assemblage at Nalakihu is dominated by undecorated sherds, and these sherds are from large jars.

Because the information from Nalakihu is more detailed, further analysis of Prescott Gray Ware types is possible. As shown in Table 10.5, rim sherds constitute 5 percent (n = 56) of the 1,127 analyzed sherds from Nalakihu. Of the rim sherds, only 11 sherds were identified as bowl fragments (Table 10.3) and all were Prescott Black-on-gray, yielding a ratio of about 1:1 (body = 12; rim = 11). The lack of rim sherds from other Prescott types renders comparisons of bowl ratios impossible.

Jar rims of all four types compose the re-

TABLE 10.5
Summary Data for Ceramic Sherds from Nalakihu Excavations: Vessel Part

Vessel Part	Number of Sherds	Percent of Total
Body	1071	95
Rim	56	5
Total	1127	100

TABLE 10.6
Summary Data for Ceramic Sherds from Nalakihu Excavations: Vessel Part Ratios

Ceramic Type	Vessel Part Ratios for Jars Body:Rim
Prescott Gray	103:1
Aquarius Orange	295:1
Prescott Black-on-gray	7:1
Aquarius Black-on-orange	82:1

maining 45 rim sherds (Table 10.6). These data indicate that only Prescott Black-on-gray rims occur with any frequency producing a body/rim ratio of 7:1 as compared with other type ratios: Prescott Gray 103:1; Aquarius Orange 295:1; and Aquarius Black-on-orange 82:1. The wide range exhibited among these ratios is unexpected, for it shows unequal ratios across types within the same vessel form. A review of the sherd frequency data indicates that with the exception of 6 sherds, all sherds from Prescott Gray, Aquarius Orange, and Aquarius Black-on-orange are jar body sherds.

In sum, observations from the Nalakihu excavation suggest that my expectations derived from Colton's assertions about general ceramic distributions of wares and types are not supported by this analysis. Sherd frequencies indicate that plain types outnumber decorated types. Also, large jars are overwhelmingly present, almost to the exclusion of small bowls, which are the expected vessel size and form that would be transported over 90 miles from the area of production. This lack of agreement raises questions regarding the distribution of the types.

A comparison of jar body/rim sherd ratios across types indicates substantial differences between these types (Table 10.6). Prescott

Gray, Aquarius Orange, and Aquarius Black-on-orange are almost exclusively identified from jar body sherds, while Prescott Black-on-gray jar rims occur much more frequently. These data indicate that the same parts of jar vessels are not equally represented in the Prescott types. If, controlling for size, jar body/rim ratios are expected to be roughly equivalent across types, these data indicate that there are very few rims represented from types other than Prescott Black-on-gray. More rim sherds would be expected based on the number of body sherds recovered. Although other factors may be responsible, invalid type distinctions are one possible factor. Excavation data of vessels recovered in the Prescott area seem to support the suggestion that certain sherd types may be representative of different vessel parts (Barnett 1970, 1973, 1974, 1978; Frampton and Gratz 1978a, 1978b).

The above analyses do not support the expectations modeled on Colton's assumptions for ceramic distributions and typological distinctions. An initial analysis of ceramic sherds in the Wupatki area indicates that there are obvious contradictions to the assertions that plain ceramic types do not circulate outside their apparent area of manufacture. Furthermore, the vessels that were transported to this area are large globular jars, not the expected small "nestable" bowls. Ceramic data from surface materials indicate that plain types outnumber decorated Prescott types and that they occur at more survey sites. The expectations for Colton's ceramic distributions and types are not met by the excavation data. Again, plain sherds outnumber decorated types, jars predominate, technological differences are not known, and the ratio of jar body to rim sherds is not comparable across types as suggested for discrete types.

DISPARITIES AND CONTRADICTIONS

Given the apparent contradictions between the proposed expectations for ceramic type distinctions and the frequencies and nature of Prescott Gray Ware types in the Wupatki area, I offer two reasons as possible explanations for the disparities. First, the location of the decorations on existing whole vessels and the excavated materials from the Prescott area suggest that the presence or absence of decoration is strongly associated with vessel form. As undertaken in this study, controlling for vessel form is necessary when working with decorated ceramics.

The second explanation concerns aspects of the manufacturing process, including location of decoration and firing condition. I discuss each in turn. The analyses of whole and reconstructible vessels suggest that designs tend to occur on specific portions of particular vessel forms and that inattention to form may be misleading. In studies conducted elsewhere in the Southwest (e.g., Plog 1980), the location of ceramic designs on different vessel parts has been found to confuse type distinctions. Distinctions between Prescott Gray and Prescott Black-on-gray are based on the presence of decoration; all of the other diagnostic type attributes defined by Colton are shared by the two types.

Originally, several Prescott Gray Ware types were identified with the caveat that the presence of designs and uncontrolled firing practices may produce the variations (Caywood and Spicer 1935; Colton 1939b; Colton and Hargrave 1937; Spicer and Cay-

wood 1936). Prescott Gray and Prescott Black-on-gray were suggested as plain and decorated variants of one type (Colton 1939b:15–16). Later, Colton stated:

For all practical purposes, there is only one definite type in this ware, although a number of types have been described: Verde Black-on-gray. . . . For practical purposes in sorting sherds, the gray sherds are called Verde Gray and the orange sherds, Aquarius Orange, but as firing methods were not well controlled, several colors may appear on the same vessel. (1958:1; emphasis added)

Recent work has provided additional information concerning Prescott decorated sherds. A series of excavations in the Prescott area (Barnett 1970, 1973, 1974, 1978) yielded ceramic vessels that indicate that Prescott jars are usually decorated at the rim, often into the interior of the rim. Furthermore, analyses of one excavated assemblage by Frampton and Gratz (1978a, 1978b) indicated that decorated jars were always decorated at the rim; there were no decorated vessel bodies without rim decoration. Also, based on their tabulations of decorated rim sherds to estimate whole vessels, 58 percent of the jar sherds were Prescott Black-on-gray. However, body and rim sherds suggest the opposite; 72 percent of the ceramics are Prescott Gray (Frampton and Gratz 1978a:60). This disparity is due, in part, to the large number of plain sherds that constitute the unpainted portions of jar bodies, thereby skewing analyses. A similar situation of sherd bias was encountered at an earlier excavation (Barnett 1970:83).

In contrast, Prescott Black-on-gray bowls are regularly decorated on the interior with design elements generally covering the majority of the surface (Barnett 1970, 1973, 1974, 1978; Spicer and Caywood 1936). Plain bowls are infrequent and exterior designs on bowls are not common (Frampton and Gratz 1978a). The predictability of design location and the vessel size seem to reduce sherd bias for identifying decorated and undecorated bowls.

Extant whole vessel collections from the

Museum of Northern Arizona, the Verde Valley, and Prescott, Arizona, support these design analyses from excavated materials. Examples in those collections indicate that jars were decorated primarily in the neck area, often on the interior of that area, and on widely spaced areas of the vessel body. Bowls were decorated on at least 50 percent of the interior, often covering the entire area. As followed in this analysis, these data suggest that vessel form should be considered when assigning sherds to particular ceramic types. Because there is apparent patterning in the location of decoration relative to form, failure to consider vessel form may render the typology invalid.

A second source of error with the Prescott types concerns the manufacturing process of Prescott wares generally and Aquarius types in particular. The validity of the Aquarius types has been a subject of debate for a number of years. The typological distinctions first proposed by Colton (1939a) included the caution that the ceramic differences may be due to poor firing practices with uncontrolled amounts of oxygen. Later researchers in the Prescott area (Euler and Dobyns 1962; Ward 1975) also argued that differences between Prescott and Aquarius types were due to firing; these studies provided sherd examples with a multitude of different colored "fire clouds" ranging from gray to brown to orange, indicating uncontrolled oxidation. Analyses of Wupatki sherd materials have prompted similar arguments regarding the orange surface manifestations (Downum 1988).

Examples from collections of whole vessels also suggest that firing processes may be responsible for the distinctive orange sherds (Euler and Dobyns 1962). Often, these whole vessels exhibit several different colors on the exteriors of the same vessel and with interiors appearing as a third distinct color (Ward 1975). Originally, questions were raised when "polychromes" were identified (Spicer and Caywood 1936) and firing problems were first suspected.

Recent work in northern Arizona supports suggestions that the Aquarius types are not independent of Prescott Gray and Prescott Black-on-gray (Mills et al. 1993: 272). Refiring of Prescott Gray and Aquarius Orange sherds under laboratory conditions indicated that the sherds oxidized to the same yellow-red hue. This experiment suggests that these types are not compositionally different. Color variations, however, indicate that the original firing was conducted in an atmosphere where the amount of oxygen was uncontrolled.

Following Colton's definition of ceramic types (Colton and Hargrave 1937:2–3), valid typological distinctions include an expectation that similar materials and firing techniques will yield similar surface colors that should be relatively consistent within types. In contrast, these attributes will vary between types. Information from the abovementioned studies suggests that surface colors are not consistent within the Aquarius types in the ceramics from the Prescott area.

The ceramic data from this study at Wupatki also do not conform to this expectation. The sherd materials are consistent with the suggestion that the Aquarius types may represent uncontrolled firing practices.

Although surface materials provide a paucity of Aquarius sherds, more interpretation is possible with the excavation data. An inspection of sherd materials indicates that a range of orange hues is attributable to Aquarius Orange and that some sherds exhibit gray portions, together suggesting variation in the overall surface color. Based on the above observations from other studies of vessel color variation, Aquarius Orange would be expected to occur less frequently than the typical surface color on the vessel body. Excavation data indicate that Aquarius Orange constitutes 26 percent of the identified sherds (less than either Prescott Gray or Black-on-gray; see Table 10.3) and that all but one of these sherds are from jar bodies.

CONCLUSIONS

This study investigated Colton's ceramic concepts regarding the distribution of plain and decorated Prescott Gray Ware ceramic types. Based on Colton's original suggestions, I formulated specific expectations for the ceramic distribution of Prescott Gray Wares in the Wupatki area of northern Arizona. A preliminary analysis of ceramic distributions was followed by survey and excavation data from the Wupatki area that were used to assess the fit between Colton's ideas and the nature and distribution of Prescott Gray ware types in northern Arizona, Flagstaff, and especially Wupatki. Analyses of sherd frequencies using traditional type distinctions appear to contradict the model expectations since plain sherds outnumber decorated sherds. Additional assessment of whole and reconstructible vessels suggests that vessel form is associated with the presence and location of decoration and that poor firing practices may be responsible for the distinctive Aquarius sherds.

I suggest that Prescott Gray Ware types are problematic unless vessel form is considered. Colton (1958:1) acknowledged the difficulty in applying his ceramic typology to this ware. The accumulation of data since that time supports his early cautionary statements. Information from this study suggests that consideration of vessel form during typological processes may provide some clarity. Extant whole vessel collections provide information that Prescott Black-on-gray jars are always decorated at the rim and may be decorated on the body as well. Plain jars (without rim decoration) are less common. Relying on sherd counts without consideration of vessel form has been known to bias assemblage interpretations (Barnett 1973; Frampton and Gratz 1978a) and may render typological distinctions for jars invalid. The analysis of Prescott Gray Ware jars raises a fundamental ceramic issue: Is the analytic unit of sherd a valid measure of the ceramic unit of vessel? The results of this study suggest that Prescott jar sherds may not be a good proxy for vessels unless vessel form is considered.

Prescott bowls are decorated on interior surfaces, generally 50 percent or more. Bowls with decorated exterior surfaces are less common and plain bowls are infrequent, but known. I suggest that sorting bowl sherds based on the presence of interior decoration may constitute an appropriate distinction.

This approach seems justified based on whole vessel collections and design layouts of Prescott bowls, and the traditional bowl type distinctions should be retained.

Interestingly, a consideration of vessel form in conjunction with typological distinctions supports Colton's general assertions of ceramic distributions. Colton stated that decorated ceramics would tend to circulate, probably for purposes of exchange (1939b). A reassessment of Prescott Gray Ware types in conjunction with vessel form suggests that jars imported into Nalakihu were probably decorated rather than the plain vessels that the sherd frequencies alone would suggest. Also, the predominance of large jars, rather than the more easily transported "nestable" but empty bowls, suggests that vessel contents played some role in ceramic transport. Colton first suggested typological problems for this ware, and more recent research indicates that the type distinctions need to be revisited. An evaluation of the validity of these differences is the initial step toward a thorough ceramic description and future interpretations.

ACKNOWLEDGEMENTS

I thank the editors for their assistance throughout the process of writing this chapter. I also thank the anonymous reviewers for their comments, which greatly improved this chapter. Thanks to the following individuals for sharing their thoughts and ideas on Prescott Gray Ware over the past few years: Bruce Anderson, Richard Boston, Patricia Crown, Chris Downum, David Wilcox, and especially Peter Pilles. Access to Museum of Northern Arizona ceramic data by David Wilcox and Richard Boston is gratefully acknowledged. This chapter is dedicated to my mother, Ruth Heemstra Lambert.

APPENDIX

According to the following definitions provided by Colton and Hargrave (1937:2–3):

Pottery Type

   A pottery type is a group of pottery vessels that are alike in every important characteristic except (possibly) form. In general these characteristics are as follows:

1. Surface color — white, buff, yellow, red, and gray.

2. Method of handling the clay — thinned by scraping ("coiled") or by pressure ("paddle and anvil").

3. Texture of the core — varying from almost no visible temper to coarse temper.

4. Chemical composition of the temper if difference is obviously caused by a difference in technique.

5. Chemical composition of the paint.

6. Styles of design in decorated pottery.

Ware

A ware is a group of pottery types that has a majority of (the above) characteristics in common but that differs in others.

Series

A series, therefore, is a group of pottery types within a single ware in which each type bears a genetic relation to each other, including all those types and only those types that occur

(a) in the direct line of chronological genetic development from an original primitive or ancestral type to a later type and

(b) as collateral developments or variations from any type in that line of development, but which are not themselves followed in chronological genetic sequence by derived types other than types derived through the main line of development from the type of which the collateral type is a development or variation.

Notes

1. Colton's meanings for the terms "type" and "ware" are both use-related and taxonomic (Colton and Hargrave 1937:27–28). For example, utility types and table types are use categories as previously discussed and shown in Table 10.11. He often employs utility and table types in his discussions of ceramic distributions, particularly related to trade/contact. Notations about ceramic wares, such as Prescott Gray Ware, decorated types, or plain types are descriptive and refer to his ceramic taxonomy. The two uses of the term can become intertwined when he discusses use and descriptive aspects as in decorated table types.

2. A conference on Prescott Gray Ware was held in November 1996 at the Museum of Northern Arizona in Flagstaff. The conference was convened due to the ongoing concerns of archaeologists working in the Prescott area. Recent workers have argued for revisiting the Prescott Gray Ware ceramic scheme because of the apparent variation that is now recognized in these ceramics. Although the conference proceedings have not been finalized, approximately seven new ceramic types have been proposed (Peter Pilles, personal communication 1996). These new types include Prescott Red, Prescott Buff, Prescott Polychrome, Prescott Red-on-gray, Prescott White-on-gray, Prescott White-on-red, and Prescott Red-on-buff. The types are proposed based on differences in surface finish and color and paint colors, if decorated. Initial information appears to indicate that type distinctions may be associated with geographic locales within the larger area of Prescott Gray Ware manufacture described above in the text. Together, this information suggests that the broad spatial scale of the ware may need to be partitioned to study the apparent variation in the ceramic types.

11

Theory, Measurement, and Explanation
Variable Shapes in Poverty Point Objects

Christopher Pierce

Because most of the things archaeologists study are relatively easy to observe, we have had little difficulty generating abundant descriptions of the archaeological record. However, we have been less successful at constructing useful descriptions that produce secure descriptive and explanatory knowledge of human cultural history. With the exception of dating, there are few observations archaeologists routinely make that will settle a dispute over meaning attributed to descriptions of the archaeological record. This problem derives in large part from inadequate attention paid explicitly to assessing the reliability and validity of our empirical and conceptual units. Reliability refers to the accuracy and precision or repeatability of specific observations, while validity involves the relevance of observations to the particular descriptive or explanatory goals of the research. The common admonition among archaeologists against using data generated by other investigators is a tacit recognition of a problem with data reliability. In spite of the fact that we realize various kinds of errors exist in archaeological descriptions stemming from the use of samples as well as errors introduced through the processes of collection, identification, measurement, and reporting, we frequently do not evaluate or document the reliability of these descriptions. Validity, in contrast, has received greater attention by archaeologists (see Ramenofsky and Steffen, this volume). For example, Binford's middle-range research (1981) and Schiffer's Behavioral Archaeology (1976, 1988b) are both explicitly designed to address the validity of units for generating certain kinds of behavioral descriptions. However, questions of unit validity continue to plague archaeology, particularly regarding abstract validity (see Ramenofsky and Steffen, this volume), or the coherence between the conceptual synthetic units employed in explanation and the empirical analytical units of description. The typical excavation report offers an excellent example of this problem. These reports usually contain extensive archaeological and environmental descriptions followed by a synthetic or interpretive section which bears little or no relationship to the preceding descriptions in terms of the units employed.

Although this criticism is harsh, I think there are good reasons why archaeologists have avoided assessing reliability and continue to struggle with abstract validity. We often consider reliability and validity separately, but a case can be made for a very close and hierarchical relationship between these two forms of unit evaluation. In the few cases in which archaeologists have consistently attempted to assess reliability, they have been working with valid units or units believed to be valid. For example, culture historians were concerned with both the accuracy and precision of the relative frequency data they employed in seriations (e.g., Beals et al. 1945:164–68). Thus, there seems to be a general, though implicit, recognition among archaeologists that establishing unit reliability makes sense only if you are going to *do* something meaningful with the measurements. Given the potentially high costs of assessing reliability (often involving measuring the same thing multiple times) and the limited financial resources constraining most archaeological work, performing reliability assessment only on valid units is entirely reasonable. Thus, the lack of concern for unit reliability stems from a problem with validity. However, establishing the validity of archaeological units is no simple task, particularly in the absence of a widely accepted general theory.

In this chapter, I intend to show how theory can provide the rationale for the construction and evaluation of both conceptual and empirical units employed in the investigation of a particular archaeological problem. The theory I use is an expanded form of evolutionary theory that is currently receiving considerable attention in archaeology (e.g., Dunnell 1978, 1980, 1989, 1992a; Leonard and Jones 1987; Neff 1992; Neiman 1995; O'Brien and Holland 1990, 1992; O'Brien et al. 1994; Ramenofsky 1991; Rindos 1984, 1989; Teltser, ed. 1995) as well as in a variety of other disciplines involved in the study of the human condition (e.g., Barkow et al. 1992; Basalla 1988; Boyd and Richerson 1985; Bradie 1994; Campbell 1988; Cavalli-Sforza and Feldman 1981; Cziko 1995; Dennett 1991, 1995; Durham 1991; Holland 1995; Hull 1988b; Nelson and Winter 1982; Perkinson 1993; Pinker 1994). The research problem is one of long-standing interest to archaeologists working in the lower Mississippi Valley, and involves trying to explain why Poverty Point objects (an abundant class of early ceramic artifacts used in cooking) were so variable morphologically.

THE PROBLEM: PREVIOUS ATTEMPTS TO DESCRIBE AND EXPLAIN POVERTY POINT OBJECT VARIATION

Poverty Point objects are shaped and unshaped balls of fired clay that are abundant in Late Archaic and Early Woodland midden deposits of the lower Mississippi Valley and adjacent coastal regions (Figure 11.1). The earliest dates for Poverty Point objects are from the third millennium B.C. (Dunnell and Whittaker 1990; Ramenofsky and Mires 1985), but they appear to have been used most frequently between 1500 to 1000 B.C. (Huxtable et al. 1972). Surficial impressions show that Poverty Point objects were made by rolling a small lump of moist clay between bare hands. A variety of shapes were then produced by altering the motion (circular, reciprocal, and compressive) and the part of the hand used (palms versus fingers). In some cases, further modifications such as grooves and incisions were made to the basic forms using fingers or some other instrument. Common Poverty Point object shapes include plain bicones, grooved bicones, grooved cylinders, grooved spheres (referred to as cross-grooved), grooved ellipsoids (referred to as melon-shaped), plain spheres, and disk-like forms (referred to as biscuit-shaped) (Ford and Webb 1956; Webb 1968, 1982). Less common forms vary widely in their basic shape and in having such modifications as incisions, punctations, etc. (Webb 1982: 38–39). Variation in size is less pronounced with most objects weighing between 50 and 80 grams, although very small and very large examples occur (Webb 1982:37). These shape classes are the most common form of description of Poverty Point objects. Little attention has been paid to other aspects of variation such as technology, composition, use-alteration, etc.

Poverty Point objects routinely occur dispersed in midden deposits or contained in pit features, often with other burned material. The restriction of Poverty Point objects to domestic contexts in stone-poor environments together with the fact that they were fired, warrant the common interpretation that these objects served as heating elements in earth ovens and other cooking technologies analogous to the way that stones were used in more stone-rich environments prior to the development of pottery vessels (DePratter 1979; Ford et al. 1955; Gibson 1975;

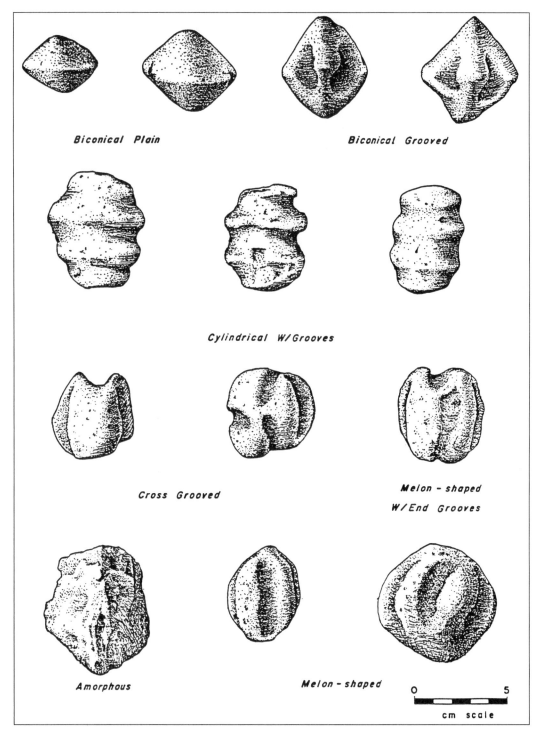

Figure 11.1. Common forms of Poverty Point objects from the Poverty Point site (reprinted from Ford and Webb [1956] with permission of the American Museum of Natural History).

Hunter 1975; Webb 1982). Other interpretations of Poverty Point objects include their use as atlatl weights (South 1970), gaming pieces (Moore 1913:73–74), pot rests, fishing-net weights, bola weights, "slingstones" for hunting, and heating elements in sweat baths (Bunn 1974). These latter interpretations have generally been rejected for lack of supporting evidence (Hunter 1975).

Archaeologists working with Poverty Point assemblages in the 1950s and 1960s treated the Poverty Point object shape variants as style markers (Webb 1968, 1982; see also Gibson 1991; Ramenofsky 1983). This approach to Poverty Point objects derived from an underlying assumption that Poverty Point object distributions and formal variation resulted from patterns of cultural interaction and transmission rather than from constraints imposed by the environment or particular uses. This assumption, together with the great abundance of Poverty Point objects in late prepottery sites in the lower Mississippi Valley, led to the use of Poverty Point objects to track the occurrence and influence of Poverty Point culture and order assemblages in time through seriation (Ford et al. 1955; Ford and Webb 1956; Gagliano and Saucier 1963; Webb 1968). Neither of these attempts to use Poverty Point objects as style markers succeeded. The unvarying association of Poverty Point objects with stone-poor environments in the lower Mississippi Valley region and the occurrence of similar clay objects in stone-poor areas of Australia (Clark and Barbetti 1982) and California's Central Valley (Heizer 1937; Schenck and Dawson 1929; Wedel 1941) undermine the notion that the distribution of these objects matches the distribution of a "Poverty Point culture." Although considerable variation exists in the relative frequencies of different Poverty Point object forms vertically and horizontally within particular deposits and among different sites, the failure to produce effective seriations suggests that morphological variation is not entirely stylistic (Webb 1982:28).

Growth of the more functionally oriented New Archaeology in the 1970s led to new interpretations of Poverty Point object variation. Gibson (1974, 1975, 1985) and Hunter (1975) in separate studies experimented with replicated Poverty Point objects to test their effectiveness as heating elements in earth oven cooking. Gibson's experiments, the details of which are unpublished, indicate to him that the different shapes of Poverty Point objects created different thermal conditions in the earth ovens both in terms of the amount or intensity of the heat and the rate of temperature change. Although Gibson did not experiment with the more elaborately decorated forms (incised, punctated, etc.), his experience with their spatial distributions at the Poverty Point site suggest to him that their variation is stylistic (1972, 1973). Hunter's experiments demonstrate that shaped clay balls work well as heating elements in earth ovens and that grooved forms were easier to handle during the cooking operation. He also found that replicated and archaeological specimens could be heated and cooled several times without significant damage to the objects. Unfortunately, Hunter's experiments were not designed explicitly to evaluate the effectiveness of different forms.

Further evidence of the possible functional nature of variation among the different forms comes from their temporal distributions. After the adoption of pottery, the diversity of Poverty Point object forms decreased dramatically, but some forms such as the small bicones continued to be made and used well after vessel ceramics became common (Dunnell and Whittaker 1990; Ford and Quimby 1945; Phillips 1970; Webb 1982). From a functional perspective, differential persistence of Poverty Point object forms may result from the use of variant forms in different activities, some of which were later usurped by pottery while others were not. However, other explanations are possible that have no implications for the differential use of Poverty Point object forms before the introduction of pottery. For example, the forms that persisted may have taken on new uses possibly created by the introduction of pottery. It is also possible that the initial use of pottery simply reduced the frequency with which Poverty Point objects were manufactured and used for the same tasks. Making fewer Poverty Point objects alone could account for the reduction in diversity of forms, particularly if the difference among forms is stylistic. Under such circumstances, chance alone would result in the most abundant forms persisting at the expense of those less frequently made.

The spatial and temporal distributions of Poverty Point objects as a whole, and of analogous objects in other parts of the world, make it clear that the use of molded clay balls for heat transfer constitutes an adaptation in stone-poor environments in the absence of vessel technology. However, the cause or causes of variation in the shape of Poverty Point objects are less clear. Gibson's and Hunter's informal experiments indicate that variation in the shape of Poverty Point objects may affect their performance in cooking activities, conferring a possible functional significance to that variation. This possibility does not explain why there is such variation within and among settlements in the lower Mississippi Valley. The variable spatial and temporal distributions of Poverty Point object forms may still result from patterns of cultural interaction and transmission (i.e, stylistic). However, it is more likely that Poverty Point object variation was caused by a complex mixture of mechanisms. Traditional empirical and conceptual units mixed style and function, crippling our ability to distinguish and evaluate particular causal mechanisms.

AN EVOLUTIONARY APPROACH TO DESCRIBING AND EXPLAINING POVERTY POINT OBJECT VARIATION

Evolutionary theory identifies selection and drift as two fundamentally distinct sets of mechanisms which can filter and structure variation that is transmitted either genetically or culturally. Selection enhances fitness and adaptation to extant conditions by promoting beneficial variation and eliminating variation that is deleterious. Drift, on the other hand, filters variation that is selectively neutral, or nonadaptive. The conceptual units of selection and drift encompass a variety of more specific mechanisms that are used to construct explanations of the differential spatial distributions and temporal persistence of particular empirical units such as traits, populations, etc. Dunnell (1978) linked these evolutionary concepts to archaeology by defining function and style in terms of selection and drift, respectively. Although function and style have long histories as conceptual units in archaeology, redefining these units in evolutionary terms unified them for the first time into a single, coherent theoretical package.

The theoretical coherence of style and function as conceptual units in archaeology has two benefits. First, the kinds of mechanisms invoked to explain patterns of style and function are theoretically constrained and logically linked. This approach creates the possibility of comparing explanations of specific cases of cultural change, and thus enhances the prospects of gaining more general knowledge of the processes of cultural change. Second, the evolutionary definitions of style and function have empirical ramifications that facilitate the construction of units used to measure the archaeological record. These empirical units are more likely to produce useful (i.e., explainable) descriptions by virtue of their logical linkage to the theory used to generate potential explanations.

The evolutionary definitions of style and function justify three kinds of descriptions of the archaeological record: engineering, distributional, and contextual (e.g., Durand 1992; Feathers 1990; Maxwell 1995; Neiman 1995; O'Brien et al. 1994; Pierce 1996). Engineering descriptions seek to measure the use and relative cost and performance of specific variants because differences in these qualities create the potential for selection. These engineering measurements, as well as other kinds of descriptions, provide the content for an analysis of the distributional characteristics of variation. Distributional descriptions document the relative frequencies of variants both spatially and temporally and provide further evidence for the work of selection or drift. Finally, descriptions of the contexts (social, technological, environmental, etc.) in which change occurred are essential for constructing hypotheses regarding the specific mechanisms involved in either the selection or drift of variation in particular cases.

Generating observations along the various dimensions of engineering, distributional, and contextual descriptions requires units with very specific and well-defined empirical referents. Here, the conceptual units and the archaeological record come together in the context of a given problem and set of archaeological materials. In producing descriptions appropriate for explaining variation of Poverty Point object shape, I employ a wide variety of observations drawn from several sources. These sources include existing published data, new observations derived from published information (mainly illustrations of Poverty Point objects), and the results of new analyses of Poverty Point objects and assemblages. As is probably apparent, many observations archaeologists currently make can be integrated into the conceptual and descriptive framework discussed here. Unfortunately though, in most cases of existing published data, the empirical validity (Is it measuring what I want it to measure?) and reliability (How accurate and precise is the measurement?) have not been assessed. Although my intentions are to establish the validity and reliability of both the existing and new descriptions, poor or missing data occasionally force me to make simplifying assumptions and use relatively coarse measures.

Despite variable success in meeting the difficult challenge of providing both valid and reliable descriptions, this new approach to explaining variation in Poverty Point object shape succeeds in revealing some intriguing, previously unrecognized qualities of Poverty Point objects and patterns among Poverty Point object assemblages. These empirical patterns further indicate the work of both functional (selection) and stylistic (drift) mechanisms through their direct linkage to theoretically defined conceptual units. In addition, the problems that arise from using published data and the potential explanations I offer to account for observed patterns

identify concrete directions for future research that can evaluate and build on my initial analyses.

ENGINEERING DESCRIPTION OF POVERTY POINT OBJECTS

Measuring the relative engineering qualities of Poverty Point objects must begin with a consideration of use, which involves documenting the conditions to which they were exposed during use and then using this information to determine if the different forms were used in the same ways. If their use was homogenous across the various forms, then the cost and performance of different Poverty Point object classes can be fruitfully compared as true use-alternatives. The goal of such a cost/benefit analysis is to assess the effectiveness of the different Poverty Point object designs as solutions to physical and chemical challenges created by the use environment.

The descriptions of Poverty Point object use, cost, and performance employed in this study include examination of recovery contexts, use-related alterations, number of production steps, use-life, heat transfer effectiveness, heat storage capacity, and ease of handling. Generating these descriptions involved combining data from new analyses with existing descriptions. I performed two new analyses. The first involved taking measurements on published illustrations of complete Poverty Point objects. The second was an examination of Poverty Point object fragments collected from the surface of the Grey Horse Lake site (23PM571), a large Late Archaic accretional mound located on the western edge of the Little River lowlands in Pemiscott County, Missouri (Dunnell and Whittaker 1990). The measurements of complete Poverty Point objects provide data on the thermal properties of different forms, while the physical and morphological studies of Poverty Point object fragments contribute information on the conditions under which Poverty Point objects were used and their use-life, or durability through multiple uses. Details on the procedures used in these studies and assessments of the empirical validity and reliability of these data are presented below along with a discussion of the results.

POVERTY POINT OBJECT USE

Two approaches exist for determining the use of Poverty Point objects: context and use-related alterations. The associations of Poverty Point objects with structural features and other artifacts in primary or use contexts can provide information from which to gauge similarities in use of the different forms. Use-related alterations (i.e., traces left by matter-energy interactions during use) indicate the nature of the interactions between Poverty Point objects and their use environment. Specifically, use-alterations permit inferences regarding the physical and chemical conditions to which Poverty Point objects were exposed during use. Alteration data complement contextual information in terms of documenting similarities in use. In addition, use-alterations can indicate the nature of the environmental challenges of use and, therefore, provide a basis for selecting relevant measures of performance.

As mentioned earlier, contextual data have been used to warrant the inference that Poverty Point objects were utilized as heating elements in earth ovens and possibly other cooking and heating activities. Within this general use as heating elements, it is possible that different forms were employed in different tasks (such as earth-oven cooking of solids versus cooking of liquids in baskets) that exposed them to different conditions and challenges. The only primary use context from which Poverty Point objects have been recovered are pit features containing burned material. Of course, Poverty Point objects used for cooking in baskets and other low visibility activities would usually not be recovered in their primary use contexts. Instead, they would probably have been deposited in middens or other secondary contexts. In both middens and pit feature contexts, Poverty Point object forms in any particular location range from the occurrence of a single form to a highly diverse assortment of forms. Consequently, contextual data are inconclusive regarding the use of Poverty Point objects in distinct kinds of cooking and heating activities, but the occurrence of different forms in the same use contexts suggests that, at least part of the time, different forms were used in the same way.

The dominant use-related alterations of Poverty Point objects consist of physical and chemical changes resulting from exposure to heat. However, the only published analysis focuses on chemical changes. From a site along the coast of South Carolina, Trinkley (1986:211–12) analyzed the phosphate content of sherds of fiber-tempered pottery and a baked clay object similar to Poverty Point objects. He found that the pottery sherds are higher in phosphate than the baked clay ball. Based on these results and Duma's suggestion (1972) that the phosphate content of pottery is affected by organic enrichment through use, Trinkley argues that the baked clay object was not used to boil liquids, but may have been used to roast food in an earth oven. However, differences in the phosphorus content of raw clay materials can also account for a variation between pottery and clay ball phosphate content (Dunnell and Hunt 1990).

I examined numerous Poverty Point object fragments from the Grey Horse Lake site to obtain data on physical changes that can provide data on the temperature, atmosphere, and rates of temperature change that occurred during use. I used two characteristics, degree of sintering and patterns of thermoremanant magnetization, to evaluate the maximum temperature reached during heating. Observations of freshly broken surfaces of numerous Poverty Point object fragments under low magnification (10X–40X) show no sintering, suggesting that Poverty Point objects were fired at relatively low temperatures, probably well below 900°C. Stepwise thermal demagnetization of fragments from one biconical Poverty Point object resulted in a substantial decline in magnetic intensity between 500° and 600°C with the clearing of magnetism associated with the mineral magnetite and a very slight decrease in remanent magnetism with the clearing of hematite between 650° and 700°C (Pierce 1993). These patterns indicate the maximum temperature during heating was probably between 500° and 700°C, a temperature range commonly reached in open fires.

The interior and exterior color on fragments of five biconical Poverty Point objects from the Grey Horse Lake site were measured to obtain data on the atmosphere during heating and cooling (Pierce 1993). Reddish exterior colors of all five fragments and reddish exteriors on objects observed by Webb (1982:37) indicate cooling in an oxidizing atmosphere. Interior colors in the Grey Horse Lake sample range from red to grayish brown. This variation in interior color indicates that although the atmosphere during cooling was consistent among different objects, the atmosphere during heating may have differed.

Finally, I examined fracture patterns for evidence of the rate of temperature change during heating and cooling. Most Poverty Point objects appear to have been fractured by thermal shock or thermal fatigue. A cursory examination of all of the Poverty Point object fragments from Grey Horse Lake revealed two kinds of fracture patterns, surface spalls and deep angular fractures. Data on nonelastic strain (physical failure) resulting from thermal stress in solids indicate that rapid heating generates spall fractures whereas relatively rapid cooling creates deep angular fractures (Blackwelder 1927; Finnie et al. 1979; Gray 1965; Schalk and Meatte 1988). Based on these observations, I was unable to discern any clear association of particular fracture patterns with specific forms. However, this observation should be considered with caution given the difficulty of identifying the form of Poverty Point objects from small fragments.

The importance of accurately describing the use of different Poverty Point object forms certainly warrants a more thorough evaluation than is currently possible. However, both existing contextual *and* alteration data lack any clear evidence for differential use of particular forms, although some evidence does exist for different use conditions among objects of the same form. Given the

data available, it seems likely that all the different forms of Poverty Point objects were used to meet a variety of heating and cooking needs, but different forms were not used exclusively in ways that would have exposed them to radically different environmental challenges. Thus, for this study, I treat the different forms of Poverty Point objects as true alternatives for the same use and thus comparable in terms of cost and performance. This assumption facilitates and simplifies the evaluation of relative performance because the only knowledge needed to select relevant performance measures is that Poverty Point objects were exposed to heat during use.

POVERTY POINT OBJECT COST

The use of tools can incur costs at five stages: production, transport, use, maintenance, and discard. Production costs involve the amount of materials and energy used in the acquisition of raw materials and the transformation of these raw materials into a useful form. Transport costs can vary depending on the transport technology, transport distance, and the condition (mass, volume, shape, temperature, toxicity, etc.) of the things being transported. During use, the costs of tools can vary in terms of the amount of time and energy required to do a specified amount of work and the length of time different tools can be used before maintenance and/or replacement becomes necessary (use-life or durability). Although largely a function of durability, maintenance costs can vary with the design of the technology—for example, serial versus modular designs (Bleed 1986). Discard can incur potentially variable costs due to the need to manage movement and placement of wastes and their impacts on the environment.

Variation in costs among different tools at any of these stages creates an opportunity for selection to act on these differences. Since there is no evidence that Poverty Point objects were differentially maintained or discarded, potential variation in costs among different forms can appear in the energy invested in production and their durability during use. Potential differences in energy re-

TABLE 11.1
Production-Step Measures for Poverty Point Objects from the Poverty Point Site

Production Step	Poverty Point Object Forms									
	AMP	CYG	BIP	SPP	BSP	ELG	SPG	BIG	BIN	ELT
Raw Mat.	1	1	1	1	1	1	1	1	1	1
Raw Mat.	1	1	1	1	1	1	1	1	1	1
Basic	—	1	1	1	1	1	1	1	1	1
Grooving	—	—	—	—	—	1	1	1	—	1
Incising	—	—	—	—	—	—	—	—	1	—
Punching	—	—	—	—	—	—	—	—	—	—
Twisting	—	—	—	—	—	—	—	—	—	1
TOTAL	2	3	3	3	3	4	4	4	4	5

AMP = amorphous; CYG = grooved cylinder; BIP = plain bicone; SPP = plain sphere; BSP = plain biscuit-shaped; ELG = grooved, ellipsoid melon-shaped; SPG = grooved sphere, cross-grooved; BIG = grooved bicone; BIN = incised bicone; ELT = twisted, grooved, ellipsoid melon-shaped twisted.

quirements during use and transport are considered in the next section on performance.

In using currently available information, relative production costs are best measured ordinally by counting the number of different production steps (Feinman et al. 1981). The production steps for Poverty Point objects include acquisition of raw materials, preparation of raw materials, basic shaping of the object, grooving, punching, incising, and twisting. When this ordinal measure is used, the cost involved in each step is treated equally—which realistically cannot be the case. However, the apparent use of local raw materials and relative ease of manufacture of Poverty Point objects may minimize the distortions introduced by ordinal measurement. In addition, I performed informal replication experiments that indicate potentially significant differences in the amount of time needed to perform the different shaping steps. Basic shaping of biconical Poverty Point objects required between seven and ten seconds per object. Grooved cylinders required two to three seconds longer per object and amorphous forms were made in about one third the amount of time of bicones. Added grooves, incisions, and punches also required approximately three seconds for each step in addition to the basic shaping.

Potential values for the production-step measure range from two for unshaped (amorphous) objects to seven for highly decorated objects. As an example of the common range of actual values, Table 11.1 shows the production-step measures for the 10 most common Poverty Point object forms at the Poverty Point site. These forms account for over 96 percent of the identifiable objects recovered from the site (Webb 1982:39). The number of production steps ranges from two to five, although the five most common forms, consisting of 88 percent of the assemblage, differ only in one production step. Given that Poverty Point objects were made in great quantities, small differences in the production cost of the most common forms could be significant.

The durability of Poverty Point objects affects their cost by limiting the number of times an object can be used before replacement becomes necessary. Since Poverty Point objects were exposed to heat during use and do not appear to have been used in ways that generated significant impact or frictional stresses, resistance to failure due to thermal stress through shock and fatigue constitutes the most relevant measure of durability. Resistance to thermal shock and fatigue is a function of both material and object properties. Material properties include porosity, thermal diffusivity, elasticity, and tensile strength, while object properties include size and shape (Rice 1987:363–69; Steponaitis 1984). Although none of these characteristics has been adequately documented for Poverty Point objects, current knowledge permits some assumptions regarding the relative resistance of different forms. The generally low thermal diffusivity of ceramics suggests that the critical temperature difference for the initiation of thermal shock is relatively low for all forms. However, Poverty Point objects tend to be quite porous, which can increase their resistance to the propagation of cracks once initiated (Hasselman 1969). Analyses of five biconical Poverty Point object fragments from the Grey Horse Lake site yielded apparent porosity values ranging from 35 percent to 50 percent with a mean of 42.3 percent and standard deviation of 6.1 percent (Pierce 1993). These porosity values are almost twice as large as values measured in the same way on early sand-tempered pottery also from sites in southeastern Missouri (Feathers 1990:579). Since the different shapes all tend to be fairly rounded and made of similar material in similar ways, the most important dimension of form affecting thermal stress resistance is probably absolute size (Crandall and Ging 1955). Although size variation exists among different forms (discussed in more detail shortly), most of the objects for which size data are available fall within a fairly narrow range.

The only experimental data on durability comes from Hunter's informal observations (1975) made during the use of replicated Poverty Point objects in earth ovens. He found that Poverty Point objects lasted through several heating and cooling cycles, which matches expectations for Poverty Point object durability given the physical properties described above. It is also likely that little variation in durability exists among the different Poverty Point object forms since they are so similar in the physical properties that control durability.

POVERTY POINT OBJECT PERFORMANCE
Performance refers to the effectiveness of alternative forms of technology in carrying out specific kinds of work. Thus, measures of performance must be linked to the kinds of work actually being done (Kleindienst and Keller 1976) and the organizational context in which that work takes place (Nelson 1991). Because current evidence indicates that Poverty Point objects were used to store and transfer heat in domestic contexts, performance measures should provide data on the relative effectiveness of different forms as portable heating elements. Three properties can be used to evaluate the relative effectiveness of alternative forms: transient heat transfer effectiveness, heat storage capacity, and ease of handling.

Transient Heat Transfer Effectiveness
Transient heat transfer effectiveness refers to the rate at which heat energy is transferred between Poverty Point objects and their environment during heating and cooling (Holman 1990; Schneider 1955). Assuming a uniform temperature within an object, its rate of heat gain or loss is described by the following differential equation:

$$q = -cpV\frac{dT}{d\tau} = hA(T-T_f)$$

where

q = heat-transfer rate,
τ = time,
T = temperature of the object at time τ,
T_f = ambient temperature of the surrounding environment,
h = surface convection heat-transfer coefficient,
A = surface area for convection,
c = specific heat of the object,
p = density of the object,
V = volume of the object.

Although Poverty Point objects almost certainly did not function under uniform internal temperatures, this assumption vastly simplifies the treatment of transient heat transfer and does not compromise the validity of the analysis presented here. The solution to the heat-transfer equation above for the temperature of the body at a specific time during heating ($T_f > T_i$) or cooling ($T_f < T_i$) takes the following form:

$$\frac{T - T_f}{T_o - T_f} = e^{-(\frac{hA}{\rho cV})\tau}$$

where T_o = initial temperature of the object.

The left side of this solution describes the boundary conditions or the temperature change to which the object is exposed. The right side of the solution describes the conditions of the object and its relation to the surrounding environment. The solution indicates that the uniform temperature of an object changes exponentially with time, and the time required to undergo a specified temperature change is directly proportional to the object's surface resistivity, specific heat, density, and surface area to volume ratio. To solve this equation for different Poverty Point object forms would require measurements of the surface convection coefficient and specific heat as well as knowledge of boundary conditions, none of which we possess. However, if we assume, as I argued for earlier, that the composition and forming techniques (which determine specific heat and density) and conditions of use (temperature change, time, and convective environment) are similar across forms, we can treat all terms in the solution equation as constants except the surface area to volume ratio. Assuming reasonably uniform composition, construction, and use conditions, surface area to volume ratio provides a suitable measure of the relative heat transfer effectiveness of Poverty Point objects.

Because archaeologists have not measured or reported the surface area and volume of Poverty Point objects, I generated these data from published illustrations. Accordingly, I made photocopies of all scaled drawings and photographs I could locate in the archaeological literature. Using a ZIDAS digitizing tablet, I digitized the scale from the illustration and then traced the outline of each Poverty Point object three times with the digitizing wand. With each outline trace, the digitizer measured the perimeter and area of

the Poverty Point object illustration. Taking multiple measurements allows evaluation of the measurement accuracy and precision and controls for measurement blunders. The measured sample consists of 197 whole illustrated objects collected from at least 22 different sites located in eight states extending from southern Indiana to the mouth of the Mississippi River and east to Florida and South Carolina (Pierce 1993).

Three problems may affect this data set: sample bias, two-dimensionality, and spatial autocorrelation. First, biases certainly exist in the kinds of objects selected for illustration. The most pronounced bias is that all of the illustrated objects are complete. Since objects must be complete to obtain the measurements, using only the illustrated artifacts sidesteps this problem. The formation processes responsible for leaving some objects whole while reducing the vast majority to fragments are not well documented. Choices of objects for illustration also tend to emphasize shaped forms over amorphous forms. Of the hundreds of illustrated Poverty Point objects, I could find only four examples of amorphous forms despite the great abundance of amorphous objects in some assemblages. The potential biasing effects of these and other formation processes and illustration choices cannot be evaluated without a more thorough study of Poverty Point object fragments and other objects not chosen for illustration.

Second, the illustrations allow measurements in two dimensions, but surface area and volume are three-dimensional attributes. To approximate surface area and volume, the perimeter length and cross-sectional area of the illustrated Poverty Point objects were measured by digitizing the perimeter of each illustrated object. For objects with a single axis of symmetry, digitized perimeter-to-area ratios are directly related to surface-area–to–volume ratios in a linear fashion with a y intercept of 0 and a slope close to 1.5. With forms that do not meet the axial symmetry requirement, such as those possessing grooves parallel to the axis of symmetry, like grooved ellipses, spheres, and bicones, the

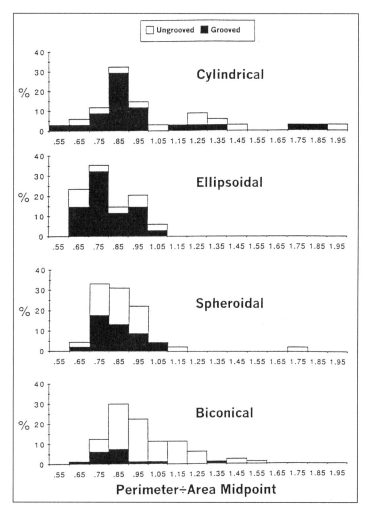

Figure 11.2. Digitized perimeter-to-area ratios for different Poverty Point object forms.

surface-area–to–volume ratio may be underestimated by the perimeter to area ratio.

Finally, 35 percent (69 objects) of the sample used here is from one site, the Poverty Point site in northeast Louisiana. No other single site accounts for more than 5 percent of the sample. Because of the possibility that a large number of objects from one site could skew the sample as a whole, I assessed the values for objects from Poverty Point against the rest of the sample. The two-sample t-test statistics comparing the mean values of area and perimeter-to-area ratio indicate that the objects from Poverty Point are statistically indistinguishable (p =.05) from the rest of the

sample in these two dimensions. Since spatial autocorrelation does not adversely affect aspects of the data set relevant to thermal properties, and impacts of two-dimensional measurements are known, it is reasonable to assume that the measurements of perimeter and area from illustrations provide a suitable data set for this initial evaluation of performance.

Figure 11.2 shows that the distributions of perimeter-to-area ratios are quite similar for grooved and ungrooved variants of the four most common forms. The greater variation of cylindrical forms is expected since they are manufactured using a reciprocal

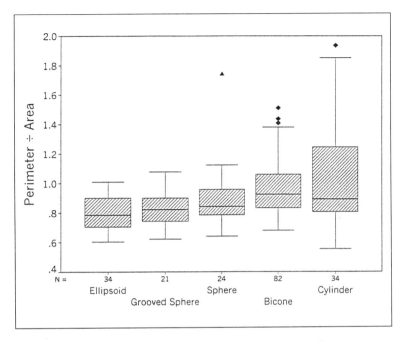

Figure 11.3. Box plots of perimeter-to-area ratios for different Poverty Point object forms.

motion that provides less control over size and shape than do the circular motions used in making the other forms. Figure 11.3 presents box plots of the perimeter-to-area ratio for five forms. Although the box plot shows little variance in median values among the forms, a Tukey-type test of a Kruskal-Wallis ANOVA indicates that significant ($p < .05$) differences exist between the mean-rank perimeter-to-area ratios of the ellipsoidal forms and the bicones and cylinders. However, the digitizing technique employed to measure perimeter and area underestimates the ratios of the ellipsoidal forms, suggesting that the significant differences are probably an artifact of measurement rather than an indication of significant difference in heat transfer effectiveness.

Heat Storage Capacity

The heat storage capacity of an object is a function of its size and composition. Since different Poverty Point object forms appear to be very similar in composition, size provides an adequate measure of the relative quantity of heat stored by different forms.

Two sources of data are available on the size of Poverty Point objects. The first consists of the measurements derived from the scaled illustrations used in the discussion of heat transfer effectiveness. Figure 11.4 shows the distributions of digitized cross-sectional area for grooved and ungrooved variants of the four most common Poverty Point object forms. The histograms show some variation in size among different forms, and a one-way ANOVA demonstrates significant ($p < .05$) differences in the mean size of some forms. As a second source of data, Webb (1982:37–40) published the ranges of dimensions for common and extreme sizes of different Poverty Point object types. He noted that biconical forms tend to be smaller and that grooved cylinders and spheres tend to be larger, but the form of his data does not allow statistical comparisons. Although both sources indicate that variation in size exists among the shape classes of Poverty Point objects, the extensive overlap in size among different forms casts doubt on the performance significance of these differences. The quantity of heat brought to a particular use event

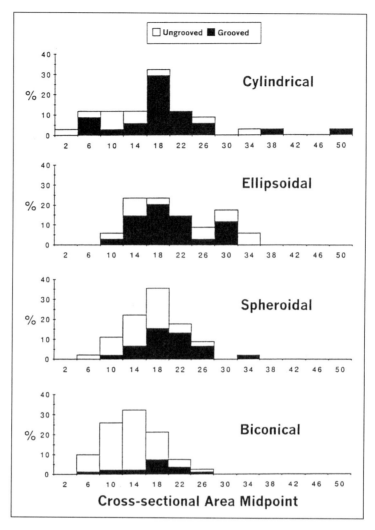

Figure 11.4. Digitized cross-sectional area for different Poverty Point object forms.

can be adjusted by either altering the size of individual objects or varying the number of individual objects. Consequently, other constraints on size may have a stronger influence than heat storage capacity. These constraints include the effects of size on heat transfer performance, durability, and handling. Figure 11.5 depicts the relation between size measured as area and the perimeter-to-area ratio of illustrated Poverty Point objects plotted with a curve showing the same relation for a circle of varying radius. The hyperbolic relation between size and

perimeter-to-area ratio dictates that, for small objects, changes in size have a pronounced effect on heat transfer performance whereas changes in size of larger objects produce little effect. The clustering of measured Poverty Point objects around the inflection region of the curve suggests that heat transfer performance was under stronger selective pressure than was heat storage capacity. Larger objects are also more susceptible to structural failure during drying and use. Stresses created by moisture gradients during drying and thermal gradients during heating

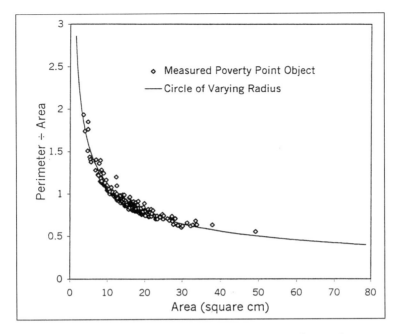

Figure 11.5. Scatter plot of perimeter-to-area ratio and size of Poverty Point objects.

and cooling increase with the size of the object if composition and structure remain constant, which, in itself, may select against the production of large objects. However, it is also possible that differential breakage of objects according to size could create a bias against the recovery of complete larger objects in relation to smaller objects. Finally, use conditions may place strong constraints on size. The size of Poverty Point objects can affect air flow, thereby either promoting or inhibiting combustion. Individual objects can also be either too small or too large for effective handling and transport. Selection for certain sizes may result from uses involving different forms of handling and transport. Given the potential for multiple constraints on size variation, some of which are unrelated to performance (i.e., differential preservation), and the considerable overlap in size among different forms, it seems prudent to avoid overemphasizing the observed variation and to treat the different forms as roughly equivalent in terms of heat storage capacity.

Ease of Handling

This third aspect of performance is the most difficult to measure with existing information. If heated Poverty Point objects were moved from one location to another, some means of handling them would have been necessary. If the handling technology involved clasping individual objects, then objects with rough or irregular surfaces would be easier to handle. While conducting experiments with Poverty Point object replicas, Hunter (1975) noted that grooved forms were more easily handled using two sticks than were ungrooved forms. If promoting ease of handling is the purpose of grooves, then one would expect other forms of surface roughening as well, but no such forms exist. Without additional information on the conditions of use, in particular whether Poverty Point objects were used in ways that required transport of individual objects—to heat liquids, for example—it is impossible to evaluate this performance factor. However, the inability to evaluate ease of handling may have little impact on this analysis if I am correct in assuming that different Poverty Point object forms were used in similar ways.

SUMMARY OF ENGINEERING DESCRIPTION

Differences in cost and performance under comparable production and use conditions constitute the basis for determining the relative engineering effectiveness of variant Poverty Point object forms. The analysis of recovery contexts and use-alterations suggests that different kinds of Poverty Point objects were used as heating elements under similar conditions. This assessment of use established the comparability of Poverty Point objects for the engineering analysis. Poverty Point objects constitute true alternatives or states of the same trait. In addition, the use analysis indicated the kinds of measurements needed to evaluate the relative cost and performance of different Poverty Point object forms. Based on the engineering analyses presented above, production cost differences appear to be the most significant among the alternative forms of Poverty Point objects. The data on size showing a fairly narrow range and optimality (in terms of the relation between heat transfer and heat storage) indicate that this dimension was constrained by selective pressure acting equally on all Poverty Point object forms. In addition, the wide variety of shapes appear to have no impact on performance.

If differences in the cost of making Poverty Point objects were large enough to affect the fitness of the people who made them, the spatial and temporal distribution of variation in production costs of particular assemblages should display a nonrandom pattern attributable to selection. However, variation in the shape of Poverty Point objects with little or no effect on cost or performance should display a stylistic distribution attributable to patterns of cultural transmission and drift.

DISTRIBUTIONAL DESCRIPTION OF POVERTY POINT OBJECTS

The relative success of different Poverty Point object forms can be evaluated by examining their distributions in time and space. Unfortunately, patterns of temporal varia-

tion in Poverty Point object forms are difficult to document because assemblages either are poorly dated or were accumulated over long periods of time. Webb (1982:37) suggests that the earliest forms tend to be spheroidal, ellipsoidal, and biscuit-shaped (see also Ramenofsky 1983). It is also apparent that during the 500 years or so the Poverty Point site was occupied, a wide variety of forms were made. After the large-scale adoption of pottery vessel technology, the diversity of forms decreased radically and small biconical forms dominate assemblages. However, as discussed earlier, the causes of this reduction in diversity remain unclear. The addition of temper in some areas may also coincide with the introduction of pottery vessels (Dunnell and Whittaker 1990; Klippel 1969), but this aspect of Poverty Point object technology has not been adequately studied. The nature of these changes suggests some sorting of different forms and technologies through time, but the quality of the data does not allow a more thorough analysis of temporal patterns.

Spatial distributions are more easily documented because of the wealth of data on Poverty Point object assemblages from roughly contemporary sites throughout the lower Mississippi Valley. The engineering analysis indicates that variation in Poverty Point objects will likely display distinct spatial patterns in the similarity of assemblages. However, before examining the similarity of assemblages, I must first determine the reliability of the assemblages data used in these comparisons. Evaluating the sources of potential data biases is important in any comparison of assemblages, but takes on increased significance in this study because of my heavy reliance on published data and the great deal of variation in sample size, collection method, and analysis represented by these data.

UNIT RELIABILITY: ASSESSING AND COPING WITH BIASES IN ASSEMBLAGE DATA

Two kinds of biases can reduce the reliability of assemblage data. First, samples used to

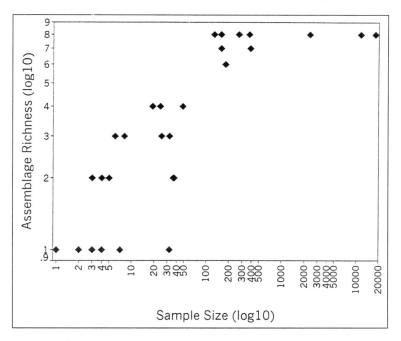

Figure 11.6. Scatter plot of Poverty Point object assemblage richness against sample size.

characterize assemblages can be biased beyond normal sampling error if they are generated in such a way that they do not adequately represent the larger population. Inadequate sample size and flawed sampling design are two ways that unrepresentative or biased samples can be produced. Second, decisions made during the collection, analysis, and reporting of a sample can introduce bias through systematic removal, misidentification, or neglect of certain classes in an assemblage. In this section, I evaluate the reliability of published descriptions of Poverty Point object assemblages and adopt strategies for dealing with identified biases.

Inadequate sample size can bias assemblage data by significantly altering the richness (number of classes represented) and evenness (relative class abundance) of the sample away from the true population value (Leonard and Jones 1989). Consequently, when dealing with samples, it is necessary to evaluate and control for the effects of sample size. Figure 11.6 shows the log-log relation between sample size and the number of shape classes present out of eight possible classes

(biconical, cylindrical, grooved spheres, ellipsoidal, spherical, biscuit-shaped, amorphous, and other). Although sample sizes below 100 items have a strong effect on shape class richness, collections with more than 100 artifacts show little or no sample size effect. Since this comparison includes samples of different sizes drawn from the same sites, we can be fairly certain that these differences are driven by sample size and are not a population characteristic. Thus, we can compare the occurrence of shape classes in the 10 collections with more than 100 artifacts without concern for different sample sizes. Table 11.2 presents relevant information on these 10 assemblages, and Figure 11.7 shows the locations of these sites in the lower Mississippi Valley.

Although class richness in the 10 selected assemblages is apparently unaffected by sample size problems, the number of objects in each class is still potentially subject to biased sampling designs and preferential recovery, analysis, and reporting procedures. Before evaluating the morphological and production cost similarities of the assemblages, the

TABLE 11.2
Data for Sites Included in Analysis of Spatial Distributions of Poverty Point Objects

Site Name	Poverty Point Object Form Frequencies								
	BIC	CYL	ELI	SPH	SPG	BIS	AMP	OTH	Total
Caney Mounds	29	5	1	7	1	58	55	1	157
Claiborne	3259	1230	3476	824	2014	22	476	143	11444
Copes	67	78	130	2	17	11	56	1	362
Hearnes	57	—	5	6	—	8	90	12	178
Jaketown	485	1411	3	29	410	—	—	—	2338
Linsley	58	7	33	4	8	4	7	6	127
Poverty Point	3122	4718	5103	355	3434	138	866	187	17923
Shoe Bayou	23	3	1	1	—	12	116	1	157
Teoc Creek	228	12	2	16	2	2	4	1	267
Terral Lewis	104	—	108	5	93	12	56	4	382

BIC = biconical; CYL = cylindrical; ELI = ellipsoidal; SPH = spheroidal; SPG = grooved sphere; BIS = biscuit; AMP = amorphous; OTH = other.

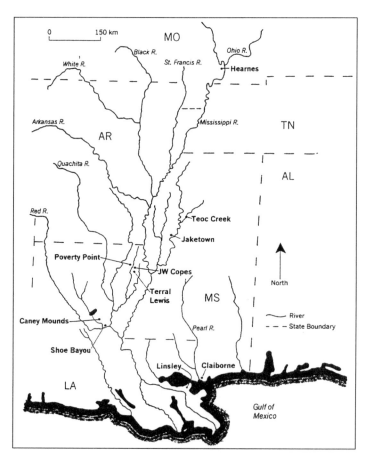

Figure 11.7. Locations within the Mississippi Valley of the 10 sites included in the distributional analysis.

TABLE 11.3
Frequencies of Poverty Point Objects in Multiple Collections from the
Poverty Point Site and the J. W. Copes Site

| Forms | Poverty Point Site Collections[a] | | | J. W. Copes Site Collections[b] | |
	A.M.N.H.	WEBB-BECKMAN	FORD-WEBB[c]	HILLMAN	JACKSON
Amorphous	13	0	282	47	6
Biconical	14	176	73	35	6
Biscuit-shaped[d]	—	—	—	2	6
Ellipsoidal	19	111	167	48	67
Grooved Cylinders	56	401	577	38	22
Grooved Spheres	40	257	559	4	0
Spheroidal	2	6	17	1	0
Production Steps					
Two	13	0	282	47	6
Three	67	464	622	75	34
Four	74	487	1273	53	67

[a]From Ford and Webb 1956:Table 2.
[b]From Webb 1982:Table 2.
[c]Cuts 1–4, 7, 8, and 10.
[d]Biscuit form not identified in Poverty Point collections.

extent to which biases affect the representativeness of the samples must be determined for both dimensions of variation. One way to test the representativeness of samples is to re-sample the same population. Data from multiple samples are available from two sites, the Poverty Point site and the J. W. Copes site (Table 11.3). Ford and Webb (1956:45) report the frequencies of Poverty Point objects in three different collections (each exceeding 100 objects) from the Poverty Point site. Two of the collections were obtained through uncontrolled surface collection, and the third is a compilation of data from several excavation units. Webb (1982:Table 2) presents data on Poverty Point object frequencies in five collections from the J. W. Copes site, two of which (Hillman's and Jackson's) were generated by excavation and contain more than 100 objects.

Focusing first on morphological variation, a chi-square test shows significant (p > .05) differences in frequencies of different Poverty Point object classes among all three collections from the Poverty Point site. This indi-

cates that either different populations were sampled or at least two of the collections did not adequately represent the relative frequencies of different Poverty Point object forms. The locations within the site from which the surface collections were made are not identified in a published report, but the excavated collections came from trenches scattered across the site (Ford and Webb 1956:21–23). Since Poverty Point is a very large, complex site with considerable internal spatial variation (Gibson 1970, 1973), it is possible that the samples are representative of different populations (different areas of the surface and subsurface) within the site. However, a chi-square test of the two collections from the considerably smaller and less complex J. W. Copes site (Webb 1982:27) also shows significant differences in frequencies between the two collections.

A similar pattern occurs in the production cost data. To compare production costs among the samples from the Poverty Point site and the J. W. Copes site, I summed the frequencies of all the Poverty Point object classes with the same number of production steps for each sample. As with the form frequency data, a chi-square test shows significant (p > .05) differences in the frequencies of objects with different production steps among all of the collections from the two sites respectively.

These results strongly suggest that recovery and possibly analytic and publication biases have had a significant, widespread impact on the relative frequencies of different form and production cost classes in collections of Poverty Point objects. One approach in dealing with biased frequency data is to reduce the level of measurement to an ordinal (rank order) or even nominal (presence/absence) scale. This approach can work because rank order or simple presence of classes is less sensitive to biases than are class frequencies. I examine ordinal scale comparisons first because rank orders contain more information on assemblage content than nominal scale does.

To assess the impact of biases on ordinal scale comparisons, I first converted the shape and production cost class frequencies to rank orders and then calculated rank-order correlation coefficients to compare the different samples from each site. Hillman's and Jackson's samples from the J. W. Copes site show significant correlations ($r_s = .88$; $p < .05$; corrected for ties following Siegel [1956: 206–10]) between both the rank orders of different Poverty Point object forms, and the rank order of production cost classes. Two of the three combinations of samples from the Poverty Point site display significant rank order correlations of form classes (AMNH-Ford $r_s = .91$; $p < .05$; AMNH-Webb $r_s = .94$; $p < .05$) whereas the third combination (Ford-Webb $r_s = .80$) falls just below the critical value at the .05 significance level. The rank orders of objects with different production steps are identical in the three Poverty Point site samples.

Thus, it appears that by comparing collections on an ordinal scale for both morphology and production costs, we eliminate most of the variation introduced by biases, and differences among collections from the same

site fall within the range expected due to normal sampling error. However, converting to ordinal level measurement introduces some new problems in determining assemblage similarity. Because ordinal measures give equal weight to very frequent and very rare types as well as very large and very small differences in abundance, measures of assemblage similarity based on rank orders can be sensitive to possibly random variation in frequencies of rare types (Grayson 1984: 93–115). In assemblages with frequencies that are widely separated, rank orders accurately reflect the relative abundance of types. When frequencies are closely spaced, such as occurs with very low abundances, rank orders are susceptible to greater fluctuation, and the likelihood of ties increases. The influence of ties on rank-order correlation coefficients used as measures of assemblage similarity can be corrected quantitatively (Siegel 1956:206–19). In addition, most of the problems with correlation coefficients as measures of assemblage similarity discussed recently by Cowgill (1990b) do not extend to rank-order correlation coefficients because they are not constrained by the closed-array problem introduced by the use of relative frequency data. However, the impact of closely spaced frequencies on shifting rank orders can be evaluated only through comparisons of assemblage content and rank order similarity.

ASSEMBLAGE SIMILARITY

Describing the spatial patterns of variant forms involves comparing the similarity of Poverty Point object assemblages to their arrangement in space in terms of both proximity and context. The engineering analysis indicates that variation in production costs may have affected fitness and thus been subject to selection. Figure 11.8 shows the patterns of similarity in the rank orders of production costs among the 10 assemblages listed in Table 11.2, using cluster analysis dendrograms with three different linkage methods. The same two groups appear in all sets of dendrograms. The group containing Jaketown, Teoc Creek, Poverty Point, Terral

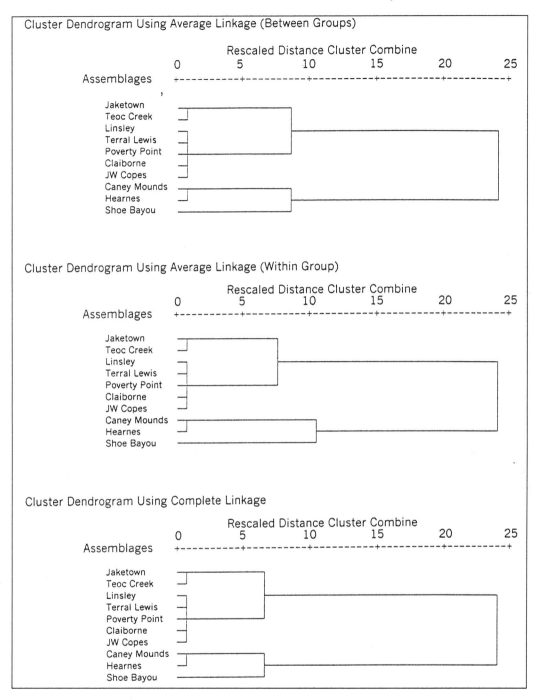

Figure 11.8. Cluster dendrograms based on rank-order correlation coefficient of production costs as the distance measure and three different linkage methods.

Lewis, Claiborne, Copes, and Linsley includes assemblages with the greatest amount of Poverty Point objects requiring three or four production steps. Assemblages in the remaining group of Hearnes, Caney Mounds, and Shoe Bayou are dominated by amor-

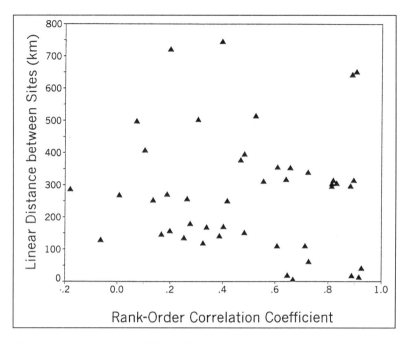

Figure 11.9. Scatter plot of linear distance between sites and formal similarity among all assemblages.

phous objects that involve only two production steps. Timed replicative experiments indicate that the amorphous objects require considerably less time to make than the objects with three and four production steps, while the difference between three and four steps appears to be relatively minor. Two of the three assemblages (Caney and Shoe Bayou) in the group with potentially significantly lower production costs come from sites in the Catahoula Lake region of central Louisiana, and the third (Hearnes) comes from a site located at the far northern end of the lower Mississippi Valley near the confluence of the Mississippi and Ohio Rivers.

Figure 11.9 shows the relationship of linear distance between sites to the similarity in rank orders of different Poverty Point object forms for the 10 assemblages. The scatter plot shows no clear pattern between distance and similarity. However, since some Poverty Point object assemblages may differ significantly in their production costs, the distributions shown in this figure could be a mixture of stylistic and functional variation. In Figure 11.10, the distance-similarity relations for assemblages dominated by low-cost amorphous forms (Shoe Bayou, Caney Mounds, and Hearnes) are plotted separately from the remaining assemblages dominated by higher cost forms. For the lower cost assemblages, the lack of clear relationship between distance and similarity continues. However, the assemblages dominated by higher cost Poverty Point objects form two groups, both of which display strong, linear inverse relations between distance and similarity. To the extent that distance between settlements serves as a good proxy for transmission or interaction intensity, the presence of two different patterns of similarity in space for low- and high-cost assemblages supports the inference that Poverty Point object assemblages include both functional (selected) and stylistic (nonselected) variation.

TOWARD EXPLAINING POVERTY POINT OBJECT VARIATION

In an evolutionary approach, distinguishing between stylistic and functional variation is critical because each indicates the work of

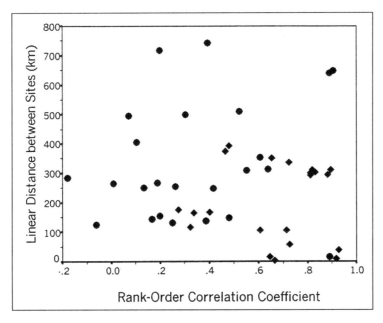

Figure 11.10. Scatter plot of linear distance between sites and formal similarity for low-cost (circles) and high-cost (diamonds) assemblages.

different kinds of mechanisms. Functional variation is usually sorted by a combination of transmission and selection, whereas patterns of stylistic variation are generated by transmission and drift. Thus, attempting to explain the patterns of variation in Poverty Point object assemblages in evolutionary terms requires different kinds of hypotheses to account for the functional and stylistic variation. Explanations of functional variation must describe how the particular selected variants affected the fitness of their possessors. Explanations of stylistic variation must demonstrate how the structure of trait transmission and stochastic processes can account for particular observed patterns. To be useful, these potential explanations must also be testable in that they specify the nature of phenomena that are observable and measurable in the archaeological record.

FUNCTIONAL VARIATION

The preliminary set of engineering analyses of Poverty Point objects conducted for this study indicates that different forms vary in the amount of energy involved in their manu-facture and that these differences in cost do not appear to be offset by improved performance. Comparisons of Poverty Point object assemblages from the lower Mississippi Valley further show that assemblages vary in their overall production costs and that low-cost assemblages display a different kind of spatial pattern than high-cost assemblages do. Thus, selective sorting of production cost appears to have played a role in structuring Poverty Point object variation.

The spatial structure of low-cost assemblages does not conform to a transmission-based sorting model, and probably resulted from selection in certain environments (physical and/or social) favoring a low-energy investment in Poverty Point objects. The small number of low-cost assemblages and lack of good environmental descriptions currently limit the ability to construct detailed, testable hypotheses to account for the observed pattern. However, it is possible to offer a general sketch of what these hypotheses might look like and specify the kinds of environmental descriptions required to account for the observed functional variation.

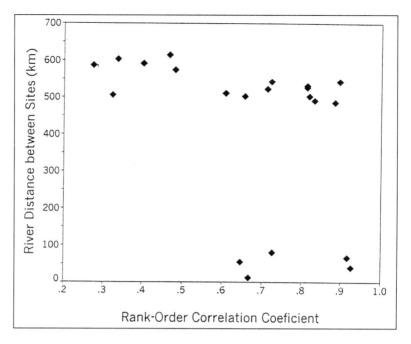

Figure 11.11. Scatter plot of river distance between sites and formal similarity for high-cost assemblages

Competition for energy resources is one context in which selection for low-cost technologies can occur. In the case of Poverty Point objects, I can imagine two possible, but not necessarily exclusive, scenarios. First, in the areas where low-cost assemblages occur, perhaps another low-cost alternative existed. The alternative could take the form of different raw materials for performing the same task, such as a readily available source of suitable stones or a different technology that performs the same function (e.g., heat storage and transfer) in a different way. Competition can also occur within the total energy budget of the population. If conditions allow for population growth, selection would favor groups investing more energy resources in productive areas that fuel growth, such as food acquisition. Under these conditions, energy resources might be diverted away from technologies and behaviors that are not directly involved in energy production, thus selecting for low-cost alternatives.

A similar hypothesis can be constructed to explain the occurrence of high-cost assem-blages. If population growth is constrained, selection can favor groups that invest energy in nonproductive areas (Dunnell 1989; Durand 1992; Graves and Ladefoged 1995). The added cost of elaborating Poverty Point objects in the apparent absence of performance benefits may fit this type of selection. Further formulation and testing of these hypotheses will require considerably more data on demographics and the resource and technological environments than currently exist. However, regardless of the specific selective conditions that fostered increased investment in Poverty Point object production, the data presented here demonstrate that the elaboration resulting from this investment was necessary for the appearance of stylistic variation.

STYLISTIC VARIATION

The pattern of decreasing similarity with increased distance found among the high-cost assemblages fits the expected pattern for stylistic variation sorted by transmission frequency when distance is the primary determinate of transmission (Dunnell 1978, Neiman 1995). However, the occurrence of two groups of comparisons among high-cost assemblages in Figure 11.10 displaying the same linear relationship, but over different distances, indicates that a more complex situation exists. Either linear distance between sites is not the best proxy for transmission rate or an extremely unusual pattern of transmission existed.

In this case, linear distance between settlements probably does not adequately map patterns of transmission because, until quite recently, rivers and other waterways provided the easiest routes of travel and interaction in the lower Mississippi Valley. To further evaluate the relations between assemblage similarity and spatial proximity and provide an initial test of the transmission rate hypothesis, I measured the river distance between sites and plotted this against assemblage similarity for high-cost assemblages (Figure 11.11). Based on river distance, most of the points representing assemblage comparisons collapse into one group of widely separated settlements with a significant negative correlation (r_p = -.663; p = .003) between distance and similarity. However, closely spaced settlements (< 100 km) still form a separate group with more variation in similarity than expected and no clear relationship between distance and similarity.

It is possible that for closely spaced settlements, spatial distance is not a reasonable surrogate for transmission rate. Instead, the structured nature of human groups (e.g., kinship, work groups, etc.) probably has a greater influence on the nature of trait transmission (DeBoer 1990; Douglas and Kramer 1992 [and papers therein]; Graves 1985; Hodder 1982). Unfortunately, several issues, including poor chronology, too few assemblages, and problems with assemblage data and measures of similarity, make it difficult to know at this time whether the patterns in style distributions are real or a product of poor or missing data. Obtaining better collected and analyzed assemblages, particularly from settlements located at moderate river distances from one another, will help answer this question.

CONCLUSIONS

My intentions in this chapter were to show how theory validates the choice of and linkage between conceptual and empirical units used to describe and explain shape variation in Poverty Point objects. Figure 11.12 shows the various units employed in this study arranged along spectra of unit content (from mostly conceptual to mostly empirical) and validation (from abstract to empirical). On the conceptual side, I used evolutionary theory to establish the abstract validity of different units. As the empirical content of units increases, abstract validity becomes less important and issues of empirical validity dominate the validation process. In empirical validation, physical theory justifies unit selection.

Although I used evolutionary and physical theories to validate my units, these are not the only concepts that can serve this function. Archaeologists currently employ a wide variety of concepts (including social agency, complexity, analogy, correlates, etc.) that serve to validate the use of particular units. However, the linkages between general theories that establish the abstract validity of conceptual units and the various notions used to justify empirical validity are rarely explicitly evaluated. Rather than presenting arguments for the superiority of my theory choices over others, I focused instead on the benefits derived from making the validation process explicit. By demonstrating the role that general theory plays in validating and linking conceptual and empirical units, I have drawn attention to the importance of theory in both description and explanation. One cannot expect to generate explainable descriptions unless the units employed in making those descriptions are empirically *and* conceptually valid. Constructing such valid units involves working back and forth between abstract and empirical issues. However, a coherent general theory ultimately provides the glue that holds together a sufficient framework of descriptive and explanatory units.

Conceptual <--------------------------------	Unit Content	--------------------------------> Empirical
		Feature/Artifact Associations
		Chemical Alteration
		Degree of Sintering
		Thermoremnant Magnetization
		Object Color Patterns
		Object Fracture Patterns
		Number of Production Steps
		Object Porosity
	Recovery Context	Use Experiments
	Use-Alterations	Surface Area to Volume Ratio
	Production Steps	Object Size
Use	Use-Life/Durability	Object Surface Roughness
Cost	Heat Transfer Effectiveness	Distance & Similarity among
Engineering Performance	Heat Storage Effectiveness	High Cost Assemblages
Function Distribution Spatial Pattern	Ease of Handling	Distance & Similarity among
Style Context Temporal Pattern	Distribution by Assemblage Cost	Low Cost Assemblages

Evolutionary Theory ···
Abstract   **Unit Validation**   **Empirical**
·· Physical Theory

Figure 11.12. Content and validation of units employed in the study of variation in Poverty Point object shapes.

The descriptions of Poverty Point objects and assemblages presented in this chapter produced intriguing patterns that appear to indicate the presence of both functional and stylistic variation. Because the engineering and distributional descriptions I employed are linked directly to evolutionary theory, I was also able to offer outlines of some possible explanations for the observed patterns that are logically coherent and provide direction for future research. This logical coherence between my descriptions and explanations of morphological variation in Poverty Point objects follows directly from working with a set of conceptually and empirically valid units.

Because the validity of units has been established, the reliability of the particular descriptions becomes an important issue. Through my efforts to assess the reliability of the various measurements of Poverty Point objects and assemblages, it is clear that the heavy use of published information has diminished the reliability of some of these descriptions. Before focusing too much attention on possible explanations for the observed patterns, we need more thorough and reliable descriptions of the use, cost, and performance of Poverty Point object variants. These future engineering studies should in-

volve detailed analyses of actual Poverty Point objects and well-designed and documented experiments with replicas. In addition, we need better descriptions of existing Poverty Point object assemblages and contexts as well as more collections that are adequately dated, sampled, analyzed, and reported so that more robust distributional analyses can be conducted.

If these future studies provide reliable support for my initial descriptions, the hypotheses regarding patterns in the spatial distributions of production costs and elaborate forms can be more fully developed and tested. Should these subsequent studies support the conclusion that considerable variation in Poverty Point objects is stylistic, these synthetic style units constructed at the object scale can then be employed as analytic units at the settlement and regional scales to investigate patterns of interaction and transmission during the Late Archaic in the lower Mississippi Valley.

ACKNOWLEDGMENTS

Discussions with Robert Dunnell, Felice Pierce, Jim Pullen, Pat McCutcheon, Jim Feathers, and Martha Jackson enhanced the design and execution of this project. I received helpful comments on earlier versions of this chapter from Robert Dunnell, Felice Pierce, Carol Barnes, Robert Leonard, Fraser Neiman, Jon Gibson, and the editors of this volume. In addition, Jon Gibson graciously offered his ideas and experience with Poverty Point objects. Professor Dunnell gave me access to his collection of Poverty Point objects from the Grey Horse Lake site. Professor H. Paul Johnson and his research team, particularly Janet Pariso, in the Oceanography Department at the University of Washington provided access to and training in the use of equipment in their paleomagnetism lab as well as valuable information on the nature of thermoremanant magnetization. This study was partially supported by a grant from the University of Washington, Graduate School Research Fund to Professor Dunnell and by funds from the Department of Anthropology to purchase equipment and supplies needed for the thermal demagnetization research.

References

Abbott, A. L., R. D. Leonard, and G. T. Jones
  1996 Explaining the Change from Biface to Flake Technology: A Selectionist Application. In *Darwinian Archaeologies*, edited by H. D. G. Maschner, 33–42. Plenum Press, New York.

Adams, R. McC.
  1981 *Heartland of Cities: Surveys of Ancient Settlement and Land Use on the Central Floodplain of the Euphrates.* The University of Chicago Press, Chicago.

Adams, W. Y.
  1988 Archaeological Classification: Theory vs. Practice. *Antiquity* 61:40–56.

———, and E. W. Adams
  1991 *Archaeological Typology and Practical Reality: A Dialectical Approach to Artifact Classification and Sorting.* Cambridge University Press, Cambridge.

Adovasio, J. M., J. Donahue, and R. Stuckenrath
  1990 The Meadowcroft Rockshelter Radiocarbon Chronology, 1975–1990. *American Antiquity* 55:348–55.
  1992 Never Say Never Again: Some Thoughts on Could Haves and Might Have Beens. *American Antiquity* 57:327–31.

———, J. D. Gunn, J. Donahue, and R. Stuckenrath
  1975 Excavations at Meadowcroft Rockshelter, 1973–1974: A progress Report. *Pennsylvania Archaeologist* 45:1–30.

———, J. D. Gunn, J. Donahue, R. Stuckenrath, J. Guilday, and K. Lord
  1980 Yes Virginia, It Really Is That Old: A Reply to Haynes and Mead. *American Antiquity* 45:588–95.

Agogino, G. A.
  1969 The Midland Complex: Is it Valid? *American Anthropologist* 71 (6): 1117–18.
  1970 Occasional, Purposeful Fluting of Agate Basin Points. *New Mexico Academy of Science Bulletin* 11 (2):13–15.

———, and W. D. Frankforter
  1960 The Brewster Site: An Agate-Basin Folsom Multiple Component Site in Eastern Wyoming. *Masterkey* 34 (3):102–7.

Ahler, S. A.
  1972 "Mass Analysis of Flaking Debris." Paper presented at the 30th annual Plains Anthropological Conference, Lincoln, Nebraska.
  1986 *The Knife River Flint Quarries: Excavations at Site 32DU508.* State Historical Society of North Dakota, Bismarck.
  1989a Experimental Knapping with KRF and Midcontinent Cherts: Overview and Applications. In *Experiments in Lithic Technology*, edited by D. S. Amick and R. P. Mauldin, 199–234. BAR International Series 528. British Archaeological Reports, Oxford.
  1989b Mass Analysis of Flaking Debris: Studying the Forest Rather Than the

Trees. In *Alternative Approaches to Lithic Analysis*, edited by D. O. Henry and G. H. Odell, 85–118. Archaeological Papers of the American Anthropological Association no. 1. Washington, D.C.

Aikens, C. M.
1970 *Hogup Cave*. University of Utah Anthropological Papers no. 93. University of Utah Press, Salt Lake City.

———, D. L. Cole, and R. Stuckenrath
1977 *Excavations at Dirty Shame Rockshelter, southeastern Oregon*. Miscellaneous Papers no. 4. Idaho State Museum of Natural History, Pocatello.

———, J. D. Wilde, and R. Stuckenrath
1982 "Cave and Dune Excavations in the Steens Mountain Region." Paper presented at the 18th Biennial Meeting of the Great Basin Anthropological Conference, Reno.

Aldenderfer, M. S.
1987a Assessing the Impact of Quantitative Thinking on Archaeological Research: Historical and Evolutionary Insights. In *Quantitative Research in Archaeology: Progress and Prospects*, edited by M. S. Aldenderfer, 9–29. Sage Publications, Newbury Park.

———, ed.
1987b *Quantitative Research in Archaeology: Progress and Prospects*, edited by M. S. Aldenderfer. Sage Publications, Newbury Park.

Allen, K. M. S., S. W. Green, and E. B. W. Zubrow, eds.
1990 *Interpreting Space: GIS and Archaeology*. Taylor & Francis, New York.

Allen, M. S.
1996 Style and Function in East Polynesian Fish-Hooks. *Antiquity* 70: 97–116.

Altschul, J. H.
1978 The Development of the Chacoan Interaction Sphere. *Journal of Anthropological Research* 34:109–46.

Amick, D. S.
1994 Folsom Diet Breadth and Land Use in the American Southwest. Ph.D. diss., Department of Anthropology, University of New Mexico, Albuquerque.

———, and R. P. Mauldin
1989 Comments on Sullivan and Rozen's "Debitage Analysis and Archaeological Interpretation." *American Antiquity* 54:166–68.

———, and R. P. Mauldin, eds.
1989 *Experiments in Lithic Technology*. BAR International Series 528. British Archaeological Reports, Oxford.

———, R. P. Mauldin, and L. R. Binford
1989 The Potential of Experiments in Lithic Technology. In *Experiments in Lithic Technology*, edited by D. S. Amick and R. P. Mauldin, 1–14. BAR International Series 528. British Archaeological Reports, Oxford.

———, R. P. Mauldin, and S. A. Tomka
1988 An Evaluation of Debitage Produced by Experimental Bifacial Core Reduction of a Georgetown Chert Nodule. *Lithic Technology* 17 (1):26–36.

Ammerman, J. T.
1981 Surveys and Archaeological Research. *Annual Review of Anthropology* 10:63–88.

Amsden, C. A.
1937 The Lake Mohave Artifacts. In *The Archeology of Pleistocene Lake Mohave*, 51–97. Southwest Museum Papers no. 11. Los Angeles.

Anderson, B., ed.
1990 *The Wupatki Archaeological Inventory Survey Project: Final Report*. Professional Paper no. 35. National Park Service, Santa Fe.

Arnold, D. E., H. Neff, and R. L. Bishop
1991 Compositional Analysis and "Sources" of Pottery: An Ethnoarchaeological Approach. *American Anthropologist* 93:70–90.

Asaro, F., H. V. Michel, R. Sidrys, and F. Stross
1978 High-Precision Chemical Characterization of Major Obsidian Sources in Guatemala. *American Antiquity* 43:436–43.

Ashmore, W., and R. J. Sharer
1988 *Discovering Our Past: A Brief Introduction to Archaeology*. Mayfield Publishing, Mountain View, California.

Aston, M., and T. Rowley
  1974   *Landscape Archaeology: An Intro-
          duction to Fieldwork Techniques on
          Post-Roman Landscapes.* David and
          Charles, London.
Athanassopoulos, E.-F.
  1993   *Intensive Survey and Medieval Rural
          Settlement: The Case of Nemea.*
          Ph.D. diss., University of Pennsylva-
          nia. University Microfilms, Ann Ar-
          bor.
Bacon, C. R., R. Macdonald, R. L. Smith, and
  P. A. Baedecker
  1981   Pleistocene High-Silica Rhyolites of
          the Coso Volcanic Field, Inyo
          County, California. *Journal of Geo-
          physical Research* 86:10, 233–41.
Baedecker, P. A., and D. M. McKown
  1987   Instrumental Neutron Activation
          Analysis of Geochemical Samples. In
          Methods for Geochemical Analysis,
          edited by P. A. Baedecker. U.S.
          Geological Survey Bulletin 1770:
          H1–H14. Washington, D.C.
Bailey, R. A.
  1974   *Preliminary Geologic Map and
          Cross-Sections of the Casa Diablo
          Geothermal Area, Long Valley
          Caldera, Mono County, California.*
          U.S. Geological Survey Open File-
          Map, 2 sheets (unnumbered), 1:
          40,000 scale. Washington, D.C.
Baldwin, G. C.
  1939   The Material Culture of Kinishba.
          American Antiquity 4:314–28.
Bamforth, D. B.
  1988   *Ecology and Human Organization
          on the Great Plains.* Plenum Press,
          New York.
  1991a Flintknapping Skill, Communal
          Hunting, and Paleoindian Projectile
          Point Typology. *Plains Anthro-
          pologist* 36 (137):309–22.
  1991b Technological Organization and
          Hunter-Gatherer Land Use. *Ameri-
          can Antiquity* 56:216–35.
Barbour, E. H., and C. B. Schultz
  1932a The Mounted Skeleton of Bison Oc-
          cidentalis, and Associated Dart-
          Points. *Nebraska State Museum
          Bulletin* 1 (32, October):263–70.
  1932b The Scottsbluff Bison Quarry and Its
          Artifacts. *Nebraska State Museum
          Bulletin* 1 (34, December):283–86.
  1936   Paleontologic and Geologic Consid-
          eration of Early Man in Nebraska.
          Nebraska State Museum Bulletin 1
          (45, April):431–49.
Barkow, J. H., L. Cosmides, and J. Tooby
  1992   *The Adapted Mind: Evolutionary
          Psychology and the Generation of
          Culture.* Oxford University Press,
          Oxford.
Barnett, F.
  1970   *Matli Ranch Ruins: A Report of Ex-
          cavation of Five Small Prehistoric
          Indian Ruins of the Prescott Culture
          in Arizona.* Museum of Northern
          Arizona Technical Series no. 10.
          Flagstaff.
  1973   *Lonesome Valley Ruin in Yavapai
          County, Arizona.* Museum of
          Northern Arizona Technical Series
          no. 13. Flagstaff.
  1974   *Excavation of Main Pueblo at Fitz-
          maurice Ruin: Prescott Culture in
          Yavapai County, Arizona.* Museum
          of Northern Arizona Special Publi-
          cation. Flagstaff.
  1978   *Las Vegas Ranch Ruin-East and Las
          Vegas Ranch Ruin-West: Two Small
          Prehistoric Prescott Indian Cul-
          ture Ruins In West Central Arizona.*
          Museum of Northern Arizona Bul-
          letin 51. Flagstaff.
Basalla, G.
  1988   *The Evolution of Technology.* Cam-
          bridge University Press, Cambridge.
Basgall, M. E.
  1979   To Trade or Not to Trade: A Pomo
          Example. *Journal of California and
          Great Basin Anthropology* 1:178–81.
Baumhoff, M. A., and R. F. Heizer
  1965   Postglacial Climate and Archaeol-
          ogy of the Desert West. In *The Qua-
          ternary of the United States,* edited
          by H. E. Wright, Jr., and D. G. Frey,
          697–708. Princeton University
          Press, Princeton.
Baumler, M. F., and C. E. Downum
  1989   Between Micro and Macro: A Study
          in the Interpretation of Small Sized
          Lithic Debitage. In *Experiments in
          Lithic Technology,* edited by D. S.
          Amick and R. P. Mauldin, 101–16.
          BAR International Series 528.
          British Archaeological Reports,
          Oxford.

Beals, R. L., G. W. Brainerd, and W. Smith
1945 *Archaeological Studies in Northeast Arizona*. University of California Publications in American Archaeology and Ethnology, vol. 44, no. 1. University of California Press, Berkeley and Los Angeles.

Beauchamp, W. M.
1897 *Aboriginal Chipped Stone Implements of New York*. Bulletin of the New York State Museum, vol. 4, no. 16. University of the State of New York, Albany.

Beck, C.
1984 *Steens Mountain Surface Archaeology: The Sites*. Ph.D. diss., University of Washington. University Microfilms, Ann Arbor.
1995 Functional Attributes and Differential Persistence of Great Basin Dart Forms. *Journal of California and Great Basin Anthropology* 17: 222–43.

———, ed.
1994 *Dating in Exposed and Surface Contexts*. University of New Mexico Press, Albuquerque.

———, and G. T. Jones
1989 Bias and Archaeological Classification. *American Antiquity* 54:244–62.
1994 On Site Artifact Analysis as an Alternative to Collection. *American Antiquity* 59:304–15.

Bedwell, S.F.
1973 *Fort Rock Basin: Prehistory and Environment*. University of Oregon Press, Eugene.

Beier, T., and H. Mommsen
1994 Modified Mahalanobis Filters for Grouping Pottery by Chemical Composition. *Archaeometry* 36:287–306.

Bell, E. H., and W. Van Royen
1934 An Evaluation of Recent Nebraska Finds Sometimes Attributed to the Pleistocene. *Wisconsin Archeologist* 13 (3):49–70.

Bernard, H. R.
1994 *Research Methods in Anthropology: Qualitative and Quantitative Approaches*. 2d ed. Sage Publications, Beverly Hills.

Bescherer Metheny, K., J. Kratzer, A. E. Yentsch, and C. M. Goodwin
1995 Method in Landscape Archaeology: Research Strategies in a Historic New Jersey Garden. In *Landscape Archaeology*, edited by R. Yamin and K. Bescherer Metheny. University of Tennessee Press, Knoxville.

Bettinger, R. L.
1976 *The Surface Archaeology of Owens Valley, Eastern California: Prehistoric Man-Land Relationships in the Great Basin*. Ph.D. diss., University of California, Riverside. University Microfilms, Ann Arbor.
1977 Aboriginal Human Ecology in Owens Valley: Prehistoric Change in the Great Basin. *American Antiquity* 42:3–17.

———, R. Boyd, and P. J. Richerson
1996 Style, Function, and Cultural Evolutionary Processes. In *Darwinian Archaeologies*, edited by Maschner, 133–64. Plenum Press, New York.

———, and J. Eerkins
in press Evolutionary Implications of Metrical Variation in Great Basin Projectile Points. In *Rediscovering Darwin: Evolutionary Theory in Archeological Explanation*, edited by C. M. Barton and G. A. Clark. Archeological Papers of the American Anthropological Association 7. Washington, D.C.

———, J. F. O'Connell, and D. H. Thomas
1991 Projectile Points as Time Markers in the Great Basin. *American Anthropologist* 93:166–72.

Bettis, E. A., III, and D. W. Benn
1989 Geologic Context of Paleoindian and Archaic Occupations in a Portion of the Mississippi Valley, Iowa and Illinois. *Current Research in the Pleistocene* 6:85–86.

Bieber, A. M., Jr., D. W. Brooks, G. Harbottle, and E. V. Sayre
1976 Application of Multivariate Techniques to Analytical Data on Aegean Ceramics. *Archaeometry* 18:59–74.

Binford, L. R.
1961 A New Method of Calculating Dates From Kaolin Pipe Stem Samples.

Southeastern Archaeological Conference Newsletter 9 (1):19–21.

1962 Archaeology as Anthropology. *American Antiquity* 28:217–25.

1964 A Consideration of Archaeological Research Design. *American Antiquity* 29:425–41.

1965 Archaeological Systematics and the Study of Culture Process. *American Antiquity* 31:203–10.

1967 Smudge Pits and Hide Smoking: The Use of Analogy in Archaeological Reasoning. *American Antiquity* 32:1–12.

1968a Archaeological Perspectives. In *New Perspectives in Archaeology*, edited by S. R. Binford and L. R. Binford, 5–32. Aldine, Chicago.

1968b Some Comments on Historical versus Processual Archaeology. *Southwest Journal of Anthropology* 24:267–75.

1972 Contemporary Model Building: Paradigms and the Current State of Paleolithic Research. In *Models in Archaeology*, edited by D. L. Clarke, 109–66. Methuen, London.

1973 Interassemblage Variability—The Mousterian and the "Functional" Argument. In *The Explanation of Culture Change*, edited by C. Renfrew, 227–54. Duckworth, London.

1977 Forty-Seven Trips: A Case Study in the Nature of Archaeological Formation Processes. In *Stone Tools as Culture Markers*, edited by R. V. S. Wright, 24–36. Australian Institute of Aboriginal Studies, Canberra.

1978 Dimensional Analysis of Behavior and Site Structure: Learning from an Eskimo Hunting Stand. *American Antiquity* 43:330–61.

1979a *Nunamiut Ethnoarchaeology*. Academic Press, New York.

1979b Organization and Formation Processes: Looking at Curated Assemblages. *Journal of Anthropological Research* 35:255–73.

1980 Willow Smoke and Dogs' Tails: Hunter-gatherer Settlement Systems and Archaeological Site Formation. *American Antiquity* 45:1–17.

1981 *Bones: Ancient Men and Modern Myths*. Academic Press, New York.

1982a The Archaeology of Place. *Journal of Anthropological Archaeology* 1: 5–31.

1982b Objectivity—Explanation—Archaeology 1981. In *Theory and Explanation in Archaeology: The Southampton Conference*, edited by C. Renfrew, M. J. Rowlands, and B. A. Segraves, 125–37. Academic Press, New York.

1989 "Culture" and Social Roles in Archaeology. In *Debating Archaeology*, by L. R. Binford, 3–11. Academic Press, New York.

1994 Systematic Integration of "Fragmentary Oddments": The Challenge of Settlement Pattern Approaches. In *Archaic Hunter-Gatherer Archaeology in the American Southwest*, edited by B. J. Vierra, 527–65. Eastern New Mexico University Contributions in Anthropology, vol. 13, no. 1. Portales.

———, and S. R. Binford

1966 Preliminary Analysis of Functional Variability in the Mousterian Levallois Facies. In *Recent Studies in Paleo-anthropology*, edited by J. D. Clarke and F. C. Howell. *American Anthropologist* 38 (2):238–95.

———, and J. A. Sabloff

1982 Paradigms, Systematics, and Archaeology. *Journal of Anthropological Research* 38 (2):137–53.

Bintliff, J. L., and A. M. Snodgrass

1985 The Cambridge/Bradford Boeotia Expedition: The First Four Years. *Journal of Field Archaeology* 12: 123–61.

1988 Off-Site Pottery Distribution: A Regional and Interregional Perspective. *Current Anthropology* 29:506–13.

Bishop, R. L.

1992 Instrumentation and the Future of Archaeology. In *Quandaries and Quests: Visions of Archaeology's Future*, edited by L. Wandsnider, 160–69. Center for Archaeological Investigations Occasional Paper no.

20. Southern Illinois University, Carbondale.

———, and H. Neff
1989 Multivariate Analysis of Compositional Data in Archaeology. *Archaeological Chemistry IV*, edited by R. O. Allen, 576–86. Advances in Chemistry Series 220. American Chemical Society, Washington, D.C.

———, R. L. Rands, and G. R. Holley
1982 Ceramic Compositional Analysis in Archaeological Perspective. In *Advances in Archaeological Method and Theory*, vol. 5, edited by M. B. Schiffer, 275–330. Academic Press, New York.

Blackman, M. J.
1992 The Effect of Human Size Sorting on the Mineralogy and Chemistry of Ceramic Clays. In *Chemical Characterization of Ceramic Pastes in Archaeology*, edited by H. Neff, 113–24. Prehistory Press, Madison, Wisconsin.

Blackwelder, E.
1927 Fire as an Agent in Rock Weathering. *Journal of Geology* 35:134–40.

Blackwell, B. A., and H. P. Schwarcz
1993 Archaeochronology and Scale. In *Effects of Scale on Archaeological and Geoscientific Perspective*, edited by J. K. Stein and A. R. Linse. Geological Society of America Special Paper no. 23. Boulder, Colorado.

Blaine, J. C.
1968 A Preliminary Report of an Early Man Site in West Texas. *Transactions of the Third Regional Archeological Symposium for Southeastern New Mexico and Western Texas.* South Plains Archeological Society, Lubbock.

Blalock, H. M., Jr.
1979 *Social Statistics.* Rev. 2d ed. McGraw-Hill, New York.

Bleed, P.
1986 The Optimal Design of Hunting Weapons: Maintainability or Reliability. *American Antiquity* 51:737–47.

———, and A. Bleed
1987 Energetic Efficiency and Hand Tool Design: A Performance Comparison of Push and Pull Stroke Saws.

Journal of Anthropological Archaeology 6:189–97.

Boldurian, A. T.
1990 "Lithic Technology at the Mitchell Locality of Blackwater Draw: A Stratified Folsom Site in Eastern New Mexico." Memoir 24. *Plains Anthropologist* 35 (130).

Boone, J. L., and E. A. Smith
1998 Is It Evolution Yet? A Critique of "Evolutionary Archaeology." In press for *Current Anthropology.*

Bordes, F.
1961 *Typologie du Paléolithique Ancien et Moyen.* Institute Quaternair de L'Université de Bordeaux Mémoire 1. Bordeaux.

1969 Reflections on Typology and Technology in the Upper Paleolithic. *Arctic Anthropology* 6:1–29.

———, and D. E. Crabtree
1969 The Corbiac Blade Technique and Other Experiments. *Tebiwa* 11 (2):1–21.

———, and D. de Sonneville-Bordes
1970 The Significance of Variability in Paleolithic Assemblages. *World Archaeology* 2:61–73.

Boston, R. L.
1995 Sourcing Volcanic Ash Temper in Sunset Red Ceramics. Master's thesis, Department of Anthropology, Northern Arizona University, Flagstaff.

Boyd, R., and P. J. Richerson
1985 *Culture and the Evolutionary Process.* The University of Chicago Press, Chicago.

Bradie, M.
1994 Epistemology from an Evolutionary Point of View. In *Conceptual Issues in Evolutionary Biology*, 2d ed., edited by E. Sober, 453–75. MIT Press, Cambridge.

Bradley, B. A.
1975 Lithic Reduction Sequences: A Glossary and Discussion. In *Lithic Technology: Making and Using Stone Tools*, edited by E. Swanson, 5–13. Mouton, The Hague.

1982 Flaked Stone Technology and Typology. In *The Agate Basin Site: A Record of the Paleoindian Occupation of the Northwestern High*

Plains, edited by G. C. Frison and D. J. Stanford, 181–208. Academic Press, New York.

1993 Paleo-Indian Flaked Stone Technology in the North American High Plains. In *From Kostenki to Clovis: Upper Paleolithic–Paleo-Indian Adaptations*, edited by O. Soffer and N. D. Praslov, 251–62. Plenum Press, New York.

Braidwood, R.

1937 *Mounds on the Plain of Antioch: An Archaeological Survey*. University of Chicago Oriental Publication no. 48. Chicago.

Brain, J. P.

1980 *Tunica Treasure*. Papers of the Peabody Museum of Archaeology and Ethnology, vol. 71. Harvard University, Cambridge.

Brand, D. D., F. M. Hawley, F. C. Hibben et al.

1937 *Tseh So, a Small House Ruin, Chaco Canyon, New Mexico*. Anthropological Series, vol. 2, no. 2. University of New Mexico Press, Albuquerque.

Braun, D. P.

1983 Pots as Tools. In *Archaeological Hammers and Theories*, edited by A. Keene and J. Moore, 107–34. Academic Press, New York.

1985 Absolute Seriation: A Time-Series Approach. In *For Concordance in Archaeological Analysis: Bridging Data Structure, Quantitative Technique, and Theory*, edited by C. Carr, 509–39. Westport Press, Kansas City.

Brew, J. O.

1946a *Archaeology of Alkali Ridge, Southern Utah*, 44–66. Papers of the Peabody Museum of American Archaeology and Ethnology, vol. 21. Harvard University, Cambridge.

1946b The Use and Abuse of Taxonomy. In *Archaeology of Alkalai Ridge, Southeastern Utah*, 44–66. Papers of the Peabody Museum of American Archaeology and Ethnology, vol. 21. Harvard University, Cambridge.

Broilo, F. J.

1971 An Investigation of Surface Collected Clovis, Folsom, and Midland Projectile Points from Blackwater Draw and Adjacent Localities. Master's thesis, Department of Anthropology, Eastern New Mexico University, Portales.

Browman, D. L.

1981 Isotopic Discrimination and Correction Factors in Radiocarbon Dating. In *Advances in Archaeological Method and Theory*, vol. 4, edited by M. B. Schiffer, 241–95. Academic Press, New York.

Brown, C. S.

1926 *Archeology of Mississippi*. Mississippi Geological Survey.

Brown, J. A.

1989 The Beginnings of Pottery as an Economic Process. In *What's New? A Closer Look at the Process of Innovation*, edited by S. E. van der Leeuw and R. Torrence, 203–24. Unwin Hyman, London.

Browne, J.

1938 Antiquity of the Bow. *American Antiquity* 3:358–59.

Bryan, K., and L. L. Ray

1940 *Geologic Antiquity of the Lindenmeier Site in Colorado*. Smithsonian Miscellaneous Collections, vol. 99, no. 2. Smithsonian Institution, Washington, D.C.

Bryant, V. M., and H. J. Shafer

1977 The Late Quaternary Paleoenvironment of Texas: A Model for the Archeologist. *Bulletin of the Texas Archeological Society* 48:1–25.

Bunn, J. W., Jr.

1974 Clay Balls: Ceremonial or Utilitarian? *Florida Anthropologist* 27:47–48.

Burton, J.

1980 Making Sense of Waste Flakes: New Methods for Investigating the Technology and Economics behind Chipped Stone Assemblages. *Journal of Archaeological Science* 7:131–48.

Bushnell, D. I., Jr.

1935 *The Manahoac Tribes in Virginia, 1608*. Smithsonian Miscellaneous Collections, vol. 94, no. 8. Smithsonian Institution, Washington, D.C.

1940 *Evidence of Early Indian Occupancy near the Peaks of Otter, Bedford County, Virginia*. Smithsonian

Miscellaneous Collections, vol. 99, no. 15. Smithsonian Institution, Washington, D.C.

1941 Trailing Early Man in Virginia. In *Explorations and Field-Work of the Smithsonian Institution in 1940*, 75–78. Smithsonian Institution, Washington, D.C.

Callahan, E.

1979 The Basics of Biface Knapping in the Eastern Fluted Point Tradition: A Manual for Flint Knappers and Lithic Analysts. *Archaeology of Eastern North America* 7:1–180.

Camilli, E. L., and J. I. Ebert

1992 Artifact Reuse and Recycling in Continuous Surface Distributions and Implications for Interpreting Land Use Patterns. In *Space, Time, and Archaeological Landscapes*, edited by J. Rossignol and L. Wandsnider, 113–36. Plenum Press, New York.

———, L. Wandsnider, and J. I. Ebert

1988 *Distributional Survey and Excavation of Archaeological Landscapes in the Vicinity of El Paso, Texas*. Bureau of Land Management, Las Cruces, New Mexico.

Campbell, D. T.

1988 A General "Selection Theory," as Implemented in Biological Evolution and in Social Belief-Transmission-with-Modification in Science. *Biology and Philosophy* 3:171–77.

Campbell, E. W. C., and W. H. Campbell

1940 A Folsom Complex in the Great Basin. *Masterkey* 14 (1):7–11.

Campbell, S. K.

1990 *Post-Columbian Culture History in the northern Columbia Plateau, A.D. 1500–1900*. Garland Press, New York.

Cann, J. R., and C. Renfrew

1964 The Characterization of Obsidian and Its Application to the Mediterranean Region. *Proceedings of the Prehistoric Society* 30:111–33.

Carmines, E. G., and R. A. Zeller

1979 *Reliability and Validity Assessment*. Sage University Papers on Quantitative Applications in the Social Sciences no. 17. Sage Publications, Beverly Hills.

Carr, C.

1985 Alternative Models, Alternative Techniques, Variable Approaches to Intrasite Spatial Analysis. In *For Concordance in Archaeological Analysis: Bridging Data Structure, Quantitative Technique, and Theory*, edited by C. Carr, 302–473. Westport Press, Kansas City.

1987 Dissecting Intrasite Artifact Palimpsests Using Fourier Methods. In *Method and Theory for Activity Area Research: An Ethnoarchaeological Approach*, edited by S. Kent, 236–91. Columbia University Press, New York.

———, ed.

1985 *For Concordance in Archaeological Analysis: Bridging Data Structure, Quantitative Technique, and Theory*. Westport Press, Kansas City.

Carr, P. A., ed.

1994 *The Organization of North American Prehistoric Chipped Stone Tool Technologies*. Archaeological Series 7. International Monographs in Prehistory, Ann Arbor, Michigan.

Cavalli-Sforza, L. L., and M. Feldman

1981 *Cultural Transmission and Evolution: A Quantitative Approach*. Princeton University Press, Princeton.

Caywood, L. R., and E. H. Spicer

1935 *Tuzigoot: The Excavation and Repair of a Ruin on the Verde River near Clarkdale, Arizona*. Field Division of Education, National Park Service. Berkeley, California.

Chaisson, E. J.

1981 *Cosmic Dawn: The Origins of Matter and Life*. Little, Brown and Co., Boston.

1988 *Relatively Speaking: Relativity, Black Holes, and the Fate of the Universe*. W. W. Norton, New York.

Chandler, S. M., and J. A. Ware

1976 The Identification of Technological Variability through Experimental Replication and Empirical Multivariate Analysis. *Newsletter of Lithic Technology* 5 (3):24–26.

Chang, K. C., ed.

1968 *Settlement Archaeology*. National Press, Palo Alto, California.

Cherry, J.

1983 Frogs Round the Pond: Perspectives on Current Archaeological Survey Projects in the Mediterranean Region. In *Archaeological Survey in the Mediterranean Area*, edited by D. R. Keller and D. W. Rupp, 394–97. BAR International Series 155. British Archaeological Reports, Oxford.

———, J. L. Davis, A. Demitrack, E. Mantzourani, T. F. Strasser, and L. E. Talalay

1988 Archaeological Survey in an Artifact-Rich Landscape: A Middle Neolithic Example from Nemea, Greece. *American Journal of Archaeology* 92:159–76.

———, J. L. Davis, and E. Mantzourani

1991 *Landscape Archaeology as Long-Term History*. Monumenta Archaeologica no. 16. Institute of Archaeology, University of California, Los Angeles.

Christenson, A. L.

1986 Projectile Point Size and Projectile Aerodynamics: An Exploratory Study. *Plains Anthropologist* 31: 109–28.

———, and D. W. Read

1977 Numerical Taxonomy, r-Mode Factor Analysis and Archaeological Classification. *American Antiquity* 42:163–79.

Clark, G. A.

1987 Quantifying Archaeological Research. In *Advances in Archaeological Method and Theory*, vol. 5, edited by M. B. Schiffer, 217–73. Academic Press, New York.

1994 Migration as an Explanatory Concept in Paleolithic Archaeology. *Journal of Archaeological Method and Theory* 1:305–43.

Clark, P., and M. Barbetti

1982 Fires, Hearths, and Paleomagnetism. In *Archaeometry: An Australian Perspective*, edited by W. Ambrose and P. Duerden, 144–50. Australian National University, Canberra.

Clark, R. B.

1956 Species and Systematics. *Systematic Zoology* 5:1–10.

Cogswell, J. W., H. Neff, and M. D. Glascock

1993 "An Analysis of Shell Tempered Pottery Replicates: Implications for Provenience Studies." Paper presented at the 1993 Society for American Archaeology meetings, St. Louis.

1996 The Effect of Firing Temperature on the Elemental Characterization of Pottery. *Journal of Archaeological Science* 23:283–87.

Collins, M. B.

1975 Lithic Technology as a Means of Processual Inference. In *Lithic Technology: Making and Using Stone Tools*, edited by E. Swanson, 15–34. Mouton, The Hague.

Colman, S. M.

1986 Levels of Time Information in Weathering Measurements, with examples from Weather Rinds or Volcanic Clasts in the Western United States. In *Rates of Chemical Weathering in Rocks and Minerals*, edited by S. M. Colman and D. P. Dethier, 379–93. Academic Press, New York.

———, K. L Pierce, and P. W. Birkeland

1987 Suggested Terminology for Quaternary Dating Methods. *Quaternary Research* 28:314–19.

Colton, H. S.

1922 The Geographical Distribution of Potsherds in the San Francisco Mountains of Arizona. In *Annales do XX Congresso Internacional de Americanistas*, vol. 2, pt. 1, 119–21. Rio De Janeiro.

1932 *A Survey of Prehistoric Sites in the Region of Flagstaff, Arizona*. Bureau of American Ethnology Bulletin 104. Washington, D.C.

1935 Stages in Northern Arizona Prehistory. *Museum Notes* 8 (1):1–7.

1939a *An Archaeological Survey of Northwestern Arizona*. Museum of Northern Arizona Bulletin 16. Flagstaff.

1939b *Prehistoric Culture Units and Their Relationships in Northern Arizona*. Museum of Northern Arizona Bulletin 17. Flagstaff.

1946 *The Sinagua*. Museum of Northern Arizona Bulletin 22. Flagstaff.

1953 *Potsherds: An Introduction to the*

Study of Prehistoric Southwestern Ceramics and Their Use in Historic Reconstruction. Museum of Northern Arizona Bulletin 25. Flagstaff.

1958 *Pottery Types of the Southwest. Wares 14, 17, 18: Revised Descriptions, Alameda Brown Ware, Prescott Gray Ware, San Francisco Mountain Gray Ware*. Museum of Northern Arizona Ceramic Series 3D. Flagstaff.

1968 Frontiers of The Sinagua. In *Collected Papers in Honor of Lyndon Lane Hargrave*, edited by Albert H. Schroeder, 9–16. Papers of the Archaeological Society of New Mexico no. 1. Museum of New Mexico Press, Santa Fe.

———, and L. Hargrave

1937 *Handbook of North Arizona Pottery Types*. Museum of Northern Arizona Bulletin 11. Flagstaff.

Colton, M. R. F., and H. S. Colton

1918 The Little-Known Small House Ruins in the Coconino Forest. *Memoirs of the American Anthropological Association* 5 (4):101–26.

Conkey, M. W.

1990 Experimenting with Style in Archaeology: Some Historical and Theoretical Issues. In *The Uses of Style in Archaeology*, edited by M. Conkey and C. Hastorf, 5–17. Cambridge University Press, Cambridge.

Cook, H. J.

1928 Glacial Age Man in New Mexico. *Scientific American* 139:38–40.

1931 More Evidence of the "Folsom Culture" Race. *Scientific American* 144 (2):102–3.

Corliss, D. W.

1972 *Neck Width of Projectile Points: An Index of Culture Continuity and Change*. Idaho State University Museum of Natural History Occasional Paper no. 29. Pocatello.

Cotter, J. L.

1937a The Occurrence of Flints and Extinct Animals in Pluvial Deposits near Clovis, New Mexico. Part 4, Report on Excavation at the Gravel Pit, 1936. *Proceedings of the Academy of Natural Sciences of Philadelphia* 89:1–16.

1937b The Significance of Folsom and Yuma Artifact Occurrences in the Light of Typology and Distribution. In *Twenty-fifth Anniversary Studies*, edited by D. S. Davidson, 27–35. Publications of the Philadelphia Anthropological Society, vol. 1. University of Pennsylvania Press, Philadelphia.

1938 The Occurrence of Flints and Extinct Animals in Pluvial Deposits near Clovis, New Mexico. Part 6, Report on Field Season of 1937. *Proceedings of the Academy of Natural Sciences of Philadelphia* 90:113–17.

1939 A Consideration of "Folsom and Yuma Culture Finds." *American Antiquity* 5 (2):152–55.

Cowgill, G. L.

1972 Models, Methods and Techniques of Seriation. In *Models in Archaeology*, edited by D. L. Clarke, 381–424. Methuen, London.

1982 Clusters of Objects and Associations between Variables: Two Approaches to Archaeological Classification. In *Essays on Archaeological Typology*, edited by R. Whallon and J. A. Brown, 30–55. Center for American Archaeology, Kampsville.

1990a Artifact Classification and Archaeological Purposes. In *Mathematics and Information Science in Archaeology: A Flexible Framework*, edited by A. Voorrips. Studies in Modern Archaeology no. 3:61–78. Holos-Verlag, Bonn.

1990b Why Pearson's r Is Not a Good Similarity Coefficient for Comparing Assemblages. *American Antiquity* 55:512–21.

Crabtree, D. E.

1968 Mesoamerican Polyhedral Cores and Prismatic Blades. *American Antiquity* 33:446–78.

Crandall, W. B., and J. Ging

1955 Thermal Shock Analysis of Spherical Shapes. *Journal of the American Ceramic Society* 38:44–54.

Crouse, H. Y.

1954 A Folsom Point from the Uinta Basin, Utah. *Masterkey* 28(2):50–51.

Crumley, C. L.

1979 Three Locational Models: An Epistemological Assessment for Anthropology and Archaeology. In *Advances in Archaeological Method and Theory*, vol. 2, edited by M. B. Schiffer, 141–73. Academic Press, New York.

———, W. H. Marquardt, and T. L. Leatherman

1987 Certain Factors Influencing Settlement during the Later Iron Age and Gallo-Roman Periods: The Analysis of Intensive Survey Data. In *Regional Dynamics: Burgundian Landscapes in Historical Perspective*, edited by C. L. Crumley and W. H. Marquardt, 121–72. Academic Press, San Diego.

Cunningham, G. K.

1986 *Educational and Psychological Measurement*. MacMillan, New York.

Cziko, G.

1995 *Without Miracles, Universal Selection Theory and the Second Darwinian Revolution*. MIT Press, Cambridge.

Dale, W. S. A.

1987 The Shroud of Turin: Relic or Icon? In *Nuclear Instruments and Methods in Physics Research: Section B, Beam Interactions With Materials*, edited by H. H. Anderson and S. T. Picraux, 187–92. Proceedings of the 4th International Symposium on Accelerator Mass Spectrometry B29.

Dancey, W. S.

1973 *Prehistoric Land Use and Settlement Patterns in the Priest Rapids Area, Washington*. Ph.D. diss., University of Washington. University Microfilms, Ann Arbor.

Daniel, G.

1976 *A Hundred and Fifty Years of Archaeology*. Harvard University Press, Cambridge.

Davies, P.

1995 *About Time: Einstein's Unfinished Revolution*. Simon and Schuster, New York.

Davis, C. A., and Gerald A. Smith

1981 *Newberry Cave*. San Bernardino County Museum Association, Redlands, Calif.

Davis, E. L.

1963 The Desert Culture of the Western Great Basin: A Lifeway of Seasonal Transhumance. *American Antiquity* 29:202–12.

1975 The "Exposed Archaeology" of China Lake, California. *American Antiquity* 40:39–53.

Davis, L. B., and S. T. Greiser

1992 Indian Creek Paleoindians: Early Occupation of the Elkhorn Mountains' Southeast Flank, West-Central Montana. In *Ice Age Hunters of the Rockies*, edited by D. J. Stanford and J. S. Day, 225–83. Denver Museum of Natural History, Denver.

Dawkins, R.

1982 *The Extended Phenotype: The Gene as the Unit of Selection*. Oxford University Press, Oxford.

1989 *The Selfish Gene*. [new edition] Oxford University Press, Oxford.

Dean, J. S.

1978 Independent Dating in Archaeology. In *Advances in Archaeological Method and Theory*, vol. 1, edited by M. B. Schiffer, 223–65. Academic Press, New York.

DeAtley, S. P., and R. L. Bishop

1991 Toward an Integrated Interface for Archaeology and Archaeometry. In *The Ceramic Legacy of Anna O. Shepard*, edited by R. L. Bishop and F. P. Lange, 358–82. University of Colorado Press, Boulder.

DeBoer, W. R.

1990 Interaction, Imitation, and Communication as Expressed in Style: The Ucayali Experience. In *Uses of Style in Archaeology*, edited by M. Conkey and C. Hastorf, 82–104. Cambridge University Press, Cambridge.

Dennett, D. C.

1991 *Consciousness Explained*. Little, Brown and Company, Boston.

1995 *Darwin's Dangerous Idea*. Simon & Schuster, New York.

DePratter, C. B.

1979 Shellmound Archaic on the Georgia Coast. *South Carolina Antiquities* 112:1–69.

Deuel, T.

1937 The Application of a Classificatory Method to Mississippi Valley Archaeology. In *Rediscovering Illinois*, by F-C. Cole and T. Deuel, 207–19. University of Chicago Press, Chicago.

Dewar, R. E.
1992   Incorporating Variation in Occupation Span in Settlement-Pattern Analysis. *American Antiquity* 56: 604–20.

———, and K. McBride
1992   Remnant Settlement Patterns. In *Space, Time, and Archaeological Landscapes*, edited by J. Rossignol and L. Wandsnider, 227–56. Plenum Press, New York.

Dibble, D. S.
1968   The Archeology. In *Bonfire Shelter: A Stratified Bison Kill Site, Val Verde County, Texas*, edited by D. S. Dibble and D. Lorrain, 7–16. Texas Memorial Museum Miscellaneous Papers no. 1. University of Texas, Austin.
1970   On the Significance of Additional Radiocarbon Dates from Bonfire Shelter, Texas. *Plains Anthropologist* 15 (50, pt. 1):251–54.

Dibble, H. L., and J. C. Whittaker
1981   New Experimental Evidence on the Relation between Percussion Flaking and Flake Variation. *Journal of Archaeological Science* 8:283–96.

Dixon, J. E., J. R. Cann, and C. Renfrew
1968   Obsidian and the Origins of Trade. *Scientific American* 218 (3):38–46.

Dobzhansky, T.
1982   *Genetics and the Origin of Species.* Columbia University Press, New York.

Doran, J. E., and F. R. Hodson
1975   *Mathematics and Computers in Archaeology.* Cambridge University Press, Cambridge.

Douglas, J. E, and C. Kramer
1992   Interaction, Social Proximity, and Distance: A Special Issue. *Journal of Anthropological Archaeology* 11:103–10.

Douglass, A. E.
1935   *Dating Pueblo Bonito and Other Ruins of the Southwest.* Pueblo Bonito Series no. 1. National Geographic Society, Washington, D.C.

1938   Southwestern Dated Ruins: V. *Tree-Ring Bulletin* 5 (2):10–13.

Downum, C.
1988   "One Grand History": A Critical Review of Flagstaff Archaeology, 1851 to 1988. Ph.D. diss., Department of Anthropology, University of Arizona, Tucson.

———, and A. Sullivan
1990   Settlement Patterns. In *The Wupatki Archaeological Inventory Survey Project: Final Report*, edited by B. A. Anderson. Professional Paper no. 35. National Park Service, Santa Fe.

Driver, H. E.
1969   *Indians of North America.* University of Chicago Press, Chicago.

Duma, G.
1972   Phosphate Content of Ancient Pots as Indication of Use. *Current Anthropology* 13:127–29.

Dunnell, R. C.
1970   Seriation Method and Its Evaluation. *American Antiquity* 33:305–19.
1971   *Systematics in Prehistory.* Free Press, New York.
1978   Style and Function: A Fundamental Dichotomy. *American Antiquity* 43:192-202.
1980   Evolutionary Theory and Archaeology. In *Advances in Archaeological Theory and Method*, vol. 3, edited by M. B. Schiffer, 35–99. Academic Press, New York.
1981   Seriation, Groups, and Measurements. In *Manejos de Datos y Matemáticos de Arqueología*, edited by G. L. Cowgill, R. Whallon, and B. S. Ottaway, 67–90. Unión Internacional de Ciencias Prehistórica y Protohistóricas. Mexico City, D.F.
1982   Science, Social Science, and Common Sense: The Agonizing Dilemma of Modern Archaeology. *Journal of Anthropological Research* 38:1–25.
1986a Five Decades of American Archaeology. In *American Archaeology Past and Future*, edited by D. J. Meltzer, D. D. Fowler, and J. A. Sabloff, 23–52. Smithsonian Institution Press, Washington D. C.
1986b Methodological Issues in American-

ist Artifact Classification. In *Advances in Archaeological Method and Theory*, vol. 9, edited by M. B. Schiffer, 149–207. Academic Press, New York.

1989   Aspects of the Application of Evolutionary Theory in Archaeology. In *Archaeological Thought in America*, edited by C. C. Lamberg-Karlovsky, 35–49. Cambridge University Press, Cambridge.

1991   Methodological Impacts of Catastrophic Depopulation on American Archaeology and Ethnology. In *Columbian Consequences*, vol. 3, *The Spanish Borderlands in Pan-American Perspective*, edited by D. H. Thomas, 561–80. Smithsonian Institution Press, Washington, D.C.

1992a   Archaeology and Evolutionary Science. In *Quandaries and Quests: Visions of Archaeology's Future*, edited by L. Wandsnider, 209–24. Center for Archaeological Investigations Occasional Paper no. 20. Southern Illinois University, Carbondale.

1992b   The Notion Site. In *Space, Time, and Archaeological Landscapes*, edited by J. Rossignol and L. Wandsnider, 21–42. Plenum Press, New York.

1993   Why Archaeologists Don't Care about Archaeometry. *Archeomaterials* 7:161–65.

1995   What Is It that Actually Evolves? In *Evolutionary Archaeology: Methodological Issues*, edited by P. A. Teltser, 33–50. University of Arizona Press, Tucson.

———, and W. S. Dancey

1983   The Siteless Survey: A Regional Scale Collection Strategy. In *Advances in Archaeological Method and Theory*, vol. 6, edited by M. B. Schiffer, 267–87. Academic Press, New York.

———, and J. K. Feathers

1991   Late Woodland Manifestations on the Malden Plain, Southeast Missouri. In *Stability, Transformation, and Variation: The Late Woodland Southeast*, edited by M. S. Nassaney

and C. R. Cobb, 21–45. Plenum Press, New York.

———, and T. L. Hunt

1990   Elemental Composition and Inference of Ceramic Vessel Function. *Current Anthropology* 31:330–36.

———, and M. L Readhead

1988   The Relation of Dating and Chronology: Comments on Chatters and Hoover (1986) and Butler and Stein (1988). *Quaternary Research* 30:232–33.

———, and F. H. Whittaker

1990   The Late Archaic of the Eastern Lowlands and Evidence of Trade. *Louisiana Archaeology* 17:13–36.

Durand, S. R.

1992   Architectural Change and Chaco Prehistory. Ph.D. diss., Department of Anthropology, University of Washington, Seattle.

Durham, W. H.

1991   *Coevolution: Genes, Culture, and Human Diversity*. Stanford University Press, Stanford.

Dutton, B. P.

1938   *Leyit Kin, a Small House Ruin, Chaco Canyon, New Mexico*. Bulletin 333, Monograph Series 1, no. 6. University of New Mexico, Albuquerque.

Earle, T. K., and J. E. Ericson, eds.

1977   *Exchange Systems in Prehistory*. Academic Press, New York.

Ebert, J. I.

1992   *Distributional Archaeology*. University of New Mexico Press, Albuquerque.

Einstein, A.

1961   *Relativity: The Special and General Theory*. Crown Publishers, New York.

Elston, R. G.

1971   *A Contribution to Washo Archaeology*. Research Paper no. 2. Nevada Archaeological Survey, Reno.

———, and E. E. Budy

1989   *The Archaeology of James Creek Shelter*. University of Utah Anthropological Papers no. 115. University of Utah Press, Salt Lake City.

Ensor, H. B., and E. Roemer, Jr.

1989   Comments on Sullivan and Rozen's "Debitage Analysis and Archaeological Interpretation." *American Antiquity* 54:175–78.

Ereschefshy, M.
1991 Metaphysics and Biological Systematics. *Studies in the History and Philosophy of Science* 22:525–32.

Ericson, J. E., T. A. Hagan, and C. W. Chesterman
1976 Prehistoric Obsidian in California II: Geologic and Geographic Aspects. In *Advances in Obsidian Glass Studies: Archaeological and Geochemical Perspectives*, edited by R. E. Taylor, 218–39. Noyes Press, Park Ridge, New Jersey.

Euler, R., and H. Dobyns
1962 Excavations West of Prescott, Arizona. *Plateau* 34 (3):69–84.

Evans, G. L.
1951 Prehistoric Wells in Eastern New Mexico. *American Antiquity* 17:1–9.

Evans, O. F.
1957 Probable Uses of Stone Projectile Points. *American Antiquity* 23: 83–84.

Ewers, J. C.
1955 *The Horse in Blackfoot Indian Culture*. Bulletin 159. Bureau of American Ethnology Bulletin 159. Smithsonian Institution, Washington, D.C.

Fagan, B. M.
1994 *In the Beginning: An Introduction to Archaeology*. Harper Collins College Publishers, New York.

Falconer, S. E., and S. H. Savage
1995 Heartlands and Hinterlands: Alternative Trajectories of Early Urbanization in Mesopotamia and the Southern Levant. *American Antiquity* 60:37–58.

Fawcett, W. B., and M. Kornfeld
1980 Projectile Point Neck-Width Variability and Chronology on the Plains. *Wyoming Contributions to Anthropology* 2:66–79.

Feathers, J. K.
1990 *Explaining the Evolution of Prehistoric Ceramics in Southeastern Missouri*. Ph.D. diss., University of Washington, Seattle. University Microfilms, Ann Arbor.

Feinman, G. M., S. Upham, and K. G. Lightfoot
1981 The Production Step Measure: An Ordinal Index of Labor Input in Ceramic Manufacture. *American Antiquity* 46:871–84.

Fenenga, F.
1953 The Weights of Chipped Stone Points: A Clue to their Functions. *Southwestern Journal of Anthropology* 9:309–23.

Ferring, C. R.
1986 Rates of Fluvial Sedimentation: Implications for Archaeological Variability. *Geoarchaeology: An International Journal* 1 (3):259–74.
1990 Archaeological Geology of the Southern Plains. In *Archaeological Geology of North America*, edited by N. P. Lasca and J. Donahue, 253–66. The Geological Society of America, Boulder, Colorado.

Fewkes, J. W.
1898 Preliminary Account of an Expedition to the Pueblo Ruins near Winslow, Arizona, in 1896. In *Annual Report of the Smithsonian Institution for 1896*, 517–39. Washington, D.C.
1904 Two Summers' Work in Pueblo Ruins. In *Report of the Bureau of American Ethnology*, vol. 22, pt. 1:3–195. Washington, D.C.
1909 *Antiquities of Mesa Verde National Park: Spruce Tree House*. Bureau of American Ethnology Bulletin 41. Washington, D.C.
1911a *Antiquities of Mesa Verde National Park: Cliff Palace*. Bureau of American Ethnology Bulletin 51. Washington, D. C.
1911b *Preliminary Report on a Visit to the Navajo National Monument, Arizona*. Bureau of American Ethnology Bulletin 50. Washington, D.C.

Figgins, J. D.
1927 The Antiquity of Man In America. *Natural History* 27 (3):229–39.
1931 An Additional Discovery of the Association of a "Folsom" Artifact and Fossil Mammal Remains. In *Proceedings of the Colorado Museum of Natural History* 10 (4):23–24. Denver.

1933 A Further Contribution to the Antiquity of Man in America. In *Proceedings of the Colorado Museum of Natural History* 12 (2):4–8. Denver.

1934 Folsom and Yuma Artifacts. *Proceedings of the Colorado Museum of Natural History* 13 (2). Denver.

1935 Folsom and Yuma Artifacts, Part 2. *Proceedings of the Colorado Museum of Natural History* 14(2). Denver.

Finnie, I., G. A. Cooper, and J. Berlie
1979 Fracture Propagation in Rock by Transient Cooling. *International Journal of Rock Mechanics, Mineral Science, and Geomechanics Abstracts* 16:11–21.

Fischel, H. E.
1939 Folsom and Yuma Culture Finds. *American Antiquity* 4(3):232–64.

Fish, P. R.
1978 Consistency in Archaeological Measurement and Classification: A Pilot Study. *American Antiquity* 43: 86–89.

Fish, S. K., and S. A. Kowalewski, eds.
1990 *The Archaeology of Regions: A Case for Full-Coverage Survey*. Smithsonian Institution Press, Washington, D.C.

——, P. R. Fish, and J. H. Madsen
1990 Analyzing Regional Agriculture: A Hohokam Example. In *The Archaeology of Regions: A Case for Full-Coverage Survey*, edited by S. K. Fish and S. A. Kowalewski, 189–218. Smithsonian Institution Press, Washington, D.C.

Flanagan, F. J.
1986 *Reference Samples in Geology and Geochemistry*. U.S. Geological Survey Bulletin 1582. Washington, D.C.

Flannery, K. V., ed.
1976 *The Early Mesoamerican Village*. Academic Press, New York.

Flenniken, J. J.
1981 *Replicative Systems Analysis: A Model Applied to the Vein Quartz Artifacts from the Hoko River Site*. Reports of Investigations, no. 59. Washington State University Laboratories of Anthropology, Pullman.

1984 The Past, Present, and Future of Flintknapping: An Anthropological Perspective. *Annual Review of Anthropology* 13:187–203.

——, and T. Ozbun
1988 "Lithic Analysis of Artifacts from Site A461-0683, Bear Valley District, Malheur National Forest, Oregon." Submitted to the Malheur National Forest, John Day, Oregon. PO no. 43-04kk-7-00713.

——, and A. W. Raymond
1986 Morphological Projectile Point Typology: Replication Experimentation and Technological Analysis. *American Antiquity* 51:603–14.

——, and P. J. Wilke
1989 Typology, Technology, and Chronology of Great Basin Dart Points. *American Anthropologist* 91: 149–58.

Flexner, S. B., ed.
1993 Typology. In *Unabridged Dictionary*. Random House, New York.

Foley, R.
1981a A Model of Regional Archaeological Structure. *Proceedings of the British Prehistoric Society* 47:1–17.

1981b Off-site Archaeology: An Alternative Approach for the Short-Sited. In *Patterns in the Past: Studies in Honour of David Clark*, edited by I. Hodder, G. Isaac, and N. Hammond, 157–83. Cambridge University Press, Cambridge.

1981c *Off-site Archaeology and Human Adaptation in Eastern Africa: An Analysis of Regional Artifact Density in the Amboseli, Southern Kenya*. Cambridge Monographs in African Archaeology no. 3, BAR International Series 97. British Archaeological Reports, Oxford.

Forbis, R. G., and J. D. Sperry
1952 An Early Man Site in Montana. *American Antiquity* 18:127–33.

Ford, J. A.
1936 *Analysis of Village Site Collections from Louisiana and Mississippi*. Louisiana State Geological Survey, Department of Conservation, Anthropological Study no. 2. Baton Rouge.

1952 *Measurements of Some Prehistoric*

*Design Developments in the South-
eastern United States.* American
Museum of Natural History Anthropological Papers, vol. 44, no. 3.
New York.

1954a Comment on A. C. Spaulding's Statistical Techniques for the Discovery
of Artifact Types. *American Antiquity* 19:390–91.

1954b Spaulding's Reply to Ford. *American
Anthropologist* 56:109–12.

1954c The Type Concept Revisited. *American Anthropologist* 56:42–53.

1961 In Favor of a Simple Typology.
American Antiquity 27:113–14.

1962 *A Quantitative Method for Deriving
Cultural Chronology.* Pan American
Union Technical Manual no. 1.
Organization of American States,
Washington, D.C.

———, P. Phillips, and W. G. Haag

1955 *The Jaketown Site in West-
Central Mississippi.* Anthropological
Papers of the American Museum of
Natural History, vol. 45, pt. 1. New
York.

———, and G. I. Quimby, Jr.

1945 *The Tchefuncte Culture, an Early
Occupation of the Lower Mississippi Valley.* Society for American
Archaeology Memoir no. 2. Washington, D.C.

———, and C. H. Webb

1956 *Poverty Point, a Late Archaic Site in
Louisiana.* Anthropological Papers
of the American Museum of Natural
History, vol. 46, pt. 1. New York.

Forman, R. T. T., and M. Godron

1986 *Landscape Ecology.* John Wiley and
Sons, New York.

Fowke, G.

1896 Stone Art. In *Annual Report of the
Bureau of Ethnology,* vol. 13:
57–178. Washington, D.C.

Fowler, D. D.

1968 *The Archaeology of Newark Cave,
White Pine County, Nevada.* Desert
Research Institute Technical Report
no. 3. Reno.

———, D. B. Madsen, and E. M. Hattori

1973 *Prehistory of Southeastern Nevada.*
Desert Research Institute Publica-
tions in the Social Sciences no. 6.
Reno.

Fowler, M. G.

1935 Appendix A: Spectroscopic Examination of Potsherds. In *Tuzigoot:
The Excavation and Repair of a
Ruin on the Verde River near Clarkdale, Arizona,* edited by L. R. Caywood and E. H. Spicer, 109–11.
Field Division of Education, National Park Service. Berkeley, California.

Frampton, F., and K. Gratz

1978a Analysis of Potsherds and Ceramic
Wares: Las Vegas Ranch Ruin-East.
In *Las Vegas Ranch Ruin-East and
Las Vegas Ranch Ruin-West: Two
Small Prehistoric Prescott Indian
Culture Ruins in West Central Ari-
zona,* edited by Franklin Barnett,
52–64. Museum of Northern Ari-
zona Bulletin 51. Flagstaff.

1978b Analysis of Potsherds and Ceramic
Wares: Las Vegas Ranch Ruin-West.
In *Las Vegas Ranch Ruin-East and
Las Vegas Ranch Ruin-West: Two
Small Prehistoric Prescott Indian
Culture Ruins in West Central Ari-
zona,* 97–103. Museum of Northern
Arizona Bulletin 51. Flagstaff.

Franklin, U. M., and V. Vitali

1985 The Environmental Stability of Ancient Ceramics. *Archaeometry* 27:
3–15.

Fredrickson, D. A.

1994 Archaeological Taxonomy in
Central California Reconsidered. In
*Toward a New Taxonomic Frame-
work for Central California Archaeology: Essays by J. A. Bennyhoff
and D. A. Fredrickson,* edited by
R. E. Hughes, 91–103. Contributions of the University of California
Archaeological Research Facility no.
52. Berkeley.

Frison, G. C.

1973 *The Wardell Buffalo Trap 48SU301:
Communal Procurement in the Up-
per Green River Basin, Wyoming.*
Anthropological Papers no. 48.
University of Michigan Museum
of Anthropology, Ann Arbor.

1976 Cultural Activity Associated with
Prehistoric Mammoth Butchering
and Processing. *Science* 194:728–30.

1982a Paleo-Indian Winter Subsistence

Strategies on the High Plains. In *Plains Indian Studies: A Collection of Essays in Honor of John C. Ewers and Waldo R. Wedel*, edited by D. H. Ubelaker and H. J. Viola, 193–201. Smithsonian Contributions to Anthropology no. 30. Smithsonian Institution Press, Washington, D.C.

1982b Radiocarbon Dates. In *The Agate Basin Site: A Record of the Paleoindian Occupation of the Northwestern High Plains*, edited by G. C. Frison and D. J. Stanford, 178–180. Academic Press, New York.

1984 The Carter/Kerr-McGee Paleoindian Site: Cultural Resource Management and Archeological Research. *American Antiquity* 49:288–314.

1991 *Prehistoric Hunters of the High Plains*. 2d ed. Academic Press, San Diego.

———, and B. A. Bradley
1980 *Folsom Tools and Technology at the Hanson Site, Wyoming*. University of New Mexico Press, Albuquerque.

———, and G. M. Zeimens
1980 Bone Projectile Points: An Addition to the Folsom Cultural Complex. *American Antiquity* 45:231–37.

Gagliano, S. M., and R. T. Saucier
1963 Poverty Point Sites in Southeastern Louisiana. *American Antiquity* 28:320–27.

Galloway, E., and G. A. Agogino
1961 The Johnson Site: A Folsom Campsite. *Plains Anthropologist* 6 (13):205–8.

García Heras, M.
1993 Deposiciones Invisibles: Micro-Procesos de Calcitización Postdeposicional en Cerámicas Celtibéricas. *Procesos Postdeposicionales, Arqueología Espacial* 16–17: 391–406.

Getis, A., and B. Boots
1978 *Models of Spatial Processes: An Approach to the Study of Point, Line and Area Patterns*. Cambridge University Press, Cambridge.

Getty, H. T.
1935 New Dates for Spruce Tree House, Mesa Verde. *Tree-Ring Bulletin* 1 (4):28–29.

Ghiselin, M. T.
1966 On Psychologism in the Logic of Taxonomic Controversies. *Systematic Zoology* 15 (3):207–15.

1969 The Principles and Concepts of Systematic Biology. In *Systematic Biology; 1962 Publication of the National Academy of Sciences*, edited by C. G. Sibley, 45–55. National Academy of Sciences, Washington, D.C.

Giauque, R. D., F. Asaro, F. Stross, and T. R. Hester
1993 High-Precision Non-Destructive X-ray Fluorescence Method Applicable to Establishing the Provenance of Obsidian Artifacts. *X-Ray Spectrometry* 22:44–53.

Gibson, J. L.
1970 Intersite Variability at Poverty Point: Some Preliminary Considerations on Lapidary. *Southeastern Archaeological Conference Bulletin* 12:13–20.

1972 Patterns at Poverty Point: Empirical and Social Structure. *Southeastern Archaeological Conference Bulletin* 15:119–25.

1973 Social Systems at Poverty Point: An Analysis of Intersite and Intrasite Variability. Ph.D. diss., Department of Anthropology, Southern Methodist University, Dallas.

1974 Poverty Point: The First North American Chiefdom. *Archaeology* 2:97–105.

1975 Fire Pits at Mount Bayou (16CT35), Catahoula Parish, Louisiana. *Louisiana Archaeology* 2:201–28.

1985 *Poverty Point: A Culture of the Lower Mississippi Valley*. Louisiana Archaeological Survey and Antiquities Commission Anthropological Study no. 7. Baton Rouge.

1991 Catahoula—An Amphibious Poverty Point Period Manifestation in Eastern Louisiana. In *The Poverty Point Culture: Local Manifestations, Subsistence Practices, and Trade Networks*, edited by K. M. Byrd, 61–88. Geoscience and Man no. 29. Louisiana State University, Baton Rouge.

Gifford, J. C.
1960 The Type-Variety Method of Ce-

ramic Classification as an Indicator of Cultural Phenomena. *American Antiquity* 25:341–47.

Gladwin, H. S.
1945 *The Chaco Branch: Excavations at White Mound and in the Red Mesa Valley*. Medallion Papers no. 33. Gila Pueblo, Globe, Arizona.

Gladwin, W., and H. S. Gladwin
1930a *An Archaeological Survey of Verde Valley*. Medallion Papers no. 6. Gila Pueblo, Globe, Arizona.
1930b *A Method of Designation of Southwestern Pottery Types*. Medallion Papers no. 7. Gila Pueblo, Globe, Arizona.
1934 *A Method for Designation of Cultures and Their Variations*. Medallion Papers no. 15. Gila Pueblo, Globe, Arizona.

Glascock, M. D., and M. P. Anderson
1993 Geologic Reference Materials for Standardization and Quality Assurance of Instrumental Neutron Activation Analysis. *Journal of Radioanalytical and Nuclear Chemistry* 174:229–42.

Glennan, W. S.
1971 Concave-Based Lanceolate Fluted Projectile Points from California. *Masterkey* 45 (1):27–32.

Godfrey-Smith, D. I., and N. Haywood
1984 Obsidian Sources in Ontario Prehistory. *Ontario Archaeology* 41:29–35.

Gonzalez, R. C., and P. Wintz
1987 *Digital Image Processing*. 2d ed. Addison-Wesley, Reading, Massachusetts.

Gorodzov, V. A.
1933 The Typological method in Archaeology. *American Anthropologist* 35:95–102.

Gould, R. A., and P. J. Watson
1982 A Dialogue on the Meaning and Use of Analogy in Ethnoarchaeological Reasoning. *Journal of Anthropological Archaeology* 1:355–81.

Gould, S. J.
1987 *Time's Arrow, Time's Cycle: Myth and Metaphor in the Discovery of Geological Time*. Harvard University Press, Cambridge.

Gove, H. E.
1987 Turin Workshop on Radiocarbon Dating the Turin Shroud. *Nuclear Instruments and Methods in Physics Research* B29 (1, 2):193–95.

Graebner, F.
1905 Kulturkriese und Kulturschichten in Ozeanian. *Zeitschrift für Ethnologie* 37:28–53.

Graham, R. W.
1986a Plant-Animal Interactions and Pleistocene Extinctions. In *Dynamics of Extinction*, edited by D. K. Elliott, 131–54. John Wiley and Sons, New York.
1986b Responses of Mammalian Communities to Environmental Changes during the Late Quaternary. In *Community Ecology*, edited by J. Diamond and T. J. Case, 300–313. Harper and Row, New York.
1987 Late Quaternary Mammalian Faunas and Paleoenvironments of the Southwestern Plains of the United States. In *Late Quaternary Mammalian Biogeography and Environments of the Great Plains and Prairies*, edited by R. W. Graham, H. A. Semken, Jr., and M. A. Graham, 24–86. Illinois State Museum, Springfield.

Graves, M. W.
1985 Ceramic Design Variation within a Kalinga Village: Temporal and Spatial Processes. In *Decoding Prehistoric Ceramics*, edited by B. A. Nelson, 5–34. Southern Illinois University Press, Carbondale.
———, and T. N. Ladefoged
1995 The Evolutionary Significance of Ceremonial Architecture in Polynesia. In *Evolutionary Archaeology: Methodological Issues*, edited by P. A. Teltser, 149–74. University of Arizona Press, Tucson.

Gray, W. M.
1965 Surface Spalling by Thermal Stresses in Rocks. In *Proceedings of the Rock Mechanics Symposium, University of Toronto, January, 1965*. Mines Branch, Department of Mines and Technical Surveys, Ottawa.

Grayson, D. K.

1983   *The Establishment of Human Antiquity*. Academic Press, New York.

1984   *Quantitative Zooarchaeology*. Academic Press, New York.

1993   *The Desert's Past: A Natural Prehistory of the Great Basin*. Smithsonian Institution Press, Washington, D.C.

Grebinger, P.

1973   Prehistoric Social Organization in Chaco Canyon, New Mexico: An Alternative Reconstruction. *The Kiva* 39 (1):3–23.

1978   Prehistoric Social Organization in Chaco Canyon, New Mexico: An Evolutionary Perspective. In *Discovering Past Behavior: Experiments in the Archaeology of the American Southwest*, edited by P. Grebinger, 73–100. Gordon and Breach Science Publishers, New York.

Green, R. C., R. R. Brooks, and R. D. Reeves

1967   Characterization of New Zealand Obsidians by Emission Spectroscopy. *New Zealand Journal of Science* 10:675–82.

Grenander, U.

1996   *Elements of Pattern Theory*. Johns Hopkins University Press, Baltimore.

Grieg-Smith, P.

1983   *Quantitative Plant Ecology*. 3d ed. Blackwell, London.

Griffin, J. B.

1952a Culture Periods of the Eastern United States. In *Archaeology of the Eastern United States*, edited by J. B. Griffin, 352–64. The University of Chicago Press, Chicago.

1952b *Prehistoric Pottery of the Eastern United States*. Department of Anthropology, University of Michigan, Ann Arbor.

1952c Radiocarbon Dates for the Eastern United States. In *Archaeology of the Eastern United States*, edited by J. B. Griffin, 365–70. The University of Chicago Press, Chicago.

1967   Eastern North American Archaeology: A Summary. *Science* 156 (3772):175–91.

1985   Changing Concepts of the Prehistoric Mississippian Cultures of the Eastern United States. In *Alabama and the Borderlands: From Prehistory to Statehood*, edited by R. R. Badger and L. A. Clayton, 40–63. University of Alabama Press, Tuscaloosa.

Gruhn, R.

1979   Excavation in Amy's Shelter, Eastern Nevada. In *The Archaeology of Smith Creek Canyon*, edited by D. R. Tuohy and D. L. Randall, 90–160. Nevada State Museum Anthropological Papers no. 17. Carson City.

Guernsey, S. J.

1931   *Explorations in Northeastern Arizona*. Papers of the Peabody Museum of American Archaeology and Ethnology, vol. 12, no. 1. Harvard University, Cambridge.

———, and A. V. Kidder

1921   *Basket-Maker Caves of Northeastern Arizona*. Papers of the Peabody Museum of American Archaeology and Ethnology, vol. 8, no. 1. Harvard University, Cambridge.

Guthe, C. E.

1917   The Pueblo Ruin at Rowe, New Mexico. *El Palacio* 4 (4):33–39.

Haag, W. G.

1942   Early Horizons in the Southeast. *American Antiquity* 7:209–22.

Hagerstrand, T.

1967   *Innovation Diffusion as a Spatial Process*. University of Chicago Press, Chicago.

Hall, A. F.

1933   *General Report on the Rainbow Bridge–Monument Valley Expedition of 1933*. University of California Press, Berkeley.

Hall, R. L.

1991   Cahokia Identity and Interaction Models of Cahokia Mississippian. In *Cahokia and the Hinterlands*, edited by T. E. Emerson and R. B. Lewis, 3–34. University of Illinois Press, Urbana.

Hally, D. J.

1983   Use Alteration of Pottery Vessel Surfaces: An Important Source of Evidence for the Identification of Vessel Function. *North American Archaeologist* 4:1–25.

Hanes, R. C.
1977 *Lithic Tools of the Dirty Shame Rockshelter: Typology and Distribution.* Idaho State Museum of Natural History Miscellaneous Papers no. 6. Pocatello.

Harbottle, G.
1976 Activation Analysis in Archaeology. In *Radiochemistry*, vol. 3, edited by G. W. A. Newton, 33–72. The Chemical Society, London.
1982a Chemical Characterization in Archaeology. In *Contexts for Prehistoric Exchange*, edited by J. E. Ericson and T. K. Earle, 13–51. Academic Press, New York.
1982b Provenience Studies Using Neutron Activation Analysis: The Role of Standardization. In *Archaeological Ceramics*, edited by J. S. Olin and A. D. Franklin, 67–77. Smithsonian Institution Press, Washington, D.C.

Hargrave, L. L.
1932 *Guide to Forty Pottery Types from the Hopi Country and the San Francisco Mountains, Arizona.* Museum of Northern Arizona Bulletin 1. Flagstaff.
1933 *Pueblo II Houses of the San Francisco Mountains, Arizona.* Museum of Northern Arizona Bulletin 4. Flagstaff.
1935 *Report on Archaeological Reconnaissance in the Rainbow Plateau Area of Northern Arizona and Southern Utah.* University of California Press, Berkeley.

Harrington, J. C.
1954 Dating Stem Fragments of Seventeenth and Eighteenth Century Clay Tobacco Pipes. *Quarterly Bulletin of the Archaeological Society of Virginia* 9 (1):9–13.

Harrington, M. R.
1938a Folsom Man in California. *Masterkey* 12 (4):132–37.
1938b Pre-Folsom Man in California. *Masterkey* 12 (5):173–75.

Harris, J.
1986 Silicic Volcanics of the Volcan Tequila, Jalisco, Mexico. Master's thesis, Department of Geology, University of California, Berkeley.

Hasselman, D. P. H.
1969 Unified Theory of Thermal Shock Fracture Initiation and Crack Propagation in Brittle Ceramics. *Journal of the American Ceramic Society* 52 (11):600–604.

Hatch, J. W., J. W. Michels, C. M. Stevenson, B. E. Scheetz, and R. A. Geidel
1990 Hopewell Obsidian Studies: Behavioral Implications of Recent Sourcing and Dating Research. *American Antiquity* 55:461–79.

Haury, E. W.
1938 Southwestern Dated Ruins: II. *Tree-Ring Bulletin* 4 (3):3–4.
———, and L. L. Hargrave
1931 *Recently Dated Pueblo Ruins in Arizona.* Smithsonian Institution Miscellaneous Collections, vol. 82, no. 11. Washington, D.C.

Hawking, S. W.
1988 *A Brief History of Time: From the Big Bang to Black Holes.* Bantam Books, Toronto.

Hawley, F.
1937 The Place of Tseh So in the Chaco Culture Pattern. In *Tseh So, a Small House Ruin, Chaco Canyon, New Mexico*, edited by D. D. Brand, F. M. Hawley, F. C. Hibben, et al., 115–19. Anthropological Series, vol. 2, no. 2. University of New Mexico Press, Albuquerque.

Hayden, B., and W. K. Hutchings
1989 Whither the Billet Flake. In *Experiments in Lithic Technology*, edited by D. S. Amick and R. P. Mauldin, 235–57. BAR International Series 528. British Archaeological Reports, Oxford.

Haynes, C. V., Jr.
1980 Paleoindian Charcoal from Meadowcroft Rockshelter: Is Contamination a Problem? *American Antiquity* 45:582–87.
1991a More on Meadowcroft Radiocarbon Chronology. *The Review of Archaeology* 12:8–14.
1991b Clovis–Folsom–Midland–Plainview Geochronology, Climatic Change and Extinction. Paper presented at the 56th Annual Meeting of the Society for American Archaeology. New Orleans. [Revised 1991 draft]

1992   Contributions of Radiocarbon Dating to the Geochronology of the Peopling of the New World. In *Radiocarbon after Four Decades*, edited by R. E. Taylor, A. Long, and R. S. Kra, 355–74. Springer-Verlag, New York.

———, R. P. Beukens, A. J. T. Jull, and O. K. Davis

1992   New Radiocarbon Dates for Some Old Folsom Sites: Accelerator Technology. In *Ice Age Hunters of the Rockies*, edited by D. J. Stanford and J. S. Day, 83–100. Denver Museum of Natural History, Denver.

———, D. J. Donahue, A. J. T. Jull, and T. H. Zabel

1984   Application of Accelerator Dating to Fluted Point Paleoindian Sites. *Archaeology of Eastern North America* 12:184–91.

Heizer, R. F.

1937   Baked Clay Objects of the Lower Sacramento Valley, California. *American Antiquity* 3:34–50.

1938   A Folsom-Type Point from Sacramento Valley. *Masterkey* 12 (5): 180–82.

1940   A Note on Folsom and Nepesta Points. *American Antiquity* 6:79–80.

1949   *The Archaeology of Central California I: The Early Horizon*. University of California Anthropological Records 12 (1). Berkeley.

1974   Studying the Windmiller Culture. In *Archaeological Researches in Retrospect*, edited by G. R. Willey, 179–204. Winthrop Publishers, Cambridge, Massachusetts.

1975   Some Thoughts on California Archaeology at the Moment. *Journal of New World Archaeology* 1 (1).

1978   Trade and Trails. In *California*, edited by R. F. Heizer, 690–93. Handbook of North American Indians, vol. 8, W. C. Sturtevant, general editor. Smithsonian Institution, Washington, D.C.

———, M. A. Baumhoff, and C. W. Clewlow, Jr.

1968   *Archaeology of South Fork Shelter (NV-EL-11), Elko County, Nevada.* Archaeological Survey Reports 20:119–49. University of California, Berkeley.

———, H. Williams, and J. A. Graham

1965   *Notes on Mesoamerican Obsidians and Their Significance in Archaeological Studies.* Contributions of the University of California Archaeological Research Facility 1:94–103. Berkeley.

Henry, D. O., C. V. Haynes, Jr., and B. Bradley

1976   Quantitative Variations in Flaked Stone Debitage. *Plains Anthropologist* 21 (7):57–61.

Hester, J. J.

1972   *Blackwater Locality No. 1.* Fort Burgwin Research Center Publication no. 8. Ranchos de Taos, New Mexico.

Hewett, E. L.

1909   The Excavations at Tyuonyi, New Mexico, in 1908. *American Anthropologist*, n.s., 11:434–55.

1921a   The Chaco Canyon and Its Ancient Monuments. *Art and Archaeology* 11:3–28.

1921b   The Excavation of Chetro Ketl. *Art and Archaeology* 11:45–62.

1922   The Chaco Canyon in 1921. *Art and Archaeology* 14:115–31.

Hibben, F. C.

1960   *Digging Up America.* Hill and Wang, New York.

Hill, J.

1972   The Methodological Debate in Archaeology: A Model. In *Models in Archaeology*, edited by D. Clarke, 61–107. Methuen, London.

———, and R. Evans

1972   A Model for Classification and Typology. In *Models in Archaeology*, edited by D. Clarke, 231–73. Methuen, London.

Hodder, I.

1982   *Symbols in Action.* Cambridge University Press, Cambridge.

———, and C. Orton

1976   *Spatial Analysis in Archaeology.* Cambridge University Press, Cambridge.

Hodge, F. W.

1918   *Excavations at Hawikuh, New Mexico.* Smithsonian Institution Miscellaneous Collections, vol. 68, no. 12:61–72. Washington, D.C.

1922   Recent Excavations at Hawikuh. *El Palacio* 12 (1):1–11.

Hodson, F. R.
1982   Some Aspects of Archaeological Classification. In *Essays in Archaeological Typology*, edited by R. Whallon and J. A. Brown, 21–29. Center for American Archaeology Press, Evanston, Ill.

Hofman, J. L.
1989   Prehistoric Culture History: Hunters and Gatherers in the Southern Great Plains. In *From Clovis to Comanchero: Archeological Overview of the Southern Great Plains*, 25–60. Arkansas Archeological Survey Research Series no. 35. Fayetteville.
1991   Folsom Land Use: Projectile Point Variability as a Key To Mobility. In *Raw Material Economies among Prehistoric Hunter-Gatherers*, edited by A. Montet-White and S. Holen, 335–55. University of Kansas Publications in Anthropology no. 19. Lawrence.
1992   Recognition and Interpretation of Folsom Technological Variability on the Southern Plains. In *Ice Age Hunters of the Rockies*, edited by D. J. Stanford and J. S. Day, 193–224. Denver Museum of Natural History, Denver.
1994   Kansas Folsom Evidence. *Kansas Anthropologist* 15:31–43.

———, D. S. Amick, and R. O. Rose
1990   Shifting Sands: A Folsom-Midland Assemblage from a Campsite in Western Texas. *Plains Anthropologist* 35 (129):221–53.

Hole, F.
1982   Finding Problems for All the Solutions. In *Future Directions in Archaeometry*, edited by J. S. Olin, 80–84. Smithsonian Institution, Washington, D.C.

Holland, J. H.
1995   *Hidden Order, How Adaptation Builds Complexity*. Addison-Wesley, Reading.

Holliday, V. T., and B. L. Allen
1987   Geology and Soils. In *Lubbock Lake: Late Quaternary Studies on the Southern High Plains*, edited by

E. Johnson, 14–21. Texas A&M University Press, College Station.

———, and A. B. Anderson
1993   "Paleoindian," "Clovis" and "Folsom": A Brief Etymology. *Current Research in the Pleistocene* 10:79–81.

Holman, J. P.
1990   *Heat Transfer*. 7th ed. McGraw-Hill, New York.

Holmer, R. N.
1980   Chipped Stone Projectile Points. In *Cowboy Cave*, edited by J. D. Jennings, 31–38. University of Utah Anthropological Papers no. 104. University of Utah Press, Salt Lake City.

Holmes, W. H.
1897   Stone Implements of the Potomac-Chesapeake Tidewater Province. In *Annual Report of the Bureau of Ethnology (1893–94)*, vol. 15:3–152. Washington, D.C.
1903   Aboriginal Pottery of the Eastern United States. *Annual Report of the Bureau of American Ethnology*, vol. 20:1–237. Smithsonian Institution, Washington, D.C.
1914   Some Areas of American Culture Characterization Tentatively Outlined as an Aid in the Study of Antiquities. *American Anthropologist* 16:413–46.

Howard, E. B.
1932   Caves along the Slopes of the Guadalupe Mountains. *Bulletin of the Texas Archeological and Paleontological Society* 4:7–19.
1934   Grooved Spearpoints. *Pennsylvania Archaeologist* 3 (6):11–15.
1935a   Evidence of Early Man in North America. *The Museum Journal* 24 (2–3). University Museum, University of Pennsylvania, Philadelphia.
1935b   The Occurrence of Flints and Extinct Animals in Pluvial Deposits near Clovis, New Mexico. Part 1, Introduction. *Proceedings of the Academy of Natural Sciences of Philadelphia* 87:299–303.
1936   An Outline of the Problem of Man's Antiquity in North America. *American Anthropologist* 38 (3):394–413.
1938   Minutes of the International Sympo-

sium on Early Man Held at the Academy of Natural Sciences of Philadelphia, March 17th–20th, *1937. Proceedings of the Academy of Natural Sciences of Philadelphia (for 1937)* 89:439–447.

1939   Folsom and Yuma Points from Saskatchewan. *American Antiquity* 4:277–79.

1943a   The Finley Site. *American Antiquity* 8:224–34.

1943b   Folsom and Yuma Problems. *Proceedings of the American Philosophical Society* 86:255–59.

Hudson, J., ed.

1993   *From Bones to Behavior*. Center for Archaeological Investigations Occasional Paper no. 21. Southern Illinois University, Carbondale.

Hughes, R. E.

1984   Obsidian Sourcing Studies in the Great Basin: Problems and Prospects. In *Obsidian Studies in the Great Basin*, edited by R. E. Hughes, 1–19. Contributions of the University of California Archaeological Research Facility no. 45. Berkeley.

1986   *Diachronic Variability in Obsidian Procurement Patterns in Northeastern California and Southcentral Oregon*. University of California Publications in Anthropology no. 17. Berkeley and Los Angeles.

1988a   Archaeological Significance of Geochemical Contrasts among Southwestern New Mexico Obsidians. *Texas Journal of Science* 40: 297–307.

1988b   The Coso Volcanic Field Reexamined: Implications for Obsidian Sourcing and Hydration Dating Research. *Geoarchaeology* 3:253–65.

1989   A New Look at Mono Basin Obsidians. In *Current Directions in California Obsidian Studies*, edited by R. E. Hughes, 1–12. Contributions of the University of California Archaeological Research Facility no. 48. Berkeley.

1992a   Another Look at Hopewell Obsidian Studies. *American Antiquity* 57:515–23.

1992b   California Archaeology and Linguis-

tic Prehistory. *Journal of Anthropological Research* 48:317–38.

1994a   Intrasource Chemical Variability of Artifact-Quality Obsidians from the Casa Diablo Area, California. *Journal of Archaeological Science* 21: 263–71.

1994b   Methodological Observations on Great Basin Prehistory. In *Across the West: Human Population Movement and the Expansion of the Numa*, edited by D. B. Madsen and D. Rhode, 67–70. University of Utah Press, Salt Lake City.

1994c   Mosaic Patterning in Prehistoric California—Great Basin Exchange. In *Prehistoric Exchange Systems in North America*, edited by T. G. Baugh and J. E. Ericson, 363–83. Plenum Press, New York.

———, and R. L. Smith

1993   Archaeology, Geology, and Geochemistry in Obsidian Provenance Studies. In *Effects of Scale on Archaeological and Geoscientific Perspectives*, edited by J. K. Stein and A. R. Linse, 79–91. Geological Society of America Special Paper no. 283. Boulder, Colorado.

Hull, D. L.

1967   The Metaphysics of Evolution. *The British Journal for the History of Science* 3 (12):309–37.

1969   The Natural System and the Species Problem. In *Systematic Biology; 1962 Publication of the National Academy of Science*, edited by C. G. Sibley, 56–61. National Academy of Sciences, Washington, D.C.

1970   Contemporary Systematic Philosophies. *Annual Review of Ecology and Systematics* 1:19–54.

1980   Individuality and Selection. *Annual Review of Ecology and Systematics* 11:311–32.

1988a   Interactors versus Vehicles. In *The Role of Behavior in Evolution*, edited by H. C. Plotkin, 19–50. MIT Press, Cambridge.

1988b   *Science as Progress: An Evolutionary Account of the Social and Conceptual Development of Science*. The University of Chicago Press, Chicago.

1989 *The Metaphysics of Evolution.* State University of New York press, Albany.

Hunter, D. G.

1975 Functional Analysis of Poverty Point Clay Objects. *Florida Anthropologist* 28:57–71.

Hurst, C. T.

1941 The Folsom-Yuma Problem. *Southwestern Lore* 7 (4):65–67.

Huxtable, J, M. J. Aitken, and J. C. Weber

1972 Thermoluminescent Dating of Baked Clay Balls of the Poverty Point Culture. *Archaeometry* 14:269–75.

Hyland, D. C., and T. R. Anderson

1990 Blood Residue Analysis of the Lithic Assemblage from the Mitchell Locality, Blackwater Draw, New Mexico. In *Lithic Technology at the Mitchell Locality of Blackwater Draw: A Stratified Folsom Site in Eastern New Mexico*, edited by A. T. Boldurian, 105–10. Memoir 24. *Plains Anthropologist*, 35 (130).

Ingbar, E. E.

1992 The Hanson Site and Folsom on the Northwestern Plains. In *Ice Age Hunters of the Rockies*, edited by D. J. Stanford and J. S. Day, 169–92. Denver Museum of Natural History, Denver.

———, M. L. Larson, and B. A. Bradley

1989 A Nontypological Approach to Debitage Analysis. In *Experiments in Lithic Technology*, edited by D. S. Amick and R. P. Mauldin, 117–36. BAR International Series 528. British Archaeological Reports, Oxford.

Irwin, H. T.

1971 Developments in Early Man Studies in Western North America, 1960–1970. *Arctic Anthropology* 8 (2):42–67.

Irwin-Williams, C., ed.

1972 *The Structure of Chacoan Society in the Northern Southwest: Investigations at the Salmon Site—1972.* Eastern New Mexico University Contributions in Anthropology, vol. 4, no. 3. Portales, New Mexico.

———, H. Irwin, G. Agogino, and C. V. Haynes, Jr.

1973 Hell Gap: Paleo-Indian Occupation on the High Plains. *Plains Anthropologist* 18 (59):40–53.

Jablow, J.

1951 *The Cheyenne in Plains Indian Trade Relations 1795–1840.* Monographs of the American Ethnological Society no. 19. J. J. Augustin, New York.

Jack, R. N.

1971 The Source of Obsidian Artifacts in Northern Arizona. *Plateau* 43:103–114.

1976 Prehistoric Obsidian in California I: Geochemical Aspects. In *Advances in Obsidian Glass Studies: Archaeological and Geochemical Perspectives*, edited by R. E. Taylor, 183–217. Noyes Press, Park Ridge, New Jersey.

———, and I. S. E. Carmichael

1969 The Chemical "Fingerprinting" of Acid Volcanic Rocks. *California Division of Mines and Geology Special Report* no. 100:17–32. San Francisco.

———, and R. F. Heizer

1968 *"Finger-Printing" of Some Mesoamerican Obsidian Artifacts.* Contributions of the University of California Archaeological Research Facility no. 5:81–100. Berkeley.

Jackson, T. L.

1974 The Economics of Obsidian in Central California Prehistory: Applications of X-ray Fluorescence Spectrography in Archaeology. Master's thesis, Department of Anthropology, San Francisco State University.

1989 Late Prehistoric Obsidian Production and Exchange in the North Coast Ranges, California. In *Current Directions in California Obsidian Studies*, edited by R. E. Hughes, 79–94. Contributions of the University of California Archaeological Research Facility no. 48. Berkeley.

James, M. A., J. Bailey, and J. M. D'Auria

1996 A Volcanic Glass Library for the Pacific Northwest: Problems and Prospects. *Canadian Journal of Archaeology* 20:93–122.

Jelinek, A. J.
1976 Form, Function, and Style in Lithic Artifacts. In *Cultural Change and Continuity: Essays in Honor of James Bennett Griffin*, edited by C. E. Cleland, 19–33. Academic Press, New York.

Jenks, A. E.
1934 The Discovery of an Ancient Minnesota Maker of Yuma and Folsom Points. *Science* 80 (2070):205.

1935 Recent Discoveries in Minnesota Prehistory. *Minnesota History* 16 (1):1–21.

1937 *Minnesota's Browns Valley Man and Associated Burial Artifacts*. Memoirs of the American Anthropological Association no. 49. Washington, D.C.

Jennings, J. D.
1957 *Danger Cave*. University of Utah Anthropological Papers no. 27. University of Utah Press, Salt Lake City.

———, ed.
1980 *Cowboy Cave*. University of Utah Anthropological Papers no.104. University of Utah Press, Salt Lake City.

———, A. R. Schroedl, and R. N. Holmer
1980 *Sudden Shelter*. University of Utah Anthropological Papers no. 103. University of Utah Press, Salt Lake City.

Jeske, R. J.
1992 Energetic Efficiency and Lithic Technology: An Upper Mississippian Example. *American Antiquity* 57:467–81.

Jodry, M. A.
1987 Stewart's Cattle Guard Site: A Folsom Site in Southern Colorado. A Report of the 1981 and 1983 Field Seasons. Master's thesis, Department of Anthropology, University of Texas, Austin.

———, and D. J. Stanford
1992 Stewart's Cattle Guard Site: An Analysis of Bison Remains in a Folsom Kill–Butchery Campsite. In *Ice Age Hunters of the Rockies*, edited by D. J. Stanford and J. S. Day, 101–68. Denver Museum of Natural History, Denver.

Johnson, E.
1987 Cultural Activities and Interactions. In *Lubbock Lake: Late Quaternary Studies on the Southern High Plains*, edited by E. Johnson, 120–58. Texas A&M University Press, College Station.

———, and V. T. Holliday
1987 Introduction. In *Lubbock Lake: Late Quaternary Studies on the Southern High Plains*, edited by E. Johnson, 3–13. Texas A&M University Press, College Station.

Johnson, J. K., and C. A. Morrow
1987 *The Organization of Core Technology*. Westview Special Studies in Archaeological Research. Westview Press, Boulder, Colorado.

Johnson, L. L.
1978 A History of Flint-Knapping Experimentation, 1938–1976. *Current Anthropology* 19 (2):337–72.

Johnson, R. G., and B.-S. L. King
1987 Energy-Dispersive X-ray Fluorescence Spectrometry. In *Methods for Geochemical Analysis*, edited by P. A. Baedecker. U.S. Geological Survey Bulletin 1770:F1–F5. Washington, D.C.

Jones, G. T.
1984 *Prehistoric Land Use in the Steens Mountain Area, Southeastern Oregon*. Ph.D. diss., University of Washington. University Microfilms, Ann Arbor.

———, and C. Beck
1992 Chronological Resolution in Distributional Archaeology. In *Space, Time, and Archaeological Landscapes*, edited by J. Rossignol and L. Wandsnider, 167-92. Plenum Press, New York.

———, R. D. Leonard, and A. L. Abbott
1995 The Structure of Selectionist Explanations in Archaeology. In *Evolutionary Archaeology: Methodological Issues*, edited by P. A. Teltser, 13–32. University of Arizona Press, Tucson.

Judd, N. M.
1922a *Archaeological Investigations at Pueblo Bonito, New Mexico*. Smithsonian Institution Miscellaneous

Collections, vol. 72, no. 15, 106–17. Washington, D.C.

1922b The Pueblo Bonito Expedition of the National Geographic Society. *National Geographic Magazine* 41 (3):322–31.

1923 *Archaeological Investigations at Pueblo Bonito, New Mexico.* Smithsonian Institution Miscellaneous Collections, vol. 74, no. 5, 134–43. Washington, D.C.

1924 Two Chaco Canyon Pithouses. In *Smithsonian Institution Annual Report for 1922.* Washington, D. C.

1925a Everyday Life in Pueblo Bonito. *National Geographic Magazine* 48 (3):227–66.

1925b *Exploration in Pre-Historic Pueblo Bonito, Chaco Canyon, New Mexico.* The Geographical Society of Philadelphia Bulletin, vol. 23. Philadelphia.

1926 *Archeological Investigations at Pueblo Bonito and Pueblo del Arroyo, New Mexico. Explorations and Field-Work of the Smithsonian Institution in 1925.* Smithsonian Institution Miscellaneous Collections, vol. 78, no. 1. Washington, D. C.

1927a *Archeological Investigations in Chaco Canyon, New Mexico. Explorations and Field-work of the Smithsonian Institution in 1926.* Smithsonian Institution Miscellaneous Collections, vol. 78, no. 7, 158–68. Washington, D.C.

1927b The Architectural Evolution of Pueblo Bonito. *Proceedings of the National Academy of Sciences* 13 (7):561–63.

Judge, W. J.

1970 Systems Analysis and the Folsom-Midland Question. *Journal of Anthropological Research* 26 (1):40–51.

1973 *Paleoindian Occupation of the Central Rio Grande Valley in New Mexico.* University of New Mexico Press, Albuquerque.

1979 The Development of a Complex Cultural Ecosystem in the Chaco Basin, New Mexico. In *Proceedings of the First Conference on Scientific Research in the National Parks,* vol.

2, edited by R. M. Linn, 901–6. National Park Service Transactions and Proceedings Series 5. Washington, D.C.

Kaplan, A.

1964 *The Conduct of Inquiry: Methodology for Behavioral Science.* Chandler Publishing Company, San Francisco.

Keeley, L. H., and M. H. Newcomer

1977 Microwear Analysis of Experimental Flint Tools: A Test Case. *Journal of Archaeological Science* 4:29–62.

Kelly, A. R.

1938 *A Preliminary Report on Archaeological Explorations at Macon, Ga.* Bureau of American Ethnology Anthropological Papers no. 1, Bulletin 119. Washington, D.C.

Kelly, R. L.

1988 The Three Sides of a Biface. *American Antiquity* 53:717–34.

Kidder, A. V.

1917 A Design-Sequence from New Mexico. *Proceedings of the National Academy of Sciences* 3:369–70. Baltimore.

1924 *An Introduction to the Study of Southwestern Archaeology.* Papers of the Southwestern Expedition, Phillips Academy no. 1. Yale University Press, New York. Reprinted 1962, Yale University Press, New Haven.

1927 Southwestern Archeological Conference. *Science* 66 (1716):489–91.

1936 Speculations on New World Prehistory. In *Essays in Anthropology Presented to A. L. Kroeber,* edited by R. H. Lowie, 143–52. University of California Press, Berkeley.

1962 *An Introduction to the Study of Southwestern Archaeology.* Yale University Press, New Haven. Reprint of 1924 edition. (Page references are to reprint edition.)

———, and A. O. Shepard

1936 *The Pottery of Pecos,* vol. 2. Yale University Press, New Haven.

———, and S. J. Guernsey

1919 *Archaeological Explorations in Northeastern Arizona.* Bureau of American Ethnology Bulletin 65. Washington, D.C.

Kilikoglou, V., Y. Maniatis, and A. P. Grimanis
  1988   The Effect of Purification and Firing of Clays on Trace Element Provenance Studies. *Archaeometry* 30:37–46.
King, D.
  1949   *Nalakihu.* Museum of Northern Arizona Bulletin 23. Flagstaff.
Kleindienst, M. R., and C. M. Keller
  1976   Toward a Functional Analysis of Handaxes and Cleavers: The Evidence from Eastern Africa. *Man* 2:176–87.
Klejn, L. S.
  1982   *Archaeological Typology.* Translated by Penelope Dole. BAR International Series 153. British Archaeological Reports, Oxford.
Klemptner, L. J., and P. F. Johnson
  1985   An Analytical Approach to the Technological Development of Mississippian Pottery. *Ceramics and Civilization*, vol. 1, *Ancient Technology to Modern Science*, edited by W. D. Kingery and E. Lense, 101–12. American Ceramic Society, Columbus, Ohio.
  1986   Technology and the Primitive Potter: Mississippian Pottery Development Seen through the Eyes of a Ceramic Engineer. In *Ceramics and Civilization*, vol. 2, *Technology and Style*, edited by W. D. Kingery and E. Lense, 251–71. American Ceramic Society, Columbus, Ohio.
Klippel, W. E.
  1969   The Hearnes Site, a Multicomponent Occupation Site and Cemetery in the Cairo Lowland Region of Southeast Missouri. *Missouri Archaeologist* 31.
Kluckhohn, C.
  1939   Discussion. In *Preliminary Report on the 1937 Excavations, Bc 50–51, Chaco Canyon, New Mexico*, edited by C. Kluckhohn and P. Reiter, 151–62. Anthropological Series, vol. 3, no. 2. University of New Mexico Press, Albuquerque.
———, and P. Reiter, eds.
  1939   *Preliminary Report on the 1937 Excavations, Bc 50–51, Chaco Canyon, New Mexico.* Anthropological Series, vol. 3, no. 2. University of New Mexico Press, Albuquerque.
Knudson, R.
  1973   Organizational Variability in Late Paleo-Indian Assemblages. Ph.D. diss., Department of Anthropology, Washington State University, Pullman.
Krieger, A. D.
  1944   The Typological Concept. *American Antiquity* 9:271–88.
  1946   Certain Projectile Points of the Early American Hunters. *Bulletin of the Texas Archeological and Paleontological Society* 17:7–27.
  1960   Archeological Typology in Theory and Practice. In *Selected Papers of the Fifth International Congress on Anthropological and Ethnological Sciences*, edited by A. F. C. Wallace, 141–51. University of Pennsylvania Press, Philadelphia.
Kroeber, A. L.
  1931   The Culture-Area and Age-Area Concepts of Clark Wissler. In *Methods in Social Science*, edited by S. Rice, 248–65. University of Chicago Press, Chicago.
———, and C. Kluckhohn
  1952   *Culture: A Critical Review of Concepts and Definitions.* Papers of the Peabody Museum of American Archaeology and Ethnology, vol. 47, no. 1. Harvard University, Cambridge.
Kroll, E. M., and T. D. Price, eds.
  1991   *The Interpretation of Archaeological Spatial Patterning.* Plenum Press, New York.
Krone, M. F.
  1975   A Report on Folsom Points Found in the El Paso Area. *The Artifact* 13 (4):1–19.
  1978   The Soto Ranch Site. *The Artifact* 16 (4):23–53.
Kuijt, I., W. C. Prentiss, and D. L. Pokotylo
  1995   Bipolar Reduction: An Experimental Study of Debitage Variability. *Lithic Technology* 20 (2):116–27.
Kunselman, R.
  1991   Durable Paleoindian Artifacts: XRF Variability of Selected Wyoming Source Materials. *Wyoming Archaeologist* 34:15–25.

1994 Prehistoric Obsidian Utilization in the Central Rocky Mountains: The Lookingbill Site 48FR308. *Wyoming Archaeologist* 38:1–17.

Kurtén, B., and E. Anderson
1980 *Pleistocene Mammals of North America.* Columbia University Press, New York.

Lange, F. W., ed.
1993 *Precolumbian Jade: New Geological and Cultural Interpretations.* University of Utah Press, Salt Lake City.

Lanning, E. P.
1963 *Archaeology of the Rose Spring Site INY-372.* Publications in American Archaeology and Ethnology no. 49:237–336. University of California, Berkeley.

Largent, F. B., Jr., M. R. Waters, and D. L. Carlson
1991 The Spatiotemporal Distribution and Characteristics of Folsom Projectile Points in Texas. *Plains Anthropologist* 36 (137):323–41.

Larralde, S.
1984 Quality Control in Lithics Analysis: A Test of Precision. *Haliksa'i* 31:1–8.

Leese, M. N., and P. L. Main
1994 The Efficient Computation of Unbiased Mahalanobis Distances and Their Interpretation in Archaeometry. *Archaeometry* 36:307–16.

Lemoine, C., and M. Picon
1982 La Fixation du Phosphore par les Céramiques lors de Leur Enfouissement e Ses Incidences Analytiques. *Revue d'Archéométrie* 6:101–12.

Leonard, R. D., and G. T. Jones
1987 Elements of an Inclusive Evolutionary Model for Archaeology. *Journal of Anthropological Archaeology* 6:199–219.

———, and G. T. Jones, eds.
1989 *Quantifying Diversity in Archaeology.* University of Cambridge Press, Cambridge.

———, and H. Reed
1993 Population Aggregation in the Prehistoric American Southwest: A Selectionist Model. *American Antiquity* 58:648–61.

LeTourneau, P. D.
1992a "Folsom Raw Material Use on the Southern Plains." Paper presented at the 57th Annual Meeting of the Society for American Archaeology, Pittsburgh, Pennsylvania.

1992b Folsom Use of Alibates and Edwards Cherts: Raw Material Procurement and Technological Organization. *Current Research in the Pleistocene* 9:66–69.

n.d. How Did Folsom Procure Their Toolstone? In preparation. Ph.D. diss., Department of Anthropology, University of New Mexico, Albuquerque.

Lewontin, R.
1974 *The Genetic Basis of Evolutionary Change.* Columbia University Press, New York.

Linse, A.
1993 Geoarchaeological Scale and Archaeological Interpretation: Examples from the Central Jornada Mogollon. In *Effects of Scale on Archaeological and Geological Perspectives,* edited by J. K. Stein and A. R. Linse, 11–28. Geological Society of America Special Paper no. 283. Boulder, Colorado.

Literary Digest
1934a Scientist Describes True Folsom Points. *Literary Digest,* 28 July, 18.
1934b Stone Relics of Oldest Americans? *Literary Digest,* 9 June, 22.

Lock, G. R., and Z. Stančič, eds.
1995 *Archaeology and Geographical Information Systems: A European Perspective.* Taylor & Francis, London.

Longacre, W. A., and J. M. Skibo, eds.
1994 *Kalinga Ethnoarchaeology: Expanding Archaeological Method and Theory.* Smithsonian Institution Press, Washington, D.C.

Luedtke, B. E.
1979 The Identification of Sources of Chert Artifacts. *American Antiquity* 43:413–23.

Lycett, M.
1995 *Archaeological Implications of European Contact: Demography, Settlement, and Land Use in the Middle Rio Grande Valley, New Mexico.* Ph.D. diss., University of New Mexico. University Microfilms, Ann Arbor.

Lyman, R. L.
1984 Bone Density and Differential Survivorship of Fossil Classes. *Journal of Anthropological Archaeology* 3(4):259–99.

McCary, B. C.
1951 A Workshop Site of Early Man in Dinwiddie County, Virginia. *American Antiquity* 17:9–17.

McDonald, J. N.
1981 *North American Bison: Their Classification and Evolution.* University of California Press, Berkeley.

Macdonald, R., R. L. Smith, and J. E. Thomas
1992 *Chemistry of the Subalkalic Silicic Obsidians.* U.S. Geological Survey Professional Paper no. 1523. Washington, D.C.

McGlade, J.
1995 Archaeology and the Eco-Dynamics of Human-Modified Landscapes. *Antiquity* 69:113–32.

McGregor, J. C.
1932 *Additional Prehistoric Dates from Arizona.* Museum Notes, vol. 5, no. 3. Museum of Northern Arizona, Flagstaff.
1934 Dates from Tsegi. *Tree-Ring Bulletin* 1 (1):6–8.
1936 Additional Dates From Tsegi. *Tree-Ring Bulletin* 2 (4):37.

McKern, W. C.
1939 The Midwestern Taxonomic Method as an Aid to Archaeological Culture Study. *American Antiquity* 4:301–13.

Magne, M. P. R.
1985 *Lithics and Livelihood: Stone Tool Technologies of Central and Southern Interior British Columbia.* Mercury Series no. 133. National Museum of Man, Ottawa.

———, and D. Pokotylo
1981 A Pilot Study in Bifacial Reduction Sequences. *Lithic Technology* 10 (2–3):34–47.

Mahood, G. A.
1981 Chemical Evolution of a Pleistocene Rhyolitic Center: Sierra La Primavera, Jalisco, Mexico. *Contributions to Mineralogy and Petrology* 77:129–49.
1988 Obsidian Source Heterogeneity and Uniqueness: An Example in Western Mexico. In *Obsidian Dates IV: A Compendium of the Obsidian Hydration Determinations Made at the UCLA Obsidian Hydration Laboratory,* edited by C. W. Meighan and J. L. Scalise, 105–12. Institute of Archaeology Monograph no. 29. University of California, Los Angeles.

Marquardt, W. H.
1978 Advances in Archaeological Seriation. In *Advances in Archaeological Method and Theory,* vol. 1, edited by M. B. Schiffer, 257–314. Academic Press, New York.

———, and C. L. Crumley
1987 Theoretical Issues in the Analysis of Spatial Patterning. In *Regional Dynamics: Burgundian Landscapes in Historical Perspective,* edited by C. L. Crumley and W. H. Marquardt, 1–18. Academic Press, San Diego.

Martinez, V. L.
1991 "An Analysis of Folsom and Midland Points from Several Sites in the Southern High Plains." Paper presented at the 56th Annual Meeting of the Society for American Archaeology, 24–28 April. New Orleans.

Mason, R. J.
1962 The Paleo-Indian Tradition in Eastern North America. *Current Anthropology* 3 (3):227–78.

Mauldin, R. P., and D. S. Amick
1989 Investigating Patterning in Debitage from Experimental Biface Core Reduction. In *Experiments in Lithic Technology,* edited by D. S. Amick and R. P. Mauldin, 67–88. BAR International Series 528. British Archaeological Reports, Oxford.

Maxwell, T. D.
1995 The Use of Comparative and Engineering Analyses in the Study of Prehistoric Agriculture. In *Evolutionary Archaeology: Methodological Issues,* edited by P. A. Teltser, 113–28. University of Arizona Press, Tucson.

Mayr, E.
1942 *Systematics and the Origin of Species.* Columbia University Press, New York.

1949 The Species Concept. *Evolution* 3: 371–72.

1969 *Principles of Systematic Zoology.* McGraw-Hill, New York.

1994 Typological versus Population Thinking. In *Conceptual Issues in Evolutionary Biology*, 2d ed., edited by E. Sober, 157–60. MIT Press, Cambridge.

Mead, J. I.

1980 Is It Really that Old? A Comment about the Meadowcroft "Overview." *American Antiquity* 45: 579–82.

Meltzer, D. J.

1979 Paradigms and the Nature of Change in American Archaeology. *American Antiquity* 44:544–57.

1981 A Study of Style and Function in a Class of Tools. *Journal of Field Archaeology* 8:313–26.

1983 The Antiquity of Man and the Development of American Archaeology. In *Advances in Archaeological Method and Theory*, vol.6, edited by M. B. Schiffer, 1–51. Academic Press, New York.

1989 Was Stone Exchanged among Eastern North American Paleoindians? In *Eastern Paleo-Indian Lithic Resource Procurement and Processing*, edited by J. Lothrop and C. Ellis, 11–39. Westview Press, Boulder, Colorado. Academic Press, New York.

1991a On "Paradigms" and "Paradigm Bias" in Controversies over Human Antiquity in America. In *The First Americans: Search and Research*, edited by T. D. Dillehay and D. J. Meltzer, 13–49. CRC Press, Boca Raton.

1993 Is There a Clovis Adaptation? In *From Kostenki to Clovis: Upper Paleolithic–Paleo-Indian Adaptations*, edited by O. Soffer and N. D. Praslov, 293–310. Plenum Press, New York.

1995 Clocking the First Americans. *Annual Review of Anthropology* 24: 21–45.

1991b Status and Ranking at Folsom. Paper presented at the 56th Annual Meeting of the Society for American Archaeology. New Orleans. [Revised 1991 draft]

Meserve, F. G., and E. H. Barbour

1932 Association of an Arrow Point with Bison Occidentalis in Nebraska. *Nebraska State Museum Bulletin* 1 (27, February):239–42.

Metz, J. M., and G. A. Mahood

1991 Development of the Long Valley, California, Magma Chamber Recorded in Precaldera Rhyolite Lavas of Glass Mountain. *Contributions to Mineralogy and Petrology* 106:379–97.

Mills, B. J., C. E. Goetze, and M. Nieves Zedeno

1993 Interpretation of Ceramic Artifacts. In *Across the Colorado Plateau: Anthropological Studies for the Transwestern Pipeline Expansion Project*, vol. 16. Office of Contract Archaeology and Maxwell Museum of Anthropology, University of New Mexico, Albuquerque.

Mommsen, H. T. Beier, U. Diehl, and Ch. Podzuweit

1992 Provenance Determination of Mycenaean Sherds Found in Tell el Amarna by Neutron Activation Analysis. *Journal of Archaeological Science* 19:295–302.

Moore, C. B.

1913 Some Aboriginal Sites in Louisiana and Arkansas. *Journal of the Academy of Natural Science of Philadelphia*, Series 2, vol. 16, pt. 1, art. 1.

Moorehead, W. K.

1910 *The Stone Age in North America.* Houghton Mifflin, Boston.

Morley, S. G.

1908 The Excavation of Cannonball Ruins in Southwestern Colorado. *American Anthropologist*, n.s., 10: 596–610.

———, and A. V. Kidder

1917 The Archaeology of McElmo Canyon, Colorado. *El Palacio* 4 (4):42–70.

Morris, E. H.

1919a *The Aztec Ruin.* Anthropological Papers of the American Museum of Natural History, vol. 26, pt. 1. New York.

1919b Further Discoveries at the Aztec Ruin. *El Palacio* 6(2):19–26.

1919c *Preliminary Account of the Antiquities of the Region between the Mancos and La Plata Rivers in Southwestern Colorado.* Bureau of American Ethnology Bulletin 33, 157–205. Washington, D.C.

1921a Chronology of the San Juan Area. *Proceedings of the National Academy of Sciences* 7:18–22. Easton, Pennsylvania.

1921b *The House of the Great Kiva at the Aztec Ruin.* Anthropological Papers of the American Museum of Natural History, vol. 26, pt. 2. New York.

1924 *Burials in the Aztec Ruin, the Aztec Ruin Annex.* Anthropological Papers of the American Museum of Natural History, vol. 26, pts. 3 and 4. New York.

1925 Exploring the Canyon of Death. *National Geographic Magazine* 48 (3):263–300.

1927 *The Beginnings of Pottery Making in the San Juan Area.* Anthropological Papers of the American Museum of Natural History, vol. 28, pt 2, 125–98. New York.

1928a *The Aztec Ruin.* Anthropological Papers of the American Museum of Natural History, vol. 26. New York.

1928b *Notes on Excavations in the Aztec Ruin.* American Museum of Natural History, New York.

1938 Mummy Cave. *Natural History* 42:127–38.

Morrison, K. D.
1995 *Fields of Victory: Vijayanagara and the Course of Intensification.* Contributions of the University of California Archaeological Research Facility no. 53. Berkeley.

———, and C. M. Sinopoli
1992 Economic Diversity and Integration in a Pre-Colonial Indian Empire. *World Archaeology* 23 (3):335–52.

Mueller, J. W., ed.
1975 *Sampling in Archaeology.* University of Arizona Press, Tucson.

Munson, P. J.
1990 Folsom Fluted Projectile Points East of the Great Plains and Their Biogeographical Correlates. *North*

American Archaeologist 11 (3): 255–72.

Murdock, G. P.
1967 Ethnographic Atlas: A Summary. *Ethnology* 6 (2):109–236.

Muto, G. R.
1971 A Technological Analysis of the Early Stages in the Manufacture of Lithic Artifacts. Master's thesis, Department of Anthropology, Idaho State University, Pocatello.

Myers, J. E., J. S. Olin, and M. J. Blackman
1992 "Archaeological Implications of the Leaching of Calcium Compounds from Calcareous Ceramics at Sites in the Southeastern United States and Caribbean." Poster presented at the 57th Annual Meeting of the Society for American Archaeology meetings, Pittsburgh.

Nance, J. D.
1987 Reliability, Validity, and Quantitative Methods in Archaeology. In *Quantitative Research in Archaeology: Progress and Prospects*, edited by M. S. Aldenderfer, 244–93. Sage Publications, Beverly Hills.

———, and B. F. Ball
1986 The Reliability and Validity of Test Pit Sampling. *American Antiquity* 51:457–83.

Naveh, Z., and A. Lieberman
1994 *Landscape Ecology: Theory and Application.* 2d ed. Springer-Verlag, New York.

Neff, H.
1992 Ceramics and Evolution. In *Archaeological Method and Theory*, vol. 4, edited by M. B. Schiffer, 141–93. University of Arizona Press, Tucson.

1993 Theory, Sampling, and Analytical Techniques in the Archaeological Study of Prehistoric Ceramics. *American Antiquity* 58:23–44.

1995a A Role for "Sourcing" in Evolutionary Archaeology. In *Evolutionary Archaeology: Methodological Issues*, edited by P. A. Teltser, 69–112. University of Arizona Press, Tucson.

1995b Stylistic Variation in Evolutionary Perspective: Implications for Decorative Diversity and Inter-Assemblage Distance in Illinois Woodland

Ceramic Assemblages. *American Antiquity* 60:7–36.

———, R. L. Bishop, and D. E. Arnold
1988   Reconstructing Ceramic Production from Ceramic Compositional Data: A Guatemalan Example. *Journal of Field Archaeology* 15:339–48.
1990   Reexamination of the Compositional Affiliations of Formative Period Whiteware from Highland Guatemala. *Ancient Mesoamerica* 1:171–80.

———, R. L. Bishop, and F. J. Bove
1989   Compositional Patterning in Ceramics from Pacific Coastal and Highland Guatemala. *Archeomaterials* 3:97–109.

———, R. L. Bishop, and E. V. Sayre
1988   Simulation Approach to the Problem of Tempering in Compositional Studies of Archaeological Ceramics. *The Journal of Archaeological Science* 15:159–72.
1989   More Observations on the Problem of Tempering in Compositional Studies of Archaeological Ceramics. *The Journal of Archaeological Science* 16:57–69.

———, F. J. Bove, B. Lou, and M. F. Piechowski
1992   Ceramic Raw Materials Survey in Pacific Coastal Guatemala. In *Chemical Characterization of Ceramic Pastes in Archaeology*, edited by H. Neff, 59–84. Prehistory Press, Madison, Wisconsin.

Neiman, F. D.
1995   Stylistic Variation in Evolutionary Perspective: Inferences from Decorative Diversity and Interassemblage Distance in Illinois Woodland Ceramic Assemblages. *American Antiquity* 60:7–36.

Nelson, F. W., Jr.
1984   X-ray Fluorescence Analysis of Some Western North American Obsidians. In *Obsidian Studies in the Great Basin*, edited by R. E. Hughes, 27–62. Contributions of the University of California Archaeological Research Facility no. 45. Berkeley.

———, and R. D. Holmes
1979   *Trace Element Analysis of Obsidian Sources and Artifacts from Western*

Utah. Antiquities Section Selected Paper no. 6 (15). Utah Division of State History, Salt Lake City.

———, R. V. Sidrys, and R. D. Holmes
1978   Trace Element Analysis by X-ray Fluorescence of Obsidian Artifacts from Guatemala and Belize. In *Excavations at Seibal, Department of Peten, Guatemala. Artifacts*, edited by G. R. Willey, 153–61. Memoirs of the Peabody Museum of Archaeology and Ethnology no. 14 (1).

Nelson, M. C.
1991   The Study of Technological Organization. In *Archaeological Method and Theory*, vol. 3, edited by M. B. Schiffer, 57–100. University of Arizona Press, Tucson.

Nelson, N. C.
1914   *Pueblo Ruins of the Galisteo Basin, New Mexico*. Anthropological Papers of the American Museum of Natural History, vol. 15, pt. 1. New York.
1916   Chronology of the Tano Ruins, New Mexico. *American Anthropologist* 18:159–80.

Nelson, R. R., and S. G. Winter
1982   *An Evolutionary Theory of Economic Change*. Harvard University Press, Cambridge.

Newcomer, M. H., and L. H. Keeley
1979   Testing a Method of Microwear Analysis with Experimental Flake Tools. In *Lithic Use Wear Analysis*, edited by B. Hayden, 195–205. Academic Press, New York.

Nusbaum, J. L.
1922   *A Basket-Maker Cave in Kane County, Utah, with Notes on the Artifacts by A. V. Kidder and S. J. Guernsey*. Indian Notes and Monographs, Miscellaneous Series no. 29. Museum of the American Indian, Heye Foundation, New York.

O'Brien, M. J., and T. D. Holland
1990   Variation, Selection, and the Archaeological Record. In *Archaeological Method and Theory*, vol. 2, edited by M. B. Schiffer, 31–80. University of Arizona Press, Tucson.
1992   The Role of Adaptation in Archaeological Explanation. *American Antiquity* 57:36–59.

1995   Behavioral Archaeology and the Ex-
        tended Phenotype. In *Expanding Ar-
        chaeology*, edited by J. M. Skibo,
        W. H. Walker, and A. Nielsen,
        143–61. University of Utah Press,
        Salt Lake City.
———, T. D. Holland, R. J. Hoard, and
        G. L. Fox
1994   Evolutionary Implications of Design
        and Performance Characteristics of
        Prehistoric Pottery. *Journal of Ar-
        chaeological Method and Theory*
        1:259–304.

O'Connell, J. F.
1971   The Archaeology and Cultural Ecol-
        ogy of Surprise Valley, Northeast
        California. Ph.D. diss., University of
        California, Berkeley.
1975   *The Prehistory of Surprise Valley.*
        Archaeological Papers no. 4. Ballena
        Press, Ramona, California.
1995   Ethnoarchaeology Needs a General
        Theory of Behavior. *Journal of Ar-
        chaeological Research* 3 (3):205–55.
———, and C. M. Inoway
1994   Surprise Valley Projectile Points
        and their Chronological Indica-
        tions. *Journal of California and
        Great Basin Anthropology* 16:
        162–98.

Odell, G. H.
1989   Experiments in Lithic Reduction. In
        Experiments in Lithic Technology,
        edited by D. S. Amick and R. P.
        Mauldin, 163–98. BAR Interna-
        tional Series 528. British Archaeo-
        logical Reports, Oxford.
———, and F. Cowan
1986   Experiments with Spears and Ar-
        rows on Animal Targets. *Journal of
        Field Archaeology* 13:195–212.
———, and F. Odell-Vereecken
1980   Verifying the Reliability of Lithic
        Use-Wear Assessments by Blind
        Tests: The Low-Power Approach.
        Journal of Field Archaeology
        7:87–120.

Orton, C. R.
1982   Stochastic Process and Archaeologi-
        cal Mechanism in Spatial Analysis.
        Journal of Archaeological Science
        9:1–23.

Pais, A.
1982   *Subtle Is the Lord: The Science and
        Life of Albert Einstein.* Oxford Uni-
        versity Press, New York.
1994   *Einstein Lived Here.* Clarendon
        Press, Oxford.

Parry, W. J., and R. L. Kelly
1987   Expedient Core Technology and
        Sedentism. In *The Organization of
        Core Technology*, edited by
        J. K. Johnson and C. A. Morrow,
        285–304. Westview Press, Boulder,
        Colorado.

Parsons, J. R.
1972   Archaeological Settlement Patterns.
        Annual Review of Anthropology
        1:127–50.

Patterson, L. W.
1982   The Importance of Flake Size Distri-
        bution. *Contract Abstracts and
        CRM Archaeology* 3:70–72.
1985   Distinguishing between Arrow and
        Spear Points on the Upper Texas
        Coast. *Lithic Technology* 14:81–89.
1990   Characteristics of Bifacial-Reduction
        Flake-Size Distributions. *American
        Antiquity* 55:550–58.

Pauketat, T. R.
1994   *The Ascent of Chiefs.* The University
        of Alabama Press, Tuscaloosa.

Peck, L. C.
1964   *Systematic Analysis of Silicates.* U.S.
        Geological Survey Bulletin 1170.
        Washington, D.C.

Pepper, G. H.
1902   The Ancient Basket Makers of
        Southeastern Utah. *American
        Museum Journal* 2 (4):Supplement.
1920   *Pueblo Bonito.* Anthropological
        Papers of the American Museum of
        Natural History, vol. 27. New York.

Perkinson, H. J.
1993   *Teachers without Goals/Students
        without Purposes.* McGraw-Hill,
        New York.

Perlman, I., and F. Asaro
1969   Pottery Analysis by Neutron
        Activation. *Archaeometry* 11:21–52.

Perttula, T. K.
1992   *"The Caddo Nation": Archaeolog-
        ical and Ethnohistorical
        Perspectives.* University of Texas
        Press, Austin.

Peterson, A.
1935   Specimens from the Pueblo Area
        Collected by the First Beam Expedi-

tion 1923. *Tree-Ring Bulletin* 1 (3):23–24.

Petrie, W. M. F.
  1899   Sequences in Prehistoric Remains. *Journal of the Royal Anthropological Institute*, n.s., 29:295–301.

Phagan, C. R.
  1976   A Method for the Analysis of Flakes in Archaeological Assemblages: A Peruvian Example. Ph.D. diss., Department of Anthropology, Ohio State University, Columbus.

Phillips, P.
  1958   Application of the Wheat-Gifford-Wasley Taxonomy to Eastern Ceramics. *American Antiquity* 24:117–25.
  1970   *Archaeological Survey in the Lower Yazoo Basin, Mississippi, 1949–1955*. Papers of the Peabody Museum of Archaeology and Ethnology, vol. 60, pts. 1 and 2. Harvard University, Cambridge.
  ———, J. A. Ford, and J. B. Griffin
  1951   *Archaeological Survey in the Lower Mississippi Alluvial Valley*. Papers of the Peabody Museum of American Archaeology and Ethnology, vol. 25. Harvard University, Cambridge.

Picon, M.
  1985   Un Exemple de Pollution aux Dimensions Kilometriques: La Fixation du Baryum par les Ceramiques. *Revue d'Archéometrie* 9:27–29.
  1987   La Fixation du Baryum et du Strontium par les Ceramiques. *Revue d'Archéometrie* 11:41–47.

Pierce, C.
  1993   Evolutionary Theory and the Explanation of Formal Variation: An Application to Poverty Point Objects from the Lower Mississippi Valley. M.A. Paper, Department of Anthropology, University of Washington, Seattle.
  1996   "Why Corrugated? A Functional and Historical Analysis of the Change from Smooth to Corrugated Cooking Pots in the American Southwest." Paper presented at the 61st Annual Meeting of the Society for American Archaeology, New Orleans.

Pinker, S.
  1994   *The Language Instinct*. William Morrow, New York.

Plog, S.
  1980   *Stylistic Variation in Prehistoric Ceramics*. Cambridge University Press, New York.
  1983   Analysis of Style in Artifacts. *Annual Review of Anthropology* 12:125–45.

Prentiss, W. C., and E. J. Romanski
  1989   Experimental Evaluation of Sullivan and Rozen's Debitage Typology. In *Experiments in Lithic Technology*, edited by D. S. Amick and R. P. Mauldin, 89–99. BAR International Series 528. British Archaeological Reports, Oxford.

Prudden, T. M.
  1903   The Prehistoric Ruins of the San Juan Watershed in Utah, Arizona, Colorado, and New Mexico. *American Anthropologist* 5:224–88.
  1914   The Circular Kivas of Small Ruins in the San Juan Watershed. *American Anthropologist* 16:33–58.
  1918   *A Further Study of Prehistoric Small House Ruins in the San Juan Watershed*. American Anthropological Association Memoir, vol. 5, no. 1. Washington, D.C.

Quimby, G. I.
  1966   *Indian Culture and European Trade Goods*. University of Wisconsin Press, Madison.

Ramenofsky, A. F.
  1983   The Persistence of Late Archaic Subsistence-Settlement in Louisiana. In *Foraging, Collection, and Harvesting: Archaic Period Subsistence and Settlement in the Eastern Woodlands*, edited by S. W. Neisius, 289–312. Center for Archaeological Investigations Occasional Paper no. 6. Southern Illinois University, Carbondale.
  1987   *Vectors of Death: The Archaeology of European Contact*. University of New Mexico Press, Albuquerque.
  1991   Historical Science and Contact Period Studies. In *Columbian Consequences*, vol. 3, edited by D. H. Thomas, 437–52. Smithsonian Institution Press, Washington, D.C.

1995   Evolutionary Theory and Native American Artifact Change in the Postcontact Period. In *Evolutionary Archaeology, Methodological Issues*, edited by Patrice A.Teltser, 129–48. The University of Arizona Press, Tucson.

1997   Evolutionary Theory and the Native Record of Artifact Replacement. In *Studies in Culture Contact: Interaction, Culture Change, and Archaeology*, edited by J. G. Cusick. Center for Archaeological Investigations Monograph 12. Southern Illinois University, Carbondale.

———, and A. M. Mires

1985   *The Archaeology of Cowpen Slough, 16CT147*. Department of Culture, Recreation, and Tourism, Baton Rouge.

Rathje, W. I., and C. Murphy

1992   *Rubbish! The Archaeology of Garbage*. Harper Collins, New York.

Rau, C.

1876   The Archaeological Collections of the United States Museum. *Smithsonian Contributions to Knowledge* 22 (287):1–104.

Read, D. W.

1982   Toward a Theory of Archaeological Classification. In *Essays on Archaeological Typology*, edited by R. Whallon and J. A. Brown, 56–92. Center for American Archaeology, Kampsville, Ill.

1989   Intuitive Typology and Automatic Classification: Divergence or Full Circle. *Journal of Anthropological Archaeology* 8: 156–88.

———, and G. Russell

1996   A Method for Taxonomic Typology Construction and an Example: Utilized Flakes. *American Antiquity* 61:663–84.

Redman, C. L.

1973   Multistage Fieldwork and Analytic Techniques. *American Antiquity* 38: 61–79.

Reid, J. J., M. B. Schiffer, and W. L. Rathje

1975   Behavioral Archaeology: Four Strategies. *American Anthropologist* 77:864–69.

Renaud, E. B.

1931a   *Archaeological Survey of Eastern Colorado*. University of Denver, Denver.

1931b   Prehistoric Flaked Points from Colorado and Neighboring Districts. *Proceedings of the Colorado Museum of Natural History* 10 (2). Denver.

1932   Yuma and Folsom Artifacts (New Material). *Proceedings of the Colorado Museum of Natural History* 11 (2). Denver.

1934   *The First Thousand Yuma-Folsom Artifacts*. Department of Anthropology, University of Denver, Denver.

1935   Arrowhead Types of Colorado. *Southwestern Lore* 1 (1):4–6.

1937   Folsom and Yuma Points as Known Today. *Bulletin of the Texas Archeological and Paleontological Society* 9:74–88.

1940   Flaked Weapon Points. *Bulletin of the Texas Archaeological and Paleontological Society* 12:138–68.

1941   Classification and Description of Indian Stone Artifacts. *Southwestern Lore* 6 (3-4):1–36.

1945   About the "Disappearance" of Folsom Man and Folsom Points. *Southwestern Lore* 11 (1):1–8.

Renfrew, C.

1973   *Before Civilization: The Radiocarbon Revolution and Prehistoric Europe*. Alfred A. Knopf, New York.

1982   Interfacing Problems in Archaeological Science. In *Future Directions in Archaeometry*, edited by J. S. Olin, 93–99. Smithsonian Institution, Washington, D.C.

Rice, P. M.

1978   Clear Answers to Vague Questions: Some Assumptions of Provenience Studies of Pottery. In *The Ceramics of Kaminaljuyu, Guatemala*, edited by R. K. Wetherington, 511–42. The Pennsylvania State University Monograph Series on Kaminaljuyu. University Park, Pennsylvania.

1987   *Pottery Analysis: A Sourcebook*. The University of Chicago Press, Chicago.

Rindos, D.

1984   *The Origins of Agriculture: An Evo-*

lutionary Perspective. Academic Press, New York.

1989 Undirected Variation and the Darwinian Explanation of Cultural Change. In *Archaeological Method and Theory*, vol. 1., edited by M. B. Schiffer, 1–45. University of Arizona Press, Tucson.

Roberts, F. H. H., Jr.

1929 *Shabik'eshchee Village: A Late Basket Maker Site in the Chaco Canyon, New Mexico.* Bureau of American Ethnology Bulletin 92. Washington, D.C.

1930 *Early Pueblo Ruins in the Piedra District, Southwestern Colorado.* Bureau of American Ethnology Bulletin 96. Washington, D.C.

1931 *The Ruins at Kiatuthlanna Eastern Arizona.* Bureau of American Ethnology Bulletin 100. Washington, D.C.

1932 *The Village of the Great Kivas on the Zuni Reservation, New Mexico.* Bureau of American Ethnology Bulletin 111. Washington, D.C.

1935a A Folsom Camp Site and Workshop. In *Explorations and Field-Work of the Smithsonian Institution in 1934*, 61–64. Washington, D.C.

1935b *A Folsom Complex: Preliminary Report on Investigations at the Lindenmeier Site in Northern Colorado.* Smithsonian Miscellaneous Collections, vol. 94, no. 4. Smithsonian Institution, Washington, D.C.

1935c A Survey of Southwestern Archaeology. *American Anthropologist*, n.s., 37:1–35.

1936 *Additional Information on the Folsom Complex: Report on the Second Season's Investigations at the Lindenmeier Site in Northern Colorado.* Smithsonian Miscellaneous Collections, vol. 95, no. 10. Smithsonian Institution, Washington, D.C.

1937a Archaeology of the Southwest. *American Antiquity* 3:3–33.

1937b The Folsom Problem in American Archaeology. In *Early Man (As Depicted by Leading Authorities at the International Symposium, The Academy of Natural Sciences, Philadelphia, March 1937)*, edited by G. G. MacCurdy, 153–62. J. B. Lippincott, Philadelphia.

1937c The Material Culture of Folsom Man as Revealed at the Lindenmeier Site. *Southwestern Lore* 2 (4):67–73.

1937d New Developments in the Problem of the Folsom Complex. In *Explorations and Field-Work of the Smithsonian Institution in 1936*, 69–74. Smithsonian Institution, Washington, D.C.

1938 Review of J. L. Cotter's "The Significance of Folsom and Yuma Artifact Occurrences in Light of Typology and Distribution." *American Antiquity* 4:172–73.

1939a The Folsom Problem in American Archaeology. In *Annual Report of the Smithsonian Institution (1938)*, 531–46. Smithsonian Institution, Washington, D.C

1939b On the Trail of Ancient Hunters in the Western United States and Canada. In *Explorations and Field-Work of the Smithsonian Institution in 1938*, 103–10. Smithsonian Institution, Washington, D.C.

1940 Developments in the Problem of the North American Paleo-Indian. In *Essays in Historical Anthropology of North America Dedicated to John R. Swanton*, 51–116. Smithsonian Miscellaneous Collections, vol. 100. Smithsonian Institution, Washington, D.C.

1941 Latest Excavations at Lindenmeier Site Add Information on the Folsom Complex. In *Explorations and Field-Work of the Smithsonian Institution in 1940*, 79–82. Smithsonian Institution, Washington, D.C.

1945 The New World Paleo-Indian. In *Annual Report of the Smithsonian Institution Annual (1944)*, 403–33. Smithsonian Institution, Washington, D.C.

1951 Radiocarbon Dates and Early Man. In *Radiocarbon Dating*, edited by F. Johnson, 20–22. Memoirs of the Society for American Archaeology no. 8. Washington, D.C.

Rogers, A.

1982 Data Collection and Information

Loss in the Study of Spatial Pattern. *World Archaeology* 14 (2):249–58.

Rogers, R. A., and L. D. Martin
1984   The 12 Mile Creek Site: A Reinvestigation. *American Antiquity* 49: 757–64.

Root, M. J.
1992   The Knife River Flint Quarries: The Organization of Stone Tool Production. Ph.D. diss., Washington State University, Pullman. University Microfilms, Ann Arbor.

Ross, C. S., and R. L. Smith
1961   *Ash-Flow Tuffs: Their Origin, Geologic Relations and Identification.* U.S. Geological Survey Professional Paper no. 366. Washington, D.C.

Rossignol, J., and L. Wandsnider, eds.
1992   *Space, Time, and Archaeological Landscapes.* Plenum Press, New York.

Rouse, I.
1939   *Prehistory of Haiti: A Study in Method.* Yale University Publications in Anthropology no. 21. New Haven.
1960   The Classification of Artifacts in Archaeology. *American Antiquity* 25:313–23.

Rovner, I., and G. Agogino
1967   An Analysis of Fluted and Unfluted Folsom Points from Blackwater Draw. *Masterkey* 41 (4):131–37.

Rozen, K. C., and A. P. Sullivan III
1989a   Measurement, Method, and Meaning in Lithic Analysis: Problems with Amick and Mauldin's Middle Range Approach. *American Antiquity* 54:169–75.
1989b   The Nature of Lithic Reduction and Lithic Analysis: Stage Typologies Revisited. *American Antiquity* 54:179–84.

Sabloff, J. A., and G. Tourtellot
1991   *The Ancient Maya City of Sayil: The Mapping of a Puuc Region Center.* Middle East Research Institute, Tulane University, New Orleans.

Sackett, J. R.
1973   Style, Function, and Artifact Variability in Paleolithic Assemblages. In *The Explanation of Culture Change,* edited by C. Renfrew, 317–25. Duckworth, London.

1981   From de Mortillet to Bordes: A Century of French Paleolithic Research. In *Towards a History of Archaeology,* edited by G. Daniel, 85–99. Thames and Hudson, London.
1982   Approaches to Style in Lithic Archaeology. *Journal of Anthropological Archaeology* 1:59–112.

Sampson, C. G.
1985   *Nightfire Island: Later Holocene Lakemarsh Adaptation on the Western Edge of the Great Basin.* University of Oregon Anthropological Papers no. 33. Eugene.

Sanders, W. T., J. R. Parsons, and R. S. Santley
1979   *The Basin of Mexico Survey: Ecological Processes in the Evolution of a Civilization.* Academic Press, New York.

Sappington, R. L.
1984   Procurement without Quarry Production: Examples from Southwestern Idaho. In *Prehistoric Quarries and Lithic Production,* edited by J. E. Ericson and B. A. Purdy, 23–34. Cambridge University Press, Cambridge.

Sayre, E. V.
1975   *Brookhaven Procedures for Statistical Analyses of Multivariate Archaeometric Data.* Brookhaven National Laboratory Report BNL-23128. New York.

———, and R. W. Dodson
1957   Neutron Activation Study of Mediterranean Potsherds. *American Journal of Archaeology* 61:35–41.

Schacht, R. M.
1984   The Contemporaneity Problem. *American Antiquity* 49:678–95.

Schalk, R., and D. Meatte
1988   The Archeological Features. In *The Archaeology of Chester Morse Lake: The 1986–87 Investigations for the Cedar Falls Improvement Project,* edited by R. Schalk and R. Taylor, 8:1–11. Center for Northwest Anthropology, Washington State University. Submitted to The Seattle Water Department, Contract no. C86-189.

Schelberg, J. D.
1984   Analogy, Complexity, and Regionally-Based Perspectives. In *Recent*

Research on Chaco Prehistory, edited by W. J. Judge and J. D. Schelberg, 5–21. Reports of the Chaco Center no. 8. Division of Cultural Research, National Park Service, Albuquerque.

Schenck, W. E., and E. J. Dawson
1929 *Archaeology of the Northern San Joaquin Valley*. University of California Publications in American Archaeology and Ethnology, vol. 25, no. 4, 289–413. University of California Press, Berkeley and Los Angeles.

Schiffer, M. B.
1972 Archaeological Context and Systemic Context. *American Antiquity* 37:148–57.
1976 *Behavioral Archaeology*. Academic Press, New York.
1983 Toward the Identification of Formation Processes. *American Antiquity* 48:675–706.
1987 *Formation Processes of the Archaeological Record*. University of New Mexico Press, Albuquerque.
1988a The Effects of Surface Treatment on Permeability and Evaporative Cooling Effectiveness of Pottery. In *Proceedings of the 26th International Archaeometry Symposium*, edited by R. M. Farquhar, R. G. V. Hancock, and L. A. Pavlish, 23–29. Archaeometry Laboratory, Department of Physics, University of Toronto, Toronto.
1988b The Structure of Archaeological Theory. *American Antiquity* 53:461–85.
1990a The Influence of Surface Treatment on Heating Effectiveness of Ceramic Vessels. *Journal of Archaeological Science* 17:373–81.
1990b Technological Change in Water-Storage and Cooking Pots: Some Predictions from Experiments. In *The Changing Roles of Ceramics in Society: 26,000 B.P. to the Present*, edited by W. D. Kingery, 119–36. American Ceramic Society, Westerville, Ohio.
1995 Social Theory and History in Behavioral Archaeology. In *Expanding Archaeology*, edited by J. M. Skibo,

W. H. Walker, and A. Nielsen, 22–35. University of Utah Press, Salt Lake City.
1996 Some Relationships between Behavioral and Evolutionary Archaeologies. *American Antiquity* 61:643–62.
———, and J. M. Skibo
1987 Theory and Experiment in the Study of Technological Change. *Current Anthropology* 28:595–622.
———, J. M. Skibo, T. C. Boelke, M. A. Neupert, and M. Aronson
1994 New Perspectives on Experimental Archaeology: Surface Treatments and Thermal Response of the Clay Cooking Pot. *American Antiquity* 59:197–217.
———, A. P. Sullivan III, and T. C. Klinger
1978 The Design of Archaeological Surveys. *World Archaeology* 10:1–28.

Schneider, D. C.
1994 *Quantitative Ecology: Spatial and Temporal Scaling*. Academic Press, San Diego.

Schneider, P. J.
1955 *Conduction Heat Transfer*. Addison-Wesley Publishing Company, Reading.

Schultz, C. B.
1932 Association of Artifacts and Extinct Mammals in Nebraska. *Nebraska State Museum Bulletin* 1 (33, November):271–82.
1943 Some Artifact Sites of Early Man in the Great Plains and Adjacent Areas. *American Antiquity* 8:242–49.
———, and L. C. Eiseley
1935 Paleontological Evidence for the Antiquity of the Scottsbluff Bison Quarry and its Associated Artifacts. *American Anthropologist* 37:306–19.
1936 An Added Note on the Scottsbluff Quarry. *American Anthropologist* 38:521–24.

Schumm, S. A.
1991 *To Interpret the Earth: Ten Ways to be Wrong*. Cambridge University Press, New York.

Science News Letter
1935 Uncovers Evidence of Early Mammoth Hunters. *Science News Letter* 27 (722, 9 February):92.

Sebastian, L.
1992 *The Chaco Anasazi.* Cambridge University Press, Cambridge.
Sellards, E. H.
1952 *Early Man in America.* University of Texas Press, Austin.
———, and G. L. Evans
1960 The Paleo-Indian Culture Succession in the Central High Plains of Texas and New Mexico. In *Men and Cultures: Selected Papers of the Fifth International Congress of Anthropological and Ethnological Sciences, Philadelphia, September 1–9, 1956,* edited by A. F. C. Wallace, 639–47. University of Pennsylvania Press, Philadelphia.
Sellet, F., and G. Frison
1994 "Hell Gap Revisited." Paper presented at the 59th Annual Meeting of the Society for American Archaeology, April 20–24. Anaheim, California.
Senter, F. H.
1938 Southwestern Dated Ruins: IV. *Tree-Ring Bulletin* 5 (1):6.
Shackley, M. S.
1991 Tank Mountains Obsidian: A Newly Discovered Archaeological Obsidian Source in East-Central Yuma County, Arizona. *The Kiva* 57:17–25.
1992 The Upper Gila River Gravels as an Archaeological Obsidian Source Region: Implications for Models of Exchange and Interaction. *Geoarchaeology* 7:315–26.
Sheets, P.
1975 Behavioral Analysis and the Structure of a Prehistoric Industry. *Current Anthropology* 16:369–78.
Shennan, S.
1988 *Quantifying Archaeology.* Edinburgh University Press, Edinburgh.
Shetrone, H. C.
1936 The Folsom Phenomena as Seen from Ohio. *Ohio State Archaeological and Historical Quarterly* 45: 240–56.
Shott, M. J.
1989 Diversity, Organization, and Behavior in the Material Record. *Current Anthropology* 30 (3):283–315.
1990 Stone Tools and Economics: Great

Lakes Paleoindian Examples. In *Early Paleoindian Economies of Eastern North America,* edited by K. B. Tankersley and B. L. Isaac, 3–43. Research in Economic Anthropology Supplement 5. JAI Press, Greenwich.
1993 Spears, Darts, and Arrows: Late Woodland Hunting Techniques in the Upper Ohio Valley. *American Antiquity* 58:425–43.
1994 Size and Form in the Analysis of Flake Debris: Review of Recent Approaches. *Journal of Archaeological Method and Theory* 1:69–110.
Siegel, S.
1956 *Nonparametric Statistics for the Behavioral Sciences.* McGraw-Hill, New York.
Simpson, J. C.
1948 Folsom-Like Points from Florida. *Florida Anthropologist* 1 (1–2): 11–15.
Sinopoli, C. M., and K. D. Morrison
1995 Dimensions of Imperial Control: The Vijayanagara Capital. *American Anthropologist* 97:83–96.
Skibo, J.
1992 *Pottery Function: A Use-Alteration Perspective.* Plenum Press, New York.
Smith, B. D.
1978 Variation in Mississippian Settlement Patterns. In *Mississippian Settlement Patterns,* edited by B. D. Smith, 475–503. Academic Press, New York.
1989 Introduction. In *Mississippian Emergence,* edited by B. D. Smith, 1–8. Smithsonian Institution Press, Washington D.C.
Smith, C. B.
1970 Evidence of a Distinctive Midland Complex in Southeastern New Mexico. *New Mexico Academy of Science Bulletin* 11 (2):16–19.
Smith, M. T.
1987 *Archaeology of Aboriginal Culture Change in the Interior Southeast: Depopulation during the Early Historic Period.* Riply P. Bullen Monographs in Anthropology and History no. 6. Florida State Museum, Gainesville.

Smith, R. L.
1960   *Ash-Flows.* Geological Society of America Bulletin 71:796–842. Boulder, Colorado.

Smith, W.
1952   *Excavations at Big Hawk Valley.* Museum of Northern Arizona Bulletin 24. Flagstaff.

Snow, D. R.
1995   Microchronology and Demographic Evidence Relating to the Size of Pre-Columbian North American Indian Populations. *Science* 268:1601–4.

Sober, E.
1980   Evolution, Population Thinking, and Essentialism. *Philosophy of Science* 47:350–83.
1984   *The Nature of Selection.* MIT Press, Cambridge.

Sollberger, J. B.
1985   A Technique for Folsom Fluting. *Lithic Technology* 14 (1):41–50.

South, S. A.
1970   *Baked Clay Objects from the Site of the 1670 Settlement at Charles Towne, South Carolina.* Notebook no. 2:3–16. South Carolina Institute of Archaeology and Anthropology, University of South Carolina, Charleston.

Spaulding, A. C.
1953a   Review of "Measurements of Some Prehistoric Design Elements of the Southeastern United States." *American Anthropologist* 55:588–91.
1953b   Statistical Techniques for the Discovery of Artifact Types. *American Antiquity* 18:305–13.
1954   Reply to Ford. *American Antiquity* 19:391–92.
1960   The Dimensions of Archaeology. In *Essays in the Science of Culture in Honor of Leslie A. White*, edited by A. C. Spaulding, G. E. Dole, and R. L. Carneiro, 437–56. Thomas Crowell, New York.
1977   On Growth and Form in Archaeology: Multivariate Analysis. *Journal of Anthropological Research* 33:1–15.

Spector, P. E.
1981   *Research Designs.* Sage University Papers on Quantitative Applications in the Social Sciences no. 23. Sage Publications, Beverly Hills.

Speth, J. D.
1981   The Role of Platform Angle and Core Size in Hard-Hammer Percussion Flaking. *Lithic Technology* 10 (1):16–21.

Spicer, E., and L. Caywood
1936   *Two Pueblo Ruins in West Central Arizona.* University of Arizona Bulletin, Social Science Bulletin no. 10. Tucson.

Stahl, A. B.
1992   Concepts of Time and Approaches to Analogical Reasoning in Historical Perspective. *American Antiquity* 58:235–60.

Stahle, D. W., and J. E. Dunn
1982   An Analysis and Application of the Size Distribution of Waste Flakes from the Manufacture of Bifacial Stone Tools. *World Archaeology* 14 (1):84–97.

Stallings, W. S.
1937   Southwestern Dated Ruins: I. *Tree-Ring Bulletin* 4 (2):3–5.

Stanislawski, M. B.
1990   Ceramics. In *The Wupatki Archaeological Inventory Survey Project: Final Report*, edited by B. Anderson. Professional Paper no. 35. National Park Service, Santa Fe.

Stein, B.
1983   Idiom and Ideology in Early Nineteenth Century South India. In *Rural India: Land, Power, and Society under British Rule*, edited by P. Robb, 23–58. Curzon Press, London.
1992   Introduction. In *The Making of Agrarian Policy in British India, 1770–1900*, edited by B. Stein, 1–32. Oxford University Press, Delhi.

Stein, J. K.
1993   Scale in Archaeology, Geosciences, and Geoarchaeology. In *Effects of Scale on Archaeological and Geological Perspectives*, edited by J. K. Stein and A. R. Linse, 1–10. Geological Society of America Special Paper no. 283. Boulder, Colorado.

Steponaitis, V. P.
1984   Technological Studies of Prehistoric Pottery from Alabama: Physical

Properties and Vessel Function. In *The Many Dimensions of Pottery*, edited by S. E. Van Der Leeuw and A. C. Pritchard, 81–122. Universiteit van Amsterdam, Amsterdam.

Strauss, S.
1994 *The Sizesaurus*. Kodansha International, New York.

Stross, F. H., T. R. Hester, R. F. Heizer, and R. N. Jack
1976 Chemical and Archaeological Studies of Mesoamerican Obsidians. In *Advances in Obsidian Glass Studies: Archaeological and Geochemical Perspectives*, edited by R. E. Taylor, 240–58. Noyes Press, Park Ridge, New Jersey.

———, P. Sheets, F. Asaro, and H. V. Michel
1983 Precise Characterization of Guatemalan Obsidian Sources, and Source Determination of Artifacts from Quirigua. *American Antiquity* 48:323–46.

Stuiver, M.
1982 A High-Precision Calibration of the A.D. Radiocarbon Time Scale. *Radiocarbon* 24:1–26.

———, and R. Kra, eds.
1986 Proceedings of the Twelfth International Radiocarbon Conference—Trondheim, Norway. *Radiocarbon* 28 (2A).

Sullivan, A. P., III
1992 Investigating the Archaeological Consequences of Short-Duration Occupations. *American Antiquity* 57:99–115.

———, and K. C. Rozen
1985 Debitage Analysis and Archaeological Interpretation. *American Antiquity* 50:755–79.

Tankersley, K. B., and C. A. Munson
1992 Comments on the Meadowcroft Rockshelter Radiocarbon Chronology and the Recognition of Coal Contaminants. *American Antiquity* 57:321–26.

Taylor, C. C.
1972 The Study of Settlement Patterns in Pre-Saxon Britain. In *Man, Settlement and Urbanism*, edited by P. J. Ucko, R. Tringham, and G. W. Dimbleby, 109–13. Duckworth, London.

Taylor, R. E., ed.
1976 *Advances in Obsidian Glass Studies: Archaeological and Geochemical Perspectives*. Noyes Press, Park Ridge, New Jersey.

Taylor, W. W.
1948 *A Study of Archaeology*. American Anthropology Memoir no. 69. Washington, D.C.

1957 What the Archaeologist Needs from the Specialist. In *The Identification of Non-Artifactual Archaeological Materials*, edited by W. W. Taylor, 11–13. National Academy of Sciences—National Research Council Publication no. 565. Washington, D.C.

Teltser, P. A.
1991 Generalized Core Technology and Tool Use: A Mississippian Example. *Journal of Field Archaeology* 18:363–75.

1995a Culture History, Evolutionary Theory, and Frequency Seriation. In *Evolutionary Archaeology: Methodological Issues*, edited by P. A. Teltser, 51–68. University of Arizona Press, Tucson.

1995b The Methodological Challenge of Evolutionary Theory in Archaeology. In *Evolutionary Archaeology: Methodological Issues*, edited by P. A. Teltser, 1–12. University of Arizona Press, Tucson.

1997 Settlements. *Journal of Archaeological Method and Theory* 4 (in press).

———, ed.
1995 *Evolutionary Archaeology: Methodological Issues*. University of Arizona Press, Tucson.

Thomas, C.
1985 [1894] *Report on the Mound Explorations of the Bureau of Ethnology*. Reprint, Smithsonian Institution Press, Washington, D.C.

Thomas, D. H.
1971 *Prehistoric Subsistence-Settlement Patterns of the Reese River Valley, Central Nevada*. Ph.D. diss., University of California, Davis. University Microfilms, Ann Arbor.

1973 An Empirical Test of Steward's Model of Great Basin Settlement

Patterns. *American Antiquity* 38: 155–76.

1975 Nonsite Sampling in Archaeology: Up a Creek without a Site? In *Sampling in Archaeology*, edited by J. W. Mueller, 61–81. University of Arizona Press, Tucson.

1976 *Figuring Anthropology: First Principles of Probability and Statistics.* Holt, Rinehart, and Winston, New York.

1978 The Awful Truth about Statistics in Archaeology. *American Antiquity* 43:231–44.

1981 How to Classify the Projectile Points from Monitor Valley, Nevada. *Journal of California and Great Basin Anthropology* 3:7–43.

1983 *The Archaeology of Monitor Valley.* American Museum of Natural History Anthropological Papers no. 58, pt. 1. New York.

1986 Points on Points: A Reply to Flenniken and Raymond. *American Antiquity* 51:619–27.

1988 *Archaeology.* 2d ed. Holt, Rinehart, and Winston, New York.

———, ed.
1985 *The Archaeology of Hidden Cave.* American Museum of Natural History Anthropological Papers no. 61, pt. 1. New York.

Thompson, R. M.
1948 Notes on the Archaeology of the Utukok River, Northwestern Alaska. *American Antiquity* 14:62–65.

Thruston, G. P.
1890 *The Antiquities of Tennessee and Adjacent States and the State of Aboriginal Society in the Scale of Civilization Represented by Them: A Series of Historical and Ethnological Studies.* Robert Clarke.

Titmus, G. L., and J. C. Woods
1986 An Experimental Study of Projectile Point Fracture Patterns. *Journal of California and Great Basin Anthropology* 8:37–49.

Todd, L. C.
1987 Analysis of Kill—Butchery Bonebeds and Interpretation of Paleoindian Hunting. In *The Evolution of Human Hunting*, edited by

M. H. Nitecki and D. V. Nitecki, 225–66. Plenum Press, New York.

1991 Seasonality Studies and Paleoindian Subsistence Strategies. In *Human Predators and Prey Mortality*, edited by M. C. Stiner, 217–38. Westview Press, Boulder, Colorado.

Tomka, S. A.
1989 Differentiating Lithic Reduction Techniques: An Experimental Approach. In *Experiments in Lithic Technology*, edited by D. S. Amick and R. P. Mauldin, 137. BAR International Series 528. British Archaeological Reports, Oxford.

Trigger, B. G.
1968 The Determinants of Settlement Patterns. In *Settlement Archaeology*, edited by K. C. Chang, 53–78. National Press, Palo Alto, California.

1989 *A History of Archaeological Thought.* Cambridge University Press, Cambridge.

1995 Expanding Middle-Range Theory. *Antiquity* 69:449–58.

Trinkley, M. B., ed.
1986 *Indian and Freedman Occupation at the Fish Haul Site (38BU805), Beaufort County, South Carolina.* Research Series 7. Chicora Foundation, Columbia, South Carolina.

Truncer, J.
1995 "Provenance as a Measure of Transport Cost: A Study of Steatite Vessel Manufacture Using Evolutionary Theory." Paper presented at the 60th Annual Meeting of the Society for American Archaeology, Minneapolis.

Tunnell, C.
1977 Fluted Projectile Point Production as Revealed by Lithic Specimens from the Adair-Steadman Site in Northwest Texas. In *Paleoindian Lifeways*, edited by E. Johnson, 140–68. The Museum Journal, vol. 17. West Texas Museum Association, Texas Tech University, Lubbock.

Ucko, P. J., R. Tringham, and G. W. Dimbleby, eds.
1972 *Man, Settlement and Urbanism.* Duckworth, London.

Upham, S.

1987　The Tyranny of Ethnographic Analogy in Southwestern Archaeology. In *Coasts, Plains and Deserts: Essays in Honor of Reynold J. Ruppé*, edited by S. W. Gaines. Arizona State University Anthropological Research Papers no. 38:265–79. Tempe.

Van Buren, G. E.

1974　*Arrowheads and Projectile Points.* Arrowhead Publishing, Garden Grove, California.

Vivian, G., and T. W. Mathews

1973　*Kin Kletso, a Pueblo III Community in Chaco Canyon, New Mexico.* Southwestern Monuments Association Technical Series 6. Globe, Arizona.

Vivian, R. G.

1970　An Inquiry into Prehistoric Social Organization in Chaco Canyon, New Mexico. In *Reconstructing Prehistoric Pueblo Societies*, edited by W. A. Longacre, 59–83. School of American Research Advanced Seminar Series. University of New Mexico Press, Albuquerque.

1990　*The Chacoan Prehistory of the San Juan Basin.* Academic Press, New York.

Voorrips, A., ed.

1990　*Mathematics and Information Science in Archaeology: A Flexible Framework.* Studies in Archaeology no. 3. Bonn.

Walter, V., and Y Besnus

1989　Un Exemple de Pollution en Phosphore et en Manganèse de Céramiques Anciennes. *Revue d'Archéométrie* 13:55–64.

Wandsnider, L.

1995　The Results of Education: Natural Formation Research and Scaler Analysis of Archaeological Deposits. In *Quaternary Environments and Geoarchaeology of India: Essays in Honour of Professor S. N. Rajaguru*, edited by S. Wadia, R. Korisettar, and V. S. Kale, 435–45. Geological Society of India Memoir no. 32.

1996　Describing and Comparing Archaeological Spatial Structures. *Journal of Archaeological Method and Theory* 3 (4):319–84.

1997　Landscape Element Configuration, Lifespace, and Occupation History: Ethnoarchaeological Observations and Archaeological Applications. In *The Interpretative Potential of Surface Archaeological Phenomena*, edited by A. P. Sullivan, III. University of New Mexico Press, Albuquerque.

———, and E. L. Camilli

1992　The Character of Surface Deposits and Its Influence on Survey Adequacy. *Journal of Field Archaeology* 19 (2):169–88.

1996　Land Use Histories from the Mesilla Bolson (South-Central New Mexico): Evidence from Spatial Patterning in Surface Artifact Distributions. In *Interpreting Southwestern Diversity: Underlying Principles and Overarching Patterns*, edited by P. R. Fish and J. J. Reid, 211–40. Arizona State University Anthropological Research Papers no. 48. Tempe.

Ward, A. E.

1975　The PC Ruin: Archaeological Investigations in the Prescott Tradition. *The Kiva* 40 (3).

Watkins, T., ed.

1975　*Radiocarbon: Calibration and Prehistory.* University Press, Edinburgh.

Watson, P. J.

1986　Archaeological Interpretation, 1985. In *American Archaeology Past and Future*, edited by D. J. Meltzer, D. D. Fowler and J. A. Sabloff, 439–57. Smithsonian Institution Press, Washington, D.C.

Weaver, J., and F. Stross

1965　*Analysis by X-ray Fluorescence of Some American Obsidians.* Contributions of the University of California Archaeological Research Facility no. 1:89–93.

Webb, C. H.

1968　The Extent and Content of Poverty Point Culture. *American Antiquity* 33:297–321.

1982　*The Poverty Point Culture.* 2d ed., revised. Geoscience and Man, vol. 17. Louisiana State University

School of Geoscience, Baton Rouge.

Wedel, W. R.

1941 *Archaeological Investigations at Buena Vista Lake, Kern County, California*. Bureau of American Ethnology Bulletin 130, Washington, D.C.

Weigand, P. C., G. Harbottle, and E. V. Sayre

1977 Turquoise Sources and Source Analysis: Mesoamerica and the Southwestern U.S.A. In *Exchange Systems in Prehistory*, edited by T. K. Earle and J. E. Ericson, 15–34. Academic Press, New York.

Wendorf, F.

1954 A Reconstruction of Northern Rio Grande Prehistory. *American Anthropologist* 56:200–227.

———, and A. D. Krieger

1959 New Light on the Midland Discovery. *American Antiquity* 25:66–77.

———, A. D. Krieger, C. C. Albritton, and T. D. Stewart

1955 *The Midland Discovery: A Report on the Pleistocene Human Remains from Midland, Texas*. University of Texas Press, Austin.

Whallon, R., Jr.

1972 A New Approach to Pottery Typology. *American Antiquity* 37:13–33.

1982 Variables and Dimensions: The Critical Step in Quantitative Typology. In *Essays on Archaeological Typology*, edited by R. Whallon and J. A. Brown, 127–60. Center for American Archaeology, Kampsville, Ill.

1984 Unconstrained Clustering for the Analysis of Spatial Distributions in Archaeology. In *Intrasite Spatial Analysis in Archaeology*, edited by H. J. Nietala and P. Larson. Cambridge University Press, Cambridge.

———, and J. A. Brown

1982 *Essays on Archaeological Typology*. Center for American Archaeology, Kampsville, Ill.

Wheat, J. B., J. Gifford, and W. Wasley

1958 Ceramic Variety, Type Cluster, and Ceramic System in Southwestern Pottery Analysis. *American Antiquity* 24:34–47.

White, A. M.

1963 Analytic Description of the Chipped Stone Industry from the Snyders Site, Calhoun County, Illinois. In *Miscellaneous Studies in Typology and Classification*, edited by A. M. White, L. R. Binford, and M. L. Papworth, 1–70. Anthropological Papers no. 19. Museum of Anthropology, University of Michigan, Ann Arbor.

Whittlesey, S. M.

1974 Identification of Imported Ceramics through Functional Analysis of Attributes. *The Kiva* 40 (1–2):101–12.

Wiessner, P.

1983 Style and Social Information in Kalahari San Projectile Points. *American Antiquity* 49:253–76.

1990 Is There a Unity to Style? In *The Uses of Style in Archaeology*, edited by M. Conkey and C. Hastorf, 105–12. Cambridge University Press, Cambridge.

Wilde, J. D.

1985 Prehistoric Settlements in the Northern Great Basin: Excavation and Collections Analysis in the Steens Mountain Area, Southeastern Oregon. Ph.D. diss., Department of Anthropology, University of Oregon.

Wilke, P. J., and J. J. Flenniken

1991 Missing the Point: Rebuttal to Bettinger, O'Connell, and Thomas. *American Anthropologist* 93:172–73.

Willer, D., and M. Webster, Jr.

1970 Theoretical Concepts and Observables. *American Sociological Review* 35:748–57.

Willey, G. R.

1953 *Prehistoric Settlement Patterns in the Virú Valley, Peru*. Bureau of American Ethnology Bulletin 155. Washington, D.C.

1968 Settlement Archaeology: An Appraisal. In *Settlement Archaeology*, edited by K. C. Chang, 208–26. National Press, Palo Alto, California.

———, and P. Phillips

1958 *Method and Theory in American Archaeology*. The University of Chicago Press, Chicago.

———, and J. Sabloff

1980 *A History of American Archaeology*. 2d ed. W. H. Freeman, New York.

1993 *A History of American Archaeology,*

3d ed. W. H. Freeman, San Francisco.

Williams, G. C.

1965 *Adaptation and Natural Selection: A Critique of Some Current Evolutionary Thought.* Princeton University Press, Princeton.

1992 *Natural Selection: Domains, Levels, and Challenges.* Oxford University Press, New York.

Williston, S. W.

1902 An Arrow-Head Found with Bones of Bison Occidentalis Lucas, in Western Kansas. *American Geologist* 30 (5):313–15.

1905 On the Occurrence of an Arrow-Head with Bones of an Extinct Bison. *Proceedings of the International Congress of Americanists (1902)* 13:335–37.

Wills, W. H.

1990 Cultivating Ideas: The Changing Intellectual History of the Introduction of Agriculture to the American Southwest. In *Perspectives in Southwest Prehistory*, edited by P. E. Minnis and C. L. Redman, 319–32. Westview Press, Boulder, Colorado.

Wilmsen, E. N.

1970 *Lithic Analysis and Cultural Inference: A Paleo-Indian Case.* University of Arizona Anthropological Papers no. 16. University of Arizona Press, Tucson.

——, and F. H. H. Roberts, Jr.

1978 *Lindenmeier, 1934–1974: Concluding Report on Investigations.* Smithsonian Contributions to Anthropology no. 24. Smithsonian Institution Press, Washington, D.C.

Wilson, D. S., and E. Sober

1994 Reintroducing Group Selection to Human Behavioral Sciences. *Behavioral and Brain Sciences* 17:585–654.

Wilson, T.

1891 Forms of Ancient Arrow-Heads. *American Anthropologist* 4:58–60.

1899 Arrowheads, Spearheads, and Knives of Prehistoric Times. In *Annual Report of the United States National Museum (1897)*, pt. 1, 811–988. Washington, D.C.

Wobst, H. M.

1978 The Archaeo-Ethnology of Hunter-Gatherers or The Tyranny of the Ethnographic Record in Archaeology. *American Antiquity* 43:303–9.

Wolpert, L.

1992 *The Unnatural Nature of Science.* Faber and Faber, London.

Wormington, H. M.

1939 *Ancient Man in North America.* Popular Series no. 4. Colorado Museum of Natural History, Denver.

1944 *Ancient Man in North America.* Popular Series no. 4. 2d (revised) ed. Colorado Museum of Natural History, Denver.

1948 A Proposed Revision of Yuma Point Terminology. *Proceedings of the Colorado Museum of Natural History* 18 (2). Denver.

1949 *Ancient Man in North America.* Popular Series no. 4. 3d ed. Denver Museum of Natural History, Denver.

1950 The Need for Changes in Terminology Used in Studies of Early Stone Industries. In *Proceedings of the Sixth Plains Archeological Conference (1948)*, edited by J. D. Jennings, 26–31. Anthropological Papers No. 11. University of Utah Press, Salt Lake City.

1957 *Ancient Man in North America.* Popular Series no. 4. 4th ed. Denver Museum of Natural History, Denver.

Wylie, A.

1985 The Reaction Against Analogy. In *Advances in Archaeological Method and Theory*, vol. 8, edited by M. B. Schiffer, 63–111. Academic Press, New York.

Yamin, R. A., and K. Bescherer Metheny

1995 *Landscape Archaeology: Reading and Interpreting the American Historical Landscape.* University of Tennessee Press, Knoxville.

Yellen, J. E.

1977 *Archaeological Approaches to the Present.* Academic Press, New York.

Young, D. E., and R. Bonnichsen

1985 Cognition, Behavior, and Material Culture. In *Stone Tool Analysis: Essays in Honor of Don E. Crabtree*, edited by M. G. Plew, J. C. Woods, and M. G. Pavesic, 91–131. University of New Mexico Press, Albuquerque.

Zeimens, G. M.

1982   Analysis of Postcranial Bison Remains. In *The Agate Basin Site: A Record of the Paleoindian Occupation of the Northwestern High Plains*, edited by G. C. Frison and D. J. Stanford, 213–40. Academic Press, New York.

Index

Note: Use of the term "passim" after a range of page numbers indicates coverage of a topic throughout a chapter.

Contributors

Peter W. Ainsworth
Department of Anthropology
University of Utah
Salt Lake City, Utah 84112

Charlotte Beck
Department of Anthropology
Hamilton College
Clinton, New York 13323

Richard E. Hughes
Geochemical Research Laboratory
20 Portola Green Circle
Portola Valley, California 94028-7833

Ruth E. Lambert
Grand Canyon Monitoring and
Research Center
2255 N. Gemini Drive
Flagstaff, Arizona 86002

Philippe D. LeTourneau
Department of Anthropology
University of New Mexico
Albuquerque, New Mexico 87131

Hector Neff
Research Reactor Center and
Department of Anthropology
University of Missouri
Columbia, Missouri 65211

Christopher Pierce
212 Spruce St.
Santa Fe, New Mexico 87501

Ann F. Ramenofsky
Department of Anthropology
University of New Mexico
Albuquerque, New Mexico 87131

Heidi E. Reed
Chaco Culture National Historical Park
Maxwell Museum
University of New Mexico
Albuquerque, New Mexico 87131

Elizabeth J. Skinner
SWCA Inc.
56 West 400 South
Salt Lake City, Utah 84101

Anastasia Steffen
Department of Anthropology
University of New Mexico
Albuquerque, New Mexico 87131

John R. Stein
Navajo Nation Historic Preservation
Department
Window Rock, Arizona 86515

LuAnn Wandsnider
Department of Anthropology
University of Nebraska
Lincoln, Nebraska 68588